THE DYNAMIC
ASSESSMENT OF
RETARDED PERFORMERS

THE DYNAMIC ASSESSMENT OF RETARDED PERFORMERS
The Learning Potential Assessment Device, Theory, Instruments, and Techniques

by
Reuven Feuerstein
Director, Hadassah-Wizo-Canada
   Research Institute, Jerusalem
Director, Youth Aliyah–Hadassah-Wizo-Canada
   Child Guidance Clinic, Jerusalem
Professor, Bar Ilan University, Ramat Gan, Israel
Adjunct Professor, George Peabody College of
   Vanderbilt University, Nashville

in collaboration with
Ya'acov Rand
Co-director, Hadassah-Wizo-Canada
   Research Institute, Jerusalem
Dean, Faculty of Social Sciences, Bar Ilan University,
   Ramat Gan, Israel
and
Mildred B. Hoffman
Director, Teachers' Training and Field Operations,
   Hadassah-Wizo-Canada Research Institute, Jerusalem
Adjunct Assistant Professor, George Peabody College of
   Vanderbilt University, Nashville

Illustrations by **Eitan Vig**

University Park Press
Baltimore

UNIVERSITY PARK PRESS
International Publishers in Science, Medicine, and Education
300 North Charles Street
Baltimore, Maryland 21201

Typeset by American Graphic Arts Corporation.
Manufactured in the United States of America by
The Maple Press Company.

Library of Congress Cataloging in Publication Data

Feuerstein, Reuven.
The dynamic assessment of retarded performers.

Bibliography: p.
Includes index.
1. Socially handicapped children — Testing. 2. Psychological tests for children.
3. Intelligence tests. I. Rand, Ya'acov, joint author. II. Hoffman, Mildred B.,
joint author. III. Title. [DNLM: 1. Cognition — In adolescence. 2. Learning —
In adolescence. 3. Mental retardation. 4. Psychological tests — In adolescence.
WS463 F423d]

BF432.S63F48   618.9'28'588075   79-9063
ISBN O-8391-1505-9

This book is partially based upon research supported by a grant from the
Ford Foundation, through the Israeli Foundation Trustees. The research was
conducted by the principal author and has enjoyed the participation of the
following contributors:

Research design and instruments:	Haim Shalom, Professor I. M. Schlesinger, Levia Kiram, and Irit Harari
Field work:	Evelyn Bloomfield Schachter, Levia Kiram, Dalia Katz, Tamar Schwartz-Gruenwald, Ruth Zanger, and Yitzhak Rand
Statistical elaboration:	Mendel Hoffman and Yehiel Friedlander
Editorial work:	Prof. Harvey Narrol, Mogens Jensen, and Dr. Ronald Miller
Graphics:	Eitan Vig
Consultants:	Prof. Martin Hamburger, Prof. A. Harry Passow, and Prof. Abraham J. Tannenbaum

Contents

Foreword

This fascinating and important book is the work of a gifted behavioral observer and clinician who has used his clinical observations as the basis for radical modifications of conventional psychometric theory. It describes an innovative approach to the assessment of educability that reverses several of the long-honored presuppositions of conventional psychometric theory and practice.

Conventional, norm-referenced tests of intelligence measure intellectual achievements that exist at the time of testing. They employ these measures to predict what the individual will be able to achieve or do in the future. Such conventional practice has presumed either that intelligence is a faculty that develops with little influence from experience or that the variation existing in the development-fostering quality of experience across cultures and social classes is slight. The "Learning Potential Assessment Device" (LPAD) described in this book, on the other hand, was inspired by considering seriously the possibility that the development-fostering quality of past experience can have large effects on the attainment of those cognitive achievements that constitute the items on intelligence tests. Its goal is to determine the degree to which the effects of cultural deprivation can be reversed by appropriate experience. The LPAD, therefore, attempts to assess how much an individual's level of intellectual functioning can be modified with what amount of investment in teaching effort. In place of the conventional psychometric focus on the products of intellectual functioning with a presumptive assumption that the future will reflect the past, the LPAD focuses on the process of intellectual functioning with a view to discerning ways it can be improved.

This shift of focus from product to process and from existing abilities to modifiability as an indicator of educational potential demands fundamental changes in psychometric practice. Items sensitive to learning are usually eliminated from norm-referenced tests of intelligence because they tend to damage the reliability of measures of the stable characteristics of an individual. The LPAD, on the other hand, utilizes problems the solution of which demand that the examinee have a grasp of relevant cognitive principles. Grasp of these principles demands in turn the mastery of more elementary cognitive principles and also motivation. The examinee is given the training required to master the initial problem; then he is presented with a series of tasks representing a progressively more complex application of the basic principle. The LPAD is less a battery of tests than a model for the construction of what Feuerstein calls "dynamic tests."

The LPAD calls for other modifications in psychometric practice. One is a shift in the examiner-examinee interaction, from one in which the examiner remains neutral and unresponsive while issuing "dry, standardized instruction," to one of teacher-pupil in which the examiner/teacher "constantly intervenes, makes remarks, requires and gives explanations whenever and wherever they are necessary, sums up experience, anticipates difficulties and warns the child about them, and creates reflective insightful thinking in the child not only concerning the task but also regarding the examinee's reactions to it." Thus, examiner and examinee become "engaged in a common quest for mastery of the material." A second is the introduction of training as an integral part of the assessment. This training "is not merely oriented toward a specific content, but includes the establishment of the prerequisites of cognitive functioning for a wide array of problem-solving behavior." A third is a modification of the approach to interpreting the results. Whereas conventional psychometric practice, based on a "product orientation," has ignored occasional responses of higher than typical quality because they are presumed to be deviant and to represent error, the LPAD approach, based on a "process orientation," finds "such rare, high-quality responses . . . illuminating . . . for purposes of remediation and education."

Reuven Feuerstein, who studied in Geneva under the direction of Professors André Rey and Jean Piaget, was moved to do the studies leading, over a period of 28 years, to the LPAD by the low level of functioning of some of the children and adolescents migrating to Israel. Their performances on conventional tests of intelligence lagged from 3 to 6 years behind the norms for European children of middle class. They raised etiological questions: low genetic endowment? membership in a particular socioeconomic group? Also, important decisions of educational policy rested on the issue of reversibility of what were recognized as genuine cognitive deficiencies. After examinations with "nonverbal," "culture-free," "culture-fair," and "development" tests, as well as tests of practical intelligence, had all revealed corroborative evidence of genuine cognitive deficits, Feuerstein turned to the question of whether the deficit could be reversed in school-age children and adolescents.

It is no accident that it was a psychologist trained at the University of Geneva who found his way to a solution of the problem presented. Feuerstein had acquired the entry skill required there, where his professor, André Rey, and Jean Piaget shared a hierarchical conception of knowledge and skills. It was noting the prevalent use of "elementary and primitive schemata that did not take into account the nature of the object and the specificity of the task," which characterized not only the test performances but also the characteristic daily functioning of these children, that led Feuerstein toward a solution involving the hierarchical conception of knowledge and skills.

[When an adolescent examinee] "showed incapacity to structure the human figure, as reflected in his drawing an undifferentiated body made of a circle that included the head and body, from which the four extremities emerged (*homunculus tetard*), we attempted to change the internal model of the examinee. We would point to the different parts of the body, using touch; and if it were still necessary, we would draw in front of him a more differentiated, though simple and schematic, model of the human figure. The subsequent productions of the child, as shown in later retests, gave us insight into his capacity to modify his internal body image and his graphic expression . . . . This training-assessment approach . . . required a great deal of intuitive, creative latitude from the examiner. In a way we investigated the ability of the deprived examinee to learn a mathematical operation by providing him with the necessary principles, skills, and techniques, followed by the opportunity to apply them to new tasks. The results were then interpreted in terms of the capacity of the individual to become involved in and affected by the learning process despite his initial low level of functioning in the described areas. The evaluation also hinted, again in a very intuitive way, at the manner in which the examinee had to be approached in order to produce positive results. Clinical-anecdotal and statistical-empirical follow-up studies have demonstrated a relatively high validity for the techniques we have been developing . . . Many of the children who demonstrated a retarded level of performance when examined in adolescence have reached a relatively high level of adaptation, as seen in the state of their academic and professional performance and in the state of their general mental health. Throughout the years, both the assessment and training approaches were systematized and formulated into the LPAD model, which in turn has generated a series of instruments and techniques."

The importance of this fascinating book resides in a variety of contributions. These include the audacious revisions of conventional psychometric practice and the evidences of modifiability or plasticity in cognition and motivation still present at adolescence. They include Feuerstein's concept of "mediated experience" as distinct from "direct experience" of the environment and the suggestions for compensatory education in his elaboration of the process of "mediating the environment." They include the information about the learnings, or "metalearnings," as Feuerstein has sometimes termed them, that enable individuals to cope with new situations and to learn in the usual sense. They include the evidence of the validity of Feuerstein's approach, the examples of its uses for deciding questions of educational policy, and especially its usefulness for investigating cognitive modifiability and uncovering the nature of the "metalearning" to be taught through "mediated experience."

My own introduction to Feuerstein and his LPAD occurred early in 1969. In early February of that year, I had met and traveled with Professor Abraham Minkovitch of the Hebrew University in Jerusalem on a tour, financed by the Kettering Foundation, of the infant schools of England. I was on my way to Tehran to plan with my collaborators the next steps in our program of interventions in the child-rearing at the Orphanage of the Queen Farah Pahlavi Charity Society. Professor Minkovitch invited me to visit the Hebrew University on my return from Tehran. At this university, I was invited to lecture on the plasticity of early development and the importance of early experience. Reuven Feuerstein, whom I had not yet met, was in the audience. He questioned what he considered to be my overemphasis on early experience and wondered if there were not substantial plasticity still present at adolescence if it were exploited with appropriately "mediated" experiences. When I did not immediately grasp what he meant by "mediated experience," he invited me to visit the Hadassah-Wizo-Canada Child Guidance Clinic of Youth Aliyah, of which he was Director. I accepted. There, he demonstrated his method of examining culturally deprived adolescents. I observed him use his LPAD version of Raven's Progressive Matrices with a boy of 12, conventional IQ of 60, and the LPAD version of Grace Arthur's Stencil Design Test with a girl of 16, conventional IQ in the 60s. It was abundantly evident, even though the interchanges in Hebrew had to be communicated to me through simultaneous translation, that these adolescents could, with Feuerstein's encouragement and questioning, appreciate and use conceptual schemata of which their conventional IQs indicated they were devoid. I was impressed. Later, Feuerstein showed me the test record at age 13 (conventional IQ of 70) of a young man whom I had met. When I met him, he had earned a Ph.D. in psychology from the Sorbonne in Paris. And there were others. I was even more impressed. When I discovered that Feuerstein had written a preliminary paper on the LPAD, I requested a copy and asked permission to have it mimeographed for limited distribution in the United States. Permission was granted. It is a pleasure now to be invited to write a foreword for this fascinating book.

Even though conventionally objective psychometricians may still have qualms about the clinical ingenuity required of the examiner/teacher and about the subjectivity still involved in quantifying the amount of effort the examiner/teacher must invest in getting examinees to appreciate the cognitive and motivational schemata required of them, psychometric assessment of educability should never again be the same after this book has been read and its message appreciated. Other investigators can build upon the very substantial foundation that Feuerstein has constructed.

J. McVicker Hunt, Ph.D.
Professor Emeritus of Psychology and Early Education
University of Illinois

Preface

> Be heedful not to neglect the children of the poor,
> for from them Torah [teachings] goeth forth,
> As it is written, "the water shall flow out
> of their buckets"...
> And why is it not usual for scholars to give birth to
> sons who are scholars? Said Rabbi Joseph, "That no one
> may claim the Torah as his inherent birthright."
>
> *Talmud Nidorim 81.1*

This book, introducing the Learning Potential Assessment Device, attempts to solve the difficult and hitherto unyielding problems of the cognitive assessment of low functioning, retarded performing adolescents. The Learning Potential Assessment Device is but one part of a larger framework concerned both conceptually and practically with the theory of human cognitive modifiability.* Cognitive modifiability is defined in this framework as a transformation in the structure of the intellect that may reflect as well as determine a sharp departure from the individual's expected course of development. Thus defined, modifiability refers not to changes produced by developmental and maturational processes but rather to changes in a person's cognitive structure that noticeably deviate from the expected developmental course.

Some developmental and behavioral scientists consider such a departure, even when in the desired direction, to be an aberration and therefore not a phenomenon one can reliably and deliberately produce. The expectations regarding an individual's course of development are derived from the predictive power attributed to certain performance characteristics that typify the individual at a given point in his† development. The characteristics are reflected in the individual's manifest level of functioning and are usually considered reliable predictors of his expected level of functioning in the near and more distant future. Predictions of this nature permit and even encourage the plotting of a developmental trajectory in

---

*Also see *Instrumental Enrichment: Redevelopment of Cognitive Functions of Retarded Performers* by Reuven Feuerstein (Baltimore: University Park Press, in press).

†Masculine pronouns are used throughout this book for grammatical clarity and simplicity, they are not meant to be exclusionary.

order to characterize the individual's performance throughout his life. The expectations generated by this trajectory are translated into more specific formulations of developmental and educational goals, appropriate treatments, and conducive environmental settings. When the predicted course of development occurs, it is often considered indicative of the individual's immutable, irreversible, and stable condition. Yet, the realization of goals determined initially from a trajectory of expected development represents the fulfillment of predictions based on prior labeling and classification, both of which are very powerful determinants of the activities selected for and engaged in by the individual.

The concept of modifiability presented here is concerned mainly with those changes that represent deviations from the predicted course of development. Changes in an individual's cognitive structure materialize as a function of specific, identifiable events and produce deviations from an otherwise expected course of development. Dramatic changes that reflect the essential modifiability of the individual are sometimes regarded as originating from accidental and random circumstances. The unexpected alterations described in many anecdotal accounts of individuals' developmental histories may be traced to specific changes in their environmental conditions. The interactional patterns resulting from such changes may generate the need and provide the appropriate conditions for the emergence of higher levels of cognitive functioning than those that could previously be expected. Accidental changes, however, are limited in occurrence and are unpredictable. They serve only to indicate that such significant departures are indeed possible and that the so-called "remission" is in fact associated with a very specific set of events. But the same dramatic changes can be produced intentionally through a systematic, focused, and intensive attack on those deficiencies responsible for the low manifest level of functioning in the retarded performer.

This book deals with the search for modifiability of the retarded performer in an "in vitro" learning situation. It attempts to describe the underlying philosophy, theory, and techniques by means of which changes in cognitive functioning may be produced, measured, and assessed as an index of the individual's potential for modifiability. As a diagnostic tool and method, the Learning Potential Assessment Device attempts to identify the deficient cognitive functions that produce low levels of manifest performance. This provides a basis for modifiability because appropriate techniques and training can be formulated in accordance with the specific problems experienced by the individual. The author's companion volume,

Instrumental Enrichment, deals specifically with the rationale, techniques, and instrumentation of the intensive intervention needed to produce meaningful and permanent changes in the individual. The Instrumental Enrichment Program is based on the observations and experience gained from the Learning Potential Assessment Device, which has provided evidence that retarded performers can indeed be modified and attain higher levels of functioning than their initial performance would lead us to expect. Thus, the Learning Potential Assessment Device is the source of the detailed information needed for the planning and execution of meaningful intervention strategies.

Chapter 1 of this volume provides an overview of educational policy, management of human resources, and research on the use of psychometric tests. It argues the inadequacy of conventional static psychometric methods for the assessment of retarded performers from a variety of distal etiological determinants, such as ethnocultural and socioeconomic subgroups and neurophysiological conditions, and points to the considerable damage that can be caused by such methods.

In Chapter 2, the sources of cognitive impairment characteristic of retarded performers are outlined. A theoretical basis for cognitive development—the concept of mediated learning experience derived from adult–child interactions—is presented in light of the theory of modifiability.

Chapter 3 proposes the Learning Potential Assessment Device (LPAD) as a possible alternative to conventional testing methods, and presents the theoretical model by means of which the conditions necessary for dynamic (vs. static) assessment can be created. Clinical and experimental data are discussed in Chapter 4, and the use of the instruments in group situations is described in Chapter 5.

In Chapter 6, the ways in which conventional methods have failed to disclose cognitive potential, and the use of the individual clinically oriented LPAD approach to point out cognitive modifiability, are illustrated by a series of case studies. These case studies are derived from the author's clinical experience with the assessment and treatment of retarded performers, those with and without diagnosed neurophysiological, organic, familial, or culturally determined deficiencies.

Analogical thinking, fundamental to cognitive functioning, is used to study the impact of differential intervention for changing the level of functioning of the retarded performer. The group study presented in Chapter 7 represents an attempt to partially implement the model presented in Chapter 3 by using two languages of presentation, figural and verbal, and a series of training procedures related to the characteristics of the manifest functioning of the children as established on a pretest. Chapter 7 is presented mainly as a paradigm of the methodology of research into strategies for cognitive modifiability and as a suggestion for a model for the establishment of an index of modifiability. Excerpts from the LPAD Group Test Manual are detailed in the appendix.

The final chapter, Chapter 8, summarizes the theory and implementation of the LPAD in both individual and group settings as they have been used thus far. It recommends areas for future development and implementation of the suggested model.

This book does not present the reader with the full details for administering the Learning Potential Assessment Device. This is reserved for the future manuals accompanying the instruments themselves.

It is the author's hope that in this book he will convey to the reader not only his concern with the current state of the art in psychometry, but his optimism regarding the contribution a dynamic assessment can make in the evaluation and treatment of retarded performers. Children are the most precious natural resource of a society. Not even a part of that resource should be wasted.

Acknowledgments

A long-term program of clinical systems development, theoretical formulation, and supportive research such as ours cannot be carried out without owing thanks to many people. It is our hope that, in our acknowledgment of specific debts, we can convey our gratitude to those who more than deserve it and, at the same time, convey to the reader the broad base of support that was required and enjoyed.

Our first thanks must go to Youth Aliyah, that singular institution charged with the ingathering and nurturance of Jewish youth whose living conditions abroad make it necessary for them to immigrate to Israel. Youth Aliyah's total commitment to the child in need placed us in a position where we could not help but search for solutions to problems that might otherwise have been too easily dismissed as impossible to solve. The children were ours and we had to cope. We express our gratitude to Moshe Kol, former Head of Youth Aliyah; Dr. Hanoch Rinott, former Education Director; David Umanski, former Director General; and Shimon Tuchman, former Deputy Director and Treasurer of Youth Aliyah and member of the Board of the Hadassah-Wizo-Canada Research Institute.

Eleanor Roosevelt, former World Patron of Youth Aliyah, encouraged our work and had a deep and stimulating understanding of the theoretical and clinical aspects of our attempts to help the culturally different and culturally deprived child. Her interest in our work started in the early 1950s, and was nurtured by her abiding concern for the integration of the culturally different child in the United States.

It is with special pleasure that we recognize the World Patron of Youth Aliyah, Baroness Alix de Rothschild, who has followed and supported our work since we began it with the children in North Africa.

The late Professor André Rey had a great impact upon the author and was personally involved in the evolvement of the research leading to the establishment of the LPAD model. Professors Jean Piaget and Barbel Inhelder were inspiring teachers who were extremely helpful in establishing the clinical approach that proved so useful in studying the basic structures behind the cognitive operations of deprived adolescents. Professors Marc Richelle and Maurice Jeannet should be mentioned as the first to cooperate with the author in his studies on the Moroccan children.

Dr. David Krasilowsky, Co-director of the Hadassah-Wizo-Canada Research Institute, has been thoroughly involved in both our clinical and theoretical work and has given his valuable assistance over many years. Dr. Harry Feldman participated in many discussions regarding the construction of materials for assessing modifiability of psychomotor functions. Tangible encouragement was provided by Professor J. McVicker Hunt, who was among the first to disseminate our shorter monograph on which much of the present book is based. Professors Lee Cronbach and Louis Guttman provided valuable counsel in elaborating the experimental aspects of our work.

At a relatively early stage, a number of colleagues recognized the value of the Learning Potential Assessment Device and its supporting theory as a means of transcending the issue of normative individual assessment by focusing on the structure of the thought processes and the remediation of cognitive deficiencies. For their many valuable contributions we thank Professors Cynthia and Martin Deutsch, Alfred Freedman, Martin Hamburger, A. Harry Passow, Milton Schwebel, and Abraham J. Tannenbaum. Special mention must be made of Professor H. Carl Haywood. Not only has he contributed many insightful clarifications of the theoretical and practical applications of the Learning Potential Assessment Device, but he also is presently engaged with the author in the preparation of manuals for the practical application of the LPAD (Feuerstein et al., in preparation). The faith displayed by all connected with our work inspired us with the confidence necessary to proceed with the fuller publication and dissemination of our theory and techniques, despite the trepidation we often felt at the prospects of flaunting some of our "heresies" before a large and respectable segment of the profession that seriously advocates using conventional psychometry for the assessment of the culturally deprived.

Treasured colleagues at the Youth Aliyah Child Guidance Clinic, especially Rivka Klots, and at the Hadassah-Wizo-Canada Research Institute have done yeoman service in applying the Learning Potential Assessment Device and providing the invaluable feedback and observations that have been included in our work. In this regard, Juliette Goldberg, Tamar Schwartz-Gruenwald, Dalia Katz, Yael Levy, Yitzhak Rand, Ruth Zanger, Sidney Singer, and Paola Weisz deserve special mention.

We are most grateful for the confidence bestowed upon us and for the generous financial support given specifically to this work by the Ford Foundation, through the Israel Foundation Trustees. Over the years, we have been fortunate to have the faith, interest, and personal encouragement of the Hadassah-Wizo Organization of Canada and its presidents, Clara Balinsky, Neri Bloomfield, Blanche Weisenthal, Anne Eisenstadt, Nina Cohen, and the late Lotte Riven. Their encouragement has been manifested in both a personal and financial manner. We have been aided in the preparation of this manuscript by a gift from the Bloomfield family of Montreal and Mrs. Evelyn Bloomfield Schachter. Mrs. Schachter was among the first to study the application of the LPAD with EMR children.

We express our indebtedness to The Psychological Corporation for granting us the permission to use the Arthur Design Test in its new form of the Representational Stencil Design Test (RSDT). We also thank Les Editions du Centre de Psychologie Appliquée and Delachaux Niestlé for their permission to use Rey's Complex Figure test, and the editors of the Monographs de Psychologie Appliquée for their permission to use Rey and Dupont's Organization of Dots test.

We acknowledge the generous support of the National Institute of Child Health and Human Development, through its Grant 1 ROI HD04634-01, in the development of the theoretical framework dealing with mediated learning experience as the proximal etiological determinant of differential cognitive development, as well as in the construction of an inventory of impaired functions that is at the basis of our intervention program, Instrumental Enrichment.

To Dr. Ronald Miller and to our publisher, University Park Press, especially to our editor Janet S. Hankin, we express our gratitude for editorial advice and assistance.

Finally, our deepest gratitude goes to the children with whom we worked. In helping them, we were helped.

THE DYNAMIC
ASSESSMENT OF
RETARDED PERFORMERS

CHAPTER 1   # Liberating Human Potential: *The Growing Anti-Test Movement*

The finding that individuals from certain ethnocultural and low socioeconomic subgroups regularly perform below the levels of functioning characteristic of the mainstream culture has become a major issue in the last two to three decades. The finding has led behavioral scientists to question the degree to which psychometric data accurately reflect the qualitative and quantitative differences they are said to measure.* The existence of manifest differences between the mainstream culture and its subgroups is not denied since the differences represent pervasive phenomena that transcend the limited areas of functioning tapped by the measuring instruments. Low scores, for example, on a test of linguistic behavior or on a numerical or on a reasoning test often represent a wide variety of activities characterized by the same or a similar level of functioning as the one revealed by the test. The issue raised by the behavioral scientists, therefore, has not been related to establishing this fact, but rather to interpreting it.

* Abel, 1973; Anastasi, 1950, 1965, 1976; Bereiter, 1970; Bernstein, 1960, 1961; Bortner and Birch, 1970; Clarke and Clarke, 1973; Cronbach, 1970, 1971, 1975; Cronbach and Drenth, 1973; Cronbach and Furby, 1970; Deutsch et al., 1964; Eells et al., 1951; Engelmann, 1970; Erdman and Olson, 1966; Feuerstein, 1968, 1970a, 1972, 1973a; Feuerstein and Rand, 1977; Findley and Bryan, 1971; Gagné, 1962, 1968, 1974; Gordon, 1963; Havighurst, 1964; D. E. Hunt, 1973; J. McV. Hunt, 1961, 1973; Karp and Sigel, 1965; Lennon, 1964; Lindsley, 1971; Luria, 1973; MacMillan, Jones, and Aloia, 1974; McClearn, 1964, 1970; Mercer, 1975; Narrol and Bachor, 1975; Patterson, Cobb, and Ray, 1972; Riessman, 1962; Rivers et al., 1975; Samuda, 1975; Schwebel, 1968; Skinner, 1968, 1972; Stott, 1972, 1974; Vale and Vale, 1969; Vernon, 1969; Vygotsky, 1962; Wesman, 1968; White, 1973; Williams, 1974.

Two groups of questions are especially relevant to the differences in cognitive performance found both in cross-cultural studies and in those of individual low performers belonging either to the mainstream culture or to socioeconomic, ethnic, or cultural subgroups. The first relates to the organism's ability to adapt to its environment, and the second pertains to the predictive value of psychometric measures:

1. What is the significance of the observed differences on psychometric measures in terms of the individual's ability to adapt? To what extent do these differences reflect the ability of the organism to adapt to its own environment and ecological conditions? What do these differences mean for the individual's capacity to adapt to conditions of life other than his own (Berry, 1971)?

2. To what extent can the reported manifest level of functioning be considered a stable, immutable condition of the organism and, consequently, a highly reliable predictor of the organism's future development? In other words, to what extent is the measured condition amenable to change, and, if it is, what is the meaning of the results obtained by psychometric testing for this process (Clarke and Clarke, 1975; Kagan, 1975)?

This chapter analyzes how psychological theories have attempted to answer these questions.

THE MEANING OF COGNITION FOR HUMAN ADAPTATION: MEASUREMENT, ASSESSMENT, AND MODIFIABILITY

Predictability vs. Change (Modifiability)

Because the field of psychometric measurement is a relatively young discipline, its development has largely relied on traditional research procedures and it has adopted the criteria suggested by purely conventional statistical considerations. This has led to a very prominent emphasis on statistical concerns such as validity and reliability coefficients. The field of psychometric measurement has been rather defensive about inquiries like those listed in the second group of questions above. This is hardly surprising, since such questioning suggests that psychometric testing is less relevant than previously thought, and is possibly damaging. The response to this kind of questioning typically has been in the direction of seeking to reinforce previously established theory and techniques, thus providing psychometrics with even further increased powers of prediction—higher validities and reliabilities. But the possibility, in principle, of generating these strong statistics in psychometric measurement has not been the object of dispute. The argument is, rather, that the striving for increased validity and reliability may be like an application of medicine that worsens the illness it is supposed to cure. The critical issues cannot be solved by raising the levels of test reliability and validity, which are of little relevance if the major concern of education is, as it should be, changing the individual's cognitive structure, not stabilizing it.

Bereiter (1962) commented early on the paradox between our commitment to education and our evaluation of educational practice: ". . . the only reasonable evaluation of an educational practice is one that measures . . . changeable traits. But the tests available for use in such evaluations are designed as predictors of future status, and in order to be good predictors they must be insensitive to the very changes the educator is trying to produce and measure" (p. 8). Yet given the traditional concern with impressive reliabilities and validities, it is hardly any wonder that developments in psychometrics have been so little concerned with the production of instruments for measuring change. For psychometricians, change in an individual whose *expected course* of development was predicted by conventional psychometric devices can be menacing. Change is therefore often denied, neglected, or ignored, or when it does appear it is conceptualized as an error or a random deviation from the expected course of development, instead of being understood as a genuine phenomenon that one may produce at will and measure scientifically. Contrasting the "prediction" approach to the "educational" approach, Bereiter noted that: "It is curious that the first approach, which is manifestly inferior in principle to the second, should appear familiar and workable, whereas the second . . . should appear strange and risky" (p. 7).

The defensive stance taken by representatives of the field of psychometric measurement has, unfortunately, continued, despite evidence that the assumptions underlying the measurement procedure have been shown to be highly suspect. "The traditional method by which psychometrists estimate the intelligence of individuals is to measure achievement relative to age norms, that is, individuals are compared with respect to their relative mastery of the products of prior learning. Such an approach assumes that the individuals being compared have had equal opportunity to learn . . . [This] assumption is patently untenable" (Haywood et al., 1975, p. 97).

There is, indeed, overwhelming evidence of the great impact of environment on the individual's development and manifest level of functioning, observed in groups whose varying experiential, cultural, educational, and social backgrounds nonetheless are compared (Ferron, 1965; Adams, 1973). "Scores on standardized individual and group intelligence tests have been known to vary according to the child's membership in a particular socioeconomic class, the number of years of his schooling, the area in which he lives, the level of education of his parents and his ethnic origin" (Karp and Sigel, 1965, pp. 401–402). Yet: "Race, regional, nationality and sex differences on test scores have been used without justification as data supporting genetic causation of those differences, and in turn as justification for discrimination" (Cleary et al., 1975, p. 15).

Variations in background are not considered by traditional psychometric approaches to invalidate the interpretation of the differences found on the tests, differences that are routinely seen to reflect variations in the tested individual's potential, and, as a corollary, to represent stable differences in the individual's expected course of development. These stable differences are ascribed either to 1) genetic, hereditary determinants, so that the differences are therefore considered immutable; 2) hypothesized organic factors, again producing irreversible effects; or 3) experiential background whose adverse effects on the individual, although avoidable in principle, are considered irreversible beyond assumed critical periods. In sum, the observed performance differences are understood to preserve their predictive and discriminative value under all of these conditions (Hebb, 1949; Jensen, 1963, 1969, 1970, 1973; Herrnstein, 1973).

One of the most pervasive and enduring assumptions underlying the traditional psychometric approach is that performance on an IQ test is largely determined by genetic factors. A great deal has been written on this topic. Reactions to researchers such as Jensen (1969, 1970, 1973), Herrnstein (1973), and Eysenck (1971) have been many and varied, but two major points emerge. The first deals with largely methodological issues. It is argued that the available data are either inadequate to support the view that intelligence test performance is mainly a function of genetic endowment or that the data in fact support the opposite view, that environment is the major determining factor. This approach is adopted by Kamin (1977), who by reanalyzing the available data demonstrates in a most convincing manner the absence of any reliable scientific evidence to support the genetic view of intelligence. The second major point is concerned with conceptual problems: the issue of the nature of the IQ test itself and what it is that it measures. This is a more fundamental issue. Even if the correct methodology were employed, the question of the meaning or interpretation of an IQ score still remains. It is with this issue that we are primarily concerned. Beyond providing a measure of manifest performance at a given time and within a given context of past experience and opportunities to learn and benefit from such experience, there is little reason to assume or accept that performance on IQ tests provides a stable or reliable measure of future performance.

A wealth of findings from studies of the testing environment itself have pointed out very clearly that situational variables may have a very significant and adverse effect on the examinee's test performance (Cronbach, 1975; Hunt, 1975). "[Current] developments [in cognitive functioning] have shown that problem solving strategies differ not only because various individuals possess various 'abilities' but also because individuals' strategies are different under various conditions and because a level of performance in any decision making task may depend on different processes. This may mean ... [that] the overt behavior may not be the result of potential ability, but rather, behavior is brought about by environmental factors" (Gitmez, 1971, p. 191). And so: "The failure to make allowance for different work habits, interests, and levels of motivation may ... give rise to misleading conclusions" (Haynes, 1971, p. 17) when endogenous factors nevertheless are invoked explanatorily.

An attempt to use results reflecting such a heterogeneous set of determinants is in itself an inappropriate endeavor. Even if we were to admit that genetic determinants may be less accessible to change, other components in the functioning of the individual have a much heavier impact on his behavior and make predictability even less meaningful. We may question, however, the degree to which even genetic or organic determinants should be considered unchangeable under all possible conditions.

Human Adaptation and the Problem of Measurement

Psychodiagnosis, in general, and measurement of cognitive functioning, in particular, have become the subject of discussion and questioning by a large body of researchers, theorists, and practitioners (Throne, 1972; Cronbach, 1975; McReynolds, 1975; Anastasi, 1976; Block and Dworkin, 1976; Ivnik, 1977). Many professionals were once enchanted with the study and application of psychometric practice. It is a sign of the disrepute into which the field has fallen that many of these previously enthusiastic supporters have developed an aversion to testing in the last two decades (Bersoff, 1973; Cleveland, 1976; Lewandowski and Saccuzzo, 1976). Many now consider measurement a boring, ungrateful, mechanical chore—at best, a technique that should be left to the novice or the technician.

Paradoxically, this disenchantment with the measurement of cognitive functions is contrasted with the growing importance that should be attributed to gaining knowledge about cognitive functioning. The importance of adequate cognitive functioning is probably greater today than ever because it is a prerequisite for adaptation. It is even more important when the individual's cultural environment is marked by discontinuity that imposes multiple stresses on him to adapt to new situations (Sarason, Johnsonn, and Siegel, 1977). The discontinuity increasingly characteristic of living in the modern world reduces the relevance and feasibility of an individual's current adjustments (skills, jobs, attitudes) and leaves him without the preformed ways to adapt that were previously offered to him by his culture. Unable to use previously learned and transmitted modes of functioning, the individual is confronted with a need to arrive at his own ways of coping with unprecedented and unpredicted conditions impinging on his life. The only lasting, meaningful way to prepare oneself is by developing one's capacity to change, that is, developing the ability to modify oneself.

To a very large extent cognitive functioning represents autoplasticity—the way in which an organism changes itself in response to the disruption of its equilibrium by sudden changes in the internal or external environment. Accordingly, the measurement and evaluation of cognitive levels of functioning and the loci of deficiencies are of growing importance not only for selecting individuals who have the capacity to handle specific tasks efficiently—one of the traditional goals of psychometric measurement—but also for planning and instituting intervention strategies that enhance the cognitive functioning and development of individuals whose lower levels of functioning otherwise endanger their adaptation to life. As Sundberg points out (1977), development in assessment must be sensitive to rapidly changing societal conditions, new family forms, economic discrepancies, and increasing world interdependency. But the growing importance of the measurement of cognitive functioning is inversely related to the capacity of conventional assessment procedures to fulfill this need. Testing has not made much progress in the last two decades. "The part that shows as change is the one-ninth of the berg that is above water level, and the part that remains much the same is the vast underwater bulk" (Thorndike, 1971, p. 3).

The Sociological Function of Classification

The critique of conventional psychometric assessment cannot be limited to a set of issues related to the need for and the quality of assessment and discussed in learned terms by professionals from various academic viewpoints. Distal sociological, economic, and politico-ideological perspectives play a vigorous role. Their role is probably far more instrumental in producing or preventing change than are any of the well reasoned proximal arguments that influence the development of assessment theory and technique. Mercer (1975) noted that "the classification of exceptional children did not become an issue because psychologists, educators and medical practitioners were dissatisfied with the present system . . . The central issues are conceptual and ethical rather than technical and empirical. Basic assumptions are being challenged" (p. 131). On the larger social dynamics, Hamburger (1964) wrote: "The problems of disadvantage are frequently matters of power and power structure, with the disadvantaged being powerless as well as deprived and poor. Nominal or real disenfranchisement is often correlated with minority group status and poor education with nominal or real segregation. Thus, economic, political, and social issues are involved in measurement when, through pupil placement laws, tests are used to fortify a social system" (p. 79). Hamburger stated that: "The essence of the philosophical, ideological and moral issues in the application of measurement to the disadvantaged lies in the supposition that our basic concepts of human ability have been drawn from instrumentation which has been developed to conform to a particular view of human nature" (p. 77). This particular view of human nature, racial groups, and the etiology of disadvantage considers essential developments to be genetically determined and largely beyond environmental influences during the first years of life. "The great temptation in counseling is to inventory the sort of pragmatic solutions that society has produced, rather than to enter into the real effort that is involved in altering a process which has always seemed irreversible" (Hamburger, 1964, p. 77).

Any testing procedure reflects underlying value judgments in its criteria for success and in its total approach to the problems at hand. In the absence of intentional clarification, the impact of these value judgments becomes observable only over time. It is clear that professional involvement in cognitive assessment is permeated with nonscientific norms and expectations. "One is struck by the variety of ways in which testing is contaminated by political, social, and ideological questions relating to public policy as well as by the emotional, and often racist, attitudes that seem to color each new development" (Miller, 1974, p. 5). Standard psychometric measures discriminate in a way that is grossly incongruent with the basic aspirations of modern society: culturally different individuals, including immigrants from less advantaged countries, culturally deprived minorities, and low functioning individuals from the mainstream culture, represent an enormous human potential. Yet, standard psychometric procedures write off this potential as a loss or as demanding an unwanted, unprofitable investment.

As if the inherent biases of content, modality, and structure of standard psychometric tests were not sufficient to discriminate, there are abuses in their application. We cite the psychometric service in a school that cuts the time allowed for completion of a test so as to select only those students who can succeed within the shortened time limit. The use of time as a criterion automatically operates against that segment of the population which, despite its good capacity, differs in the level of its efficiency as measured by the rapidity-precision complex (see below, "Functional Efficiency vs. Cognitive Deficiency"). Thus, discrimination gains legitimacy by a quasi-objective criterion chosen by a highly biased approach.

Any approaches that include value judgments are indefensible given our knowledge of bias, the detrimental outcomes of biased procedures, and the recognition that the human resource is the most important asset of the modern world. We must bring assessment procedures into line with the best of our knowledge concerning the assumptions on which our perspectives are laid, their factual scientific defensibility, and the general worth of their criteria and purposes. The results of currently accepted procedures are disastrous, and the harm continues largely unabated.

The inadequacies of conventional assessment techniques for measuring cognitive functions have also made psychometric testing a highly disputed and problematic field on a larger sociological scale. There is a growing awareness of the injustice of conventional psychometric approaches when they are applied to children and adults from sociocultural and ethnic subgroups (Beeman, 1974; Miller, 1974; Schmidt and Hunter, 1974; Rivers et al., 1975; Samuda, 1975). The inferior performance of these groups, using the currently accepted assessment practice, is increasingly understood to have entered, with adverse and dramatic implications, the chain of interrelated decisions made by and for the individual. A multitude of vital areas are affected, including occupational status, academic orientation, civil participation, and, in general, the goals set forth to

and introjected by individuals belonging to such groups. Dispropor-
tionate numbers of individuals from low socioeconomic, ethnocultural subgroups have been diagnosed, classified, and treated
as educable mentally retarded (EMR) or lower, following recommendations based upon testing with conventional methods. About
80% of those classified as EMR and placed in special schools for the
retarded, special classes for slow learners, and other special education frameworks originate from particular socioeconomic and ethnic
subgroups (Havighurst, 1964; see also Erdman and Olson, 1966;
Mercer, 1972, 1973). Such incriminating findings have raised the
question of the validity—and the damage—of conventional diagnostic
testing on the broadest sociological level, and have resulted in court
rulings against psychometric measurement (see Leary, 1970; Ross,
DeYoung, and Cohen, 1971; Weintraub, 1972). The question of
psychometric measurement has become an issue in civil rights (see
Mercer, 1972; Segal, 1972) and is the subject of congressional investigations (see Hoffman, 1962; Black, 1963; Kirp, Kuriloff, and Buss,
1975).

Clearly, there are many attendant issues in the practice of
classification. The complexities of the question have been reviewed
and discussed in the monumental Project on the Classification of
Exceptional Children directed by Nicholas Hobbs and presented in
his book, *The Futures of Children* (1975a), and in the two-volume
Issues in the Classification of Children (1975b). In his introduction
to the latter, Hobbs states: "Serious problems are introduced by a
lack of sophistication in taxonomy, by strong-running professional
biases, by preoccupation with dominant symptoms to the neglect of
important determinants of behavior, by transposing adult-appro-
priate schemes to children, and by the use of classification to legiti-
mize social control of the individual" (1975b, p. x).

Labeling

In particular, the anti-test movement has thrived on carefully documented findings indicating that the labeling resulting from conventional psychometric measurement has massively damaging effects
upon the individual's prospects in life. Conventional testing may
often be considered largely irrelevant for determining a diagnosis of
retardation, which is also available through the observable manifest
behavior (Feuerstein et al., 1972; Haywood et al., 1975). However,
the assessment method assumes broad prerogatives in the lives of
individuals by attaching labels and by failing to supply a means of
intervention. Affixing the retardation label under such conditions,
indicating a diagnostic category, may be the most powerful determin-

ing force in the individual's personality and social interactions, virtually guaranteeing that the formulation of a prognosis, whenever undertaken, will continue to justify the diagnosis and the continued application of the label. Although only some specific aspects of the person's behavior may lead to the labeling, in practice it is the total person who is labeled and then reacted to accordingly (Ullman and Krasner, 1969). Unfortunately, "while the process of labeling is a formal procedure, the removal of labels is not" (Goldstein et al., 1975, p. 36). The label prevails.

Assigning the Labels   In her study of retardation-labeling practices in Riverside, California, Mercer (1975) found that public schools were by far the predominant labeler among the 241 organizations serving retarded persons in the community. An additional finding resembled that of Havighurst in 1964, in which 80% of the group classified as EMR originated from particular socioeconomic and ethnic subgroups. It showed Mexican Americans to be 300% and blacks 50% overrepresented in the group labeled "retarded," while only 60% as many Anglo-Americans were represented as would be expected. Mercer (1975) concluded that: "Present assessment procedures violate certain basic rights of children" (p. 132). The rising criticism against psychometric assessment, classification, and labeling may be seen as a correlate of the growing conviction that the individual testee should be served by the results of the assessment he undergoes, and that he is poorly served indeed by being tracked into what we know today is educational poverty.

In a recent review of labeling practices, Goldstein et al. (1975) found that children are typically assigned labels by a static review largely based on the ubiquitous intelligence test. "If he has scored below 75/80 on the intelligence test, he is labeled MR (Mentally Retarded)—either TMR (Trainable Mentally Retarded) or EMR (Educable Mentally Retarded). If he has scored above 75/80, he may be labeled LD (Learning Disabled), depending on the results of the educational evaluation. Children referred primarily for behavioral problems will undergo further diagnosis. This procedure is essentially one of eliminating possibilities. To be labeled LD or BD (Behaviorally Disordered), the child must score high enough not to be considered MR . . ." (p. 26).

The Damage from Labels   It is on the background of so simple and yet so powerful classification practices that the vast impact of labeling has to be unraveled and its harmful effects documented. Rivers et al. (1975), researching the problem from the perspective of the black child, wrote: "Any attempt to convey in words the brutal impact that unfair and unfortunate labeling practices have had on the lives of black children is a depressing but necessary venture. The deleterious effects of traditional labeling practices on the progress through life of black children have been manifested socially, economically, politically, and most important, within the emotional and cognitive systems of our children" (pp. 213–214). Moreover, much as Hamburger noted generally, Rivers et al. pointed out that "negative labeling of black children has been, and remains, functional to those who are responsible for the process. Classification schemes allow for control and efficiency in school and classroom administration and serve as justification for continued discrimination against black children. New labels for black children serve as substitutes for and as statements of oldfashioned prejudices" (p. 214). Mercer (1974) reached a similar conclusion and attributed "the maintenance of the subordinate social position of certain minority groups" to the "latent functions" of IQ testing in public schools (p. 83).

It is indicative of the way knowledge grows that this gross state of affairs was predicted and forcefully criticized more than half a century ago on the grounds that testing procedures do not allow for a distinction between inherited and acquired intelligence and that this practice, therefore, "could not but lead to an intellectual caste system in which the task of education has given way to the doctrine of predestination and infant damnation" (Lippman, 1922, p. 297; see also Rey, 1934). Also from the point of historical development, Haywood et al. (1975) noted that: "The principal goals of measurements of products of prior learning include prediction, selection and classification, and group planning. Such tests as the Binet-Simon scales were designed primarily for selection purposes, but rather quickly were used toward the achievement of all of these goals" (p. 98).

This confusion of goals, with its accompanying failure to develop specialized tests for each goal, has resulted in the assigning of labels. Narrol and Bachor (1975) pointed out that ". . . a host of theorists, tests constructors, and nosological categorizers have located the cause of learning failure in the learner. These theories and techniques attempted to assess an individual's capacity for future performance on the basis of the person's current success or failure in solving problems. Based on such a sample of performance, a normative label was attached to the person. Inferences were then made about the individual's expected capability in all future learning situations" (p. 4).

This pattern is certainly the established one in testing today. Conventional psychometric tests are concerned exclusively with cataloguing the respondent's current knowledge and measuring his manifest level of functioning. They operate on the basis of the tautological platitude, "if *a* then *a*." If the retarded performing child functions on a low level in school, the very behaviors that ensure poor school performance are then measured psychometrically and the child emerges from the testing with a low IQ, i.e., a low estimated intelligence level. The child, of course, performs poorly on the school-oriented intelligence test because he has not developed the requisite classroom skills; nevertheless, he is said to be deficient in these areas *because* of low intelligence.

Conventional test methods obviously do not limit themselves to describing the individual's manifest level of functioning as registered at a certain point in his development and under certain specified conditions. Rather they produce a generalized view, which perceives the results obtained by measurement as transcending the specific measured elements and the time and condition of the measurement. What for the child starts out as an episode and a fragment becomes a durable view of his total personality with the extension of the retarded label. Labels are, in principle, only useful to the extent that a generalization may apply to a specific child (Moss, 1973), but actually many investigators (Leland, 1972) feel that there are no generalized behaviors specific to mental retardation. The social implications of labeling, on the other hand, are broadly identifiable: "Whereas those around him might never have attained any consensus about his behavior before, . . . public labeling establishes a common focus for uniform community responses that carve out a role for the [labeled individual]" (Freidson, 1965, p. 85).

Labeling is an extremely effective generator of uniform attitudes and responses, and it works its way through the individual, family, community, and school finally to create whole subgroups of labeled children segregated through the institutionalization of their labels both in their own group and in the groups from which they are distinguished by the label. "The labels take on broad and diffuse generalized meanings and become institutionalized among the population. The labels, thus institutionalized, become social and linguistic devices through which people orient themselves with respect to others [distinguishable others] in the society. A whole series of behavioral expectations, images and beliefs operates under the rubric of the label. It should . . . be noted that the impact of labeling affects the black community as well as the white community and often in similar ways. That is to say, the nondeprived develop an explicit set of beliefs, images and expectations about the 'deprived,' and very often the deprived develop a similar set of beliefs about themselves" (Rivers et al., 1975, p. 221). Within such an agonizing set of generalized expectations in the social system, decisions are made and carried out, shaping the system and finally accounting for the broadly identifiable segments of the educational practice surrounding the groups of labeled, low functioning children.

Children are swept up by the labeling process even before they are given the label. "When these young children enter the school system, many of their teachers and counselors, who have adopted the labels of the dominant society, treat them in such a manner that they begin to accept the predetermined status that the society has decided that they will fulfill as adults. Many young children enter the school with an abundance of motivation, only to find it thwarted within a few short years" (Rivers et al., 1975, p. 218; see also Haynes, 1971).

Discussing the current labeling and classification practice, Kirp (1974) wrote that: "It increasingly has undermined one of the essential premises of sorting: that it benefits the students. The research concerning the educational effects of ability grouping and special education reveals that classification, as it is typically employed, does not promote individualized student learning, permit more effective teaching of groups of students of relatively similar ability or, indeed, accomplish any of the things it is ostensibly meant to do. Rather the findings indicate that classification effectively separates students along racial and social class lines, and that such segregation may well cause educational injury to minority groups. They also suggest that adverse classification stigmatizes students, reducing both their self-image and their worth in the eyes of others" (pp. 12–13).

Goldstein et al. (1975) noted that while there is relatively little research available on the relationship between labeling and self-image, "It is widely accepted that . . . negative labels create a unique atmosphere around the children, complicating their lives in significant though unmeasured ways" (p. 24). In his review of the impact of special classes, Johnson (1962) pointed out that such classes, usually composed on the basis of test scores and thought to be the best remedial environment, are shown in many studies to have no significant advantage, academically or socially, over regular classrooms. Instead, special classes, he found, usually emphasize the disability rather than concentrate on developing the abilities of their pupils. The result is that pressures for learning and achievement are effectively removed and students feel no need to progress. In a detailed summary of their research on ability grouping, Findley and Bryan (1971) concluded: "Findings of the impact of ability grouping on classroom groups have implications for residential segregation and schooling tied to it. The issues underlying ability groupings and school segregation are deeply embedded in our society and its culture. The matters reported here are integral parts of a larger social pattern, contributing to the perpetuation or change of that pattern, but largely determined by it" (p. 4).

Instead of initiating a period of development and growth for the labeled child, the attachment of the label has the effect of terminating whatever attempts were made until then to contend with the problems presented by the child. In many instances, a teacher who is confronted with the difficulties presented by the child, and is still groping for an understanding of the child's particular struggle, is freed of his attempts in this direction; his didactic involvement and hesitations are brought to an end by the label offered him by the psychometric assessment. Conventional test procedures make a very significant contribution in this way to the finalization of a label. Before the label is determined, observations of the individual's manifest behavior might have oriented the environment toward a kind of tentative "working hypothesis" of his deviancy (Rosenthal and Jacobson, 1966; Beez, 1968; Thorndike, 1968; Avery, 1971). Once reinforced by the results of psychometric measurement, the specific characteristics of the differential cognitive structure of the given individual are obfuscated by the attachment of the label. Soon the individual is stereotypically perceived as being similar, if not identical, to others with whom he shares the label. A much more impersonal approach than the one used with the normal individual— to whom we attribute variability, differentiation, and individuality— is quickly developed for handling interactions with the labeled child. The deduction of an individual's particular situation directly from a set of general expectations upheld for a group of similarly labeled individuals is bound to produce considerable misjudgment and mistreatment. Total populations of schools or school units are perceived as belonging to the group of retarded performers (individuals who function below the norm). The whole system, consequently, becomes oriented toward the level of the retarded performer, and this level of functioning is almost invariably perceived as immutable and stable. This attitude influences numerous decisions, from the choice of curriculum to the choice of teachers suited to teach concrete material on a low level. Over a short period of time it is apparent that such schools provide much lower levels of stimulation, fewer variations of tasks, and limited opportunities for learning.

Effect of Labels on Educational Goal Setting   The retarded performer is frequently described as lacking autonomous, abstract, representational cognitive functioning. But the educational system restricts his opportunity to develop in this area. The instructional material chosen and considered most appropriate for these individuals requires only simple, mechanically associative mental processes for its Level I types of tasks (see Jensen, 1969; see Chapter 2, Figures 4 and 5 and accompanying text). These do not require the individual to generate any new information or to transform acquired information, either learned or experienced. They call for a very task-bound and concrete type of learning.

Labeling an individual as being subaverage or EMR has a detrimental effect (Blatt, 1972; Jones, 1972). It ipso facto orients the teacher, and no less the whole environment, toward concrete modes of transmission, problem presentation, and response management. Very limited use is made of higher levels of thought processes, symbols, and abstract levels of communication. This concrete modality of instruction is, for the retarded performer, a central link in the vicious circle determining the perpetuation of retarded performance. Used in combination with the diagnosis derived from conventional psychometric measures, the concrete modality of transmission serves to produce a stable condition that one then interprets as endogenously produced, immutable, and irreversible. Yet the use of the concrete modality becomes a very potent determining factor for perpetuating the condition, since it does not provide the individual with opportunities to use a higher level of functioning or, even more important, to ever require such from him. As a result the child is permanently expected to continue to function on a low level. Wittingly, unwittingly, or with considerations presumably for his welfare, the individual is treated in such a way that his development will not fail to fulfill the expectation of low level functioning throughout his lifespan.

The mother of a child examined by the author was able to perceive the relationship between the concrete mode of transmission she used with her son and the low level of functioning that characterized him at the time of our assessment. When the child, following treatment, subsequently acceded to much higher levels of functioning and school achievement than she had previously expected, the mother remarked: "When my son was very young, the psychologist told me he had a limited level of functioning. And so I avoided confronting him with anything unfamiliar or too complex for him to grasp—really, anything which would have required an independent response from him. I always started the word he was supposed to give as an answer to any question of mine; he only had to complete it afterwards. I couldn't help doing this to him until recently, when he started to get really annoyed whenever I did it. My husband and I have always protected him from any pressures, problems, and situations for which we knew he didn't have a way of responding appropriately." Clearly, this mother's expectation of a low functioning child, an expectation derived from the diagnosis and resultant label, actually helped to create a low functioning child. The mother adjusted her teaching and caregiving in accordance with the limited concrete modality associated with the label. The result was that the child never acquired higher, abstract levels of functioning and the mother never realized that he even had the capacity to do so.

Despite the fact that many professionals advocate only the concrete approach to teaching children labeled "retarded" or "low functioning," recent evidence suggests that abstract material should be the preferred method of instruction. For example, Neifeind and Koch (1976) have researched the differential effect of concrete, motor-manipulative versus abstract-representational modalities of training in normal and retarded children. Their results clearly point to the greater efficiency of the representational abstract modality, which enabled the retarded children in their study to go significantly beyond the level reached by their normal peers. (For further analysis of this study, see Chapter 4.)

Effect of Homogeneous Grouping The placement policy for children diagnosed on the basis of psychometric test results as having limited capacity to function on higher cognitive levels is usually toward the homogeneous grouping of similarly functioning children. Homogeneous grouping has been considered beneficial because it permits the teacher to orient efforts to deficiencies that need remediation and to avoid exposing the child to frustrating situations where he is confronted with demanding tasks and individuals. Yet serious doubt can be leveled at all of the assumptions and predictions underlying the practice of homogeneous ability grouping. It does not appear, for example, that ability grouping tailors the classroom interaction to any meaningful degree in favor of achieving the desired remediational results, whereas "Integrating handicapped and nonhandicapped children has the potential to create a more demanding environment for the handicapped child, an environment that may assist in the continued development of the child's behavioral repertoire" (Bricker, 1978, p. 17; see also Guralnick, 1978). The ostensibly homogeneous group is "homogeneous" only because the same label has been extended to all its members. For remediational purposes, little is gained by a homogeneity of labeled individuals because traditional psychometric testing extends a label irrespective of the great variety of particular problems that may determine each individual's manifest level of functioning. There is, therefore, no reason to believe that ability grouping ever would make the teacher's task substantially easier. "The effect of grouping procedures [as opposed to the stated goals] is generally to put low achievers of all kinds together and deprive them of stimulation of middle-class children as learning models and helpers" (Findley and Bryan, 1971, p. 3).

Findley and Bryan (1971) concluded from their very extensive research that: "Assignment to low achievement groups carries a stigma that is generally more debilitating than relatively poor achievement in heterogeneous groups" (p. 3). By keeping the low functioning child away from a day-to-day confrontation with his more successful peers, labeling actually creates—in many of those affected by it—a constant and clear feeling of impairment and marginality and an incapacity to cope with the great variation of stimuli encountered in life. The failures experienced by the deprived child will, of course, then be interpreted as the natural outcome of the incapacity inherent to his label (Feuerstein, 1978a).

Homogeneous grouping based on labels affixed following the assessment of manifest behavior represents the typical approach we term "passive-acceptant." This approach assumes that regardless of the nature of intervention the low functioning individual is, and will remain, accessible to only very limited change. By accepting him as he is, one is reinforcing the retarded performer's current condition in an environment which, by its very homogeneity, does not require any amount of adaptation from the child to new situations and varied conditions (Feuerstein, 1970a).

It is not surprising, then, that while the special class ostensibly is set up to provide a framework suitable for the remediation of deficiencies first discovered in the regular class, there is only a trickle of children returning to regular educational frameworks. "Placement of children in special education programs on the basis of child-based categorization systems is often a one-way street, with little or no opportunity to escape the label or the treatment" (Goldstein et al., 1975, pp. 46–47). If the aim of the special classes is special intervention and remediation, with the goal of joining normal classes even at some more distant point in the future, it seems that this aim does not reach fulfillment by present practices. "In a number of large city school systems far less than 10 percent of the children placed in special education classes are ever returned to regular education. When one considers that the referral error could well be that high, it is easy to conclude that the bridge that should exist between special and regular education is, in fact, not really there. The traffic all goes in one direction" (Gallagher, 1972, p. 529; see also Clark, 1965; Kirp, 1974). There is a noteworthy consistency between this outcome and the underlying conceptualization of the psychometric assessment that ascribes failure to stable and immutable conditions.

In the early stages of the development of our dynamic assessment procedure, its application was limited to children originating from culturally different and disadvantaged backgrounds. The dynamic assessment did not seem at the time to be either necessary or appropriate for use with children and adolescents from middle-class backgrounds and normally functioning families. However, our experience proved otherwise, as exemplified by Roger, a 13-year-old boy from an "advantaged" family.

> Upon referral to the author, Roger was examined with conventional tests and methods and found to have an IQ of 54. This finding corresponded to results obtained on the Binet-Simon and Wechsler tests prior to his referral and with the boy's deficient cognitive functions, his lack of operational thinking, and his inadequate social behavior. Recommendations following this diagnosis were geared mainly to accepting the boy's condition as being basically immutable. The management of his behavioral and educational problems required a lessening of the considerable pressure of his highly sophisticated parents to which he was exposed and an orientation to a training program appropriate to his low capacity. Foster family placement became necessary because of the strained parent-child relationships that were considered an aggravating condition.
>
> With the failure of the treatment within the foster family setting, a reassessment was undertaken, this time with the help of our dynamic approach, and a high level of modifiability was evidenced. Following a drastic change in the setting of goals, an educational program was instituted that involved placement, cognitive redevelopment, and psychotherapy. Fourteen years later, this young man has a degree in philosophy and medieval history. (A more detailed presentation of this case is found in Chapter 6.)

Roger's mobility is a result of a process that began with the decision to revise the results previously and repeatedly obtained with conventional psychometric procedures. This revision interrupted the vicious circle that starts with diagnosing retarded performance as a stable characteristic of the individual, followed by the institution of remediational processes that usually consist of lowering educational requirements and setting goals based solely on the individual's current level of functioning. Prolonged placement in special settings and classes prescribed by the homogeneous placement policy and management do not permit the bridge from the passive-acceptant to a regular environment. The limited educational and adaptational goals set by the homogeneous low environment, implying the provision of qualitatively limited stimuli, widen the gap between the deviant and low functioning child and his normal peers, thus closing the circle around the low functioning child and confirming the label assigned to him.

PSYCHOMETRIC MEASUREMENT:
REFLECTS OR CREATES INEQUALITY?

Within the context of discussing mobility and the passing of barriers it is also necessary to mention the policy of democratization of education, which ostensibly has opened the gates of higher education to all. This policy has resulted in only a very limited increase in the number of students from ethnic minorities and the lower socioeconomic strata (Temp, 1971, 1974). One of the outcomes, however, of razing the educational barriers is the provision of yet another breeding ground for the endogenous interpretation whenever disadvantaged youngsters fail to enter the gate opened by the democratization of education. A meritocracy will easily incriminate the individual and blame his cognitive structure and the immutable nature of his level of functioning for his failure to use the so generously offered opportunities for educational progress. In their book discussing the democratization of education in France, Bourdieu and Passeron (1964) observed that the blindness exhibited toward the perception of social inequalities authorizes the interpretation of all such inequalities, especially those in scholastic achievements, as reflecting inequalities in the nature of individuals and their endowments. Such an attitude, they noted, resides within the logic of a system that, postulating the formal equality of all students as a prerequisite for the functioning of the system, is unable to accept any inequalities other than those pertaining to the individuals' endowment. It is dubious whether the formal opening up of educational opportunities for all is of any real value as long as it serves solely to reinforce the perception of cognitive functions as being endogeneously determined and leaves little room for meaningful environmental influence and possibilities for change.

The position held by many promoters of conventional psychometric measurement is that biases and injustices are not produced by these procedures, but only measured and registered by them. This is not a convincing argument. It confuses the act of registering a manifest level of functioning, which no one is denying, with its interpretation as reflecting a capacity, which conventional psychometric tests claim but fail to measure. "Great numbers of minority children are denied equal access to a quality education each year because of flaws in the testing apparatus of our schools. This situation is illegal and immoral, and it is becoming more and more untenable" (Brazziel, 1974, p. ix).

The contention that current psychometric testing only reflects the injustices and inequalities in society but contributes neither to their production nor to their perpetuation is vulnerable from many points of view including, of course, the ones already mentioned above. Additional arguments are raised below, casting even further doubt on this contention.

Assumption That Intelligence Is a Substance

One of the basic ideas underlying the development of the conventional psychometric approach is the concept of intelligence as a substance. This view of intelligence determines to a very large extent the goals of testing, the nature of the instruments, the test procedures, and the interpretation of test results. This basic assumption of the immutability of cognitive capacity, as reflected in IQ and other indices, represents a view of intelligence as a fixed entity, the evaluation of which can be made relatively accurately even at early stages of development. The acknowledged problem of this position is the need for ingenious, sophisticated "mining methods"—tests that can penetrate the layers in the total behavior that represent the natural endowment. This conception of intelligence is analogous to that of an object whose volume, at least in principle, can be measured easily and reliably and whose permanence is conserved over transformations and other external changes. Wesman (1968) referred to this conception as the "reification of intelligence" and wrote: "We have all too often behaved as though intelligence is a physical substance, like a house or an egg crate composed of rooms or cells; we might better remember that it is no more to be reified than attributes like beauty, or speed, or honesty. There are objects which are classifiable as beautiful; there are performances which may be characterized as speedy; there are behaviors which display honesty. Each of these is measurable, with greater or lesser objectivity. Because they can be measured, however, does not mean they are substances. We may agree with E. L. Thorndike that if something exists it can be measured; we need not accept the converse notion that if we can measure something it has existence as a substance" (p. 267). Because of the general impact that the conception of immutability of cognitive capacity has on so many aspects of testing, it may be seen as one of the most important sources of difficulty for the psychometric approaches.

The fact that we know that intelligence is based on the results of our measurement has not changed the traditional use of the concept of intellectual capacity as a reified substance. The results of intelligence testing have, for example, usually been understood to be represented by a normal distribution curve presumed to be the "true" distribution of natural endowment (Galton, 1967). Yet any distribution of test scores depends entirely upon the underlying view of intelligence represented in our testing materials and procedures. Of course, our minimal assumptions need only be that the individual organism is a closed system and that intelligence is related to some number of binomially distributed characteristics that, when found, are stable in the organism. Instruments and test situations can be constructed that will, indeed, show a normal distribution of scores. Yet, starting out with the normal distribution of test scores we cannot infer this view of intelligence. Tyler and Chalmers (1943) pointed to the possibility of achieving a normal distribution by making the test on which it is based a little harder or a little easier—thereby pushing the skew in the desired direction—or even manipulating the test scores so as to arrive at the kind of distribution sought.

On this subject, Hamburger (1964) has correctly noted that, "The difficulty with the normal curve from the counselor's viewpoint is not with the test construction and the norming, but with the misconceptions that follow, or are fortified by, the presumably immutable distribution of traits and talents. Thus intelligence is seen as 1) a *dimension* on 2) a *scale*. Both notions have been attacked as scientifically fallacious and practically deplorable [Hunt, 1961] . . . If persons are open systems in which change occurs as a function of unspecifiable future conditions, then the use of *dimension* and *scale* in counseling is particularly serious" (p. 74). A counter argument to the effect that the individual and his cognitive capacity do represent a closed system has to face very considerable evidence to the contrary: ". . . the hundreds of investigations . . . have made it quite clear that intellectual capacity is not a unitary function but a complex of overlapping, partially independent functions. Various test instruments measure various facets of these complex variables. The functions themselves are subject to modification by other internal developmental factors and by external environmental influences . . . The interactions of cognitive with noncognitive functions in adaptive behavior are extraordinarily complex, especially as learning accumulates over time" (Cobb, 1972, p. 144). Thus Cobb concluded that: "There is no 'real' IQ inherent in the person, but only a variety of functions which may be measured in different ways and yield various IQ's" (p. 146; see also Bloom, 1964).

The development of conventional psychometric tests came to rely upon a set of untenable assumptions regarding the nature of intelligence and its measurement; in particular, it has not been realized how complex the issue really is. "Our attempts to describe the development of intelligence have been really attempts to describe stability and change in measurements of intelligence . . . It seems likely that performance on these tests is responsive to the experiences individuals have had and that change in the general picture of stability and change could be produced by new developments in education and by different child-rearing practices . . . It is conceivable that changes in any or all of these could produce a very different picture than the one we have been able to draw" (Bloom, 1964, p. 90). We may continue this argument and note that the failure already at this point to take into account the great variations in subjects' backgrounds is, to a large extent, responsible for the results of classification and labeling of individuals (Havighurst, 1964; Mercer, 1975).

The Predictive (Stable) Approach
vs. the Educational (Modifiable) Approach

One of the major implications of the view that intelligence is an immutable, stable substance has been the need to develop psychometric measures that corroborate this point of view and that have high predictive validity. Given this view of intelligence one may, in principle, collect data at any point along the individual's development and then predict the development to be expected in the future. Prediction, indeed, becomes a major goal of a science that deals with objects said to be permanent; and, conceived over a period of time, such prediction is *necessary* whenever the planning of an individual's future is to be founded only on the foreseeable developmental course. On the assumption that financial and emotional resources are limited and therefore have to be distributed in the most efficient way, such a course of development has to be discovered and predicted as a way to single out its end points and subsequently establish the most efficient and economical ways of reaching them.

For example, when lifelong custodial care, following assessment, is considered an unavoidable end point for a given child, the parents are often advised by pediatricians and psychologists to initiate custodial care immediately. This is seen as preferable to entering into an uneconomical and emotionally stressful relationship with a child who is predicted to require later custodial care in any event. Acting on a recommendation to place the child in custodial care often leads to the fulfillment of the child's predicted development because the conditions produced for the child under these circumstances may prove powerful in perpetuating the very conditions that initially served as the basis of the prediction. On the other hand, in cases where parents and educators have not opted for "the most economical way" such predictions have not always become fulfilled (Edgerton and Bercovici, 1976). In our files are hundreds of cases, some of which represent children who were initially referred to custodial care and others with similar diagnoses who were nonetheless reared in stimulating environments by parents and educators. Some of these cases are reviewed in detail in this book (see Chapter 6). In general, high modifiability was indicated on the Learning Potential Assessment Device for many of these children, and the discovered potential has in numerous cases materialized into significantly higher levels of functioning for the children and adolescents involved. In this group also are many examples of children who were raised in environments that were so emotionally and cognitively restrictive that they could only have dwarfed the child's potential—a potential whose existence is confirmed by its residue that resisted the adverse conditions in which the child was nurtured and remained for assessment. Such a case was Joel.

Joel had been a resident in an institution for the retarded from the age of 8. This placement followed a diagnosis of severe mental retardation complicated by behavioral disorders attributable to a light, episodic, and well controlled convulsive condition. At the age of 16 Joel was referred to us for assessment. His parents, both of whom were professionals, were initially not willing to cooperate fully as they had reservations concerning Joel's ability to function without the custodial care provided by the residential institution.

When first referred Joel had the typical appearance of a long-term institutionalized youngster. He showed little interest in his new environment, was apathetic and torpid, and only interacted with the examiner in a limited manner. Joel was illiterate, had little orientation in time and space, and lacked self-care skills. His verbal output was severely restricted and was contaminated by perseveration and echolalia.

Joel's initial response to the LPAD situation was very poor. The examiner had to use a technique of modeling through imitation, exposing himself as a model for each behavior that he attempted to elicit from the boy. It was clear that before any attempt could be made to modify Joel's cognitive structure, a deeply ingrained lack of meaningful communication had to be overcome. This took five sessions to accomplish. Very elementary skills were established during this period: focusing; following a sequence; responding by pointing; simple counting; grouping of objects; and finally, comparing and establishing relationships. Once this preparatory stage was over, Joel seemed profoundly changed, at least in his eagerness to continue to work with the examiner. He displayed an alertness and vigilance that had not been apparent previously.

What followed was a dramatic change in Joel's level of functioning that manifested itself by a capacity to rapidly learn to solve tasks for which complex principles were required. Once Joel had learned the necessary principles, he was able to apply them in a stable and efficient way to situations that became progressively more complex and unfamiliar.

Very early in our assessment and work with Joel, it became clear that he had a substantial potential for modifiability. Unfortunately, in his 8 years of institutionalization this core of potential had never been recognized or assessed. Joel was placed in one of our treatment groups (Feuerstein and Krasilowsky, 1967), and we continued to work with him for 6 years. At the end of this period Joel was able to learn a vocation. He is a proficient reader and is able to communicate his thoughts and feelings. Most important, Joel is able to function independently as a self-supporting member of society.

Had Joel remained in the restrictive institutional environment for the "retarded," he would, in all probability, have conformed to the prediction of the original diagnosis and the initial expectation of his parents.

It is questionable to what extent the behavioral sciences at this point should be granted the right to predict that has been granted to physical and even biological sciences. To what extent has psychology as a science reached the point in its development where it can use the body of data with which it operates to infer developments and institute conditions to provide, rather than deprive, the organism with specific stimuli for growth? As pointed out earlier, any inference made about the developmental course of an individual will of necessity end up shaping its environmental conditions, thus helping to fulfill the prediction. This may have the effect of drastically limiting the prospects in life for the individual who presumably should have been served by the diagnosis and the prediction. It must, consequently, be considered a mistake to continue seeking the improvement of the kind of predictive capacity which has usually been the goal of psychometrics: ". . . the idea that development . . . is an open ended process puts a logical limitation to the predictive validity of tests of intelligence, or on measures of any personal characteristic" (Hunt, 1961, p. 310).

Indeed, the further that validities on standard psychometric measures are pushed up, the more stable are the characteristics measured and the less relevant they become for aiding the search for ways of meaningful intervention. "If one is interested in making a prediction about a person's future performance, it is important to have information about his most stable characteristics, for with respect to those characteristics he is likely to be functioning about the same in the future as he is now. His more changeable characteristics are likely to be modified by unforeseeable events so that predictions based upon them are much more likely to go awry. If one is interested in educating or otherwise contributing to the development of a person, however, it makes much more sense to examine those characteristics that are subject to a fair amount of alteration . . . As formulated here, the functions of prediction and of education are opposed rather than complementary" (Bereiter, 1962, p. 7).

Representatives of the view that intelligence is a stable and fixed entity could argue, of course, that whatever is measured under Bereiter's "educational" approach has nothing to do with intelligence. This position holds that whatever is commonly possessed by individuals, such as a capacity to become modified, is of little relevance for a measure of intelligence, which should search for and point to stable differences between individuals. This is reflected also in the use of norms, which are invariably referred to in order to determine the quality of each individual's performance. The "educational" approach would not be looking for stable interpersonal differences. Instead, it would seek to determine the specific capacity and specific problems of each individual, irrespective of norms. Cobb (1972) concluded: "Insofar as intellectual and academic functions have been found to be predictive, it has not been a relationship of global intellectual functioning to a global criterion of success, but of specific intellectual determinants to specific adaptive criteria" (p. 140).

Intelligence testing, therefore, must recognize heterogeneity in the criterion variables, in which, among others, one factor is training: ". . . predictive validity diminishes over time, or at least over successive stages of training. While this does not by any means rule out the possibility that *some* variables may have longer range predictive stability, it does make it clear that such stability may not be assumed. On the fact of it, the assumption that specific factors-in-person could in and of themselves predict final outcomes seems unwarranted. At best it would appear more reasonable to assume that intervening training will interact with the personal characteristics to yield variations in subsequent settings and treatments encountered" (Cobb, 1972, p. 143).

In the same vein Wesman (1968) wrote: "So preoccupied have we been with reifying intelligence as some mystical substance that we have too often neglected to take a common-sense look at what intelligence tests measure. We find ourselves distressed at our failure to predict with satisfactory accuracy the intelligence test scores of a teenager from his intelligence test scores as an infant. Why should this occasion surprise, let alone distress? If we look inside the tests, it should be obvious that the kinds of learning we typically appraise at the earlier ages bear little resemblance, and may have little relevance, to the kinds of learnings we appraise later" (p. 271). It is a curious fact that instead of discarding the use of conventional psychometric tests for classification and prediction, the development has rather been to seek to increase the validity of these tests. It should be clear that this attempt, even if successful, cannot contribute positively to the relevance of these tests.

Stable characteristics are selected with the help of reliability tests, to which each measuring instrument is subjected. Items that fail to show the appropriate level of reliability, that is, are too sensitive to the impact of environmental conditions and therefore reflect the modifiability of the organism, are rejected in favor of those that do not show such sensitivity. They thereby stay constant and efficiently measure the rigidity rather than the autoplasticity of the organism. Many functions that reflect the adaptability of the organism, because they are considered unreliable and nondiscriminating among individuals, are just not tackled by the measurement, and very little information is collected regarding their presence in the organism. In short, the concept of modifiability and change is not considered a relevant dimension characteristic of the organism, and indeed worthy of becoming itself an objective of psychometric measurement procedures and techniques. "It is indeed curious that we use intelligence tests mainly to predict capacity for learning and yet none of our tests involve any learning, instead they give us a cross-section of what has been learned" (Vernon, 1969, p. 106; also see Wesman, 1968). The danger is that, over time, it is concluded that what is not measured does not exist; that is, modifiability of the low functioning individual is not assessed *because* such modifiability does not exist. To correct this state of affairs, change should be introduced as the central goal of the assessment, and situations should be constructed in which change can be elicited and then measured. This is in line with what a famous developer and proponent of psychometric testing has said: ". . . the practice and theory of measurement are moving away from the preoccupation with assessing individual differences, and toward an attempt to describe the individual on scales that have direct meaning. Tests ought to describe what can be expected of a person; forecasting his rank on the criterion is generally insufficient" (Cronbach, 1971, pp. 413–414).

SOURCES OF EXAMINEE TEST FAILURE: PRODUCT VS. PROCESS ORIENTATION

The search for stable characteristics in the conventional psychometric approaches also shapes the test situation and especially the interaction between examiner and examinee. Interactions susceptible to producing changes in the examinee's behavior are considered noxious to the process of measuring the individual's stable characteristics. This approach has resulted in the sterilization of the relationship between examiner and examinee. This neutralization of the relationship serves the dual purpose of reaching out to the most stable and unmodifiable characteristics of the individual and of ensuring the standardized conditions necessary for first establishing and then referring to normative behaviors. Such practice may not affect the results in normal functioning individuals. However, it may limit drastically the retarded performing child's chances to demonstrate his capacity to function, in general, and his capacity to become involved in processes of higher levels of cognitive functioning, in particular, because of his strong dependency on the adult and his outerdirectedness (Yands and Zigler, 1971). Bloom (1964) has observed that psychometric methodology involves the measurement of an individual at a given point in time, using standard problems and questions, conditions of testing, and interpretation of the individual's performance. "Central to the interpretation of test results was the collection of normative data which could be used as a basis for defining and describing the results of the particular individual. Of great significance in this testing movement is the very sharp focus on the specific test performance or behavior of an individual at a particular point in time without regard to other characteristics of the individual at that point of time or without regard to the conditions under which he had lived prior to this time" (Bloom, 1964, p. 7).

Situational Variables and Effects of Environment

In their persistent search for stable characteristics in support of the concept of the immutability of cognitive functioning, conventional psychometric measures do not regard the situational and background variables as pertinent to the performance on the tests and the interpretation of results. In her study of the culturally different child and his assessment, Haynes wrote: "We now have a considerable amount of evidence concerning the complexity of factors which can effect test performance and it is now clear that a wide range of factors must be taken into account when considering the test performance of any child whose development has been impoverished by virtue of physical or intellectual limitations in his surroundings. The child already carries a handicap but there are also elements within the testing situation and test itself which may serve to put any child who has been brought up amongst different traditions and educational practices at an even further disadvantage" (Haynes, 1971, p. 19; see also Ferron, 1965).

Many situational variables have been studied, including the sex, race, and interactional style of the examiner (Abrahamson, 1969; Caldwell and Knight, 1970; Katz, 1970; Sattler, 1970; Epps et al., 1971; Williams, 1971; Savage and Bowers, 1972; Epps, 1974); familiarity with tasks, answer media, and time pressures (Ferron, 1965; Butcher, 1968; Biesheuvel, 1969; Dubin, Osburn, and Winick, 1969; Epps, 1969; Vernon, 1969; Findley and Bryan, 1971; Backman, 1972); and stress and anxiety (Zigler and Butterfield, 1968; Hawkes and Koff, 1970; Cohen and Roper, 1972; Roper, 1972). Conventional psychometric testing procedures, looking and testing for stable characteristics and interindividual and group differences, do not seek to accommodate for the very potent influence that these situational variables may have on test-taking performance. The influence of all such factors is pooled by default and assigned to endogenous differences among the individuals tested.

A comparable treatment is extended to the differential backgrounds of the examinees in determining the level and nature of the results obtained by different individuals. The fact that the child comes from a given environment that may differ greatly from that characteristic for the group used for developing the norms of the psychometric measure simply is not taken into account as a determinant of the variation in the results obtained. Rather it is considered an integral part of the predictive power of the test.

André Rey (1934) once wrote that if people are asked to evaluate which of two dogs is the more intelligent when one dog, following patient training, has a well established conditioned reflex, and the other dog has undergone no such training, the request would be met with a smile and considered absurd since the animals are not comparable on the basis of an acquired characteristic. The question that should have been asked is, if given an appropriate amount of investment, could the second dog also display the conditioned reflex. The same observation, in analogy, does of course also hold for human beings. Yet the conventional psychometric approaches, regarding intelligence as fixed and immutable, place the major emphasis on the endogenous factors with the tendency to include environmental factors as themselves reflecting certain endogenous parameters. Thus, heritability as a determinant of cognitive behavior is conceptualized as strongly linked to the environmental determinants by way of the "social drift" hypothesis, which basically considers a person's environmental conditions to be themselves produced by his hereditary endowment.

The failure to see differential environmental backgrounds as a determinant of variation in the levels of functioning observed among individuals also represents another concept underlying conventional psychometric theory and method, namely, the universality of cognitive development such as postulated in the system developed by Jean Piaget. Yet, environmental background affects not only the content matter to which the individual can make reference, but also his cognitive style and to a very large extent his cognitive structure (Feuerstein and Rand, 1973; Feuerstein et al., 1977). It is possible that cultural difference may affect only the *content* accessible to individuals, but cultural deprivation may meaningfully determine the cognitive *structure* of the individual and therefore require attention in measurement because of its influence, especially on the manifest levels of functioning measured by conventional test approaches.

The lack of consideration for the impact of differential backgrounds is deleterious because it justifies a lack of variation in test administration and finally in the interpretation of test results. It is mostly inappropriate because it determines the modalities of presentation of test material and shapes the test situation as well as the relationship between the examiner and the examinee, thus producing the standardized and sterile test-taking situation. On the subject of background variables and in-test aspects of performance, Haywood et al. (1975) wrote that: "Individuals may make poor scores on product oriented tests, not necessarily because they lack the aptitude for academic pursuits but frequently for two other reasons: opportunities to learn the associations and skills demanded by tests have not been uniformly present, [and] the tests do not measure adequately the fine grained skills and strategies required even for academic learning" (p. 99). Bloom (1964) concluded that ". . . much of what has been termed individual variation may be explained in terms of environmental variation" (p. 9). It does therefore appear much more reasonable to believe that cognitive adaptability is more the result of "ecological and cultural demands" (Berry, 1971) than of innate intelligence (see also Cobb, 1972; Clarke and Clarke, 1973).

The fact that conventional psychometric approaches are oblivious to situational and environmental background variables is seen also in the failure of these approaches to distinguish among 1) the individual's capacity for functioning, 2) his manifest level of functioning, and 3) his functional efficiency. Of these three parameters, conventional psychometric methods completely disregard the third, functional or mental efficiency, and, even so, constantly confuse the manifest level of functioning—which these tests do measure—with the individual's capacity for functioning—

which these tests claim to measure but do not and cannot measure. It is not difficult to see how this confusion comes about since the goal of prediction set forth by conventional test procedures necessitates that these two very different parameters of the individual are equated. It is by equating the two, and discounting entirely the parameter of functional efficiency, that one can turn the instantaneous and momentary performance into a supposedly credible source of information pertaining to a development whose materialization is placed in a more or less remote future. Yet, as has been noted, the conventional goal of prediction is largely discredited by the outcomes of its own implications, and there can be no doubt that the end of prediction is not justified by this means of achieving it. Manifest level of functioning and capacity are two entirely different parameters, and it is hard to imagine what gains derived from equating them would outweigh the losses of not keeping them apart.

Functional Efficiency vs. Cognitive Deficiency

Yet the relationship between manifest level of functioning and capacity is further complicated by the need also to take into account the parameter of functional or mental efficiency, which is distinct from either of the former. The concept of mental efficiency (Wishner, 1962) should be seen as an integral dimension in the measurement of cognitive functions, distinctly different from concepts such as intelligence, knowledge, mastery, and even the more emotional, affective aspects of the mental act such as motivation and anxiety. Mental efficiency may be considered a variable on a parameter that is affected on the one hand by the nature of the task, its type, its complexity, its novelty, its degree of abstraction, and the modalities in which it is presented, and on the other hand by individual variables (see the section "Cognitive Map" in Chapter 3). Individual variables may reflect permanent characteristics such as cognitive style or specific sensory and motor difficulties, or they may reflect more transient conditions such as fatigue and level of vigilance and arousal that are liable to affect efficiency *irrespective* of intellectual capacity and even irrespective of the actual mastery of the tasks involved. Thus, for example, an individual who has just mastered a given task is less efficient, slower, and less precise in performing this task when influenced by fatigue. Indeed, the precision-rapidity complex is one of the indices by which functional efficiency is measured. Functional efficiency may be considered highly unstable and therefore also accessible to a considerable degree of change.

Although fatigue is known to drastically lower the level of efficiency even of someone who has proper mastery over a criterion task, it will have much more marked effects on individuals whose level of functioning is more vulnerable because of recency of acquisition of the specific skills demanded in the criterion task. The measurement of the effect of an intervention program immediately following the termination of intervention may reveal only a very feeble representation of the acquisition of new skills because of low functional efficiency attributable to the recency of this acquisition. Functional efficiency is much enhanced with the automatization and crystallization of a given mental operation. This enhancement is apparent also when the particular operation is a component of otherwise rather different situations than the one where it was initially encountered and mastered. When testing for learning, one should make sure that the aspects of the rapidity and the precision of the subject's response are not confused with the question of whether the subject has acquired the principle he was to learn. Errors in performance cannot immediately determine the answer to this question because they may reflect problems of efficiency and recent acquisition, not lack of capacity.

Psychometric measurement, assuming uniform familiarity with test items, is biased against individuals whose level of efficiency is low because of limited exposure and reduced automatization. When functional efficiency is low and influences performance on a particular task in the measurement, however, the product of cognitive functioning will nonetheless be ascribed to low capacity.

Manifest level of functioning, whenever successfully approaching the criterion of the measuring instruments, can be explained only by the combined effects of capacity and efficiency. But whenever the criteria for successful behavior are not reached, it is highly questionable if one may equate the low manifest level of functioning with capacity. The reasons for failure on the level of measured behavior may range from transient conditions that affect efficiency, such as fatigue, familiarity, and motivation, to specific stylistic characteristics or sensorial variations, such as visual-motor difficulties.

It is also possible that the reasons for failure may be best explained by structural characteristics, which may not necessarily reflect the capacity of the individual but rather some peripheral deficiencies in cognitive style or structure that can be easily overcome or bypassed by means of specific interventions and conditions. Dealing solely with the manifest level of functioning and sampling behavior in a sterile one-way interaction with the examinee, conventional psychometric tests gather behavior that exclusively represents the products of cognitive functioning. This method of gathering data produces little if any information regarding the *process* underlying and leading toward the registered end product. The "product-oriented" approach—the approach used by conventional psychometric tests, measuring only the end product, not the process of cognitive functioning—does not distinguish among the many possible sources of error and their location in the mental act (see Chapter 3, "Cognitive Map"). Apart from the possibility that errors are attributable to low functional efficiency, errors may arise from (1) inappropriate and insufficient gathering of data at the input level, (2) inappropriate elaboration, and in some cases (3) inappropriate output. It should be clear that all three phases of the mental act (data input, data elaboration, and data output: see Chapter 2), since they are mutually interrelated, converge into the product eventually presented by the examinee in response to a test item.

The product-oriented approach does not reveal any aspects of the individual's cognitive structure at either the input, elaborational, or output phases of the mental act, or its other parameters such as content, modality of presentation, required operations, level of abstraction, or level of complexity. It will therefore not be able to discriminate among a large number of possible difficulties for the child's failure to solve a problem. The conventional systems of assessment simply do not consider at all the more molecular components of cognitive behavior, which are functional prerequisites of cognitive, operational thinking: blurred perception, lack of systematic exploratory behavior, impaired spatial and temporal orientation, lack of strategies for hypothesis testing, impaired planning behavior, and many others (see Chapter 2). As Bryant (1974) has noted, the failure, for example, to grasp Piagetian concepts such as conservation may not result at all, as Piaget (1966) suggested, from difficulties on an elaborative level. Instead, it may result from the child's more transient difficulties with storing memory data, as well as retrieving and mobilizing the data when faced with the need to do so in order to solve a task at a specific point in time (Belmont, 1966; Haywood and Heal, 1968; Haywood et al., 1970; Bryant and Trabasso, 1971).

Against this background a sharp distinction must be made between manifest level of functioning, capacity, and efficiency. This distinction generates the working hypothesis that will account for variation in the levels of cognitive development and functioning among and within individuals. Conventional psychometric test procedures use an inventory of functions claimed to be characteristic of the individual's capacity even though all they reflect is a specific segment of the behavior as collected and registered at a given moment, stage of development, and condition of the individual. This approach cannot contribute beyond the use of norms gathered for, and restricted to, manifest and stable dimensions seen to be characteristic of the average individual's capacity at a given time of his development.

Indices vs. Peaks of Performance

An additional problem, characteristic of the product orientation of conventional psychometric methods, is the associated preference for summarizing scored responses in the form of a quotient, an index, a percentile, or an average. Much as these approaches fail to research the process behind each of the products obtained from the examinee, they go on to erase whatever differential knowledge may be gathered about the examinee by preferring a round-up picture leading to a label. The exclusive sampling of products leaves little by way of understanding some of the behaviors leading to these quotients, and the intraindividual differences are further wiped out by the summation procedures applied. The fact that a given individual, for example, can give appropriate and adequate responses in one or more instances to questions of differential difficulty is totally neglected in favor of the more global index. The failure to research these peaks in the examinee's performance is a built-in fact of many psychometric tests, reflected, for example, in the instruction to discontinue scoring after the examinee fails to solve a number of consecutive tasks adequately. The assumption is that the failure on easier tasks makes success at more advanced levels not just improbable but also meaningless as a random aberration from the established level of performance. Viewed in this way, the episodic appearances of correct responses to more difficult questions (the "peaks of performance") are seen to be nonrepresentative of the individual's capacity. Such representativeness *is* attributed to his average behavior. It is questionable to what extent such an attribution of peaks to random behavior is legitimate without at all entering into a more elaborative analysis of such peaks. A process orientation, looking for the more intimate structure of behavior, becomes more efficient in understanding the specific determinants of any given behavior, including the peaks of performance, and undertakes a deliberate search for such peaks.

The absence of such a deliberate search in conventional psychometric testing reflects the idea that capacity should be measured in those areas where children show the highest level of efficiency (Jensen, 1969). Thus the subaverage Level II types of behavior seen in retarded performers are interpreted as reflecting a random "spill-over" from the Level I types of behavior, which are seen as truly representative of these children. This interpretation represents a dangerous approach since it argues in favor of accepting these individuals' incapacity to function on the hierarchically higher levels of cognitive behavior. To a certain extent, this is the solution of searching for the lost key where the light is and not where the key was lost. Such a passive-acceptant approach (Feuerstein, 1970) will very likely totally renounce attempts to produce appropriate changes by intervention, and as noted earlier the fact that Level II types of behavior are not measured may be interpreted as circumstantial evidence of their nonexistence. This is an example of the outcome that may be expected from a psychometric approach. Because the psychometric approach looks for stable interindividual differences, it does not consider it appropriate to test for aspects of performance commonly found in all individuals. The conclusion, by way of circular reasoning, is that the cognitive operations that are not tested for in the low functioning population are absent from the test because they do not exist in this population.

Jastak (1949) has argued that the peaks in the examinee's performance are indicative of his potential whereas the summed and averaged scores, that is, the global index, are representative only of the subject's manifest level of performance, since this index wipes out the saliency of the peaks. The peaks of performance must be viewed as very important hints of the existence of a capacity that does not become generally manifest because of the individual's inefficiency in using it. The inefficiency may be transient or more permanent for reasons that have to be revealed by appropriate search.

ASSESSMENT FOR INTERVENTION

It follows from the above-mentioned points of criticism that a serious problem with the product orientation in testing is almost total failure to provide detailed and reliable information about each individual's particular strengths and difficulties. Successful intervention depends entirely upon an understanding of the process that has brought about the particular level of functioning exhibited by the child. Without obtaining such information to any meaningful degree, it is no wonder that the special education programs set up in response to the recommendations produced by conventional psychometric testing have been shown to fail to bring about remediational changes in the individuals referred and even to do them harm. Lloyd Dunn (1968), a major force for many years in special education programs for the retarded, made the following evaluation of these programs: "In my view, much of our past and present practices are morally and educationally wrong. We have been living at the mercy of general educators who have referred their problem children to us, and we have been generally ill-prepared and ineffective in educating these children" (p. 5).

It is necessary to institute testing procedures that will provide the information needed for prescriptive teaching and specific intervention for each child: ". . . our efforts should be directed towards the construction of tests to measure potentiality to meet educational, vocational and social demands and to study the factors that influence modifiability of behaviour. These should be called tests of adaptability" (Biesheuvel, 1971, p. 5). Biesheuvel has also emphasized the need to provide tests with a learning component in order to obtain data from assessment relevant for instituting modification of knowledge and skills. Many authors have commented upon the inadequacy of conventional psychometric measures in the search for prescriptive, interventional strategies (Johnson, 1962; Bloom, 1964; Hamburger, 1964; Cobb, 1972; Rivers et al., 1975). It is clear that insights needed for designing such strategies may be gained only through extensive interviewing and experimental manipulation in the testing situation. "Might it not be more revealing to give some task with which he [the examinee] is partly familiar and observe and measure the progress he makes over a period of time, i.e., to institute a teaching situation in miniature? This should also give the tester better opportunities than does a conventional test to observe the child's method of tackling difficulties, his attention and perseverance" (Vernon, 1969, p. 106).

ATTEMPTED ALTERNATIVES TO CONVENTIONAL TESTING

Because of the widely recognized inadequacy of existing psychometric instruments for the assessment of the disadvantaged, low functioning child, many investigators have attempted to devise new instruments or to modify existing ones to make them more suitable for evaluating this population. While the need for a dynamic and learning element in the testing situation, in this author's opinion, is indicated by the researched criticism against the conventional psychometric method, such an element has not been included by the most well known of the attempted changes.

Conceptual Models as Basis for Assessment

The attempted changes have often, although not exclusively, used as a conceptual guideline either the cultural difference model (Labov,

1966; Labov et al., 1968; Baratz and Baratz, 1969; Rivers et al., 1975) or the deficit model (Burt, 1966; Shuey, 1966; Jensen, 1968, Bennet, 1970) to account for the constantly observed gaps in performance on conventional psychometric measures exhibited by members of low socioeconomic and ethnic subgroups when compared to the normative groups.

The cultural difference model explains the observed gaps as an artifact produced by the use of assessment instruments, which were to a large extent developed and standardized with reference to the dominant, mainstream culture. According to this view, the overlap between different cultures in the area of intellectual functioning, which can be tapped by psychometric measures, is not sufficiently large to guarantee relevance of a test for one cultural subgroup when the test was originally developed for another. The specific approaches adhering to the cultural difference model vary in the degree to which they deem it necessary that conventional psychometric procedures be changed. The changes actually attempted have included: 1) preserving the conventional tests intact but constructing separate norms for different cultural groups (Ammons and Aguero, 1950; Sattler, 1974; Wechsler, 1974); 2) translating conventional measures into languages of presentation presumably more familiar to the targeted subgroups (Labov et al., 1968; Matarazzo and Wiens, 1977); and 3) developing separate tests to be used only within the populations for which they were intended (Warburton, 1951; De Avila, Havassay, and Pascual-Leone, 1976; Mercer and Lewis, 1977).

The deficit model seeks to explain the observed differences as reflecting cognitive deficits, which are seen to characterize members of the low functioning groups. This view credits culture and environment with an impact on the observed deficits, but does not assume that different cultures and environments reflect inherently different types of intelligence such as is implied by an extreme exposition of the cultural difference model. The deficit model, rather, sees the manifest behavior of individuals from low socioeconomic and ethnocultural subgroups as reflecting a lack of certain cognitive skills or, in general, a deficit in one or more of those test-related factors that influence performance on the conventional psychometric instruments. The deficit model, like the cultural difference model, has given rise to a number of conceptually distinct approaches, differing mainly with respect to the degree of stability that should be assigned to the deficits. Jensen (1969) has proposed a deficit model that regards the deficiencies as *immutable* and *stable*. In Jensen's view, genetic factors primarily account for the deficits observed, and he does not believe that meaningful returns on investments may accrue from attempts to close these gaps through intervention. As far as assessment is concerned, Jensen's approach favors the development of instruments that focus exclusively on those simple cognitive behaviors that the low functioning population is said to perform as well as, and even better than, their socioeconomically more advantaged peers; it entirely omits tasks that demand cognitive functioning on a higher level. The latter areas should be tapped in tests designed for use with individuals and groups who may be expected to manifest cognitive behaviors beyond the stimulus-response, associative type so characteristic of the population of low scorers on conventional psychometric tests (see Chapter 2).

Another branch of the deficit model argues that the observed deficits do not reflect real incapacities in the individual and are not stable and immutable, but are determined by deficiencies in certain prerequisites of adequate cognitive functioning. The deficiencies may be overcome by appropriate approaches and techniques, and once they are corrected one may perceive the capacity of the individual which, it is claimed, was previously obscured by the deficits. This type of deficit model argues that the conventional and static psychometric procedures should be replaced with dynamic instruments incorporating possibilities for the low functioning child to show the degree to which he can profit from, and become modified by, different types of investments. The differential impact of nature and nurture is not, in this view, understood to reflect stable, immutable conditions, but is subject to change within an investment/learning ratio, the specific nature of which should be determined by assessment procedures. The approach presented in this book represents an example of this type of deficit model.

A third alternative to conventional psychometric tests takes the view that generic intelligence and levels of functioning can be measured by tests specifically constructed to overcome any differential influence of culture and environment. The term "culture free" has usually been used to describe instruments that typically emphasize pictorial and nonverbal modalities and use test items that presumably are not biased for or against any particular culture. A further alternative, developmental tests, on the other hand, views intelligence as developing in a fixed sequence of stages where the final level of development is determined by natural endowment and maturational factors only. It may be examined, for example, by tests of production such as visual-motor tests, the Bender-Gestalt test (Bender, 1938), and the Human Figure Drawing Test (Machover, 1949).

Finally, attempts have been made to modify conventional psychometric procedures by reducing the weight assigned to the performance on the tests. This is done by taking into account additional information, obtained in a nontest situation, on the degree of the examinee's social competence and successful adaptation to his own environment. This view discounts the need to develop assessment instruments for the intellectual area. The argument is that specially developed instruments would not differ greatly from the conventional ones because tests invariably become so tangled in bias and unfairness that no real gain may be hoped for in test development. The proposal, therefore, is to leave psychometric testing more or less the way it is, but additionally to assign very considerable weight to adaptational and competence information normally excluded by sole reliance on psychometric tests.

In the following brief review it is argued that attempts to modify conventional psychometric approaches remain insufficient as long as they fail to divest themselves of the static nature characteristic of the conventional approaches. Drawing support from previous investigators' efforts to introduce a dynamic element into assessment procedures, the Learning Potential Assessment Device is finally presented as a preferential method and tool for the assessment of the low functioning individual.

Cultural Difference vs. Cultural Deprivation

All of the attempts to change conventional psychometric tests suffer from a conceptual difficulty. They lack a clear distinction between culturally different and culturally deprived children. The distinction between these two phenomena, cultural difference and cultural deprivation, is of utmost importance for establishing the different needs of these two populations and for providing them with appropriate programs for their integration into society. Although low levels of manifest functioning may well be observed in culturally different individuals who are confronted with task requirements that vary from the expectations of their own familiar culture, these individuals may overcome their difficulties relatively easily since the learning of their own culture has rendered them accessible to the acquisition of cultural elements other than their own.

A very salient example of adaptability and modifiability is that of the Yemenite Jews in Israel. For centuries, in their country of origin, this ethnic group existed with their very unique culture, in nurturing conditions of life that varied greatly from those of the Occidental culture to which they had to adapt in Israel. The sudden change produced by the "flying carpet" program that whisked them from Yemen to Israel nonetheless revealed that these extremely different individuals were equipped with highly developed culturally adaptive capacities—capacities acquired through their exposure to their own and very different culture. Indeed, *one may say that the more different the culture of a group is, the less the group can be considered deprived,* since these differences, which are equated with and form the identity and the uniqueness of the group, are produced by strong cultural transmission processes characteristic of the particular culture.

The individual who has learned to function within his own culture has learned to adapt and become modified. This modifiability, while developed and expressed within the context of a particular culture, is of much general adaptive value because it has established the prerequisites for learning and for continued modifiability. Culturally different individuals may therefore show a considerable capacity to learn and adapt once they are confronted with the need to do so.

> *In distinction, the culturally deprived can be defined as an individual or a group that has become alienated* from its own culture. *This alienation may have been produced by a variety of sociological, economic, geopolitical, psychophysical, and cultural determinants affecting the individual and/or the group. Alienation is reflected in a disruption of intergenerational transmission and mediational processes. One should note that the concept of cultural deprivation, as used by the author, refers to an* intrinsic *criterion of the specific culture, namely, the lack of the process inherent to the concept of culture itself: intergenerational transmission. This differs from the usually accepted meaning of the term "cultural deprivation," which refers to an extrinsic criterion by which the culture of certain ethnic subgroups is considered as depriving their members, thereby negatively affecting their cognitive capacities. As we define it, however, culture can never be viewed as a depriving factor. It may certainly produce differences in identity and uniqueness commensurate with the degree of adherence that an individual in a group has to his particular culture. It is by this lack of such an adherence, because of poor mediating transmissional processes, that an individual, or a group, becomes culturally deprived.*

Such deprivation may strongly affect the adaptive capacities of the individual since he is devoid of the learning skills and habits that are produced by transmission processes.

The confusion between cultural difference and cultural deprivation has had unfortunate results in many ways. The exclusive concern with the manifest level of functioning has produced much confusion between the causes of the inadaptive behavior of the culturally deprived and the transient nature of the low level of functioning of the culturally different. Although the behavior of the culturally different individual is attributable to his lack of familiarity with certain tasks, cognitive styles, contents, and languages of presentation, the problem for the culturally deprived is the absence or impairment of prerequisite cognitive functions produced by the lack of mediation and cultural transmission. The lack of acceptance of the idea that cultural deprivation produces specific deficits in the deprived individual's cognitive behavior has resulted in the faulty recognition of these difficulties as reflecting either true retardation or cultural difference, depending on the socioeconomic and ethnic background of the individual. The emphasis upon cultural difference as a source of variation in the levels of functioning among individuals belonging to various socioeconomic and ethnocultural subgroups has oriented the search for more appropriate ways of assessment toward areas of functioning that do not necessarily have any affinity for the problems of large segments of the population of low functioning individuals. The problems of cognitive functioning, and hence of its assessment, must be approached differently for cultural difference and for cultural deprivation.

Inadequacies in the Alternatives

Cultural Difference or Deficits Model The attempted improvements of conventional psychometric methods under the cultural difference model fail to take into account the important distinction between cultural difference and cultural deprivation. Because they fail to recognize the reasons for the pervasive and persistent low level of functioning of the culturally deprived child, they can be of little relevance to the child's problems.

Of all the attempted improvements to conventional psychometric assessment under the attempted cultural difference model, perhaps the least imaginative is the modification of tests by creating special norms to be used with the culturally disadvantaged. In these modifications, the tests themselves are left completely as they were originally or, at most, are slightly modified in keeping with the language of specific targeted populations. New means, standard deviations, and age–score relationships are carefully worked out so that testers and educators confronted with the relatively low level of competency will not have unrealistic expectations of these children. The tests, however, are not designed for use with the low socioeconomic, ethnocultural subgroups, and the results will not shed light on these groups' cognitive functioning. The scores will at best serve for ranking purposes, that is, for locating the respondent in relation to other members of his own group. But the results for the group will always indicate that these individuals are inferior in comparison to the majority group (McNemar, 1975). The results may therefore serve to deepen the negative stereotype and the perception of differences in regard to these disadvantaged groups. The danger inherent in the development of special norms is that the culturally disadvantaged individual's functioning is eventually interpreted as substantiating the viewpoint that immutable genetic and constitutional factors determine his low level of functioning, as in the stable deficit models of Shuey (1966) and Jensen (1969).

Culture-fair and Culture-free Tests The attempts to develop somewhat more radical alternatives to the conventional psychometric measures under the cultural difference model have been the so-called culture-fair tests. These tests have been constructed with the laudable goal of presenting item arrays that will not penalize the respondent for his social, ethnic, or experiential background. "Each culture encourages and fosters certain abilities and ways of behaving, and discourages and suppresses others. It is therefore to be expected that on tests developed with the American culture, American subjects will generally excel. If a test were constructed by the same procedures within a culture differing markedly from ours, American subjects would probably appear deficient in terms of test norms. Data bearing on this type of cultural comparison are very meagre. What evidence is available, however, suggests that persons from our culture may be just as handicapped on tests prepared within other cultures as members of those cultures are on our tests" (Anastasi, 1958, pp. 741–742; see also Mercer, 1975).

All the static principles of assessment characteristic of conventional instruments have been preserved in the culture-fair tests, except that they have been incorporated into tests designed for more narrowly defined populations. Like conventional instruments, culture-fair tests do not consider the great variety of reasons for failure to function at higher levels, and they reveal little about the respondent's cognitive structure and capacity. The failure to distinguish between cultural difference and cultural deprivation ensures that the deprived child will function as poorly on the culture-fair test as on the conventional psychometric measures. The results obtained on the Davis-Eells Games (Davis and Eells, 1953) are an example of this outcome. The Davis-Eells Games require no reading and all instructions are given orally. Its items are pictorial and seek to present problems appearing in the everyday life experience of children in the urban American culture. Yielding an Index of Problem Solving Ability, the test, as pointed out by its authors, is not intended as a measure of IQ or scholastic aptitude. It may therefore be expected that scores on this test will not correlate well with educational achievement or with traditional IQ measures such as the Stanford-Binet (Anastasi, 1954). Yet the scores on the Davis-Eells Games for lower class children do correlate closely with scores on the Stanford-Binet (0.78). The same correlation for middle-class children is in the upper sixties but it is zero for upper-class children. In her review of the Davis-Eells Games, Anastasi (1961) concluded that "lower class children perform as poorly on this test as on other intelligence tests" (p. 268). Masland, Sarason, and Gladwin (1958) have suggested that children with educational advantages can bring different specialized skills to each kind of test, whereas deprived children respond in the same way to all tests, thus explaining the above correlations between a "culture-fair" measure and the conventional Stanford-Binet. Ortar (1960), studying five groups of children in Israel with variation in both social class and degree of acculturation, found that while the verbal tests of the Wechsler Intelligence Scale place the five groups in the expected rank order, the performance tests, presumably more culture-fair because of their nonverbal nature, produced even greater differences in favor of the more privileged and longer acculturated children.

The culture-free tests use item arrays that supposedly enable the measurement of functioning across cultures, while the culture-fair tests use sets of item arrays where each set is biased in favor of a specific culture. This conceptualization really represents an extension of what we call the passive-acceptant approach, which considers intelligence to be originally and uniquely determined by stable genetic and hereditary-environmental factors. "The culture-fair or culture-free test is dedicated to the proposition of the genotype. If we think in terms of diagnosis, in terms of point-to-point phenotypical sampling and then of appropriate intervention, the usefulness of such instruments is minimal" (Hamburger, 1964, p. 76).

Studies such as Ortar's in Israel (1960) and the author's *Children of the Mellah* (Feuerstein and Richelle, 1963), have exposed the fallacy of assuming that nonverbal items are more free from environmental influences than are verbal ones (Haynes, 1971). It is doubtful if any relevance of these nonverbal tests is preserved when the tests are to be used for educational predictions. On the construction of the "so-called culture-free and culture-fair tests of ability," Judith Haynes (1971) wrote: "The tests did not, in fact, involve good examples of skills relevant to educational progress and the whole approach was clearly based on the concept of intelligence as some fixed power of the mind which would reveal itself through unrelated tasks and in widely different test situations" (p. 22). Haynes therefore concluded that "Such testing cannot make an assessment of the full educational potential of the individual" (p. 21).

Tannenbaum (1965), in his review of the Cattell Culture-Free Test (Cattell, 1940, 1944), whose premise was said to be "freedom from cultural bias, [with] results reflecting individual capabilities but not differences in cultural experience" (Masland, Sarason, and Gladwin, 1958, p. 274), wrote:

> Is it, indeed, a goal worth pursuing? Even if it were possible to devise a test so antiseptic as to clean out inequality not only among sub-cultures but also among other groups showing difference in test-intelligence, such as those classified by sex, age, education, geographic origin, body-type, physical health, personality structure and family unity—what kind of an instrument would we then have? Since such a test must perforce be so thoroughly doctored as to omit tasks that reveal these group differences, or substitute others that show no difference what could it possibly measure? What could it predict? Covering up differences in this way does not erase test bias. Rather it delimits drastically the kinds of information one can gather about problem solving strengths and weaknesses associated with groups as well as individuals. (p. 723)

(See also Lorge, 1953.) The culture-free and culture-fair tests misunderstand the task to be one of trying to show that no real differences exist among individuals and groups even on the manifest level of functioning, as if the fact that such differences are found on the conventional measures is the source of the ill doing to which these tests have led. But while the conventional measures can be criticized for sampling only the manifest level of functioning, it is wrong to argue that there really are no such differences on the manifest level. They are patently revealed by the conventional measures and corroborated by a great variety of nontest data. The following quotations indicate that the weight of expert opinion no longer supports the notion of culture-free tests:

> It is safe to say at present that no test exists which can approximate to a measure of inherent mental capacity irrespective of cultural experience, or which can measure differences of intelligence between individuals of a different culture than our own along dimensions they themselves consider most "important." (Masland, Sarason, and Gladwin, 1958, p. 274)

> We concluded that sociocultural differences are so marked and are so highly correlated with test scores, both within and between racial/ethnic groups, that the usual practice of making a diagnosis of biological potential by comparing scores for persons from different sociocultural settings within the same normative framework is not justified and should be abandoned. (Mercer, 1975, p. 140)

> . . . . no test can be truly "culture-free." Since every test measures a sample behavior, it will reflect any factor which influences the behavior of individuals. (Anastasi, 1961, p. 255)

> A culture-free test would presumably probe learnings which have not been affected by environment; this is sheer nonsense. (Wesman, 1968, p. 269)

Developmental Tests   Much of the criticism against culture-free tests obviously applies to the developmental tests as well. The use of developmental tests as measures of intellectual ability assumes that the cognitive functions underlying performance on these tests are little if at all influenced by sociocultural factors and by general life experiences. It is held that, up to a certain point in the individual's development, the appearance or nonappearance of certain cognitive functions is maturationally and genetically determined. Yet scores on developmental tests such as the Bender-Gestalt, the Human Figure Drawing, the Minnesota Perceptuo-Diagnostic Test, and other visual-motor tests, contrary to what should be expected, correlate with measures of intelligence that have long been shown to be influenced by environmental factors. Thus for example, Ansbacher (1952), studying 100 fourth graders, found that scores on the Goodenough Draw-a-Man test (Goodenough, 1926; Goodenough and Harris, 1950) correlated with the Primary Mental Ability Sub-tests (Thurstone, 1938) of reasoning, spatial aptitude, and perceptual speed. The author of this test herself recognized that scores were more dependent upon cultural differences than originally assumed. "The search for a culture-free test, whether of intelligence, artistic ability, personal-social characteristics, or any other measurable trait is illusory" (Goodenough and Harris, 1950, p. 399).

This author's experience with children's figure drawings has indicated that marked differences in ability exist as a function of cultural and experiential background (Feuerstein and Richelle, 1958). Children from different social and ethnic groups demonstrate varying degrees of success even when intelligence levels are held constant (Feuerstein and Richelle, 1963). In a hitherto unpublished study, the author (1970b) found significant sociocultural differences in children's ability to convey foreground-background perspectives in drawings. Israeli school children were instructed to draw a child partially hiding behind a house, a tree partially visible behind a rock, apples partially visible behind a stone, and a child partially visible behind his mother (Figure 1). Responses were categorized as "juxtapositions," "transparencies," or "correct."

From grades one through eight, the number of correct responses per class indicated a gap from 3 to 4 years between a group ($N = 357$) of rural lower-class children, broadly defined as culturally disadvantaged, and a group of urban, middle-class children matched to the former for age and sex (Figure 2). A similar 3- to 4-year difference in favor of the middle-class sample was obtained measuring the percentage of subjects per class in the two groups who obtained at least a score of 3 on a human figure drawing, scored according to the

Figure 1.   Illustrations from the Four Drawings Test. Total transparency: examples 1, 2, and 3. Juxtaposition: examples 4, 5, and 6. Partial transparency: examples 7 and 8. Corrected transparency: example 8. Correct responses: examples 9, 10, and 11.

5-point Witkin Sophistication Scale (Witkin et al., 1962) (Tables 1 and 2). The meaning of the 3- to 4-year differences obtained on both tests is, in other words, that lower-class fourth graders were most comparable with middle-class first graders, etc. Comparing perform-ance across age levels a U-shaped curve was indicated on both tests

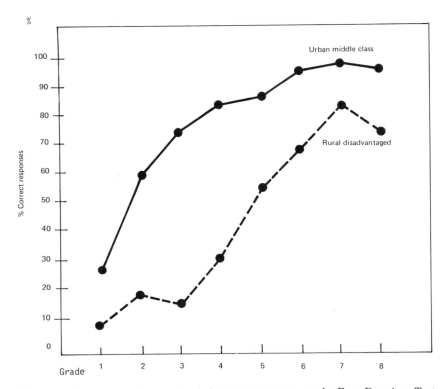

Figure 2. Comparison of percentage of correct responses on the Four Drawings Test according to school grade and socioeconomic class.

showing roughly 20% more middle-class children than lower-class children obtaining criterion scores in the first and eighth grades. In the foreground-background test middle-class children enjoyed their greatest advantage over lower-class children in the third grade (75% vs. 14%). The maximum difference between the two groups on the human figure drawing test was found to be of the same magnitude in the fifth grade (77% vs. 21%).

The Minnesota Perceptuo-Diagnostic Test, a visual-motor test known to discriminate among normal, neurotic, psychotic, and organically impaired groups, has also been investigated as a possible instrument for minimizing sociocultural differences in the assessment of the individual's psychological structure. It was found that the culturally disadvantaged, both white and black, demonstrate performance levels inferior even to those of organically impaired and psychotic individuals (Fuller and Laird, 1963).

Table 1.   The Four Drawings Test: Lower- and middle-class samples

Grade	Percentage giving correct responses		Percentage difference in favor of middle class
	Lower class (N = 357)	Middle class (N = 373)	
1	8	27	19
2	18	59	41
3	14	74	60
4	32	83	51
5	53	86	33
6	68	95	27
7	82	97	15
8	75	95	20

It may be safely concluded that all tests which supposedly capitalize on developmental-maturational processes are greatly influenced by the nature of the respondent's interaction with his environment. Certain organism-environment interactions will favor the appearance and enhance the development of even so-called maturational functions while others may ignore, belittle, or even warp the growth of these same functions. Like the culture-free and culture-fair attempts to improve conventional psychometric tests, developmental tests do not constitute a solution to the problems presented by conventional testing, as long as they preserve the status quo. In fact, under specific conditions the developmental tests may reflect and emphasize the passive-acceptant view of intelligence as a stable and immutable entity by relating the results to endogenous factors operating in the individual, rather than relating them to the environmental interaction.

Table 2.   The Witkin Sophistication Scale: Lower and middle-class samples

Grade	Percentage obtaining scores 1-3		Percentage difference in favor of middle class
	Lower class (N = 357)	Middle class (N = 373)	
1	4	26	22
2	3	35	32
3	17	58	41
4	30	64	34
5	21	77	56
6	67	89	22
7	67	90	23
8	63	77	14

Inventory of Adaptive Behavior

Recently, attempts have been made to modify conventional psychometric procedures by reducing the weight assigned to test performance and by including additional information obtained in the nontest situations in the overall evaluation. For example, Leland (1973) suggested inventorying adaptive behavior as a way to broaden the findings on pure psychometric approaches. However, this is again an example of the static approach. It leaves open the question of the diagnosis of an individual whose results on the test denote a lack of adaptive behavior even in his own culture and by criteria intrinsic to it. Does an individual's low level of functioning mean he is not modifiable and cannot acquire the adaptive behavior that is missing in the broad assessment of his cognitive level and social competence?

With the inventory type of approach, however broad-minded it may be, one again turns to the search for stable characteristics whether they are seen to be generated by genetic factors or by environmental determinants. This approach may at best do justice to the culturally different; but it will be totally unsatisfactory and, beyond a certain point, deleterious, whenever cultural difference is coupled with a cultural deprivation that reflects an individual's alienation from processes of cultural transmission. Here the lack of adaptive behavior is a corollary to a lack of efficient cognitive functions, which are absent or impaired because the individual was not involved in the processes of transmission. Individuals with cultural deprivation defined in this way may be found with greater frequency in lower socioeconomic, ethnocultural subgroups, but they may also be found in families and groups from a great variety of backgrounds. A static inventory of cognitive functioning, adaptive behavior, and social competence may just result in the continued labeling of a great portion of the population of children and adolescents whose manifest level of functioning is low. Although the condition of these culturally deprived children is not always easily or spontaneously reversed, neither is it immutable or fixed. Yet it may appear so through measurement by the static inventory approach.

Summary

We have reviewed the attempted changes of conventional psychometric procedures under the cultural difference vs. the stable deficits model, the culture-free and culture-fair tests, the developmental tests, and the inventory of adaptive behavior. We have also found, as have many other authors, that each of these attempted changes is unsatisfactory. Although they struggle in different ways to overcome some of the criticism leveled against conventional psychometrics, they still serve the static paradigm of assessment. Conventional psychometric instruments, and the attempted changes, passively aim at inventorying existing and manifest cognitive capacities. All of these instruments reveal inadequate performance patterns in culturally deprived populations, but none of them can reveal the deprived child's potential for being modified by learning. No search for such a potential is undertaken by any of the measures, and none produces information about more intimate causes of failure and the specific remediational procedures that may be instituted to overcome the difficulties.

Several authors have denounced the basic assumptions of inherited and fixed intelligence as being responsible for the inadequacy of the structure of conventional mental test procedures. Gordon (1965) along with many other authors (e.g., Rey, 1934; Hunt, 1961; Bereiter, 1962; Deutsch et al., 1964; Hamburger, 1964; Schwebel, 1968), has stressed that, if psychological appraisal is to meaningfully address the problems of educational and social planning for the culturally disadvantaged, we should concentrate our efforts on the development of instruments and techniques to evaluate patterns of learning disability, learning facility, and potential for learning, making the appraisal process one of qualitative analysis rather than of quantitative assessment (see also Vygotsky, 1962; Karp and Sigel, 1965; Biesheuvel, 1971). The next section briefly describes this dynamic approach, the attempts made to move in its direction, and the requirements of a dynamic assessment.

THE DYNAMIC APPROACH: ASSESSMENT OF MODIFIABILITY THROUGH FOCUSED LEARNING

The potential for being modified by learning should be the object of focus in psychometric assessment. This potential can be measured only by an active, involved, and involving process, and can never be revealed by a static enumeration of existing abilities. Indeed, one wonders why it has taken us so long to realize that the only way to assess potential for change is to attempt to modify the examinee in some way, while measuring the extent of the change and the means by which this was attained. As far back as 1934, the eminent professor André Rey observed that the goal of psychometric testing should be the measurement of potentiality for being modified by learning. Rey (1934) speculated that the historical preference in psychometric testing for eliciting the already existing adaptational and intellectual capacities, the "accommodat," reflects the concern with developing easy and rapid methods for investigating intellectual processes. Yet, as Rey noted, the study of *developed* capacities is unsuitable for making any meaningful comparisons of capacity. It is necessary, therefore, to abandon the making of such comparisons, using the available "accommodat," in favor of investigating processes of development and modification of adaptational and intellectual capacities.

This dynamic approach to evaluating intelligence by measuring modifiability during active learning is clearly incompatible with the view that intelligence is determined in some matrix of unchangeable, genetic-constitutional, environmental factors. Rather, intellectual functioning is seen to be the expression of a complex interaction of biogenetic, cultural, experiential, and emotional factors, and thus, reversibility of poor intellectual performance may definitely be anticipated.

The dynamic approach to assessment and the view that intelligence is reflected in the potential for being modified by learning have been supported by many investigators of intellectual development. Wesman's contribution deserves prominent mention: "Organisms may differ from one another in their susceptibility to modification. One organism may need a more potent stimulus to trigger reaction to the environment than does another. A particular organism may respond to a given class more readily than it does to other kinds of stimuli. Organisms may differ from one another in their readiness to respond to different classes of stimuli. There may be important differences in the ability of organisms to modify their behavior in effective ways as a result of experience" (Wesman, 1968, p. 267; see also Feuerstein, 1978b).

Viewing intelligence as the result of complex interaction between the organism and the environment, and as summarily expressed in the capacity for modifiability or learning, implies that assessment procedures used for educational and social intervention should not be primarily concerned with interindividual differences. Rather, they should enable a full, independent study of each particular individual. If intelligence is a summation of one's learning and learning consists of being modified, then if one sets about to induce some modification, the speed and accuracy with which learning is produced will correctly indicate the intellectual capacities. No labels are inherently useful: the need for a high level of detailing each examinee's functioning eclipses the usefulness of general categories except for describing the level of manifest behavior. But the manifest behavior, while the end point of conventional psychometric testing, is only the point of departure for the dynamic testing. Beyond this point of departure, labels become irrelevant, gross, and misleading with respect to the minute assessment of the particular individual's capacity for learning. The dynamic, interactional view of intelligence is reflected in the assessment, with the examiner and the examinee interacting as teacher and student, as helper and helped. Such an interactional approach to assessment was proposed by Luria (1961), who was strongly critical of conventional psychometric approaches: "When we know that higher psychological processes, including intellectual activity, have a complex developmental history and are formed in the course of the child's speech-based social relationships, can we continue to adhere to the . . . static principles in assessing a child's abilities and intellect? Can we continue to make confident judgments of a child's intellectual development merely on the basis of whether he performs on his own with a greater or lesser success? Would it not be more proper to set about it differently, to reject the static principle of assessing a child's independent performance of a given task in favor of that of comparing the success of his independent performance with that achieved *with adult help?*" (pp. 40–41).

Attempts at a Dynamic Approach by Other Investigators

Several investigators have already begun to work practically in this direction and have demonstrated that an entirely different impression of cognitive potential is indeed obtained when a child is asked to learn something during the test, rather than merely required to display what he has or has not learned. Else Haeussermann (1958) early developed a system of "Educational Evaluation" for young handicapped children. Her test is in many ways similar to the Binet test in form and material, yet shows much innovation and extension beyond the Binet format because the goal of assessment is dynamic, that is, it assesses *how* the child has arrived at a given solution and explores the basis for particular failures. Her goal is to supply a "painstaking evaluation of the areas significant for development and learning in the individual child" (Haeussermann, 1958, p. 46). The information provided by the assessment is naturally used to detail and plan an educational program for each examinee.

Helen Schucman (1968) developed an "Educability Index" for the trainable child. Her test procedure is explicitly based on the assumption that a child's educability may be inferred from his ability to profit from instruction, to transfer the training, and to retain the contents or principles learned. Schucman's index measures discrimination among gross shape, size and color, imitative behavior, and rote memory. She found these areas most suitable for the assessment of her young subjects (mean IQ, 36). Schucman uses a test-coach-retest model to estimate the child's learning ability in line with her acceptance of the view that a single administration of a test may not identify fundamental abilities of the trainable child. Schucman's work added to the growing body of evidence since the transfer and retention scores obtained for her children proved to be the most sensitive detectors of cognitive potential.

Milton Budoff (1968), using a task based on Koh's block design, has argued for criterion tasks to be administered a total of three times with a coaching session interspersed between the test and the first retest. The first retest is administered 1 day after the coaching session and the second retest follows 1 month later. Using this procedure, Budoff and his colleagues have identified three groups of learners: "gainers," "non-gainers," and "high-scorers prior to coaching." Budoff has found that gainers and high-scorers sampled from special classes learned as much as did their like-named peers from normal classes when all subjects were tested on a specially devised educational exercise. Non-gainers from both types of classrooms did markedly worse than the gainers and high-scorers.

Budoff's distinction between the initial level of functioning (assessed by the test), "the child's optimal level of performance following an optimizing procedure" (Budoff, 1973) assessed by the first posttraining scores, and the child's capacity to benefit from training, assessed by the posttraining scores adjusted for pretraining scores, certainly represents a step toward a more dynamic approach. However, Budoff's initial orientation to search for the stable characteristics of those who proved modifiable (gainers) and those who proved unable to profit from the coaching provided during the assessment (non-gainers) does not go far enough in adopting the principle of dynamic assessment. Rather than looking for the reason for failure of the intervention to turn the child into a gainer, he looked for some stable characteristic corollary to the failure, either in the realm of personality, motivation, or cognitive structure. An intraindividual picture has to be formed of each examinee, irrespective of the performance of other examinees, in order to identify the reasons for failure. If this examination of the reasons for failure is not undertaken, a substantial group of low functioning children will be denied constructive remediational efforts. More recently, using the approach and instruments suggested by this author, Budoff and his colleagues have begun to tackle the problems presented by the non-gainers and have also emphasized the need for "a taxonomy of necessary or appropriate skills that facilitate educability" (Budoff, 1973, p. 67; see also Budoff and Hamilton, 1976).

Research designed to explore the cognitive prerequisites that facilitate learning has been begun by Clarke and his colleagues, who studied the relationship between stimulus complexity, discrimination, and categorization. The authors found that "with appropriate conditions of training, subjects became sensitive to the categorical properties of incoming stimulus material, thereby increasing their efficiency when moved to transfer tasks based on different elements" (Clarke, Clarke, and Cooper, 1970, p. 433; see also A. D. B. Clarke and Cooper, 1966; Clarke, Cooper, and Henney, 1966; Clarke and Clarke, 1967). In another example of relevant research, Rohwer and Ammons (1971) studied elaborative behavior after they found that the tendency to spontaneously elaborate material could account for the different learning patterns observed in a sample of children from high and low socioeconomic backgrounds. Using a paired-associates task administered to second grade black children with a low socioeconomic background and white children with a high socioeconomic background, these researchers found that the high socioeconomic subjects profited from both training and practice, relative to an appropriate control group, whereas the low socioeconomic children derived virtually no learning improvement from practice but did improve sustantially with training. Rohwer (1971) has also called for the development of tests to measure learning proficiency and learning style using dynamic tests of ongoing learning rather than evoking material learned in the past.

Haywood and his associates have performed a series of experiments, replicated with different samples, attempting to enhance the ability of mildly retarded persons to form verbal abstractions (Gordon and Haywood, 1969; Foster, 1970; Call, 1973; Tymchuk, 1973; Haywood and Switzky, 1974). In some of these experiments, 20-item similarities tests were administered under regular and enriched conditions to groups of institutionalized, cultural-familially, and organically retarded persons and normal controls matched for mental age. Under the regular condition, test items were administered just as for the Wechsler similarities test, while the enriched procedure used between three and five examples for each item, depending on the experiment. The enriched procedure was tested on the hypothesis that the limited ability of the mildly retarded individuals to form verbal abstractions on conventional intelligence tests may "be the result of a secondary deficiency in information input-capacity, rather than a deficiency in the ability to form abstractions given adequate information input" (Haywood et al., 1975, p. 104).

Enriching the input for grouping and classifying discrete events indicated that subjects, whose retardation is associated with cultural deprivation, performed as well as did their normal mental age-matched peers on the enriched procedure while with the regular procedure results were distributed, in the expected way, in their disfavor. The normal subjects did not show improvement with the enriched procedure, which, the authors pointed out, would not be expected since no information-input deficit is assumed to exist for this group. The failure of the organically retarded to profit from the enriched procedure could be attributable to a more central impairment or to an insufficiency of the enrichment procedure used to overcome their deficit.

In his study of 8-year-old low ability and high ability children, all of lower social class families, Call (1973) found that using an aural-plus-picture enrichment condition for presenting the similarities tasks resulted in the low ability children functioning as well as the high ability children of the same chronological age. Moreover, the aural-plus-picture enrichment made for a significant increase in verbal abstraction over aural enrichment alone for these children, while no such differences were found for the high ability subjects between any of the enrichment and regular procedures. These results indicate that a relatively simple mechanism affecting the richness of input data may determine the level of performance of verbal abstraction of many low functioning children.

The above-mentioned authors have all contributed to and provided demonstrations showing the effectiveness of a dynamic training-assessment system that can provide a valid and prescriptively helpful estimate of the cognitive potential of the low functioning, disadvantaged child, by beginning to indicate which functions are deficient and which specific means should be taken for their correction. Haeussermann's Educational Evaluation, the most comprehensive approach in the above group and indeed a brave departure for the period during which it was developed and presented (1958), is aimed at a very young and possibly physically handicapped population and hence comprises a fairly small range of cognitive functioning. Schucman (1968), Budoff (1968, 1973), Budoff and Hamilton (1976), Clarke, Clarke, and Cooper (1970), Rohwer and Ammons (1971), and Haywood et al. (1975) have all provided clear demonstrations in support of a new philosophy of assessing cognitive potential.

Several authors have worked to develop an approach focusing on the functional analysis of behavior (Ferster, 1965; Baer, Wolf, and Risley, 1968; Bricker, 1970; Gardner, 1971; Bricker and Bricker, 1973). This approach classifies behavior rather than children. Emphasizing environmental determinants of behavior within the context of any relevant genetic and/or organic factors, the functional analysis of behavior seeks to identify antecedent and consequent events that determine the quality and quantity of the specific behaviors in need of modification. The data gathered are directly relevant for implementing changes through manipulation of controlling events. "Thus the validity of the analysis is indicated by the extent to which behavior changes systematically as recommendations derived from the evaluation are implemented" (Haywood et al., 1975, p. 126). Moreover: "Functional analysis is a continuing process, ending only when the desired change in behavior has been effected and is being maintained by the natural environment" (Haywood et al., 1975, p. 128).

Piaget's work (1952, 1954, 1966; Piaget and Inhelder, 1969) has also given rise to several attempts to improve assessment procedures. Some of these have preserved the static nature of testing. These studies have been primarily useful in pointing out that the level of cognitive functioning over a range of culturally different children may be equally developed in spite of sharp variations in performance as revealed on traditional psychometric measures (as in De Avila, Havassay, and Pascual-Leone, 1976).

The work of Uzgiris and Hunt (1975) represents an effective and successful approach in using the most basic developmental milestones conceptualized by Piaget, such as the construction of object permanency, means-end relations, and the development of imitative processes. This approach is certainly a fruitful one in cross-cultural evaluation and assessment, is easily applied in a dynamic way, and may therefore be of help in outlining the more universal developmental processes such as described by Piaget.

Bricker (1973) has developed a diagnostic and educational system, termed Constructive Interaction Adaptation, which represents an attempt to combine the developmental model proposed by Piaget with the principles of functional analysis briefly described above. The approach seeks to introduce the Piagetian concept of a fixed developmental sequence. "The test is given sequentially until the response of the child is not appropriate, at which time testing stops and instruction begins" (Filler et al., 1975, p. 222). The approach readily accommodates for failure and, indeed, uses failure as a starting point for the instructional effort.

Requirements of the Dynamic Approach

In the following chapters we present the theoretical framework, principles, and techniques of a learning potential assessment system that may reveal hidden potential lying buried beneath the surface of the manifest behavior of retarded performing and disadvantaged children. This approach represents a radical departure from conventional psychometric procedures. We propose to replace the static goal of the diagnostic procedure with a dynamic goal, which, instead of inventorying the manifest capacities of the individual and using these as a basis for making inferences regarding future development, seeks to measure the degree of the individual's modifiability by providing him with a focused learning experience. We may thereby obtain a measure of the individual's learning potential, defined as his capacity to become modified by a learning process. This assessment provides a wealth of data directly relevant to the modification of the deficient functions identified in the assessment, making meaningful intervention possible and often enabling a restructuring of the cognitive behavior. The dynamic assessment approach requires changes in the following four areas:

1. The structure of the tests   The test instruments have to be constructed in a way that provides the examiner and the examinee with tasks that can be used in a teaching process and that can enable the examiner to evaluate the effect of the teaching process on the capacity of the individual to deal with new situations.

2. The examination situation   The shift from a static to a dynamic goal implies a change in the test situation that will turn the examiner into a teacher-observer and the examinee into a learner-performer. This shift entails a variety of changes in the usual interaction and in the establishment of a two-way communication process.

3. The orientation of the tests   The shift from product to process orientation is another change necessary to turn a static approach into a dynamic one.

4. Interpretation of results   The peaks in the pattern of the obtained results should be used as an indication of the cognitive potential of the examinee.

The Learning Potential Assessment Device represents an attempt to incorporate these features into a model of assessment of the low functioning child. The following chapters present this model, the method underlying the construction of instruments, their application in individual and group assessment, and the interpretation of results obtained with their use.

CHAPTER 2 Sources of Cognitive Impairment

As has already been stated, culturally deprived and socioeconomically disadvantaged individuals demonstrate inadequate performance levels on conventional IQ measures. They lack motivation to take tests, they are deficient in the kind of information generally tapped by intelligence tests, and often they are uncertain about what is expected of them in the test situation.

The basis of this poor performance on IQ tests can be found in the wide array of cognitive deficiencies characteristic of the culturally disadvantaged. These deficient functions are not considered elements that are missing from the cognitive repertoire of the individual. Rather they are conceived of as functions that are underdeveloped, poorly developed, arrested, and/or impaired. Under certain conditions, especially when a strong need emerges in the individual, adequate functioning may appear. Such elicitation, however, is infrequent because of the lack of the requisite need system, so that the effort involved in their mobilization makes their use uneconomical. A state of impairment or deficiency is to be understood in the sense that these functions do not appear spontaneously, regularly, and predictably in the cognitive behavior of the individual, and/or when they do appear they show a marked inefficiency in the problem-solving behavior.

The nature of the deficient functions and their locus of occurrence in terms of our input, elaboration, output model are presented. Some of the more significant deficient functions are explained in greater detail. Three theoretical considerations—mediated learning experience, cultural deprivation, and reversibility of retarded performance—are then elucidated. The chapter concludes with a discussion of genetic endowment as the source of cognitive impairment in retarded performers and rejects this explanation in light of definitions of learning and intelligence and data from the Learning Potential Assessment Device.

THE NATURE AND LOCUS OF IMPAIRMENTS

The deficient cognitive functions can be analyzed into three phases of the mental act—1) the input phase, 2) the elaborational phase, and 3) the output phase—in order to help define specific problems and to suggest types of strategies for their solution. Although this division is intended to assist in diagnosis and prescription, the interactions occurring between and among the phases are of vital significance in understanding the extent and pervasiveness of cognitive impairment manifested by the retarded performer in psychometric measures of intelligence and school achievement and in real-life situations. An additional dimension, the affective-motivational factor, has a pervasive influence on the three phases of the mental act.

Since the deficient functions represent a crucial dimension in our attempts to modify the cognitive structure of the disadvantaged adolescent in a more stable way, their more detailed and elaborate description is found in our work in *Instrumental Enrichment* (Feuerstein, in press). Here we limit ourselves to listing the deficiencies and briefly discussing some of them to provide a better understanding of the reasons for the child's failure in testing situations and for any attempts to modify him during the LPAD testing sessions.

The Input Phase

Deficiencies at the input phase include all those impairments concerned with the quantity and quality of data gathered by the individual as he attempts the solution of a given problem or even as he begins to appreciate the nature of the problem. Some impairments at this phase include:

1. Blurred and sweeping perception
2. Unplanned, impulsive, and unsystematic exploratory behavior
3. Lack of or impaired receptive verbal tools that affect discrimination: objects, events, relationships, etc., do not have appropriate labels
4. Lack of or impaired spatial orientation and the lack of stable systems of reference that impair the establishment of topological and Euclidean organization of space
5. Lack of or impaired temporal concepts
6. Lack of or impaired conservation of constancies of factors such as size, shape, quantity, orientation, etc., across variations of other dimensions of the perceived object

7. Lack of or deficient need for precision and accuracy in data gathering
8. Lack of capacity for considering two or more sources of information at once, which is reflected in dealing with data in a piecemeal fashion rather than as a unit of organized facts

These factors, acting either by themselves or in clusters, result in a condition of deficiency in "readiness for response." The response will invariably be inadequate in terms of the solution expected by the examiner because the appropriate data have not become available to the examinee. If we were to trace the response back to the premises from which it originated, we might find that sound elaborational techniques were employed for the processing of inadequate data. Impairment at the input phase may also, but not necessarily, affect the ability to function at the phases of elaboration and output (see Gordon and Haywood, 1969).

The Elaborational Phase

Deficiencies at the elaborational phase include those factors that impede the individual's efficient use of the data available to him. In addition to impairments in data gathering, which may or may not have occurred at the input phase, these deficiencies operate to obstruct proper elaboration of whatever cues do exist:

1. Inadequacy in the perception of the existence and definition of an actual problem
2. Inability to select relevant vs. nonrelevant cues in defining a problem
3. Lack of spontaneous comparative behavior or limitation of its application by a restricted need system
4. Narrowness of the mental field
5. Episodic grasp of reality
6. Lack of or impaired need for pursuing logical evidence
7. Lack of or impaired interiorization
8. Lack of or impaired inferential hypothetical "iffy" thinking
9. Lack of or impaired strategies for hypothesis testing
10. Lack of or impaired planning behavior
11. Nonelaboration of certain cognitive categories because the verbal concepts are not a part of the individual's repertoire on a receptive level or are not mobilized at the expressive level

We have found these deficiencies in the elaboration of cues to occur, often in combinations, with marked frequency in the culturally disadvantaged.

It is the elaboration of cues to which we usually refer when we speak of "thinking." Inadequate or inappropriate data do not preclude an appropriate, or even original, creative elaborational response. The appropriate discovery may be contained in situations where there is a perception of inappropriate elements or where not all the elements are perceived and some must be deduced. Elaboration of such inappropriate or inadequate data, however, requires an intellectual ingenuity that will withstand frustration in face of failure. Such qualities are not often found in the culturally disadvantaged. Incomplete data may be dealt with by inadequate elaboration. The outcome may be either a personalized or a bizarre response, an impoverished one utilizing only the data meaningful to the respondent, or perhaps no response at all—a blocking in anticipation of complete failure.

The Output Phase

Deficiencies at the output phase include those that result in inadequate communication of final solutions. Even adequately gathered data and appropriate elaboration can result in inappropriate expression if difficulties exist for the individual at this phase. Specific deficiencies include:

1. Egocentric communicational modalities
2. Difficulties in projecting virtual relationships
3. Blocking
4. Trial and error responses
5. Lack of or impaired verbal tools for communicating adequately elaborated responses
6. Lack of or impaired need for precision and accuracy in communicating responses
7. Deficiencies in visual transport
8. Impulsive, acting-out behavior

Affective-Motivational Factors

Affective-motivational factors can combine negatively in such a way as to influence test-taking attitudes to the severe detriment of the culturally disadvantaged individual. These phenomena have been widely commented upon by psychologists working with this population. Deutsch et al. (1964), for example, argued that in contrast to the middle-class child the lower-class child will tend to be more fearful of strangers, less self-confident, less competitive in the intellectual realm, more "irritable," and less conforming to middle-class norms of behavior and conduct. Such children are also at a distinct disadvantage in their motivation for doing well on IQ tests. The dislike for the entire test situation combined with the feeling that the test lacks relevance may readily depress an IQ score, possibly by a few points, as admitted by Jensen (1969), but more likely by tens of points, as we found in our clinical work.

SPECIFIC IMPAIRMENTS

Unplanned, Impulsive, and Unsystematic Exploratory Behavior

Unplanned and unsystematic exploratory behavior is often demonstrated by the culturally disadvantaged. Their explorations are diffuse, probabilistic, and accidental. When these children are presented with a number of cues that must be scanned, it becomes apparent that the manner in which the proposed data are approached is so disorganized that it will never help in selecting those cues and their specific attributes that are relevant for a proper solution.

Some observations from our clinical practice may serve to illustrate this point. When given the task of placing letters in a form board, culturally disadvantaged children characteristically attempt trial-and-error placement. There is a minimal amount of investment in exploring the two objects to be matched.

Another example is our stereognostic experiment in which geometric objects have to be recognized purely by touch. Subjects manipulate objects concealed in a covered box by putting only their hands through the side of the box. Through the open side of the box we can observe their manipulations. Their explorations were limited to palming and partially touching the contours, rather than to careful fingering. Similarly, when asked to estimate the size of an object, again using only tactile cues, culturally disadvantaged children would invariably palm instead of keeping one finger in place as a point of reference. Their recognition of objects and their estimate of size were highly inaccurate as the result of partial, fragmented, and unsystematic exploratory behavior.

We had further evidence of this phenomenon when, for example, the test involved multiple choices. The children would begin searching for the answer before they had properly defined the problem. In instances when the task required reading full sentences that described a logical succession of events, the haphazard grabbing at facts would immediately preclude success because the examinee was handicapped from the start by insufficient data gathering. Thus, even if the elaborational process following such diffuse gathering of data was properly carried out, it could not yield the expected solution.

It should be emphasized that impulsive exploratory behavior is not the result of an incapacity to attend, although these two phenomena frequently accompany one another. It is the result of inadequate exploratory skills. These inadequacies reflect a poor definition of the problem to be solved and result in a lack of goal orientation; this, in turn, acts circularly to disrupt the organization and systematization of exploratory behavior. Ultimately, then, the definition of a problem is a function, inter alia, of appropriate exploratory behavioral skills.

Inadequacy in Perceiving the Existence of an Actual Problem and in Subsequently Defining the Problem

The deficiency in problem recognition involves the inability of an individual first to grasp the disequilibrium existing in a given situation and then to act to restore a comfortable balance. If the disequilibrium is not appreciated, clearly the individual will be unaware that a problem even exists. The origins of reflective thinking lie in perplexity, confusion, or doubt, noted Dewey. Thought does not rise spontaneously; it must be evoked by the situation (Dewey, 1933).

Why does the culturally deprived individual not perceive the existence of a problem readily perceived by others? We hold a number of poorly developed cognitive skills responsible. First, the perception of a problem requires the gathering of data and the establishment of relationships between the various cues. Next is an appreciation of incompatibilities, discrepancies, incongruities, missing cues, etc., established by an interaction between previously stored or currently perceived information and the cues inherent in the problem itself. Unless the necessary initial step of data gathering is undertaken with attention and skill, the understanding of a problem will be nonexistent or partial at best.

Apart from poorly developed cognitive skills, the lack of a number of culturally and experientially developed needs also contributes to the nonawareness of problems. Consider, for example, the culturally deprived youth's lack of need for logical evidence. His cognitive system, which does not demand that events necessarily follow from a given set of circumstances, will be hard pressed to appreciate existing discrepancies. On the other hand, his complete lack of interest in the field—often the reaction to intellectual, academic activities—will not lead to the arousal of a curiosity that would signal an encounter with a problem situation.

On a more superficial level, when disadvantaged youths in the classroom are presented with a problem and instructed on how to solve it, they may not understand either the phrasing of the problem or the instructions on a purely verbal level (Jensen, 1963). As has been stated above, the lack of attention to appropriate cues is a basis for the nonperception of problems; but the fact that the problem is not perceived as such acts to perpetuate the chain of not organizing the field toward a solution of the problem.

Lack of or Impaired Spontaneous Comparative Behavior

The deficiency in comparative behavior often impairs the cognitive process. Comparative behavior is a sine qua non for the establishment of relationships and is thus one of the basic cognitive elements. Through the products of spontaneous comparative behavior, an individual transcends the cognitive level of recognition and attains the judgmental, inferential level, that leads to propositional, abstract, and logical thinking. It is thus by comparative behavior that a person actually contributes to the world, for it is he who organizes aspects of outer reality into meaningful systems, defined by the relationships that he establishes among them.

In contrast with his normal peers, the socioculturally disadvantaged child is limited in the amount of spontaneous comparative behavior he demonstrates. This limitation is determined by a fragmented, episodic grasp of reality. Objects and events are not compared, so that a relationship between them cannot be established. This paucity of spontaneous comparative behavior has been evident in our clinical work with disadvantaged children and isolated through a focused interview technique. When the child is asked detailed questions about how he arrives at a particular response, a lack of spontaneous comparative behavior emerges as a determining factor of impaired functioning. In certain instances, we have asked children to describe what they see when they are presented with two geometric figures. Instead of comparing one with the other and establishing a relationship between the two, they invariably describe only one, or one at a time without reference to the other or to the relationship between the two. The use of comparative terms such as "like," "as," "similar," "different," "resembles," etc., is severely limited in the spontaneous speech of these children.

That this impairment does not reflect an incapacity to compare, inherent in the biopsychological structure of the child, can easily be demonstrated in situations in which these children *do* compare spontaneously. Spontaneous comparison is evident when the outcome of comparison concerns an immediate need. For example, given the choice of two pieces of cake, different in size, the child will typically respond by choosing the larger piece. Moreover, in studies of perceptual discrimination these children do not differ sharply from so-called normal children when comparative behavior is provoked by direct instruction. When comparative behavior is not directly provoked, however, but its need is only implied by the nature of a task or activity, comparative behavior rarely will occur spontaneously.

It should be noted especially that impaired spontaneous comparative behavior is responsible for many cryptic failures, failures that are often interpreted as reflecting a lack of ability.

Episodic Grasp of Reality

The episodic grasp of reality is closely linked to insufficient spontaneous comparative behavior and may even be viewed as its attitudinal basis. It reflects, in essence, an attitude toward life. From the point of view of cognitive behavior, an episodic grasp of reality may be defined as a lack of orientation toward seeking and projecting relationships, grouping, organizing, and summing events.

The culturally disadvantaged child's unawareness of grouping elements becomes even more apparent when he deals with temporal data. Clinical inquiry has revealed that his lack of orientation to summate temporal dimensions bears no relationship to his having these concepts in his cognitive repertoire. He knows what a "day," "week," "month," and "year" are, and that a day is less than a week, etc. He is even able to manipulate these units; but he rarely summates them for the purpose of ordering his life or solving a problem presented to him.

Succession of events is still another area impaired by an episodic grasp of reality. If culturally disadvantaged children are asked to relate a happening or to tell a story, they have difficulty telling it systematically or establishing by themselves any order that reflects a chronological, logical, or causal relationship among the events. It is conceivable that such an episodic grasp of reality will be reflected in impaired functioning at school, especially during test-taking where ordering, grouping, and summating are the basis for adequate responses.

Lack of or Impaired Spatial Organization

Our clinical observations of culturally different and culturally deprived groups demonstrate time and again an impairment in spatial organization. That this impairment definitely exists is clearly observed in positional learning tests we have used with culturally disadvantaged adolescents. In one test, for example, the children had to learn the position of five particular squares in a 5 × 5 grid. The gradualness of their learning curve, or indeed, their failure to learn at all, was easily traced to their incapacity to orient themselves by using terms like "left-up," "right-up," "left-down," etc. The fact that they had to rely on a kind of schematic image of the cues made their learning necessarily slow and unstable and, in some cases, even nonexistent.

In such cases, concepts like "up" and "down," "right" and "left," "front" and "back," are possibly known to the child on a receptive level, but he has not turned them into operational concepts, enabling their use in conditions where the more concrete, sensorial cues cannot be used for solving the problem. That is, he has not considered these relationships useful for categorizing objects and events and has not established habits for their use whenever necessary.

For example, in the task presented in Figure 3 the children are asked, "On which side is the small gray square in the second figure on the top row?" In many instances, the culturally disadvantaged child will point with his right hand to the gray square on the top right and say, "This is on the right side." This answer demonstrates that the division of space according to one's own body axis is not yet a stable system of reference for these youngsters. It is sufficient merely to cross the axis by a movement of the hand to confuse the division between right and left. This is also true for the discrimination

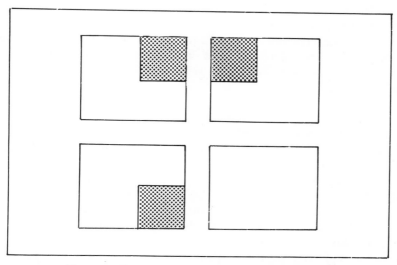

Figure 3.   Figure completion: right-left discrimination.

between horizontal and vertical. In attempting to define the orientation of a line, many children may be aided by head movements, indicating their inability to divorce the frame of spatial reference from their own body.

Many of these impairments in spatial orientation are a direct outcome of living in an environment that does not require complex responses in this sphere. When directions are asked of the culturally disadvantaged, it is frequently observed that they will use gestures rather than terms like "right" or "left" and that they might even propose accompanying you to the site rather than trying to explain by words or gestures. It seems as if it is more economical for them in terms of the time and effort necessary for them to produce an internal representation of movement and the spatial orientation accompanying it to perform the movement itself, especially since their time may be more expendable than the effort required. This is a good example of how motivational factors may affect communicational modalities and how the entrenchment of more primitive strategies can interfere with higher internalized, representational levels of structuring space.

Impairments in conceptualizing, structuring, and organizing space have far-reaching implications in psychological testing situations. Culture-free and culture-fair tests, designed mainly for the culturally deprived, usually have many items that require spatial discrimination. But the impairments of culturally deprived youths in this area preclude their succeeding on the very tests designed not to penalize them.

In our training procedure we have often found that merely by inhibiting the gestures and movements of the child, more conceptualized, interiorized handling of spatial orientation emerges. After repeated and focused training we see a marked increase in the ability to deal with spatial concepts and, accordingly, a significant reduction in the amount of failing trials.

Lack of or Impaired Need for Precision and Accuracy

The deficiency in a need for accuracy was introduced in the section on impulsive exploratory behavior. There, a lack of need for accuracy in data gathering was stressed, but these characteristics affect the responses of the examinee in another way as well.

The adequacy of any given response depends not only on the cues at the input and elaborational levels but in many instances on the individual's felt need to respond to a problem in a precise, accurate way. Again, our clinical observations have demonstrated that, in the culturally disadvantaged, even if a question is properly perceived and adequately elaborated an incorrect response may follow because there is no strongly felt need to communicate accurately. For example, in the Bender-Gestalt test, these children may characteristically count the dots and/or correctly perceive the orientation or relationship in each design, and then proceed to do a copy with more or fewer dots than the original or to separate the units in the designs. These effects are not necessarily the result of visual-motor difficulties because, if these inaccuracies are called to the children's attention, they will be able to reproduce the designs correctly. When asked why they did not reproduce exactly what they saw, their answers made it clear that they perceived correctly but had no compelling need to answer with accuracy.

We conceive the need for precision and accuracy to be the result of an interactive process between the individual and his social environment, and to reflect an attitudinal and stylistic approach to life. If the environment does not make precision so vital as to induce the required need for it, it will not emerge. If, for example, one deals with materials that have oligodynamic effects, the awareness of precision as an immanent need will become firmly established. On the other hand, if precision is not a necessity inherent in a life situation—and this is the case of culturally disadvantaged children—and if they are not required to be precise in their requests and descriptions, then being accurate will simply be uneconomical and superfluous.

The culturally different individual may show a need for precision in a specific area according to the specific structures of his culture and the needs they foster in him. The very fact that such a need exists, albeit specific and for a circumscribed area of activity, makes the culturally different individual accessible to modification and change, and turns his search for precision into a more generalized and pervasive technique when novel areas of activity are included in his repertoire. Thus, the considerable need for the Bedouin to precisely perceive animal traces is easily transferred by him to other areas once he is confronted with the need for precision required to adapt to new content or modalities of operation and communication.

In contradistinction, the culturally deprived individual, because of his limited exposure to cultural transmission and mediated learning experience, has either not acquired or only acquired to a very limited extent, the need for precision even in circumscribed and specific areas. To establish precision as a need for him will require a special strategy and training. Without such training, his failure in tests, due to a lack of precision, may obscure his elaborational capacities.

As previously mentioned, the lack of a need for precision and accuracy can affect all three phases of the mental act—input, output, and elaboration. Training specifically aimed at increasing precision in data gathering may favorably affect the precision with which responses are given. But in many cases, both the exploratory and the communicational ends of the continuum should be modified as well.

Any attempt to evaluate the intellectual capacities of the culturally disadvantaged youngsters without considering their imprecision in responding as a possible source of failure defeats its own purpose. Such evaluation will inevitably fail to discriminate between truly inadequate functioning at the elaborative level and difficulties actually located at the input or output levels. The parallel might easily be drawn with attempts to measure the understanding capacity of an expressive aphasic by asking him questions requiring verbal responses. In both cases, with the expressive aphasic and the culturally disadvantaged child, the results will be similar: a low test score and an inadequate reflection of what might have been correctly elaborated in thought, although inadequately expressed.

Egocentric Communication Modalities

This communication deficiency refers to the way the egocentric individual perceives his partner in a given transaction. The impairment involves a lack of differentiation between his own and his partner's selves. Thus, in this relationship, he does not feel the need to spell out in a detailed and clear way what he thinks, and why, since he considers this as known to the other as it is to him. This phenomenon is most apparent when it comes to providing evidence for claims and arguments. It represents an important component in the lack of need for logical evidence, often shown by the culturally deprived.

Deficiency in Projecting Virtual Relationships

The deficiency in projecting virtual relationships is closely related to a deficiency described earlier, the episodic grasp of reality. On the output level, it is mainly concerned with establishing relationships that have already been grasped or recognized but that have not been actualized in the individual's behavior. That is, they exist "virtually" in the individual, but have yet to be projected into a specific constellation of objects and events. This difficulty has to do with the need to restructure a given constellation and, thus, to shift from one type of relationship to others, as required by the task.

Deficiency of Visual Transport

The phenomenon of deficient visual transport was observed in clinical situations where it was spotted as a determinant of failure wherever the completion of a figure did not require a graphic act but, instead, the visual transport of the appropriate complementary part. This deficiency holds true for other comparison tasks when comparison requires transporting one object visually in order to compare it with another. Asked to point out or to graphically outline a missing part or different element, the child usually shows an appropriate capacity; however, when he is asked to transport visually a part needed to complete a whole, the difficulty becomes evident. He cannot carry an image in his mind's eye from one place to another without losing it on the way.

SIGNIFICANCE OF
THE DEFICIENT COGNITIVE FUNCTIONS

It should be noted that the list of the deficient cognitive functions is neither definitive nor exhaustive, nor have all those listed at the start of the chapter been discussed in detail. Our intention is to offer some observations in this highly significant area, since awareness of these impairments is crucial to the understanding of the cognitive functioning of the culturally deprived and the assessment of their modifiability.

These deficiencies do not necessarily appear in toto as a complete repertoire of the cognitive characteristics of each culturally deprived individual. Certain deficiencies may appear in an individual while others may be absent. Accordingly, the retarded performer will need more or less investment in one function rather than another, and he may be more or less resistant to change. The presence of a deficient cognitive function and its particular saliency will determine the nature of the intervention, the amount of resistance encountered, and the extent of the investment required to overcome it.

Our sources of information concerning the deficient functions stem from a great variety of situations in the life space of the culturally disadvantaged, gathered by means of a dynamic LPAD assessment. The LPAD has facilitated a deeper inquiry into the cognitive processes through the manipulation of the test situation, thereby producing insights into the relationship between the cognitive functions of the examinee and certain behavioral outcomes. Furthermore, certain types of investment, oriented toward modification of the cognitive behavior of the child, have made possible the evaluation of hypotheses concerning the role of the deficient functions, the degree to which the different functions are accessible to change, and the differential nature of the investment required to produce desired modification in specific deficient functions.

SOME THEORETICAL CONSIDERATIONS CONCERNING THE ETIOLOGY OF IMPAIRED COGNITIVE FUNCTIONS

Consideration of the list of cognitive impairments in the culturally disadvantaged child might lead to despair that anything can be done to reverse such deeply entrenched and pervasive processes. It is our conviction, however, that these impairments do not reflect any real lack of capacity, but rather ineffective attitudes, faulty work habits, and inadequate modes of thinking—in other words, functions that can be trained to operate more adequately.

Differential cognitive development and the resulting manifest level of functioning are the product of a differential capacity to learn. Those who work with the culturally deprived are often struck by the observation that learning events have limited effect on them. We consider this phenomenon to reflect structural characteristics of the retarded performer, which result in a reduced modifiability through direct exposure to sources of stimuli. These characteristics define the culturally deprived and describe a great variety of the phenomena ascribed to them. Our theoretical framework considers these characteristics accessible and modifiable through specified strategies of training and enrichment.

Insufficient Mediated Learning as Proximal Etiology

The factor we consider to be the basis of impaired cognitive functioning and reduced modifiability in the culturally deprived is *inadequate and insufficient mediated learning experience*. This concept is discussed at some length, for it serves as a theoretical guide to understanding the dynamics of cognitive impairment in our target population.

The formulation of "insufficient mediated learning experience" postulates that cognitive impairments emerge not necessarily nor directly because of poor genetic endowment or organic deficiencies. They result instead from the absence, paucity, or ineffectiveness of the adult-child interactions that produce in the child an enhanced capacity to become modified, that is, to learn (Feuerstein and Rand, 1973; Feuerstein, 1977).

Learning through direct exposure and mediated learning are conceived by us to be the two major learning modalities. They occur simultaneously but with different emphasis during different stages in any individual's development.

In learning by direct exposure, the developing human organism is modified through immediate and direct contact with sources of environmental stimulation. The learning process is conceived of as resulting from direct chance encounters with, and the spontaneous manipulations of, objects and experiences of events, resulting in continuous modification of existent schemata through the "accommodation" and "assimilation" processes described by Piaget.

Mediated learning experience, on the other hand, is defined as the interactional processes between the developing human organism and an experienced, intentioned adult who, by interposing himself between the child and external sources of stimulation, "mediates" the world to the child by framing, selecting, focusing, and feeding back environmental experiences in such a way as to produce in him appropriate learning sets and habits. The action of the adult and his activity in restricting the stimulational field and interpreting it to the infant or child constitute the major difference between mediated learning and nonmediated, direct exposure learning.

Mediated learning, as opposed to direct exposure learning, does not depend on chance confrontation with objects but on the impact of the adult's intervention in making the child focus on and/or manipulate them. In mediated learning, many techniques such as orienting an action in time and space, framing, summation, repetition, comparison, selection, labeling, and an active re-evocation of events are used by the mediating adult. It should be noted, however, that mediated learning is not necessarily limited to a specific language of mediation. In fact, it may have its greatest effect in very early mother-child relationships at a preverbal level. It occurs as well in certain pre-literate cultures where skills are passed on from generation to generation by means of provoked observation. What is significant is not so much the language or the content of the activity, but the *intentionality* on the part of the mediator. The mediator sets about mediating the meaning of the experience, and the learner is made increasingly aware that he is involved in a process of learning something that transcends the specific information and immediate needs around which the interaction takes place.

It is our contention that the more an individual has benefited from mediated learning, the greater will his capacity be to become modified through direct exposure learning. In fact, the author conceives of mediated learning experience as a prerequisite to effective, independent, and autonomous use of environmental stimuli by the child. It ultimately results in reflective thinking, inner representation, and the gradual emergence of operational behavior.

Even more important, however, over and above the specific contents the child might obtain by means of mediation is an attitude toward thinking and problem solving that is actively and efficiently involved in organizing the world of stimuli impinging on the individual from both internal and external sources. Insufficient mediated learning may be produced by any one or a combination of negative factors that are ultimately expressed in familial interactions. For example, the adults may be emotionally disturbed and therefore the communication among family members may be disrupted; or the child may be disturbed or ill and thus unable to receive or profit from any efforts expended by the adult; or prevailing socioeconomic conditions may result in a narrowed perspective that obstructs the mediational processes between the child and his mediating environment. Finally, sociopolitical circumstances may cause vast disruptions in the life style of sociocultural subgroups and in their needs and means of transmitting values.

Cultural Deprivation
as Result of Insufficient Mediated Learning

It is here opportune to offer some theoretical considerations about the proximal etiology (lack of mediated learning) of the low manifest level of functioning that is found in the culturally disadvantaged and the more direct determinants for their inadaptive modes of functioning that affect their behavior in a wide range of activities. This will provide the reader with the theoretical foundations for the concept of cognitive modifiability that the dynamic assessment aims to measure.

Although the reasons for insufficient mediated learning may be numerous, the invariable result is *cultural deprivation*. Such deprivation is characterized by impaired functioning that does not allow the individual to become modified by direct exposure to stimuli and that thereby curtails the development of hierarchically higher forms of cognition. Even though the lack of mediated learning experience is frequently observed in impoverished living conditions, they are not in themselves a necessary and sufficient cause. Poverty is not always associated with the lack of mediated learning experience and the resulting low level of functioning, and favorable material conditions of life do not preclude the lack of mediated learning experience. In fact, in our clinical work we have been confronted with cases of cultural deprivation, as defined above, in middle- and upper-class adolescents. In such cases the causes of the deprivation had nothing to do with poverty. They were related to disturbances that unfavorably affected the amount and quality of the mediated learning experiences offered to the child. Such disturbances are either the emotional condition of the family that affects interactions, or the condition of the child, either of organicity or emotional disturbances, that renders him impenetrable to the attempts at mediation offered to him by the environment.

Reversibility of Retarded Performance

The ill effects of the lack of mediated learning experience are reversible in a meaningful way above and beyond the distal etiology that has produced it and the stage of development at which intervention is initiated. Such strategies may range from the institution of mediated learning experience at the early stages of development to more radical approaches, including substitutes for mediated learning experience and changes of the milieu that has produced the specific deficiency. Redevelopment may, in fact, even occur spontaneously, given proper life circumstances, as has been shown by studies and follow-up studies on early deprivation (Skeels, 1966; Baller, Charles, and Miller, 1967; Skodak, 1968; Kagan, 1975; Clarke and Clarke, 1976).

The work of Skeels and Dye (1939), Skodak and Skeels (1949), Skeels (1966), and Skodak (1968) is especially cogent for our theoretical considerations about mediated learning. Mentally retarded preschoolers, who had been in an orphanage, were placed in a home for retarded adults. The adults actually reared the children for a short period and provided them with a mediated learning experience. As these adults were retarded, too, they did not engage in very sophisticated forms of mediation, but rather in very basic transactions. What was significant was not the quality of mediation but simply that it existed at all. The positive feelings of the adults for the children, and vice versa, created the kind of milieu in which one could be certain that mediation would take place. Active affection was probably the dynamic factor responsible for activating the whole mediational process; but it was the mediational process itself that was responsible for the changes in the cognitive structure of these children. The results of this living arrangement were that the children's IQ climbed to normal levels. The additional mediated learning, which had been minimal in the orphanage, served relatively rapidly to make these children cognitively aware. The children were then placed in normal foster homes where their mediational needs, presumably, continued to be met. Nearly all of them grew into adulthood as nonretardates.

Studies such as those cited above demonstrate reversal of retarded performance levels of youngsters at later stages in life and attest to the fact that conventional psychometric methods may measure the extent of cognitive impairment but not the actual intellectual potential. As stated previously, the degree of cognitive impairment in the culturally deprived is extensive; but the extensiveness of the impairment bears no relationship to actual intellectual potential. Thus, any attempt to evaluate the intelligence of the culturally deprived, we believe, should begin by a focused training procedure that will then be the point of departure for the assessment of their potential for modifiability by learning.

THE ISSUE OF INTELLIGENCE AND ITS RELATION TO LEARNING CAPACITY

It is widely conceded that, while definitions of intelligence abound, none is really successful in delineating the construct (Guilford, 1967; Wesman, 1968). It might be justly concluded, therefore, that any further attempts at definition would be anachronistic and futile. However, we consider it necessary to discuss and define the concept of intelligence because of its wide use by practitioners and because of the resurgence of the IQ myth, which emphasizes what we believe to be a circular and static view (e.g., Jensen, 1969).

Defining the Relationship Between Learning and Intelligence

Our concern with the examinee's modifiability through learning raises two questions: 1) What is the relationship between learning and intelligence? and 2) Which definition of intelligence would best incorporate such a relationship?

Turning to the initial question of the relationship between learning and intelligence, we maintain that certain forms of learning do reflect intelligence, and both determine and are determined by it. First, however, it would be in order to define learning. Gagné's definition of learning is concise and appropriate: "Learning is a *change* in human disposition or capability which is not simply ascribed to the process of growth" (Gagné, 1970, p. 3).

Guilford concurs that learning is a *change* in behavior, but change, he stresses, does not always mean improvement. It should be considered that although both learning ability and intelligence involve many different component abilities they share the same components, depending on the nature of the learning task and intelligence test (Guilford, 1967). These components, the nature of the learning task, and the nature of the intelligence test will essentially define whatever relationship exists between intelligence and learning. Clearly, if a learning task involves classical conditioning or some other type of neurophysiological response, intelligence factors may be minimally involved. When we enter the area of cognition, however, speed and significance of learning are very much a function of intellectual capacities. What kind of intellectual functioning the cognitive learning tasks happen to reflect and how well it is reflected are questions of both the quality of the psychometric instrument by which they are measured and the predictive needs of the examiner.

The concept of learning as a reflection of intelligence finds support in Ferguson's discussion of inferring hypothetical constructs from the measurement of specific operations. Ferguson stated: "Ability as a latent variable is a necessary logical implication of operationally determined measures of performance. Ability as a factor score is a derived measure. It also implies a latent factor variable. The use of the term 'ability' to refer to some postulated state of the organism is compelled upon us by all those circumstances that require the use of theoretical constructs in science" (Ferguson, 1963, p. 184).

As has been mentioned previously, though abilities or intelligence may be inferred from the measurement of operationally determined factors, Wesman (1968) warns against the reification of the hypothetical constructs. He emphatically underscores the consideration that just because intelligence may be measurable does not mean that it exists as a substance or an entity. Rather, it is merely a useful assumption.

Wesman's definition of intelligence is close to our operating concept. He defined intelligence as the summation of learning experiences: Learning begins with a response-capable organism subject to modification by interaction with environmental stimuli; with an interaction, the organism becomes changed and is ready to interact with the environment in a new way (Wesman, 1968). According to Ferguson's formulations, however, change or modifiability has a theoretically finite point. He holds that the state of a psychological system undergoes continuous change because of a large number of circumstances, both inside and outside the organism. Any change of state leads, theoretically, to changes in an indefinitely large number of other possible forms of performances. Certain aspects of the state of the organism, however, eventually attain a crude stability and become less susceptible than others to modification through continuing behavior. The whole process of growth and development is directed toward this very reduction of uncertainty in the behavior of the organism and toward the establishment of these invariants. Thus behavior becomes organized or structured, and to some extent, predictable (Ferguson, 1963). Ferguson holds that while biological factors create limiting conditions to the ultimate level at which invariants become affixed within these biological boundaries, the range of variation in ability attributable to learning is substantial.

Our definition of intelligence is attuned to precisely this concept, that the latitude of modifiability of intelligence, particularly in the culturally deprived, is so wide as to make for astounding growth of functioning, given proper training strategies. We define intelligence as the capacity of an individual to use *previously acquired experiences* to adjust to new situations. The two factors stressed in this definition are the capacity of the individual to be modified by learning and the ability of the individual to use whatever modification has occurred for future adjustments.

While we hold with Wesman that intelligence will be reflected in learning experiences, we add that for certain individuals, learning how to learn, that is, modifying the cognitive structure responsible for the individual's mode of learning, must first be induced. In fact, the meaningfulness and the pervasiveness of this modification are in themselves a reflection of intelligence.

We agree with Ferguson (1963), who maintains that society, through control of the environment and the educational process, can in some considerable degree determine the patterns of ability that emerge in its members. Our program of planned modification of cognitive impairments of culturally deprived adolescents is an attempt to reach this goal (see Feuerstein, in press).

Jensen's Postulation of Heredity, Learning, and Intelligence

Emphasis on the genetic hereditary basis of intellectual functioning has found renewed support in a paper by A. R. Jensen (1969). We shall dwell on this paper at some length as it is provocative and has controversial ramifications beyond the model it presents.

Level I and Level II Intelligence   Jensen conceptualized intelligence as at least a bidimensional phenomenon (Figure 4). He calls the first dimension Level I, and it consists of associative ability.

Level I: input   output

Level II: input   output

Figure 4.   Distinction between Level I and Level II cognitive activity.

The second dimension is called Level II, and it is concerned with conceptual ability. (See Figure 5.)

Associative ability, according to Jensen, involves neural registration, consolidation of stimulus inputs, and the formation of associations. Here the contribution of the individual in elaborating the stimuli is minimal. Conceptual ability, on the other hand, involves self-initiated elaboration and transformation of the stimulus input before an overt response is made. Level II abilities, then, call for much more intensive intellective undertaking on the part of the indi-

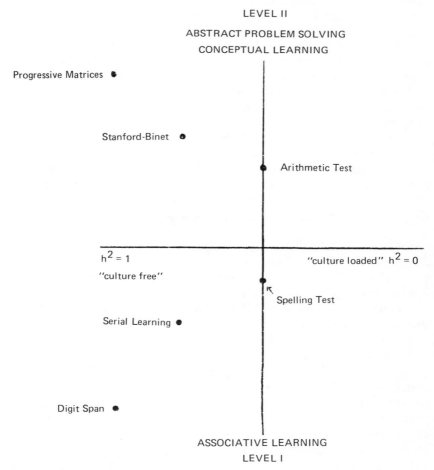

Figure 5.   Jensen's schema. (From Jensen, 1969, p. 110; reprinted by permission.)

vidual. To give a more graphic illustration, Level I might be represented as a relatively simple, tract-specific circuit, involving limited cortical activity. Psychometric tests for ability of Level I, suggests Jensen, would be digit-memory tests, serial-rote learning, selective trial-and-error learning with reinforcement for correct responses, etc. Abilities for Level II would be measured most efficiently by concept learning and problem-solving tests.

It is Jensen's contention that these two levels are genotypically distinct, and that the ability to function on only the lower level or on both is determined ultimately by hereditary factors. He argues further that Level II thinking is essentially untrainable, and for individuals who function primarily on Level I the inculcation of higher and more complex types of cognition is nearly impossible.

Jensen's hypothesis suggests, in a way, that individuals who are genetically endowed more or less favorably are characterized by the extent to which their central nervous system permits the use of higher levels of operational thinking. This position is unsupported by clinical observation and experimental data. Explaining away what appears to us to be clearcut evidence for environmentally induced cognitive differences by calling genetically linked, irrevocable hereditary factors into play, is not only highly unwarranted but is extremely dangerous. It tends to create the setting for a self-fulfilling prophecy. In his bilevel positing of genetic differences in ability to think, Jensen is not referring to those extreme retardates who frequently do show definite signs of physiological imbalance. Rather, he divides "normal" human beings into two categories: those functioning only at Level I, that is, using only associational abilities, and the exalted thinkers of Level II. The cognitive processes of Level I people, according to Jensen, come close to those of subhuman species, while Level II characterizes *Homo sapiens.*

Evidence from the LPAD That Refutes Jensen's Bidimensional Theory The Learning Potential Assessment Device deals primarily with cognitive tasks that fall into what Jensen would call the Level II category. We have considerable evidence that children of low-level functioning, with IQs between 60 and 70 on standard psychometric tests—falling into Jensen's categories as limited to Level I of intelligence—could grasp, learn, and then apply concepts requiring cognitive elaborations far transcending the simple circuit-type of associations characterizing Level I. As an example, Raven's Matrices, designated by Jensen as culture free, are a part of our LPAD battery. These matrices involve analogical thinking, permutations, seriation, and logical multiplicative types of operations. As will be subsequently demonstrated by case history presentations and group studies, retarded adolescents, some of whom were hospitalized in specialized residential settings for retarded people, were able after training to solve an average of 20 out of 30 problems, described by Raven himself as inaccessible to high-grade defectives regardless of the training (Raven, 1965).

The very key to retarded adolescents' success, however, lies precisely within the training offered to them during the test. According to Jensen's argument, such training could not possibly enable our culturally disadvantaged adolescents to accede to Level II functioning. Jensen states that Level II thinking is self-initiated. He seems to be arguing that higher levels of functioning emerge full-blown, without considering that any process of self-initiated thinking has a long and complicated history in the individual, a history which includes mediated learning experience as the broad basis of the individual's capacity for being modified by subsequent experience.

We think that if an initial principle is taught to an examinee along with specified skills and work habits, and if positive attitudes and motivations are induced in the same testing session, then the capacity of the examinee to use these newly acquired skills, insights, and operations on progressively different and more complex tasks is no less a valid indication of his potential capacities than had these principles, skills, work habits, attitudes, and motives emerged "spontaneously" or by "self-initiation."

In the LPAD we attempt to offer the examinee in vitro an intensive, focused training that aims at the induction of modifiability. The demonstration of modifiability is a prerequisite and should be the major goal of psychometric assessment for the culturally deprived. Measuring the IQs of culturally deprived adolescents without giving them the opportunity to display its modifiability is like trying to measure the volume of an iceberg by considering only its surface portion and not sounding its depth below sea level. Within the bounds of relatively short, two-hour training sessions, we do not hope to induce lasting effects in the modification of cognition. That is not our aim. For our specific and limited purpose, however, the degree of modifiability displayed during the LPAD is highly indicative to us of actual potential.

Jensen has observed that disadvantaged children of low IQ can function on Level I tasks as well as and even better in certain instances than their middle-class IQ peers. He concludes, however, that this is the most one might hope for in their attainments, and that it would be futile to expect and therefore to work for any higher levels. A more plausible explanation might be that the middle-class children are actually functioning at what is essentially their potential level, and are really the retardates, while the culturally deprived are working at far below their potential. At any rate, our clinical observations and systematic experimental studies do not at all confirm Jensen's assumptions.

According to our experience, culturally disadvantaged examinees demonstrate difficulties on Level I type tasks in many instances and for reasons other than their actual capacities. In positional learning tasks, for example, they do poorly without training because the concepts "left," "front," "right," "up," etc., are not used by them on an expressive level. In another test that involves the reproduction of a complex figure, including many details (Rey, 1959; Figure 6), culturally deprived examinees fail because they approach the task in a haphazard, perceptually accidental, probabilistic way. For example, they copy the first detail that happens to fall into their visual field (Figures 6 and 7). A simple intervention that consists of teaching the examinees to begin with the central rectangle of the figure and use it as a frame of reference for locating details proved to be highly efficient in raising scores. In other cases, when asked to redraw the figures from memory, they were able to spontaneously produce a much better organized and integrated figure than they did when they were copying directly. Memory scores were therefore paradoxically higher in many cases than original scores. Reproducing these figures from memory indicated that sound elaborative capacities existed but were masked by inadequate behavioral patterns. The latter were characterized by impulsivity, by unplanned data gathering on the input level, and by similarly rudimentary motor behavior on the output level.

This behavior pattern is, paradoxically, more often elicited in the *presence* of the visual cues than in their absence. The visual cues seem to hamper rather than to help culturally deprived individuals in the mastery of the task. Thus, in many cases, the *simple* reproduction of a given stimulus, Level I according to Jensen, is less successfully achieved than is the same task when active mobilization of a mental image is required by removing the visual cues—Level II behavior. This supports our contention concerning the role played by deficient input and output mechanisms in completing a cognitive assignment. That is, the elaborative mechanisms may be functioning relatively well, but we might come to an opposite conclusion because of poor input or output functions.

Responses to another test in our battery, called the Plateaux Test (Rey, 1950; Figure 8), also illustrate the fallaciousness of the Level I/Level II dichotomy when applied to the socioculturally disadvantaged. This test involves three tasks. The first, learning the position of a fixed peg on each of four plates, is a typical Level I task. The second, the indication of the position of the fixed peg on a schematic drawing of the peg boards, lies at an intermediate stage on the border of Level II functioning. Here the examinee is required to use a modality in answering which differs from the one in which the original task was learned. The third and final task, however, clearly transcends Level I functioning. In it, the original peg boards are rotated, and the examinee must then, by an internalized representation, indicate the position of the fixed pegs in the changed location of the peg boards following the rotation imposed on them. In order to succeed, the examinee must anticipate a nonlearned transformation of the stimulus. Success in this final task depends not only on stability of memory but on prerequisite learning and training. Through such training, examinees are able to transcend Level I thinking and operate successfully on Level II abilities. Thus, in many other test situations, our clinical observations and experimentally derived data clearly point out that Level I thinking is not necessarily an immutable, rigid end point in the cognitive development of low functioning individuals. Whether or not this level of thinking is transcended depends largely on the presence or absence of appropriate prerequisite learning experiences.

What Jensen describes as a genetic, immutable characteristic of the retarded performer, and his limitation to Level I performance, is interpreted by us as an attitudinal, motivational characteristic of the self-image of the retarded performer. His limitation to a reproductive modality of interaction with stimuli results directly from his perception of himself as a passive recipient of information rather than as an active generator of new information and ideas by inferential and constructive mental acts.

The retarded performer often considers appropriate reproduction a virtue, and whatever deviation is produced by his creativity he considers inadequate. This basic attitude is reflected in a state of passivity vis-à-vis the world and the incoming stimuli, which he registers at best in an episodic way. He does not attempt to produce the relationships that would organize the stimuli into meaningful categories. However, contrary to the findings of Jensen, our clinical data point out that the passivity affects no less the reproductive type of mental functioning wherever this type of Level I reproduction requires an active mobilization of the memory, rather than free associative processes. The retarded performing child will use expressions like "I can't remember" or "I don't know" each time the

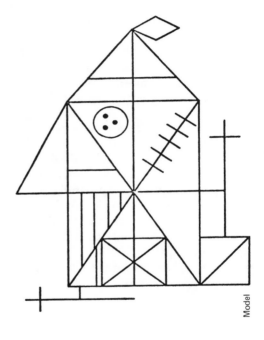

Model

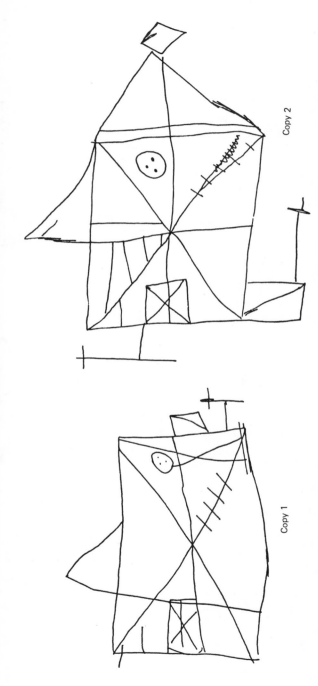

Figure 6. Complex Figure Test: model (*above*) and two copies. (From Rey, 1959. Reprinted with permission of Les Editions du Centre de Psychologie Appliquée and of Delachaux Niestlé S. A., who first printed the figure in P. A. Osterrieth, "Le test de copie d'une figure complexe," Arch. Psychol., 30:205–356, 1944.)

(1) A completely disintegrated copy of the figure, with details presented in a fragmented, unrelated, episodic way.

(2) A reproduction, term by term. The examiner copies the figure in front of the child, who then imitates it, step by step.

(3) A drawing of the figure from memory. Note the presence of the central rectangle, with the internal figures in appropriately located.

(4) Reproduction after further training.

(5) Reproduction from memory.

Figure 7. Reproduction, memory, and effect of training on Complex Figure Test (M.D., age 8).

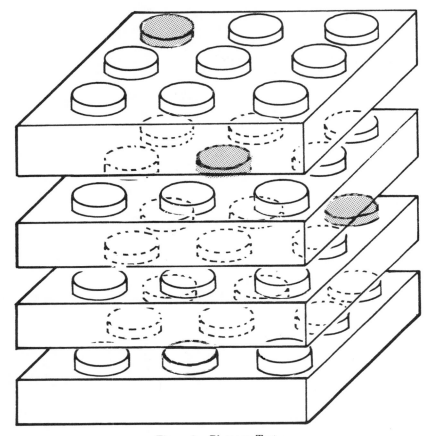

Figure 8.   Plateaux Test.

re-evocation requires an active effort of reconstruction on his part. Our intervention program has taken this characteristic as a target of attack because of its central position in the sum total of determinants for low functioning, and results obtained show that Level I is more of a highly modifiable attitude than a genetically inherited immutable state of the organism.

Implications   Finally, we should like to mention the practical implications of Jensen's approach. Jensen himself stresses the provision of a more realistic educational policy and goals for individuals he considers poorly endowed genetically. His view that, despite their limited capabilities, these individuals can contribute socially and professionally to the world, is somewhat optimistic; however, this is provided that they work in the niche Jensen has so compassionately provided for them. Is Jensen's warning on the futility and danger inherent in attempts to boost IQ levels and scholastic achievements above genetically fixed levels a helpful one? We hope that sufficient argument and evidence have been presented to encourage the reader to conclude that it is not.

CHAPTER 3 **Dynamic Assessment:**
A New Approach to
the Evaluation of
Retarded
Performance

The foregoing discussion makes clear that the manifest level of functioning of the culturally deprived individual, the possible etiology of his impairment, and the factors that determine it more directly point to the inadequacy of the attempts to evaluate the true capacity of the retarded performer by using conventional psychometric devices. This is so because the adherence to a static model of assessment, characteristic of conventional psychometric approaches, can only result in a tautological process in which a manifest level of functioning, already known to be low, is once again demonstrated by the poor results obtained by the examinee. We therefore suggest that to break this vicious circle, we must evolve, implement, and evaluate a new approach to the assessment of retarded performance. The measurement and remeasurement of existing capacities should be abandoned in favor of first inducing and then assessing modified performance right in the test situation itself. In such assessment of modifiability we must attack the cognitive functions found to be directly responsible for the usually demonstrated deficiencies. Also, we must continually take into account that these deficiencies are experienced by the examinee at the input and output phases of the mental act and/or are attributable to its motivational and emotional components and do not necessarily reflect a deficient elaborational capacity of the individual.

As set forth in Chapter 1, effective assessment of the cognitive potential of culturally deprived children requires a radical shift from a static to a dynamic goal of cognitive assessment. Departure from the conventional psychometric method must occur in the following four areas: 1) the structure of test instruments, 2) the test situation and testing procedures, 3) the interpretation of results, and 4) the orientation of the test from product to process.

In the following pages, we first present a model on the basis of which test instruments corresponding to the dynamic assessment goal might be constructed. We then describe suggested changes in the test situation and test administration and discuss the significance and modalities by which the examiner can be oriented toward a process, not a product, as the sole criterion of assessment. Finally, we present a rationale and approach that lead to a different system of interpreting the obtained test results.

STRUCTURAL MODIFICATION OF
THE MEASUREMENT INSTRUMENTS

Changing the structure of the test instruments is necessary because, as argued previously (see Chapter 1), conventional psychometric tests cannot fulfill what we consider to be the essential task in testing the culturally deprived: that of assessing the examinee's potential for being modified by learning.

Conventional test design allows only for a survey of the individual's present cognitive abilities as reflected in his spontaneous responses to given tasks. It does not permit assessment of his capacity to apply acquired skills, strategies, and operations in new situations with which he is confronted in the course of assessment. This is so because conventional tests usually lack an internal relationship between preceding and subsequent items, except for an increasing degree of difficulty in certain of these tests. In many tests, items that are known to produce changes in the readiness of the examinee to respond to subsequent tasks are often considered as contaminating the results and are therefore eliminated. In other cases, items that are considered sensitive to learning processes within the test itself are also eliminated because their sensitivity to changes occurring in the examinee renders them, ipso facto, as showing poor reliability and therefore inappropriate for assessing what is considered the most important goal of the static measure, the assessment of the stable characteristics of the individual.

Even a test such as Raven's Progressive Matrices (Raven, 1947, 1956, 1958, 1965), which makes a determined attempt to present items that induce preparation for subsequently more difficult items, fails to foster learning in the culturally deprived. When the test is presented according to standardized instructions, explanations are permitted only for the easiest items. The examinee is then left with inadequate preparation for handling subsequent items and with no feedback to enable him to know how he is doing. This is certainly helpful to the individual who has a capacity to become modified by this exposure to easy tasks. He learns through them how to approach the more difficult items. However, considering the cognitive structure of the culturally deprived individual, such an exposure does not modify him in a way that permits him to approach the more complex tasks more successfully. Thus, the scores for the culturally deprived adolescents on this test demonstrate success on the initial items of each series but usually show complete failure thereafter. This result is usually interpreted as a manifestation of limited capacity for successful solution of tasks requiring "higher mental processes," contrasted with his relatively better capacity for coping with simpler tasks involving only basic perceptual processes. Thus, Jensen uses the interpretation of Raven, himself (see page 152), as the evidence for his Level I type of intelligence, characteristic of the low functioning individuals. The data presented later positively refute such assertions.

To overcome the difficulties inherent in the psychometric approach, we suggest a model that can serve as a basis for the construction of a number of tests. Such tests respresent a sharp departure from the goals usually set for assessment. The goals of such a dynamic psychometric evaluation procedure may be defined as follows:

1. To assess the modifiability of the individual when he is confronted with conditions aiming to produce a change in him
2. To assess the extent of the examinee's modifiability in terms of levels of functioning made accessible to him by this process of modification, and the significance of the levels attained by him in the hierarchy of cognitive operations. (Here the question is to what extent the achieved modification is limited to the area of perceptual or other types of elementary functions, or whether the change enables the examinee to accede to other higher mental processes, such as abstract thinking or logical operations.)
3. To determine the amount of teaching investment necessary to bring about a given amount or type of modification
4. To determine the significance of the modification achieved in a given area for other general areas of functioning. (To what extent

are the patterns of functioning acquired in the assessment-training process applied in areas other than that of training?)
5. To search for preferential modalities of the individual, which represent areas of relative strengths and weaknesses both in terms of his existent inventory of responses and in terms of preferential strategies for affecting the desired modification in the most efficient and economical way

As can be seen, we are not interested in passively collecting data about skills that the adolescent may or may not possess. Rather, general learning modifiability is assessed by measuring the capacity of the examinee to acquire a given principle, learning set, skill, or attitude, depending on the specific task at hand. The extent of modifiability and the amount of teaching investment necessary to bring about the change are assessed, respectively, by measuring the adolescent's capacity first to grasp and then to apply these new skills to a variety of tasks progressively more distant from that one on which the principle was taught, and by measuring the amount of explanation and training investment required in order to produce the desired result. The significance of the attained modification is measured by the development of patterns of behavior that prove their efficiency in areas other than those that were actively modified by the training process.

The LPAD Model for Construction of Dynamic Tests

Figure 9 illustrates the Learning Potential Assessment Device (LPAD) model upon which a great variety of assessment tools can be constructed. The center of the diagram represents a problem, a task, or a situation that is presented to the examinee for solution and mastery. The solution or mastery of the problem entails the grasp of the given principle through the application of the relevant cognitive operation. This, in turn, is directly dependent upon more elementary functions that serve as prerequisites for cognitive processes and upon the existence of adequate attitudinal and motivational factors. The examinee is given the training necessary to enable him to solve this initial problem. Once mastery is achieved, he is then presented with a series of tasks that represent progressively more complex modifications of the initial training task, as the diverging, concentric circles indicate. To a great extent, this array of interrelated tasks of varying novelty, difficulty, and complexity simulate the adaptational requirements that often confront the growing individual in real life. The progressive novelty, difficulty, and complexity are produced by changes in one of the dimensions inherent to the solution of the task.

LPAD MODEL

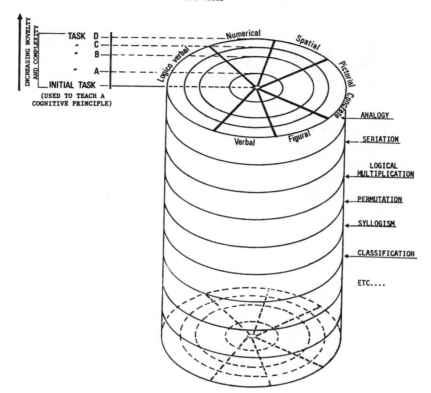

Figure 9.   LPAD model.

One can change the objects or the situation; one can change the relationship between the objects or their specific functions with regard to one another; or finally, one can change the cognitive operations that are required to solve the problem.

Thus, one may keep the operation constant while changing objects and relationships, or keep the objects and relationships constant while only varying the operations. Then any novelty can be defined by stating the number and nature of dimensions introduced in the problem, as compared with those of the initial task that was used for training purposes. The specific operations required by the problem represented by the center dot and by the diverging tasks introduced following initial training can be presented to the examinee in a variety of modalities or languages. Thus, the four segments of the circle represent different modalities for the presentation of the same problem. These can be pictorial-concrete, numerical, spatial, logico-verbal, etc. In addition, the third dimension of the model represents a selection of mental operations, such as analogies, logical multiplication, permutations, syllogisms, categorization, or seriation.

Based upon this model, one can construct many test and measurement instruments incorporating the following three dimensions:

1. Degree of novelty and complexity of the task, represented by the two concentric circles. As a source for novelty, one may use dimensions such as familiarity with the object, function, and relationship, and familiarity with the operation. Complexity can be defined by the number of units to be processed for the solution of the problem.
2. The language or modality of presentation is graphically represented by the segments of the circles. Thus, the task may be presented in any of the following modalities: figural, pictorial-concrete, verbal, numerical, etc.
3. The vertical layers of circles of the cylinder represent operations that are required to solve a given problem. One can imagine any number of operations, such as analogies, logical multiplication, permutations, syllogisms, classification, seriation, etc.

By using tests devised according to this paradigm, one may derive, from the results attained by the examinee and his interaction with the examiner in the LPAD assessment situation, data on the following criteria:

1. The capacity of the examinee to grasp the principle underlying the initial problem and to solve it
2. The amount and nature of investment required in order to teach the examinee the given principle
3. The extent to which the newly acquired principle is successfully applied in solving problems that become progressively more different from the initial task
4. The differential preference of the examinee for one or another of the various modalities of presentation of a given problem
5. The differential effects of different training strategies offered to the examinee in the remediation of his functioning; these effects are measured by using the criteria of novelty-complexity, language of presentation, and types of operation

The use of this dynamic approach in assessment assumes that the individual represents an open system that may undergo important modifications through exposure to external and/or internal stimuli. However, the degree of modifiability of the individual through direct exposure to various sources of stimulation is considered by the author to be a function of the quantity and quality of mediated learning experience. It is the mediated learning experience that sensitizes the human organism to specific characteristics of the stimuli and establishes in him sets and modalities for grasping and elaborating reality, vital for the appropriate integrated use of new experience. The retarded performer is characterized by a low level of modifiability through direct exposure, as reflected by the deficient functions described earlier. Therefore, any attempt to evaluate his true capacities by confronting him directly with problems for which he does not have the prerequisites for solution is doomed to lead to the conclusion that he has a low capacity—something that is already inferred from other areas of his behavior, such as his school achievement—and that this condition is fixed and immutable.

Static measures completely neglect separate assessment of the dimension of modifiability because they equate the measure of manifest functioning with the true and immutable capacity of the individual. The dynamic approach does not deny the fact that the functioning of the individual, as observed in his level of achievement or his general behavior, is low; but by considering this level as pertaining only to the manifest repertoire of the individual, it takes into consideration the possibility of modifying this repertoire by appropriate strategies of intervention.

In the context of this theoretical model of cognitive modifiability, intelligence is defined as the capacity of the individual to use previous experience in his adaptation to new situations. The emphasis in this definition is on the *use* of previously acquired experience. This does not preclude differential endowment, but it considers this endowment as mainly bestowing upon the individual a capacity to use experience, that is, to learn. The effect of differential endowments can be leveled by differential investments made by individuals. Still, high or normal endowment can be obscured by the lack of mediated learning experience, which becomes manifest as a low level of performance. This state is unfortunately often identified as either true mental retardation, or spuriously, as a low, though nearly normal, level of intelligence. It is only by using dynamic assessment, which attempts to substitute for the missing experiential background with a concerted and focused intervention, as well as by providing the examinee with the opportunity to demonstrate his growing capacities in a progressive way, following the focused intervention, that one can measure the modifiability of the individual in vitro.

Sample of Dynamic Tests Based on the LPAD Model

One of the tests constructed on the basis of the foregoing model can serve as an example (Figure 10). Although we discuss these figures in great detail at a later point, their introduction serves to consolidate the foregoing theoretical discussion.

Figure 10 comes from LPAD Variations I and illustrates a set of tasks that is very similar to the items in Raven's Progressive Matrices and the task presented in Raven's B_8 (Raven, 1947). B_8 presents the examinee with a problem that must be solved by an analogical operation. The examinee must supply the missing part in the item by

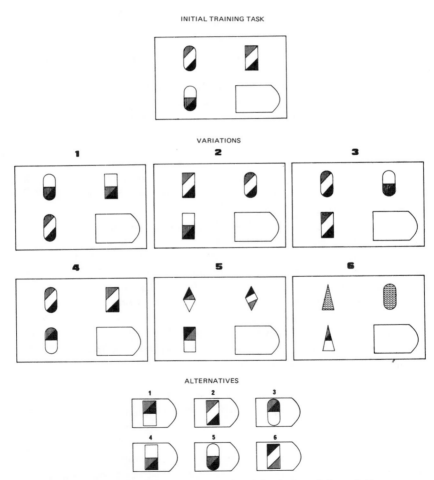

Figure 10.   LPAD Variations I: Initial training task and six variations.

deducing the relationship that exists between the two objects in the upper row. The selection of the appropriate response from within a set of distractors will be determined by the deduction of the prevailing relationship and its application to the lower row. Once this task is mastered by the examinee, through a process to be described later, a series of variations of this item, which reflect the previously elaborated principle, is presented. As can be seen in Figure 10, tasks 1 to 6 keep the operation of analogy constant and change only the relationship between the constituent terms of the problem; they end by introducing changes in certain relevant dimensions of the object, combined with changes in the relationships.

We have used changes in the placement of the objects by rows (task 1), columns (task 2), rows and columns (task 3), content orientation (task 4), figure and content orientation (task 5), and finally, the modification of the figure, its content, orientation, and the respective relationships (task 6). This procedure is similarly applied to the B_9–B_{12} tasks included in the Raven series. Figure 11 demonstrates the same procedure used in an LPAD instrument (Variations II) based this time on five tasks of the Raven Matrices. Figure 12 is also from the LPAD Variations II instrument. It demonstrates another, more remote type of task where, having acquired the principle, the examinee is confronted with tasks that are variations of all dimensions: objects, relationships, and, to a certain degree, the specific operation. Thus, the retarded performer who is confronted with such a task—after having failed in tasks of considerably less complexity—and shows a capacity to master it, should be considered to have a high level of modifiability.

A few additional words should be said about Figure 12 since we will not return to it later. This task is constructed on a principle similar to that of Raven's E_{12}. E_{12} has been empirically proven (Raven, 1965) to be the most difficult problem and is failed by a high percentage of intelligent adults. Its solution requires the discovery of a complex relationship between positive and negative numbers, symbolized by the orientation of the external and internal lines. A variety of strategies and systematic exploration is required in order to discover and deduce the rule according to which each row is formed. Thus, one must consider the sequence as reflecting a summative operation, that is, three minus four equals minus one. Then one must assign a given arithmetic sign according to the orientation of the lines. This can be done only after a careful reading of the "sentences" in the two completed rows and in the two completed columns. After the deduction of relationships in this way, one can then look for the appropriate answer among the eight distractors.

Despite the great difficulty of the task, many of the culturally deprived children whom we examined either individually or in a group test situation reached surprisingly high percentages of correct answers: 50% to 70%. This can be explained by the fact that this way of presenting the task frees the examinee of an excessive investment in both input and output processes, because certain variables of the problem are kept constant, allowing him to fully demonstrate his elaborative capacity by his success in this particularly difficult task. The achievement in this task was very high compared to that attained in another type of test used by us, whose experimental results are described in Chapter 7. The latter, a group analogy test,

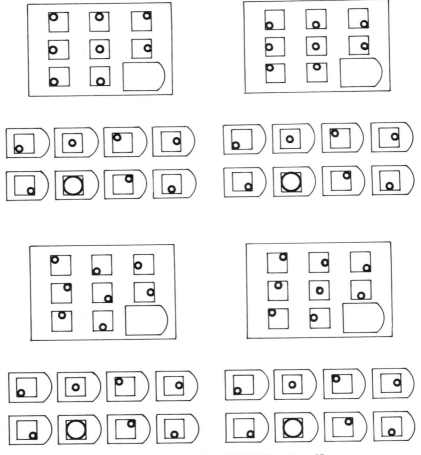

Figure 11.   Examples from LPAD Variations II.

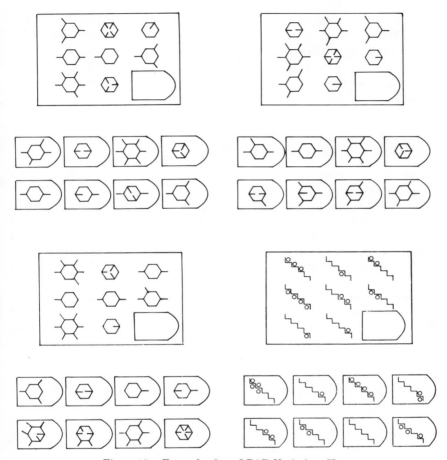

Figure 12.   Examples from LPAD Variations II.

although much easier, did not elicit such a high degree of success because it was not constructed on the principle of progressively changing the novelty, complexity, and content of the task.

The above description of the LPAD Variations serves to illustrate a number of important features of the LPAD model. By placing the emphasis on the ability to learn and apply a principle or set of principles, the model permits an assessment of the child's capacity to learn rather than providing a measure of what he knows. This approach may be extended to include any tasks, irrespective of the content, provided the purpose is to evaluate the extent to which an individual is able to become involved in a learning process. Of particular value is the structured progression of the tasks. This facilitates the evaluation of how an individual adapts to gradual increases in novelty, complexity, and difficulty rather than his performance on discontinuous and unconnected tasks. Thus, as a diagnostic and research tool, the LPAD model helps to produce insight and understanding into those processes that may be responsible for the difficulties experienced by the child.

MODIFICATION OF THE TEST SITUATION AND PROCEDURES

Changes in the instruments are not by themselves sufficiently effective to elicit and assess the modifiability of the individual, even though they are a most vital component in a more adequate system of assessing the retarded performer. The testing situation itself must be changed in a way parallel to changes in the instrumentation in order to reach the dynamic goals set by the LPAD.

Conventional psychometric tests are characterized by a uniform and controlled set of procedures from which no deviations are permitted. When the purpose is to rank an individual in terms of his manifest level of performance according to a set of established norms, such an approach may be justified. However, this is not the purpose of the LPAD, and consequently the procedures governing the assessment must be adjusted. Not only is the purpose of the assessment to evaluate the individual's ability to learn, but it is also designed to yield information regarding the manner and modality through which learning is best achieved. This necessitates a highly flexible and individualized approach in which the role of the examiner is to prod and explore for signs of modifiability and also to attend to the functions that appear to impede the progress of the child.

Two distinct aspects of the testing situation, although strongly interdependent, have to be discussed separately: 1) changes in the examiner-examinee interaction and 2) the introduction of a training process as an integral part of the LPAD measurement system.

Examiner-Examinee Relationship

The motivation of the culturally deprived examinee in the test situation is usually low because the tasks included in the test rarely have any appeal to him. His reduced level of curiosity is only one reason for his lack of motivation. Another is that the perception of novelty necessary in order to elicit an orienting reflex and an arousal followed by an exploration is not always present. Perception of novelty depends upon cognitive functions such as comparative behavior, analytic perception, and the capacity to grasp relationships and their transformations within a constant framework. The lack of a task-intrinsic motivation is then further aggravated by the negative valence with which the presented task may be endowed, provoking an avoidance reaction in the individual who associates this task with his repeated experiences of failure. Failure experiences become the source of deeply ingrained feelings of intellectual insufficiency that further increase the negative reaction evoked by the novel tasks.

Reduced motivation toward the test situation, as a particular instance of other areas of cognitive activity, can, in summary, be viewed as an outcome of three distinct determinants: 1) lack of curiosity resulting from deficiency in the prerequisite cognitive conditions needed for such an arousal to occur, 2) lack of a need system that would endow such tasks with specific meaning, and 3) the existence of a negative component—an avoidance reaction to tasks that have been associated with repeated experiences of failure, which leads to deeply ingrained feelings of intellectual inadequacy.

Given the lack of positive task-intrinsic motivation and the presence of aversive qualities, one can understand that the specific weight of emotional factors in determining the outcome of the test situation is much greater than the casual mention usually made of the meaning of the examiner-examinee relationship and the maintenance of the rapport established between them would lead one to believe. The presence of a neutral, even sympathetic, and yet basically unresponsive examiner who limits his interaction with the examinee to issuing dry, standardized instructions, cannot but add a further negative valence to the test situation. The examinee's very fragmentary grasp of the instructions and his lack of motivation toward the task will lead either to a correspondingly vague or imprecise way of dealing with the problem at hand, accompanied by a low level of anxiety and a tuning-out of the examiner, or, to the contrary, to a high level of anxiety, involving a feeling of great threat and low expectations of success. Thus the lack of interest on the part of the examiner, prescribed to him by standard test procedure, is interpreted by the examinee in two different ways, both leading to negative reactions. First, "If it doesn't matter to you, why should I be concerned with it?" This, of course, is followed by a tuning out by the child, who no longer pays much attention to the task and proceeds to respond in a random fashion. Second, the child may interpret the neutrality of the examiner, even if basically benevolent, as a manifestation of hostility and an expectation of his failure. This reduces his efficiency by lowering his motivation to cope or by energizing him with counter-hostility, which interferes with any cognitive process that might otherwise have emerged.

Any attempt by the examiner to reduce the ill effects of his prescribed neutrality by words of encouragement or by declarations of confidence are soon perceived by the examinee as lip service or even mockery, since all of these expressions prove false in relation to his continued experience of failure to cope with the array of tasks presented to him.

The Learning Potential Assessment Device technique not only allows but actually creates the conditions for a radical change in this approach. This becomes both possible and necessary in the LPAD by the shift from the roles of examiner-examinee into a relationship in which their respective roles are teacher-pupil. What follows is an elimination of the neutral, indifferent role of the examiner in exchange for the active, cooperative role of the teacher who is vitally concerned with the maximalization of the success of his pupil. It is through this shift in roles that we find both the examiner and the examinee bowed over the same task, engaged in a common quest for mastery of the material. Thus, the examiner constantly intervenes, makes remarks, requires and gives explanations whenever and wherever they are necessary, asks for repetition, sums up experiences, anticipates difficulties and warns the child about them, and creates reflective insightful thinking in the child not only concerning the task but also regarding the examinee's reactions to it. To accomplish all of this, the examiner must be alert to each one of the reactions of the individual, and in the course of behaving this way he is seen as wholly different from the usual psychometrician. He is vibrant, active, and concerned instead of aloof, distant, and neutral, and gives the examinee the feeling that the task is important, difficult, and yet quite manageable.

Following the establishment of such an interactive process, we usually observe a sharp increase in motivation. At the beginning it is purely extrinsic, with the major motive of the examinee to please the examiner. At this stage, any manifestation of reduced or discontinued interest on the part of the examiner is followed by a marked decrease in the efficiency of the trainee. Were the examiner to take a moment to answer the telephone, for example, the examinee, even when able to continue on his own, begins to make obviously incorrect responses. Later, as the teacher-trainee relationship develops and includes the task as a part of it, turning the dyad into a triad, we invariably observe a shift from extrinsic to intrinsic motivation. That is, the examinee begins to delight in the task itself, having grasped its deeper meaning through contact and interaction with the examiner.

This shift is basically produced by two factors. One is directly linked to the capacity of the individual to perceive the nature of the problem by having integrated a series of criteria, at the end of which the situations with which he is confronted become *problems*. Here, the "TOTE" (Test Operate–Test Exit) model is relevant in explaining the growing interest in the task itself, following the establishment of internal standards through previous experience (Miller, Galanter, and Pribram, 1960; Hunt, 1961). The second factor has to do with the development of a positive approach to problem solving through increased mastery of tasks, especially when the sequence of tasks follows the LPAD model of progressively increasing difficulty. Such mastery immediately raises the need in the child to repeat the experience. This repetition has functional value in that it consolidates a successful pattern of behavior in a way similar to the circular reactions described by Piaget, and at the same time raises the level of aspiration and the achievement motivation of the examinee. At this point, it is the task that becomes the center of interest and motivation of the examinee, and no longer is his motivation solely aroused by the examiner.

In the testing situation, this shift of interest is often manifested by the activity of the examinee that continues for a relatively prolonged period of time after the examiner has discontinued his instructions or active participation in the work. In clinical situations, the author has manipulated the interaction in such a way as to assess this change in the examinee, by reducing the amount of participation in the examinee's work.

This shift in motivation, achieved by assigning meaningfulness, giving encouragement, and ensuring the experience of success, will not alone suffice to make the examinee's problem-solving behavior successful and efficient. For this, it is necessary to provide the examinee with a constant fine-grained feedback of his interaction with the task that transcends the task itself and uses a variety of communicational modalities. In the usual psychometric model, feedback is often considered valueless or deleterious to either the examinee, to the standardized testing procedures, or to both. It *is* deleterious if the child is told of his failure, without helping him and permitting him to correct himself in a meaningful way. Even if correction is allowed in certain tests, it does not take the form of a thorough feedback strategy, focused on helping the examinee to master the present material in order to enable him to perform more effectively on future test items. In tests whose structure does not involve interitem dependency, the task-bound feedback has negative instead of positive implications for future test items. The child learns only that he *has* failed, not *how* or *why*. Even if he should be shown how or why, he gains little or nothing that will help him cope with subsequent items since they will be very different. No wonder the psychometrist conventionally limits the amount of feedback interactions with his examinee! The usual static test just is not suited to the use of feedback procedures.

In the case of the dynamic LPAD procedures, the feedback fulfills a variety of roles. It is used as a constituent part of the training process. The child is told the nature of his product in a differentiated way, allowing an immediate correction of a wrong answer or permitting generalization of the specific behavior he has employed if his answer was adequate. In both cases, there is neither an increase in anxiety nor a reduction of the optimal motivation needed to maintain interest in further accomplishment. Successes are acknowledged with the kind of exuberance required to convey the meaning of the experienced success. Failure, on the other hand, is acknowledged in a tone that, although it diminishes the importance of the failure, still includes the challenge to do better. In both cases, behavioral patterns leading to one or another result are analyzed and explained, thus rewarding certain types of behavior as differentiated from other facets of the response.

In summary, the personal interaction between the examiner and the examinee on the LPAD has as its basic outcome an increase in the test-taking motivation of the examinee by the fact that the examiner (turned teacher-trainer) conveys to the examinee (turned pupil-trainee) the meaning of the task, the importance of mastering it, his capacity to do so, and finally, by a process of feedback, an ability to select the appropriate behavior leading to success. By this process one aims to produce a shift from extrinsic to intrinsic motivation in the examinee, thus rendering him more independent and, to a certain extent, more reality oriented. We feel that in this kind of testing the personal relationship, which entails the change in interaction patterns as described, is a necessary condition for the appropriate assessment of the modifiability of culturally deprived adolescents. However, it is because of this that it is very difficult to conceive of this interaction being achieved in other than one-to-one relationship permitted by individual testing. The type of feedback described above, or the initial endowment of a given task with a positive emotional valence, will be acknowledged only with difficulty in the group situation, or even by use of very complex programmed learning equipment. Such equipment may become efficient after the basic remotivation process has taken place through the initially required adult mediation.

The Training Process Integral to the Test Situation

Here we describe the examiner-examinee interaction in the LPAD session that aims at inducing the cognitive prerequisites for the examinee's successful confrontation with the testing task. It should be understood that this training is not merely oriented toward a specific content but includes the establishment of the prerequisites of cognitive functioning for a wide array of behavioral patterns and the repertoire necessary for problem-solving behavior. The five areas of the training process are:

1. Regulation of behavior through inhibition and control of impulsivity
2. Improvement of deficient cognitive functions
3. Enrichment of the repertoire of mental operations
4. Enrichment of the task-related contentual repertoire (e.g., the labeling of relationships such as "up," "down," "equal to," etc.)
5. Creation of reflective, insightful thought processes

Inhibition and Control of Impulsivity   The LPAD theory and technique involve an attempt to modify the impulsive behavior of the retarded performer in two ways. First, the test is constructed to make impulsive responses nearly impossible or, at least, unnecessary. Second, the test attempts to control the behavior of the examinee in a direct way in order to restrain him from his usual impulsive response. As described in the beginning of Chapter 2, the impulsive, uncontrolled approach negatively affects the behavior of the examinee in three phases of the mental act. By its presence in the exploratory, input phase, it is directly responsible for the blurred, fragmentary, incomplete data gathered. On the elaborative level, impulsivity is reflected in the excessive use of trial and error where, instead of internalized processes marked by a high degree of flexibility, an unplanned externalized motor approach is used that hampers the culturally deprived from being modified, that is, from learning through his experience. In the output phase, impulsive behavior is manifested by a dissociation between an adequate elaborative process and a more or less adequate data gathering on the input level, thus leading to an inadequate response. In the output phase, impulsive behavior may bring about an inappropriate response because of an inadequate choice between the alternative responses available to the examinee. This may obscure appropriate data gathering at the input and elaboration phases.

As is evident from our description, we attempt to rule out, or at least control, the amount and nature of trial-and-error behavior used by the examinee as a problem-solving modality in the tasks presented to him. For many of the readers, this may raise a question, since trial and error has been considered the major method of learning available to man.

According to Hilgard (1948), Thorndike believed that most learning could be ascribed to the gradual, irregular formation of connections between certain activities and certain outcomes. The very gradualness of learning led Thorndike to conclude that by trial and error there is a piece-meal and unsteady stamping-in of correct responses and stamping-out of incorrect ones.

The expectation that varied, random attempts at problem solving will ultimately lead to success—the assumption underlying trial-and-error behavior—is evidenced, in fact, in the construction of many performance tests (e.g., Kohs' blocks (1923); object assembly, picture arrangement, and block design subtests of the WAIS (1944); Arthur's Stencil Design test (1930); etc.). In these tests, random steps are not only not prevented but are encouraged in the hope that one of them will eventually lead to the appropriate solution. Thus, performance tests involving in their construction this trial-and-error behavior were considered to be the most appropriate means of evaluating capacity in the culturally deprived because of their propensity to act motorically. What makes performance tests so attractive for use with this population is their minimal demand for expressive language and their maximal stress on motor-manual activities, which were thought to be particularly suited to the behavior patterns of the culturally deprived retarded performer, whose cognitive style is described as action oriented and impulsive rather than internalized and reflective.

However, these expectations of successful outcomes of trial-and-error activity are not fulfilled by the culturally deprived. For them, the automatic elimination of errors in favor of correct solutions rarely occurs. Each trial is an episodic, dissociated event for them. Further, even the relationship between a specific motor movement and its outcome may be only dimly perceived. This is so because actions are undertaken impulsively and there is no cognitive establishment of a cause-effect relationship. The added handicap of deficient exploratory techniques for data gathering makes it only too obvious that efficient learning following trial-and-error behavior will rarely if ever occur.

These difficulties in trial-and-error learning were illustrated in an experiment conducted by Richelle and the author (Feuerstein and

Richelle, 1957; see also Rey et al., 1955) in which problem-solving tasks were given to culturally deprived adolescents from rural and urban settlements in Morocco. Their results were compared with those in a study by Richelle (n.d.) of adolescents from the Congo and from Geneva (Table 3). The analysis of errors pointed to the fact that trial-and-error behavior in the low functioning individuals had little if any impact on the successful mastery of the tasks. The episodic grasp of reality characteristic of the culturally deprived children in our groups prevented them from becoming modified through the repeated motor experience during their trial-and-error behavior. Thus, the errors continued to appear in a rigid way, which largely denied any learning process whether gradual or insightful.

A further illustration of the failure of trial and error emerged from a variation of the presentation procedure in Raven's Progressive Matrices, when given to culturally deprived adolescents. The examinees were given the Raven designs to solve, but for some of the tasks the answers beneath the problems were concealed. Surprisingly, those who were not permitted to choose, but who had to rely instead on developing and constructing the solution internally, fared better than those presented with a number of ready-made alternatives. We credit the more successful outcome of the group that was not permitted the choice to the fact that trial-and-error behavior was inhibited when the choices were concealed. Since no ready answers were provided, they had to make a great investment in data gathering. In effect, concealing the choices created a prolonged period of exposure that fostered clearer data processing and created necessity for an internalized elaborative process. This investment on the part of the examinee then continued through the phase of data elaboration to the successful communication of the solution. Inhibition of trial-and-error responses actually served to enhance useful cognitive strategies in all three phases of the mental act.

Further confirmation of successful learning with the inhibition of trial and error occurred in a variation of the Arthur's Stencil Designs (Arthur, 1930), which is presented in detail in a later chapter

Table 3. Frequency of different types of success: Comparison of Congolese, Moroccan, and European children

Group	Immediate success (%)	Success after trial and error (%)	Failure (%)
Congolese	30	60	10.0
Moroccan	20.2	48.5	31.3
European	59.0	36.5	4.7

(see Chapter 4). Here, too, we were able to show that culturally deprived adolescents, when presented with highly complex designs, could mentally analyze and then reconstruct them by an internalized, imagined superimposition of layer upon layer, without actually manipulating the respective stencils. When they were given the opportunity to manipulate and to make random trials with the stencils themselves, as prescribed by the original Arthur test, responses were significantly less successful.

This has led us to the conclusion that solely inhibiting trial-and-error behavior in the culturally deprived examinee may contribute to the development of reflective thought, a highly significant component of formulating cognitive strategies in problem solving. Given proper assistance by the examiner, these cognitive strategies will reach fruition. Successful responses may be elicited, and the capacity to repeat the successful performance in a problem different from the initial one may be enhanced.

The inhibition of impulsive behavior requires the constant presence and unremitting attention of the examiner. The message must be conveyed to the examinee that he should not attempt to answer before planning ahead, emitting hypotheses and controlling them for their adequacy, and finally comparing his response to other existing alternatives before deciding on its appropriateness. In many instances, the examinee is asked to delay the emission of the response until the examiner specifically asks for it. In a study by Schwebel and Bernstein (1970), such a procedure has been demonstrated to enhance performance in conceptualization very significantly.

Wherever impulsive behavior has led the examinee to failure, his failure is interpreted to him by the examiner to help him to locate the determinants of his failure in his impulsive behavior in either one or more of the three phases of the mental act. In this way, although the impulsive behavior is eliminated as the product of a conscious effort on the part of the examinee, the shattered confidence of the examinee in his elaborative capacity is restored by making it clear that it is impulsivity, not an inability to think, that has caused failure.

It is interesting to observe the different effects upon various examinees with this procedure. The more impulsive among the examinees, especially the hyperkinetic children, keep their hands beneath the table following the training, to prevent themselves from impulsively pointing to the answer. Some of them even cover their mouths with their hands to keep from blurting the response verbally. Other children independently cover up the multiple choices, after having been shown how to do it a few times, later uncovering the given choices to see whether their anticipatory response was correct. Even more enjoyable is the observation that as successful problem-solving behavior develops the child progressively renounces the use of the offered multiple choices and proceeds to construct the answer in a completely internalized way. Finally he does not even pause afterwards to check the given alternatives for confirmation of his emitted response. We may see this as evidence of the process of developing a progressive internalization of control.

In an attempt to bring a change in the regulational dimension of behavior, one often is confronted with blocking, the opposite of impulsivity, which frequently occurs as a reaction to failure. This alternation between impulsive and blocking behavior is often observed in the disadvantaged, low performing individual. His motivation being too fragile and his fears too strong, he finds it difficult to approximate the adequate rhythm of work that will satisfy both the need to function and the need to produce enough control to make it adequate.

We observed this irregular control of behavior by comparing the results obtained by disadvantaged children in three tests. One was "tapping," requiring no control since it is simply a speed test in which the number of taps in 6 seconds is counted. The second was the "dotting test," where dots had to be placed within one square of a large grid, rather than randomly spread over the page. In the third test, the examinee was instructed to draw a line on a strip of paper with the slowest possible motion. Whereas in the tapping test culturally deprived children functioned very similarly to their normal peers, a gap of 3 years was observed between culturally deprived and nondeprived children in "dotting." Here requirements for precision hampered the speed previously shown by the culturally deprived.

In the third test, a phenomenon described by André Rey as commonly observed in young children and in older examinees with deficient regulation of motor behavior was a great and progressive increase in the length of the line drawn in successive 15-second segments of time. The performance of culturally deprived children equaled that of the 5- to 8-year-olds—a gap of 5 to 8 years between their performance and their chronological ages. Here again a deficiency in the regulatory process is responsible for failure. It is, therefore, understandable that the examinee, in attempting to control impulsivity, has at the same time the rather difficult task of avoiding blocking as a result of the newly established control. It is worth mentioning that this is one of the very important reasons for our objection to considering speed and timing variables as important constituents of measurement in these populations. In many cases, the very presence of a timing device interferes negatively with the performance of the culturally deprived child.

Improvement of Deficient Functions   The training for the regulation of behavior is considered by certain authors to be a sufficient strategy for enhancing the functioning of the deprived individual. This may be true for cases in which failure on the task is mostly determined by impulsive behavior. However, for the great majority of children the prevention of impulsivity represents only one of the prerequisites for adequate cognitive behavior. A host of cognitive strategies serve as prerequisites for problem solving, and to a certain extent also make the inhibition and control of impulsive behavior both possible and necessary. This leads us to the second dimension, the improvement of the deficient functions of the culturally deprived individual. We focus on a small number of the cognitive functions discussed in Chapter 2 and detail how we attempt to modify them for increased efficiency.

One of the first steps in our interaction with the child is to produce in him a state of *awareness of the existence of a problem* in the task presented to him. When he is confronted with dots to be organized into geometric figures, or with problems involving figures to be completed, or with closure, he is encouraged to find out by himself what he is expected to do. This phase is called the *definition of the problem* and can be achieved only by making the child attend to and even define the characteristics of the field, out of which he will have to select the relevant dimensions that produce the problem. This is done by a process of questioning, orienting the child's perception, and endowing him with the strategies for the selection of the relevant data. This leads to the establishment of appropriate data-gathering procedures that organize the input in such a way as to allow the projection of sets of relationships among the perceived parts by means of comparative behavior.

We have discussed spontaneous comparative behavior and its role in the eduction of relationships as a known deficiency in the culturally deprived. The induction of comparative behavior is often easily produced either by repeatedly pointing out the various objects and events to be compared by either motor or verbal behavior, or in certain instances by exposing the examinee to the comparative behavior modeled by the examiner himself. This in itself induces changes in other areas as well, such as creating a more analytical approach toward perceived entities as a product, as well as a determinant, of the comparative process. Summative behavior may be brought in to group events and objects into meaningful systems.

For instance, if a series of amorphous clouds of dots are to be organized into specified structures, such as squares and triangles, the function of counting four dots for a square and three for a triangle cannot be bypassed before proceeding to connect the dots in an appropriate way.

A solution to the problem that can be reached intuitively in certain cases, especially in perceptual completion tasks, is never left on this rudimentary level of cognitive behavior in the LPAD. Instead, when intuitive solutions are given, they are pursued further and become the point of departure for exercises in analytical, insightful thinking, brought about by a search for the logical evidence required by the examiner. By a series of inferential questions at the end of a given problem, whether it is solved adequately or inadequately, the examinee is made aware of the necessity of substantiating his response by communicating it in a way that is understandable to his partner, the examiner. The initial response of the culturally deprived child to the question "Why?" is very often limited to "Because." Upon the further questioning, "Because of what?", the child answers, "Just because." Through the pressure of further inferential questioning, the child is progressively convinced of the need to substantiate his response differently in a logical way. The examiner's requests, "Give me two reasons why this answer is right" and "Give me two reasons why this answer is wrong," induce in the child a need for logical evidence as the sole way of convincing his partner. This, in turn, compels the examinee to go back to the data with the clear goal of looking for a logical, communicable, and provable answer. His perceptual pattern thus changes from being blurred, as it often is, and becomes sharp and clear. Inferential questions such as "What would happen if . . ." create the need for logical evidence on a representational level, establishing an "iffy" hypothetical type of thinking that is important in evoking an internalized, anticipatory approach, instead of the usual trial-and-error strategy.

In many cases the need exists to organize and systematize the exploration as a necessary condition for appropriate functioning. Presented with a set of objects, the culturally deprived child frequently does not perceive them to be related in any way. Following his tendency to grasp reality as a series of unrelated episodes, he proceeds in a fragmentary way from one object to another. Training in this area consists of pointing out the required order or of establishing the sequence in which objects and events appear. Thus, the prior, apparently disparate existence is turned into a co-existence by the relationship established through an intentional, contributing action on the part of the individual. The four fixed buttons, in different positions on separate plates in the Plateaux Test (see Figure 8, Chapter 2), thus become one image organized onto a single plate.

Another area of training is the induction of the need for precision in both the input and output phases. As previously described, the lack of need for precision often characterizes children who for a variety of reasons have not had appropriate mediated learning experiences. There is a great deal of evidence that appropriate elaborative processes are not expressed appropriately because the need for precision either does not exist or exists in a very rudimentary or selective way for particular characteristics. Thus, despite their relatively good copying capacity, children will show no accuracy in reproduction in the Bender Gestalt Test. They apparently pay no attention to the relative size, location, orientation, points of contact, and number of the figures that serve to relate the various parts of the percepts. This deficiency is often interpreted as reflecting "organicity," whereas our clinical experience suggests that in many cases this reflects the lack of need for precision because of the particular experiential background of the individual. Inducing a need for precision is, in many cases, easily achieved in the LPAD session, by direct intervention through reinforced instruction, confrontation with the model, requests for more precision in verbal definitions, etc.

We have not exhausted the cognitive functions that may be tackled in the training procedure. Certain of these functions are standardly and commonly taught to all the children examined by the LPAD; others are introduced only in response to a specific need uncovered in an individual by the test. The need to approach the training-assessment process in such an individualized fashion causes difficulties in reporting on the standardization of the LPAD. One must bear in mind that the introduction of a specific training sequence is often in response to an examinee's failure, which reveals that a certain deficiency still exists or has not been appropriately corrected in another stage of the training-assessment. The readiness of the examinee to perceive a particular deficiency in his way of functioning and his need to improve may become increased by a proper interpretation of his experienced failure. Thus, the improvement-oriented interventional strategy is supported by a need established through the experience of the training-assessment situation and will be much more effective than any instructions offered to the child at the beginning of the test. Details of formal elements that are the prerequisites for adequate cognitive functioning can be found in the manuals accompanying the LPAD tests (in preparation).

Enrichment of the Repertoire of Mental Operations   In the LPAD session, the examinee is provided not only with the formal prerequisities of problem-solving behavior, but his *repertoire of mental operations is also enriched.* First a given operation is taught and then it becomes the point of departure for assessing the capacity of the examinee to apply the acquired principle. Even though such operations may have appeared in the repertoire of existent functions of many of the examinees, they were not used in a conscious, explicit way but, rather, intuitively, spuriously, and devoid of the capacity to substantiate or support their use by evidence when so required. In many cases, attempts by the examiner to elicit from the children the more general rule by which they solved the problem produced either completely tautological responses or, at best, vague answers such as "It looks good," "It fits," "There is nothing else." When pushed further, the child would retreat from his given answer, interpreting the very questioning as evidence for the inadequacy of his response. This shows the basic fragility of such children's thinking. It is completely based on intuitive processes, and the child can marshal no appropriate, logical support for his quite acceptable elaborative product. This fragility prevents the examinee from sound and stable use of his appropriate pattern of response, once he is confronted with a variation of the situation, and he proceeds in a way that leaves the impression of a randomized rather than a stable system of reference for use in solving a given set of problems.

The training of specific operations such as analogies, categorization, progressions, and seriation, presented in different languages or modalities, occurs in the LPAD session in a variety of ways, depending on the age, level of cognitive functioning, and accessibility of the child. The operational thought process thus established is then reinforced by repeated use and by extending its application to variations of the same problem and exposure to different problems. Repetition of the task, which in the LPAD always includes a certain amount of novelty, involves the examinee in a process that helps to generalize the application of the acquired principle. Training in operational thinking brings about a more profound and stable change than one would expect from such a relatively short period of intervention. (See test-retest results for groups and individuals.)

Enrichment of the Task-Related Contentual Repertoire
The LPAD is concerned with evoking and assessing the general modifiability of the individual and is, therefore, not directly concerned with the usual scholastic achievement measures. However, certain elements of content must be acquired by the individual in order to permit the measurement of modifiability of his elaborative processes; for, just as tests cannot be culture free neither can they be completely content free.

The content introduced into LPAD testing may be divided into several categories. One of these is *orientational concepts,* both spatial and temporal. These include, for example, "left," "right," "down," "between," "central," "peripheral," "before," "after." Another is *relationships between objects and events,* for which contentual concepts such as size, color, number, position, orientation, etc. are coupled with relationships such as "identical," "opposite," "common," "similar," and "different." Finally, there are objects, their characteristics and relationships that, even though recognizable as different entities, are not always appropriately used because of inappropriate *labeling on the expressive level* despite the existence of the respective concepts on the receptive level.

Without easy access to these concepts, many of the appropriate elaborative processes of the culturally deprived are completely obscured. It is surprising to find the lack of these particular contentual concepts a common denominator in culturally deprived individuals despite great differences in the more distal etiologies of their conditions. We have observed a lack of basic spatial and temporal orientation and a lack of appropriate labels for relationships in retarded performers from extremely different cultural and socioeconomic backgrounds. For example, the 13-year-old son of an official in high position was unable, as are many culturally disadvantaged children, to distinguish between right and left or to point out the difference between a horizontal and vertical line, even on a nonverbal basis. Even these simple concepts that form the basis for a spatial system of reference were not included in this child's repertoire of relational concepts. Yet these were made available to him quite easily by a short and efficient period of training, after which he was able to use them successfully in many kinds of tasks subsequently presented to him. Certainly this information and basic training had been available to this child in his rich cultural environment, but he had not benefited from them. The ease with which these difficulties were alleviated indicates that the source of the child's problem was not necessarily central nervous system impairment but rather the lack of mediated learning experience caused by the pathological relationship between him and his parents.

Of necessity, training in these contentual areas is done economically, using a variety of tasks that may be at hand for presenting and exercising the content to be acquired. This training is reinforced by renewed application on subsequent tasks or by generalization to other more remote situations. Thus, the *teaching* of discrimination among vertical, horizontal, and oblique lines uses tasks of the type found in the Raven Matrices. Subsequently, the child is asked to draw a vertical or horizontal line on a sheet of paper, and then to find a way in which the same line can take on other orientations, with the hope that he will be able to discover that this can be achieved by manipulating the sheet of paper or his own body. The same is then done with lines found in the surroundings, particularly in the objects and structure of the room. Thus the concept of orientation in space becomes alternatively linked to the orientation of one's own body, or to a more stable external frame of reference, such as the compass. The importance of establishing both stable and relative systems of reference in space and time transcends by far the particular content because these reference points supply the giant backdrop against which the entire drama of life can best be played. They supply the basis for relating all life's objects and events to each other, thereby removing them from their unique and episodic existences.

Creation of Reflective, Insightful Thought Processes
The previously described techniques of modifying the level of functioning of the deprived individual in the LPAD testing situation may have only a temporary and easily extinguishable effect, without intervention aimed at the *creation of reflective, insightful thought processes*. Insightful processes associated with cognitive operations can be considered the major factor that provides the cognitive processes with the stability required to produce their generalization to other events. It is recognized that it is insight that acts as a fixative on otherwise easily perishable experiences or on experiences that at best become either too limited or too task bound. It is, therefore, necessary that each one of the steps in the LPAD training and testing be used as a source of reflection provoked in the examinee through persistent questioning and, in many cases, by use of some manipulation of the task. Clarke and Clarke (1970) have shown that transfer of training is a direct function of the *complexity* of the task, and it is our contention that this is at least partially so because of the greater likelihood of producing insight when the individual is confronted with a complex task.

Reflective thinking is produced by provoking the child to analyze a certain sample of behaviors that have led to a given outcome. Thus, induction of comparative behavior is made possible by an awareness of the necessity of this cognitive act, of the ways in which it is best and most easily produced, and of the appropriate ordinal position of this act in a larger sequence of cognitive operations. By means of questioning and labeling, the examinee is helped to isolate this particular operation from a complex host of behavioral segments contained in his mental functioning. When confronted with failure, he will be, therefore, much more able to point to the missing behavioral segment responsible for his failure and will not use the more generalized, stereotyped explanations: "I don't know," "I can't," or "It's impossible."

The production of reflective thinking is particularly crucial in mitigating impulsive behavior that affects all three phases of the mental process. It is not sufficient merely to point out or even to help the examinee to understand that the reasons for his failure lie in his impulsive behavior. One must produce in him a deeper insight into the possible reasons for his acting impulsively. An impulsive response provoked by anxiety following failure is a frequently observed phenomenon in these children and often takes the form of erratic, absurd answers. The confrontation with failure, especially when repetitive, brings about a disintegration of the motivational system that would otherwise lead toward reasoned, logical thinking, and produces instead a fatalistic, probabilistic approach. The child acts as if to say, "Since all my logical hypotheses have proved incorrect, it's only a matter of chance as to whether I will succeed or not, so let's toss a coin." Inducing insight here is crucial in order to keep this attitude from becoming pervasive and generalized.

Another instance of impulsive behavior may be a direct outcome of an experience of success that gives the examinee an inflated feeling of security and keeps him from attending to the instructions given to him, or to some specific changes in the relevant data or in the nature of the task. What is often considered perseveration is easily explained by this type of impulsivity, which leads to a lack of discrimination between the previous stimuli and the ones to which the child is currently reacting. The persistence of the examinee in using a previously acquired set in a rigid and indiscriminate manner can be caused by his over-security with regard to the problem and therefore results in a rather superficial approach toward the gathering of the required data. On our LPAD Variations of Raven's Progressive Matrices, where the objects are kept constant and only their order of presentation is changed, an investment on the part of the examinee is required to register and properly use the crucial change in the single dimension of order. If the investment is not made, because of the prevalence of an established, rigid set engendered by the examinee's unwarranted assurance, only failure can result.

In other instances of impulsivity, the exploration of data and the search for a solution are characterized by haphazard probabilism, not task orientation. The child's expressed attitude is: "No matter what I do, I always fail, so why should I try?" Here, the very expectations of the individual for failure must be challenged and feedback regarding the successful handling of the problem must be conveyed in order to change the child's expectations and ensure a more appropriate approach.

The lack of need for precision as a source of impulsive behavior can only be challenged by setting a clear goal and conveying to the child an appreciation of the importance of this function. To require an extremely careful graphic reproduction from a culturally deprived child who has never had a real need for accuracy and to ask that he orient his drawings in a specific way will, at best, be considered "arbitrary" and dealt with accordingly. The child's whole attitude may change, however, if the request for precision is accompanied by understanding and an acceptance of the difficulty the task may hold for him.

Reflective thinking should be induced in a way as to allow the examinee to analyze his operations and to recognize the components of his actions. To orient the examinee toward the analysis of his behavior, the examiner must ask, "What did you do first?" "Next?" "Why in this order?" Precision may also be improved by not allowing the examinee to proceed until he has labeled each one of the involved functions, such as matching, separating, superimposing, linking, and relating. The awareness of the steps he has taken and his capacity to label them ensure the examinee's higher degree of accessibility to, and use of, appropriate learning opportunities.

The readiness of an individual to reflect upon his own behavior; to categorize the functions used according to their outcomes; and to evaluate these functions on the basis of their social, moral, and practical effectiveness is of great importance for the generalizability of any attainment to new tasks. The relationship between the examinee and the examiner should also become the focus of insightful, reflective thinking, with interpretation and inferential questioning by the examiner. A lack of readiness of the examinee to be controlled by the examiner, because such control is perceived by him to be a sign of submissiveness and dependency, can be changed if the nature of the interaction is properly interpreted to him. The oft-observed phenomenon of the suspicious, though not necessarily pathological, examinee who thinks the examiner is trapping him into exerting endless effort upon the solution of unsolvable problems has to be dealt with insightfully and sensitively. The examinee must be helped to understand why he tends to ascribe such intentions to the examiner, and he must be given the opportunity to realize why the opposite is actually true, with the examiner motivated by the sole interest of increasing his protégé's success.

It should be stressed that the amount of investment in this particular area and the sequence in which investments are made cannot be prescribed in a general way: they must be determined according to the need perceived by the examiner. As he continues to work with the examinee, he uses the most appropriate opportunities that present themselves during the assessment. We have experienced instances in which examinees were able to recollect such reflective processes after 15 years, although the content of the situation had been completely forgotten.

THE MODIFICATION OF THE APPROACH
TO THE INTERPRETATION OF RESULTS

In distinction to the other three major changes from conventional test procedures—in test structure, test situation, and shift from product to process orientation—the change in the approach to the interpretation of results may be possible even while conserving the more conventional aspects of assessment. In interpreting results, our major concern is the way the examiner deals with the occasional outstanding response that demonstrates a sharp, isolated, and unique departure from an otherwise well established pattern of poor responses of the individual. To a certain extent, the neglect to register and assess the significance of such a reply follows the normative model in which a deviant answer, even if positive, is considered as an aberration and therefore irrelevant when compared to the overwhelming background of the examinee's common responses. And yet, ignoring the revelations to be found in the occasional positive but deviant response can deprive us of data by far more important than the scores pooled into an average. Reactions such as, "It doesn't mean anything," or "He must have had some previous idiosyncratic training," or "Even if it has some intrinsic meaning, it really can be given little weight in the sum total of the individual's behavior," keep us from scoring or reporting extremely important material.

When the test is used for selection purposes, ignoring such occasional responses can be justified. However, if we wish to understand the person fully, or if we are assessing for purposes of remediation and education, such rare, high quality responses may be extremely illuminating. Like an apparently worthless mound that leads the archaeologist to uncover unimaginable hidden treasures (with, it should be remembered, a great deal of subsequent digging), the isolated successful response may point to the existence of a hidden repertoire of elaborational capacities that for many possible reasons are not manifested by the individual in academic or testing situations. To better appreciate this fact, one must consider the rather limited predictability of the level of functioning of the culturally or socially disadvantaged individuals who form the majority of retarded performers. The predictability of the culturally deprived individual is low because his experiential background, poor as it is in one area, may be rich in other areas. The life conditions to which he is exposed are far less standardized and controlled than those of the culturally advantaged middle-class child, whose life is organized by sets of almost immutable norms concerning the nature, intensity, and timing of his experiences. These norms are determined by the dominant culture into which one is born and reared. The culturally deprived child is certainly exposed to a greater range of experiences at a far earlier age than is the middle-class child. This is even more true for certain social situations. The socioculturally deprived child is often confronted at a premature stage of his life with complex situations that he may record in his own way and that then become a part of a repertoire that is not necessarily elicited, or, if it is, may appear in a spurious, task-irrelevant way.

The examinee's positive deviant responses may have very deep roots and meanings. Not only should they not be neglected, but the examiner should actually provoke their appearance by setting up test conditions that elicit them. This opposes the usual practice in test construction and interpretation. This neglect often becomes manifest in test procedures, with the instruction to discontinue the test after a prescribed number of failures. Discontinuing the test may be brought about by three conditions: failures are thought to be highly predictable for the subsequent performance, without needing confirmation by additional evidence; there is the economic consideration of investing as little as possible in a task that offers little promise of success; and finally, there is a wish not to frustrate the examinee by requiring him to perform tasks that failure on the previous items would indicate are beyond his capabilities. What follows then is a limited amount of systematic or incidental stimulation aimed at evoking such responses.

Even a test such as the Porteus Maze Test (1924, 1933, 1950), long considered to be culture free and to have certain characteristics of a learning process, uses the same approach and prescribes discontinuation of the test after a given number of incorrect answers, since the downgrading of correct answers follows a certain number of failures. Thus, if the examinee has to repeat the tests at age 11 and age 12, twice—or any other combination exceeding four repetitions for these two ages—the examinee can no longer proceed to the Adult items and, if given them, he cannot be credited even if he performs successfully. The actual success at the later items, Adult I or Adult II, is considered to have been produced by extensive exposure to the test by repetitions. Here, one is said to be confronted with modified and not spontaneous behavior and the occurrence of such modifications is not considered to reflect actual capacity!

As stated earlier the LPAD intervention procedures often completely change the course of the results by a sudden flash provoked in the examinee by this interactive process. In many cases, a single response has proved to be a much more valid predictive criterion than failure on a whole battery of tests. The case of Yehuda (Chapter 6) is a good illustration of this point. The failure of this boy in the whole battery was followed by a surprising and unexpected success in the Plateaux Test, particularly on the 90° and 180° rotations. On the basis of this, we decided that the boy was modifiable and chose the appropriate modificational strategies. As in many other cases, our conclusion was soon confirmed by the quick way in which Yehuda climbed from a very low level of manifest functioning. It is precisely by the use of such answers that the LPAD becomes the point of departure for further digging into the more hidden repertoire of the individual and for attempts to modify it.

This procedure is consonant with the approach of Jastak (1949). Jastak objected to the tendency to measure capacity through an inclusive use of quotients and indices of all sorts. He argued that it is inappropriate to judge the capacity of a water container by computing the average of a number of discrete measurements of the water it happened to contain at various times. Instead the water container must first be filled and then measured to find its capacity. In our case, "filling up" involves inducing in the deprived individual whatever is required to produce a given answer. It is only after all reasonable efforts have been made to induce a capacity for appropriate response that one can measure the modifiability of the individual.

THE SHIFT FROM A PRODUCT
TO A PROCESS ORIENTATION

The usual testing procedure is often criticized for its sole concern with the end product and its almost total disregard of the process that has produced it (Sigel, 1963). The shift from a product to a process orientation is an integral part of the LPAD. Conventional test construction does not usually make provision for recording, and even less for evaluating and assigning meaning to, the process by which the examinee has produced the final, recorded, scored, and weighted answer. Even more striking is the fact that conventional test constructors almost never design their tests to elicit and highlight information concerning the process by means of which an examinee arrives at any particular answer. There are certainly exceptions. The process underlying a given response is used as an important criterion in the genetic type of assessment, created by the Piagetian school for studies of stages in the development of intelligence. In the Porteus Maze test, also, the qualitative aspects of the work of the examinee *are* recorded and interpreted for their social implications.

However, the general lack of concern with process, characteristic of the conventional psychometric approaches, can be understood and to a certain extent even accepted when these techniques are mainly concerned with the selection of personnel. The pursuit of economic goals makes the reason for success or failure of little relevance to the examiner or to the consumer of his services, the employer. The fact that certain individuals within a group succeed while others fail, in itself, is sufficient basis for making decisions. However, when our goal is remediation and education, rather than mere selection, the problem is one of the extent and means by which the level of an individual's functioning can be modified rather than merely described. Here the process is of at least as much relevance as the product. Recognizing this, it is essential to distinguish among the cognitive phases to determine which has produced the inadequate final product in a particular case. Was the incorrect answer determined by inappropriate, fragmented data gathering or data integration? Many of the children show an incapacity to simultaneously use the two or more sources of information required for the solution of a given problem. Thus, they consider only, or alternately, one of the given dimensions, such as horizontal or vertical. Depending on the fragmentary information they use, they produce fragmented answers. However, from the very nature of their response, the elaborational and output phases of the mental act may be considered adequate.

There are numerous instances in which a product-oriented approach leads to unjustified conclusions regarding a failing response, assigning to it an unwarranted significant pervasiveness. Even to a conventional tester a simple strategy leading to the correct solution of a problem does not imply that the examinee might not have a more complex, sophisticated approach in his repertoire. However, whereas success may be attained by a very limited number of strategies, there can be innumerable possible reasons for failure. Yet those who are not interested in investigating the process that determined a failure are almost certain to posit the incontestable absence of required skills it demonstrates in a global and overly inferential way.

Our experience with tasks such as the Minnesota Perceptuo-Diagnostic Test (Fuller and Laird, 1963), where we attribute a high degree of rotation to inappropriate input or output based on a general lack of need for precision, helps to substantiate our belief in such potential since we find this deficit to be corrected fairly easily by a more appropriate instruction or through training that induces a need for precision in the individual. In our clinical experience, we have often been confronted with the phenomenon of children who were able to solve a problem, as evidenced by their verbalizations or gestural codes, but who failed once they had to choose the right answer from among a number of distractors or to construct the right answer as required in a motor performance test. Thus, an appropriate elaborative process was obscured by two possible phenomena: either by a high degree of imprecision in the output phase, causing the individual to neglect important aspects of the problem when communicating an obviously well elaborated response, or by the fragility of the elaborative process in a person who is easily distracted by certain other possible responses. Another phenomenon that is frequently observed is a sudden loss of the solution when it must be transported either visually or mentally for use in another task.

It is vital to distinguish when and where the failing process begins. Many failure responses are, as has been stated, determined by inappropriate input. This may even be followed by appropriate elaborative and output processes, and yet the response is still considered incorrect according to standard criteria. We also observe cases in which both input and elaboration are adequate, but impulsive, imprecise output is the cause of failure. It is only a *clinical* test approach, one that considers the locus and nature of failure, that will enable accurate assessment of the nature of cognitive behavior of the individual. This is achieved in a variety of ways with the LPAD clinical battery, where each move or response of the examinee is recorded and available for fine-grained analysis. In the interactive process, the examinee is often asked to clarify his response, giving access to the more intimate processes underlying his cognitive functioning. Finally, in the construction of the test itself, a great deal of thought has been invested in choosing and structuring items that permit such an analysis.

Cognitive Map

The following cognitive map, in conjunction with the repertoire of deficient functions described in Chapter 2, can serve as a guideline for the analysis of responses and the attribution of specific weight to the failure, in accordance with its specific determinants. The cognitive map includes seven parameters by which a mental act can be analyzed, categorized, and ordered—content, modality, phase, operations, level of complexity, level of abstraction, and level of efficiency—and enables the use of a process-oriented approach.

Content   Each mental act can be described according to the subject matter with which it deals and the universe of content on which it operates. Experiential and educational background and culturally determined saliency of a content contribute to differential levels of competence among individuals.

In clinical evaluation, it is of the utmost importance to assess and weigh the role of familiarity with the particular content in the success or failure of the child. Certain content may be so strange and different that it requires a specific and intensive investment for the examinee to reach mastery. Therefore, it is questionable whether the content that is used in evaluation should be so difficult that it absorbs all the attention of the examinee and leaves him with little capacity to focus on the cognitive operations that are the target of the assessment.

Modality   The mental act is presented in a variety of languages: verbal, pictorial, numerical, figural, or a combination of these and other codes, which range from mimicry and metalinguistic communication to conventional signs that are totally detached from the content they signify. The efficiency in use of specific modalities may differ in various socioeconomic, ethnic, or cultural groups, as well as in individuals.

The modality in which the tasks are presented deserves careful consideration, for a quasi-total failure may be converted into a correct response by shifting the modality of presentation of the task and the expression of its solution. One cannot decide that an operation, sui generis, is inaccessible to a child simply on the basis of his inability to perform it in a specific modality. On the other hand, the difficulty involved in using a particular modality must be understood in order to be challenged.

Phase   A specific mental act can be divided into three basic phases: input, elaboration, and output. The identification of a phase is neither necessary nor possible when the response is appropriate; however, with failure, it is necessary to isolate the phase responsible and to assign a differential weight to it. The individual's response may have been inadequate because of incomplete, imprecise, or inappropriate gathered data, which even if elaborated properly would lead, ipso facto, to a failure in the output phase. Failure may occur despite proper input and elaboration if the examinee is unable to communicate the response adequately because of egocentricity or the lack of verbal tools.

We frequently observe deficiencies in the phases of input and output in the retarded performer, with relatively less deficient elaboration. Input and output deficiencies are much more resistant to change than are those of elaboration. The analysis of a failure in terms of phase helps to locate deficient cognitive functions and the source of difficulties.

Operations   A mental act may be analyzed according to the operations that are required for its accomplishment. An operation may be understood as a strategy or a set of rules, in terms of which information derived from internal and external sources is organized, transformed, manipulated, and acted upon. In defining the nature of the operation, it is important to identify the prerequisites necessary for its generation and application. Operations may be relatively simple or complex. Classification, seriation, logical multiplication, or analogical, syllogistic, or inferential thinking are obviously more complex than recognition or comparison. In case of the examinee's failure because of this parameter, it is necessary to outline all of the component elements necessary for the acquisition and/or application of the required operation.

Level of Complexity   The level of complexity of a mental act may be understood as the quantity and quality of units of information it contains. The quality of the information is a function of its degree of novelty. The more familiar the units, even if they are multiple, the less complex the act; the less familiar, the more complex the mental act is. To determine the complexity of a task for an examinee, then, requires a differentiated count that considers simultaneously both the number of items and their degree of familiarity. Either teaching the examinee how to break a task into its component parts and/or familiarizing him with them, thereby making them accessible to him, may help us view the failure differently and ascribe a different meaning to it.

Level of Abstraction   The level of abstraction defines the distance between the given mental act and the object or event upon which it operates. Thus, a mental act may involve operations on the objects themselves, such as sorting, or it may involve relationships between purely hypothetical propositions without reference to real or imagined objects or events. The level of abstraction, as here defined, will be a source of interpretation of the difficulties the examinee has in acceding to a higher level of functioning and the modification that occurs when such levels become accessible to him.

Level of Efficiency   Efficiency can be perceived as both qualitatively and quantitatively different from the other six parameters although it may be determined or affected by one or more of them, either singly or in combination. For instance, a high level of complexity attributable to a lack of familiarity may lead to a relatively inefficient handling of a task. The inability to isolate efficiency from capacity is an important source of error in the assessment of an examinee's true capacity and repertoire of information and skills. It results in faulty labeling and an erroneous prognosis. The lack of efficiency, defined by slowness, reduced production, or imprecision, may be totally irrelevant to the capacity of the individual to grasp and elaborate a particular problem.

Inefficiency may be caused by a variety of task-intrinsic and/or task-extrinsic factors. Fatigue, anxiety, lack of motivation, and the amount of required investment may all affect the individual in his performance of a task. The recency of acquisition of a pattern of behavior must also be considered, inasmuch as a behavior that is neither automatic nor crystallized is more vulnerable to the impact of interfering factors. The more established and crystallized the pattern, the less it will be disrupted by emotional or extrinsic factors. Conventional test scores actually reflect efficiency in terms of rapidity and the number of correct responses, without taking into account any of the other parameters of the mental act.

An analysis using the cognitive map is undoubtedly most possible in a clinical assessment setting. However, the use of the cognitive map in the construction of instruments for group assessment enables the examiner to use examinee errors for analyzing the determinants of failure and ascribing a specific weight to them. An attempt to construct a test that permits the analysis of an error by a process-oriented approach is illustrated by the Group Shift Analogy Test (Chapter 7).

It is only opportune to conclude this chapter by pointing out that the goal of the Learning Potential Assessment Device is not to seek differences among individuals as their stable and immutable characteristics, but rather to search for the modifiability of these characteristics and concomitantly to look for strategies and modalities for the most efficient and economical way to overcome the barriers imposed by these differences. The goal of the LPAD is to know about the differences in order to overcome them.

CHAPTER 4   # Clinical and Experimental Application of the LPAD Model

The foregoing chapters have extensively discussed problems involved in testing the retarded performer and have suggested a theoretical model on the basis of which a set of instruments, testing procedures, and ways of interpretation differing from the conventional ones have emerged. This chapter presents our rationale and our experience in applying instruments based on the Learning Potential Assessment Device (LPAD) model in different settings, clinical and experimental, and under individual and group conditions of assessment.

HISTORICAL BACKGROUND FOR THE DEVELOPMENT OF THE LPAD THEORY AND INSTRUMENTS

The need for a new means of assessment arose from the confrontation of the author with culturally different and culturally deprived children from Afro-Asian countries who were referred to Youth Aliyah, the agency responsible for the ingathering and adjustment of Jewish children and adolescents to Israel. When examining these children, we were amazed by the enormous gap between their level of functioning and that of middle-class, occidental children (Feuerstein and Richelle, 1957). Even more surprising was their lack of attainment in activities and skills believed to be typical of their own culture (Feuerstein, Jeannet, and Richelle, 1954; Richelle, n. d.). This led inevitably to the question of whether we were dealing with a population showing cognitive inferiority, either because of their specific genetic endowments or their membership in a particular socioeconomic group, or whether they represented a negative selection from the total population.

The search for the etiological factors behind these deficiencies was followed by a host of practical and theoretical questions concerning the children's level of functioning. This led us to the question of whether these deficiencies could be reversed, and if so, under what conditions. Important decisions had to be made by the clinical practitioner and theoretician, decisions that were relevant not only to the educational placement of the individual but also to the course of his future development. These decisions would also be the basis for a general psychological and educational policy for large masses of children showing similar characteristics and problems. One such decision was whether the educational framework of Youth Aliyah would be able to deal with the cognitive deficits and their behavioral correlates manifested by many of these children. When looked at superficially, many of the children were considered to have only limited educational accessibility.

In view of the importance of the decisions to be made, the author could not easily accept the results obtained from assessment by regular test procedures. Attempts to use conventional tests had invariably produced a perception of these children as irreversibly retarded in a variety of areas of functioning. Our efforts to improve their assessment by use of various other tests, among them those described as "nonverbal," "culture-free," "culture-fair," "developmental," etc., not only failed to provide greater insight but added confusion to the evidence gathered by more conventional tests. For instance, the results repeatedly pointed to a gap in functional level, ranging from 3 to 6 years behind the norms for various areas of cognitive development. This was also the case when we used reductionist types of developmental tests, such as the Bender Gestalt, or geometric figure reproduction tasks. In the studies we had done, the figure drawing tests did not show a picture different from that obtained by the other conventional tests. Nor were we able to improve matters by using a specially designed set of instruments for the measurement of practical intelligence based on activities that were considered to be characteristic of the daily functioning of these children: "detour behavior," manipulation of objects for solving practical problems, etc. (Rey et al., 1953). The analysis of the children's behavior indicated a number of patterns that contributed to their test failures.

The behavior patterns that were present with great frequency and negatively affected problem-solving capacity were mainly linked to the use of elementary and primitive schemata that did not take into account the nature of the object and the specificity of the task. Children would try to break open a transparent plastic box in order to remove the coin in it, rather than use a "detour" behavior. The lack of analytic perception was responsible for the limited choice of more adequate behavior patterns. The syncretic perception did not permit the singling out of the object's characteristic that would eliminate certain acts as being inefficient compared with others leading to success. Finally, impulsivity, exacerbated by failures that the individual could not explain by his behavior, played a major role in the large percentage of total failures experienced in these tests. It seems that relative familiarity with the tasks is not necessarily helpful if the mode of the required functioning does not exist in the child's repertoire.

Our experience with these tests pointed to the heavy weight of peripheral (input and output) and attitudinal factors in the sum total of the behaviors leading to failure. After much groping, it became clear that no existing test could appropriately reflect the capacities of these children, capacities that were deeply hidden by a great amount of deficient functioning. We began by changing the techniques and procedures of testing rather than by changing the instruments themselves. Thus, many existing instruments were used within a teaching-learning situation, with the examiner providing the examinee with a learning opportunity by exposing him to models of cognitive behavior of all kinds in a way that was very unsystematic at that time.

By way of illustration, if the examinee showed a total incapacity to structure the human figure, as reflected in his drawing an undifferentiated body made of a circle that included the head and body, from which the four extremities emerged (*homunculus tetard*), we attempted to change the internal model of the examinee. We would point to the different parts of the body, using touch; and, if it were still necessary, we would draw in front of him a more differentiated, though simple and schematic, model of the human body (Figure 13).

The subsequent productions of the child, as shown in later retests, gave us insight into his capacity to modify his internal body image and its graphic expression. In other cases, we presented the examinee with ways of looking at a given stimulus and means of organizing the complex data with which he was faced. Even limited hints proved to be sufficient in certain cases to permit a more adequate level of organization, followed by a more adequate expression of the figure (for example, Figure 14).

This training-assessment approach used in psychometric and achievement testing required a great deal of intuitive, creative latitude from the examiner. In this way we investigated the ability of

Homunculus	Post-training	Post-training
Tetard	Model	Copy

Figure 13. *Homunculus tetard* and improvement: Illustration of progress through LPAD procedure.

the deprived examinee to learn a mathematical operation by providing him with the necessary principles, skills, and techniques, followed by the opportunity to apply them to new tasks. The results were then interpreted in terms of the capacity of the individual to become involved in and affected by a learning process despite his initial low level of functioning in the described areas. The evaluation also hinted, again in a very intuitive way, at the manner in which the examinee had to be approached in order to produce positive results.

Clinical-anecdotal and statistical-empirical follow-up studies have demonstrated a relatively high validity for the techniques we have been developing for the last 28 years. Many of the children who demonstrated a retarded level of performance when examined in adolescence have reached a relatively high level of adaptation, as seen in their academic and professional performance and in the state of their general mental health (Krasilowsky et al., 1971). Throughout the years, both the assessment and training approaches were systematized and formulated into the LPAD model, which in turn has generated a series of instruments and techniques.

Backed by extensive clinical experience supporting the value of the training-assessment approach, we set out to present more quantified, empirical results and a more systematic description of the Learning Potential Assessment Device.

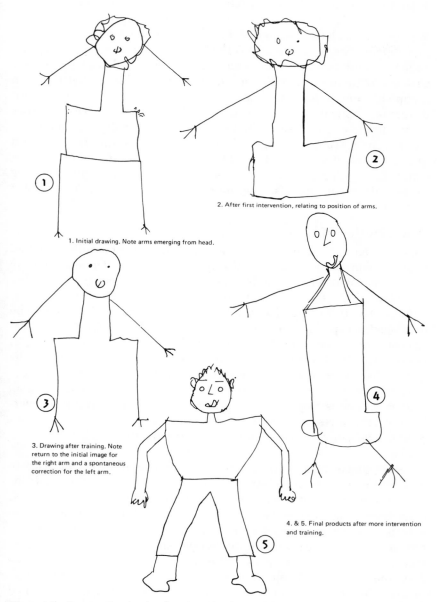

1. Initial drawing. Note arms emerging from head.

2. After first intervention, relating to position of arms.

3. Drawing after training. Note return to the initial image for the right arm and a spontaneous correction for the left arm.

4. & 5. Final products after more intervention and training.

Figure 14.   Progression in the drawing of a human figure by a culturally deprived child during LPAD procedure (I.M., age 10½).

THE CLINICAL AND EXPERIMENTAL TEST BATTERY

We first present the battery of four tests chosen from a number of instruments based on the LPAD model. We describe each test and its rationale and present data obtained in individual and group test situations. In the next chapter, the use of the clinical battery in a group situation is presented across a series of studies concerned with different applications of the LPAD. In Chapter 6, case studies illustrate the clinical use of the LPAD battery. Finally, in Chapter 7, we present a study dealing with a comparison of standardized and quantified results obtained by children exposed to different training conditions on figural and verbal analogies tests constructed according to two different models, the more conventional and the LPAD approaches.

Organization of Dots

The first test of the clinical battery presented to the child is called Organization of Dots (Figure 15) and is based on "Organisation de points" constructed by André Rey (Rey and Dupont, 1953). Rey considered the test to reflect an aptitude that differs across individuals. The test consists of amorphous clouds of dots that have to be organized according to an imposed structure. The original Organization of Dots consists of three phases: 1) a square and a triangle, 2) two squares, and 3) two squares and one triangle. Our version of the test is based on a square and two triangles. Each item has the required number of dots differently distributed within the frame. The examinee is required to organize the dots into prescribed overlapping structures by linking the discrete dots that pertain to a given figure. One point is scored for each correctly drawn figure in each frame.

   Rationale and Administration   The organization of discrete dots into a given whole or structure is not achieved, as often thought, by the sudden emergence of a Gestalt according to the law of internal organization isomorphic with the properties of the field. Both age-specific development and factors affecting the development of cognitive strategies are at work to make this structuring process more or less possible and more or less efficient. When presented with three dots, the young child will not necessarily consider them as belonging to the structure of a triangle. This occurrence is even more marked and surprising in the case of the culturally deprived school-age child and adolescent. The fact that there are regular and symmetrical distances between the dots does not necessarily imply the existence of a given regular relationship and does not compel him to perceive it

Name: Grade

Date: School

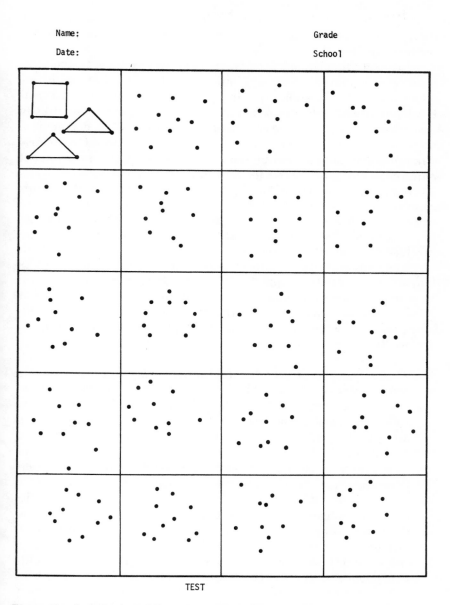

TEST

Figure 15.   Organization of Dots Test. (Adapted from Rey and Dupont, 1953 and reprinted by permission.)

as such. Thus, he will easily indulge in a free-associating type of behavior that will link anything with everything without following the specific rule, despite the instruction to bring a prescribed order to the discrete events.

In contradistinction to the young child, who may act as he does because of his relative lack of familiarity with the object or with its schematic representation, the incapacity manifested by the culturally deprived adolescent often reflects a phenomenon already described in Chapter 2, the episodic grasp of reality. The dots remain in their state of discreteness even though the required geometric structures are familiar and present. However, the active involvement required to bring the necessary organization to the particular task is not manifested because of the passive attitude characteristic of this child, who leaves everything in its original state of discreteness and episodicity. In addition, a variety of other factors characteristic of the syndrome of cultural deprivation, described earlier, are clearly involved in this particular test.

The task involves not only the projection of virtual relationships into an unorganized amorphous world but also requires that this projection follow certain rules. More important, it entails the use of specific strategies to overcome difficulties inherent in the complexity of the task. Four functions relevant to the performance of these tasks are briefly discussed.

1. *The projection of the required relationship* must undergo a process of generalization that is made possible by the conservation of the form, for example, a base-oriented square, across variations in its orientation. This generalization is not easily attained by the younger child or by the culturally deprived adolescent. To a certain extent, it is even difficult for the adult whose perceptual training has oriented him to a particular presentation of the square as base oriented.

2. The fact that two or more figures overlap requires from the examinee a capacity to segregate them. The *segregation of a given part from the whole* is known to require a capacity to *articulate the field by a process of analysis.* Defined in this way, these functions come very close to the concept of field-dependence-independence, described by Witkin as a cognitive style indicating a level of psychological differentiation (Witkin et al., 1962; see also Pascual-Leone, 1969; Rand, 1971). However, here and especially with our population, this segregation first calls on cognitive functions, such as the knowledge and understanding of criteria defining certain specific figures as compared

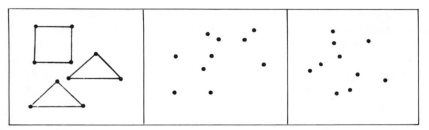

Figure 16.   Organization of Dots: Sample test items for square and two triangles.

to others. Thus, the square that can be perceived with relative ease when it is presented separately will require a search for symmetry and the parallelism of its sides as the criteria for separating it as a specific figure from others (Figure 16). There is the distraction of competing directions of contiguous dots when the square presented overlaps other figures (see Figure 16). Segregation here is a cognitive operation rather than a stylistic factor. Discriminating size and orientation will be of direct relevance to the successful fulfillment of the task.

3. *The capacity to plan ahead* is of importance here, more than in many other LPAD tasks. Any attempt to respond immediately to the appeal of a certain dot, without delaying action until this dot is perceived as belonging to the required structure, will invariably end with failure. Thus, by confronting the examinee with immediate feedback concerning his deeds, the examiner may use this task as an efficient modifier of the behavior of these children, who are known for their lack of planning and their strong propensity for acting immediately in response to the appeal of a given stimulus. The *inhibition of impulsive behavior* in the output phase is yet another factor that is relevant to this task. We frequently observed that many children failed to carry out what they had planned because of their impulsivity, which made their acts uncontrolled and uncoordinated with their previously established plans and goals.

4. The lack of *need for precision* is another attitudinal-motivational deficiency of the culturally deprived that leads to failure when they are confronted with a task such as the Organization of Dots. Even though of pervasive importance in almost any task that requires organization, the nature of the amorphous cloud of dots in this test is such that it requires a high level of precision to organize it into the proper structures. The reader should note that precision here does not refer to the sheer drawing skill necessary for the execution of the task.

The tasks in this test become more and more difficult as figures overlap more closely, the number of component figures increase, and the dots crowd together. Another problem is the change in the orientation of the figures (Figure 17). However, the learning process that is at work from the beginning of the test makes it easier for the examinee to handle more complex parts of the task, despite their increased difficulty. This reflects the change occurring in the examinee through exposure to these tasks.

Rey's and Dupont's correlations with other tests (Rey and Dupont, 1953) show very little relationship with memory or attention. A much higher correlation is found with tasks involving operational factors (from .23 to .67), pointing to the importance of general intelligence in the performance of this test. There is evidence that in our particular population the correlation with cognitive factors will be even higher. There is undoubtedly a part of this task that is determined by a spatial factor and visual perception. However, as can be seen from our correlations (see Table 4), this is not the case in the populations studied by us, and, therefore, the test can be considered to contribute to the measurement of both general intelligence and, to a certain degree, to measurement of specific abilities in the areas of spatial and perceptual activities.

Organization of Dots is presented either as a group or as an individual test. In our clinical study we presented the test individually. The test itself was preceded by a training phase, using a specially designed training sheet (Figure 18). We do not detail here the ways in which the training is done. However, we describe briefly both the structure of the training sheet and the interaction process between the examiner and the examinee that continues throughout the whole examination.

The training is oriented toward the correction of a series of functions known to be deficient in these children. Thus, the components

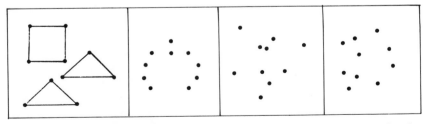

Figure 17. Organization of Dots: Test items for the square and two triangles that have changes in spatial orientation.

Table 4. Matrix of coefficients for LPAD tests, based on total study population (N = 91)*

	Raven A, Ab, B	LPAD Var.	Plat. I: trials	Plat. I: errors	Plat. II: trials	Plat. II: errors	Org. Dots	RSDT
Raven A, Ab, B	—							
LPAD Var. I	0.60†	—						
Plat. I: trials	−0.37†	−0.12	—					
Plat. I: errors	−0.29‡	−0.08	0.86†	—				
Plat. II: trials	−0.13	0.12	0.38†	0.26‡	—			
Plat. II: errors	−.08	0.01	0.44†	0.40†	0.69†	—		
Org. Dots	0.44†	0.38†	−0.50†	0.47†	0.25‡	−0.22	—	
RSDT	0.42†	0.26‡	−0.33†	−0.36†	0.08	−0.06	0.37†	—

* The study population consisted of two groups, one referred to our clinic and one recruited from a special school for the educable mentally retarded. See text (last section of chapter) for details. Abbreviations: Var., Variations Test; Plat., Plateaux Test; Org. Dots, Organization of Dots Test; and RSDT, Representational Stencil Design Test.

† Significant at the 0.01 level or better.

‡ Significant at the 0.05 level.

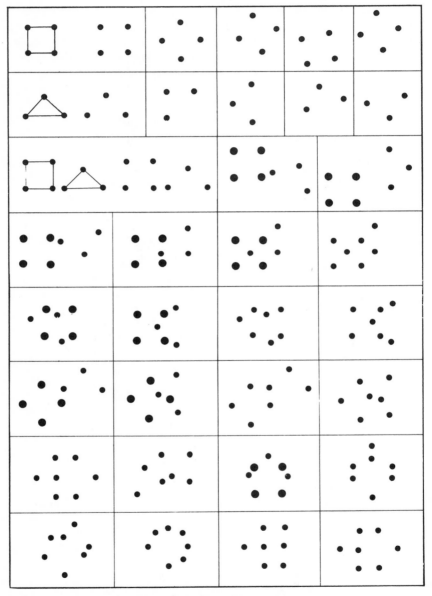

Figure 18. Organization of Dots: Training sheet. Note the use of larger dots for training.

of the task—a square and a triangle—are isolated to establish familiarity with the figure itself and with the action of linking the dots by
projecting the lines that will change the state of episodicity to the
relationship required by the particular structure. This is done on
figures whose orientation varies. The constancy of the figure,
preserved across the change in its orientation, is taught. The complexity of the task is only gradually increased, helping the trainee in
the initial stage to discriminate among the overlapping figures by
specific cues such as the varying size of the dots belonging to one
figure as contrasted with those belonging to other figures in the
frame. The gradualness in presenting the amorphous field orients the
child toward an analytical process that, it is hoped, will be mobilized
and elicited even when such cues become less visible and eventually
disappear.

The interaction between the examiner-teacher and the exam-
inee-trainee includes the following processes: induction of the appropriate attitude to the task; the correction of deficient cognitive functions, including comparative behavior required to establish the form
and size; the necessary planning behavior; the summative behavior
in which the examinee counts the number of dots belonging to a given
group; the inhibition of impulsive behavior; and, finally, the orienting of the child to read the message conveyed to him by his own
registered results and thus help him use the feedback provided to
him by his work. That orienting the child is necessary is clear to any-
body who has ever worked with the culturally deprived child who, in
many cases, may not even register an error that cries out from the
page and does not feel disturbed by it. Results of the training
process, presented later, clearly indicate its effectiveness. What is
even more important is the fact that by using such an approach we
are able to witness the emergence of a capacity to cope with the
problem and to reach a high level of mastery of tasks more complex
by far than those presented in the test.

In describing Organization of Dots we have pursued yet another
aim, namely, the evaluation of the functions involved in performing
such a task from the point of view of the quality and quantity of the
contribution required from the organism to solve it adequately. It is
clear that, in distinction to associative type of tasks in which the
human organism is involved in a process of matching, reproducing, or
copying a stimulus, here the task involves an important transformation of the stimulus by the activity of the organism. In the reproduc-
tive-associative task very little is changed by the performer; the
product is similar if not identical to the stimuli presented for copying
or reproduction. What is required from the examinee when presented

with a reproduction task is to make his product as close as possible to the stimuli presented to him. In the tasks of Organization of Dots, however, even though the given geometric figure must be copied, it cannot be copied without first rediscovering it, disentangling it, and projecting it into an otherwise dissimilar structure. From this point of view, it is clear that Organization of Dots is a task that requires an important contribution from the individual to the organization of the outer world and, therefore, draws heavily on his elaborative capacity. If judged on Jensen's Level I and Level II types of intelligence, the Organization of Dots test falls clearly in the realm of Level II.

The test itself is usually presented to subjects age 12 or older, since it is considered too difficult for younger children. The test reveals developmental characteristics, but it is influenced even more by the educational level of the examinee. It is interesting to note that the differences between the various groups tested by Rey and Dupont (1953) were related primarily to the nature of their education rather than to age or to specialized training in the visual-spatial aptitudes. Inasmuch as we did not usually impose the time limits prescribed by Rey and Dupont, it is not possible to compare our data directly with those obtained by them. However, it must be remembered that we were dealing with adolescents who were not usually exposed to tasks of this level of difficulty since such tasks are considered to be beyond the capacity for mastery by such children.

Test Data   A preliminary study that attempted to use Organization of Dots in an LPAD modality was done with a group of 70 adolescents enrolled in educational day schools for the culturally deprived. They were given the test in groups of 13 to 20 children in each. The test included three phases: testing, training, and retesting the day after training. The training involved an explanation of the salient principles required for success on the test, pointing especially to preferential strategies for approaching the task. (At that time, the training sheet used in the studies to be reported later was not yet available.) Furthermore, prerequisite attitudes and cognitive functions were stressed to the examinee, albeit in a brief and succinct way.

As can be seen in Figure 19, on the pretest the group attained a mean of 18.06 with a standard deviation of 11.07. The group retest mean was 25.47, with a standard deviation of 9.40. The significance of this change, as assessed by the Sign Test, gave a z of 6.11 ($p <$ .001). From the significant increase in the capacity of the examinees to solve these problems, the reader may see that even group training and testing demonstrate considerable effectiveness. However, group training was not nearly as effective as individualized testing and

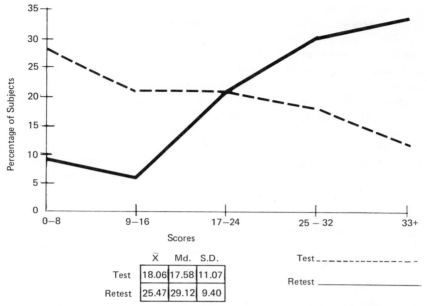

	X̄	Md.	S.D.
Test	18.06	17.58	11.07
Retest	25.47	29.12	9.40

Test _____

Retest _____

Figure 19. Organization of Dots: Distribution of obtained scores (maximum score, 34) by categories in percentages; comparison between test and retest (N = 70).

training proved to be (see results (Figures 30 and 31) obtained by the EMR and clinic groups described at the end of the chapter).

Plateaux Test

A second test selected by us for the LPAD battery is the Plateaux Test, created by Rey (1950). In his paper, "A Method for Evaluating Educability," Rey (1934) boldly presented his doubts about the legitimacy of the goals and methods set forth by the psychometric approach. He questioned the validity of such a painstakingly standardized and statistical approach to data based upon a thoroughly fallacious theory. With the Plateaux Test, Rey hoped to help the judicious clinician find better ways of evaluating and measuring the individual's capacity to be affected by an educational process. It is noteworthy to point out that Rey's paper and the instrument that it introduced appeared in a period during which psychometric theory and practice were at their highpoint and when faith was expressed in the future development of this branch of applied psychology. It is, therefore, regrettable that for a long period Rey's paper never received the proper attention of the psychological readership, or even, to a certain extent, of Rey himself. Rey's contention, that to evaluate the individual's true capacity one has to use a learning situation, is substantiated by the Plateaux Test.

This test consists of four plates, with nine buttons per plate, arranged in three parallel rows of three buttons each (refer to Figure 8, Chapter 2). One of the nine buttons on each plate is fixed; the other eight are easily removable since each has a little stud on the bottom that fits loosely into the holes in the plate. The position of the fixed buttons on each of the four plates varies, as can be seen in Figure 20. The plates are presented to the examinee stacked from 1 to 4. The task consists of learning the position of the fixed buttons on each of the four plates, repeatedly presented to the examinee in the same order and in the same position. In phase 1, the examinee is instructed to explore all the buttons by raising them until he finds

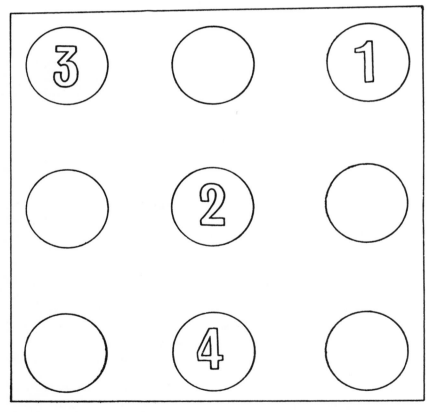

Figure 20.   Plateaux I: Unidimensional schema of position of the fixed buttons on the four plates, presented to the subject stacked from 1 to 4.

the fixed one. Then the plates are stacked again in the original order. The examinee is instructed to try to remember the position of the fixed button on each one of the plates and insofar as possible to keep from touching the other buttons. This phase is continued until all errors are eliminated, and the criterion of three errorless trials across the four plates is reached by the examinee.

Rationale, Administration, and Scoring   In phase 1, the task is clearly of an associative-positional learning type. The amount and nature of the individual's contribution in mastering the task vary according to the strategies he uses. Thus, one can learn the positions by mechanically repeating the task and associating it with a series of myokinetic afferents. The sensations associated on a perceptual, as well as on an haptic and myokinetic level, that is, learning the distances and orientations of each fixed button on each plate, are combined and thus facilitate the learning of positions. However, there are other strategies that might be more economical on the exploratory level and more effective in the learning process. One strategy could be based on the use of verbal terms and spatial orientational concepts, such as: first plate, right-up; second plate, center; third plate, left-up; fourth plate, bottom-middle. Another strategy could use a single mental image, formed by the assembly of all the four positions across the four plates, presented in a given sequence on one schemata, numbering the fixed buttons from 1 to 4, as in Figure 20. These strategies can produce differences in the criterion scores, but the outcome will also depend on a variety of other factors briefly outlined below.

First, the nature of the exploratory behavior may have a strong impact on the learning process that follows it. The systematic, planned-ahead search is economical because it allows the individual to avoid redundancy by limiting the search area and to proceed toward those parts that have not yet been tried. Furthermore, it allows the individual to register the outcome and to locate the correct position in the total field. What we have observed, in this and other tests as well, is the propensity of the culturally deprived to act and to explore in an unsystematic manner, handing the buttons in a disparate and unconnected way and moving from one button to the other until the proper one is eventually found. The "hand-to-mouth" strategy, which implies uninhibited reaction to the appeal of a certain stimulus, resembles the kind of probabilistic, random behavior that hampers the search for, and discovery of, structure. The inefficiency of such an exploration, marked by an erratic, unreasoned, and unplanned search, is best reflected in the fact that the examinee touches the same button two, three, or more times without

even attempting to eliminate it once he has learned that it is removable (Figure 21). This trial-and-error behavior necessarily interferes
with the establishment of a stable system of reference and the learning process necessary for the mastery of the task.

A second difficulty stems from the narrowness of the mental
field, clearly evident in this particular test. A frequently observed

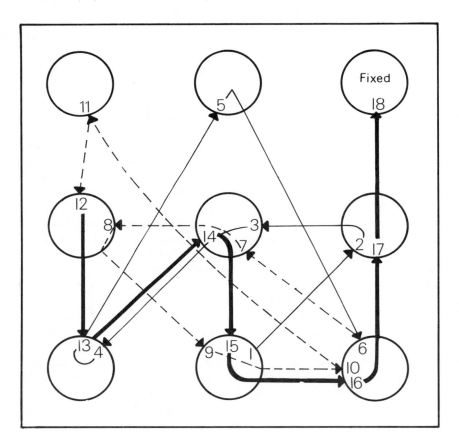

Figure 21.   Actogram of unsystematic exploration on Plateaux Test plate 1: Initial
exploration. Each move is numbered in sequence. Note the redundancy in search of
the fixed button attributable to poor internal feedback in unsuccessfully executed
trials. Compared to systematic exploration, this unsystematic exploration may render
the learning laborious and unstable.

phenomenon is the shift from success to failure on the various plates. After having finally learned the position on one of the plates, the examinee forgets the correct position on another one, and when he overcomes the difficulty in this one he loses yet another. In observing this phenomenon, we have gotten the impression that the capacity of the individual to deal simultaneously with the required number of positions is limited so that any investment in learning one position interferes in his capacity to deal successfully with another. It is as if one would use a short blanket that could cover either the arms or the legs but not both at the same time.

Considered from this angle, the first phase of this test, the learning of the four positions, only to a limited extent calls on the elaborative processes and therefore can be considered as belonging to what Jensen defines as a Level I type of task. The amount of transformation the examinee introduces in the cues is limited, even though certain strategies may hold a higher position in the hierarchy of mental functions, such as the use of spatial relations with the concepts of right-left, up-down, and center, or the assembling of the disparate positions into one image while conserving their given order. But these strategies are not necessarily used by everybody, and it might be a matter of the cognitive approach characteristic of the individual as to which of these is most economical for him at a given point. People who use a rather elementary and primitive approach when confronted with a simple task, such as finding the button, may shift to a more sophisticated conceptual approach when the task becomes more complicated, such as when two fixed buttons, instead of one per plate, are presented for positional learning. However, basically, this first phase can be dealt with by a limited investment in the elaborational phase.

The score on the first phase is based on the number of trials required by the examinee to reach the criterion of three errorless runs. A second score is formed by the number of errors accumulating over the trials until the criteria are reached. The learning process by which the examinee approaches the task can be best presented by a "learning curve," which may be helpful in demonstrating its characteristics and highlighting some of the determinants of its particular shape. Thus, one can become aware of the instability of the learning process, the alternation between gains and losses, etc.

A second phase of this test, which receives a separate score, invokes the act of *schematization.* Here the examinee is required to transpose the four fixed buttons from the four plates onto a single sheet of paper with the nine buttons represented by circles arranged in a way identical to that on the plates. The examinee is instructed to mark each fixed button with the number of the corresponding plate.

The functions involved here call for transformation of the stimuli and of the manipulation. Instead of recognizing a three-dimensional object, one has to identify its symbolic representation by its position among other similar symbols. The order of the plates has to be labeled by a number. The acquired order and orientation have to be transported to the sheet of paper. As one can see immediately, even though the mnemonic factor provides the examinee with a stable set of data, the request here is to transform these data by a process of symbolization and generalization. Therefore, we may consider this task to occupy an intermediate position between Jensen's Level I, the reproductive type of mental activity, and Level II, the transformation of the stimuli, at least from the point of view of the differential nature of the activity and of the presentation of the data at an output level. A score is given for the number of buttons properly located on the schematic diagram, with a maximum of four for the one-button plates and eight for the two-button plates.

The third phase represents a step further toward a higher level of internalized behavior and a departure from the simple reproductive Level I type of mental operations. Here the examinee is asked to represent the outcome of a change in the position of the buttons following first a 90° rotation and then a 180° rotation. The plates are rotated only after the examiner has made sure that the memory of the initial position of the buttons has been well established and consolidated, enabling the individual to respond by acting on the internalized schemata. The ability to point out the fixed button after the plates have been rotated requires mental flexibility. The examinee must be capable of operating on an internal image, freeing himself from the previously established image and the myokinetic and proprioceptive efferents in favor of a generalized and more cognitive approach. This flexibility represents a dimension of the more general capacity of the human organism to adapt to changes in the outer and internal environment. As to the nature of the required mental operation, the phase of rotation clearly involves Level II type of behavior, since it requires an internalized operation involving the transformation of stimuli. This type of operation is seldom considered to exist in the spontaneous repertoire of children functioning on moderate and even higher levels of mental retardation. The difficulties are mainly in the elaborational and output phases, whereas the input of the data necessary for this elaboration must have been acquired in order to proceed to the rotation phase. Performance during the rotation phase is scored by counting the number of buttons successfully located, to a maximum of four for the one-button plates and a maximum of eight for the two-button plates.

Test Data   The Plateaux Test was used extensively by Rey and others, and a large body of normative data is available. Our first use of the test was with groups of culturally different and deprived children from Morocco who were examined in Morocco and France (Feuerstein and Richelle, 1957). The population ranged from 10 to 16 years of age, and the results obtained by them were very comparable statistically to the results obtained by 9- to 10-year-old children from Geneva. The mean number of trials for the Swiss children was about 7.9 for phase 1 of the test and showed a mean of 29.4 errors across the four plates (for comparison, see Table 5). In Israel, we have since examined groups of children whose results are presented in Table 5. As can be seen, the level of the culturally different and deprived adolescents functioning on this test, without adequate preparation, shows a gap between 3 and 5 years when compared with their more advantaged peers. These results do not differ in any way from the similar gap in results obtained on verbal or other culturally biased tests. This points, again, to the fallacy of the assumed advantage of manipulative-motor nonverbal performance tests over the verbal and culturally dependent tests. *When used without a dynamic approach, both types of tests will result in an inadequate assessment of the retarded performer.*

By way of summary, the Plateaux Test, as conceived by Rey and used by us in the LPAD battery, provides the initiated examiner with a great variety of insights into the capacity of the individual to become modified by a learning process and into the way in which certain peripheral types of deficient functions unfavorably affect his achievement. Changes following training processes and/or induction of appropriate exploratory behavior are dramatic. As an illustration, an interesting phenomenon was observed in testing a population, described in detail at the end of this chapter, labeled educable mentally retarded. During retest after 2 months, we observed such an improvement in the functioning of the children that we decided to present them with the two-button plates, a difficult test even for

Table 5.   Plateaux Test: Number of trials, by percentiles, in Moroccan and Swiss children (N = 195)

Samples	Percentiles					Mean	N
	0	25	50	75	100		
Moroccan							
10–13 years	23	11	8	5	1	7.90	90
14–16 years	25	10	7	4	1	8.07	64
Swiss							
9–10 years	17	11	7	5	1	7.90	41

initiated adults. The results (see Figures 46–50) were surprising in that the number of trials and errors fell much *below* the number in the initial test on the one-button plates. The strategies acquired during the phase 1 testing plus training against impulsivity were used effectively in the second more complex test, enabling the retarded performers to achieve an unexpectedly good result. The modification that the examinee has undergone has acquired a structural nature, inasmuch as he has increased his capacity to learn. In other words, *the examinee has learned to learn.*

This interpretation of the result was confirmed by a study on the effects of training in positional learning for the establishment of learning sets that turn the exposure to new tasks into meaningful learning experiences (Rey, 1950). On a grid of 25 squares, five positions are presented successively to the examinee, who is then asked to recall them and to register them on a grid (Figure 22). This procedure is repeated until the criterion of three errorless trials is reached. Following this achievement, the examinee is presented with four additional sets of different positions, five positions per set. The task is presented in order to establish whether the exposure to the first two or more tasks facilitates the subsequent learning of other sets, with the number of trials and errors on each of the tasks as the criterion.

The difficulty inherent in the learning of such a chain of sets lies in the interference and retroactive inhibitory process that the acquisition of one set may have on the learning of another. However, such a difficulty could be of less importance if, instead of relying on a rote memory in which each cue is registered and recalled separately, the examinee were to use a more cognitive and structural approach to the task. Such an approach is neither spontaneously nor necessarily formed if the individual is presented with only one set and thereby not overloaded with details for storage and subsequent recall. However, the very fact that the examinee is presented with more than one set creates a need for the meaningful organization of the disparate cues, providing them with links, relationships, labels, and frameworks. The obtained results have confirmed the hypothesis, inasmuch as the retarded children have produced an increased capacity with each set learned by them. The across-set learning curve has become a typical learning curve, ⟿, with the number of trials decreasing with the number of sets presented (Figure 23).

The Raven Progressive Matrices and Its LPAD Variations

At an early stage in our work with culturally different and deprived children we used the Raven Progressive Matrices. This test has the

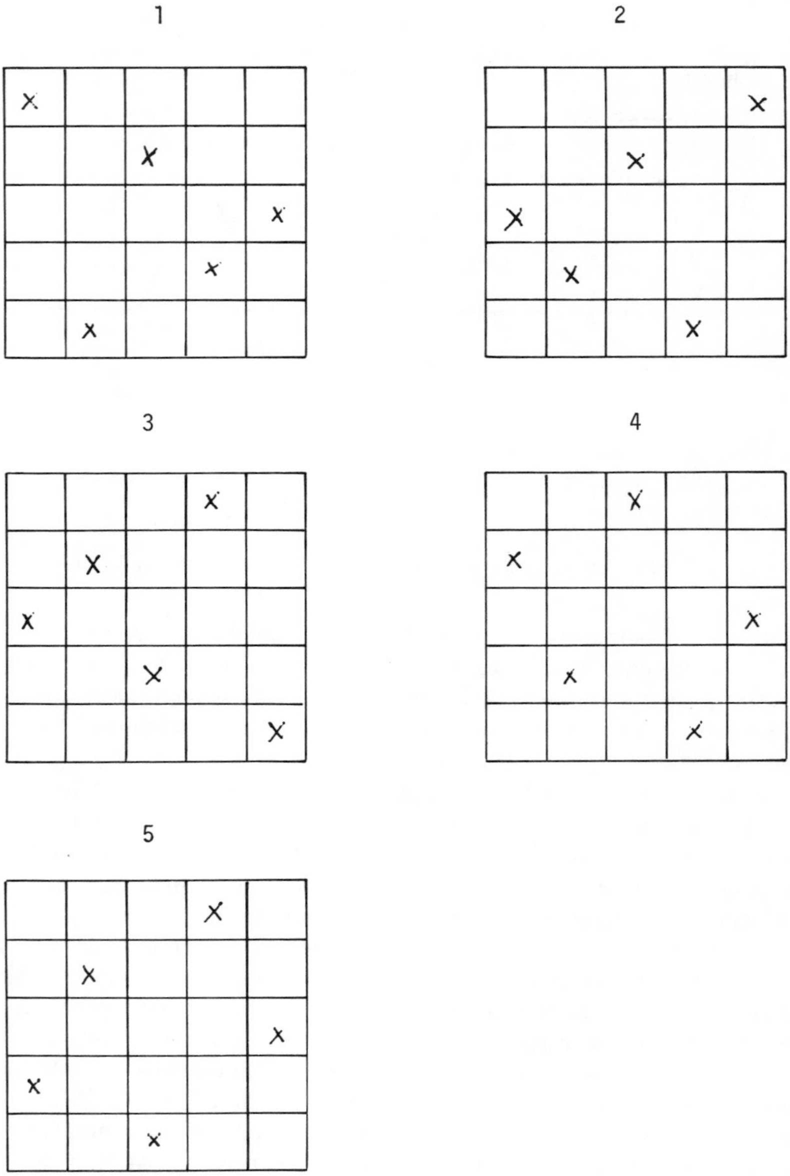

Figure 22.   Positional Learning Test (5/25): Five model sets. (Adapted from Rey, 1950.)

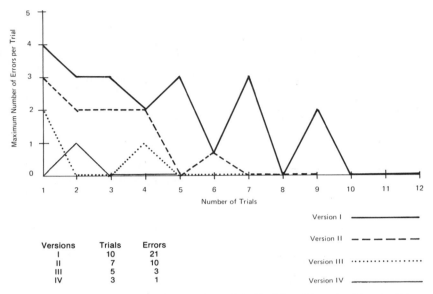

Figure 23.   Learning across four versions of the Positional Learning Test (5/25).

advantage of being attractive, colorful, and easily understood by the examinee. Since it is considered, perhaps fallaciously, to be a culture-free test and to require only a limited amount of verbal instruction or mediation, it is preferred by practitioners for use with culturally different children.

Rationale and Administration   One important advantage of the Matrices is its *progressive* sequence of tasks, which starts with rather simple Gestalt completion and builds up to levels of functioning that require more complex cognitive operations, such as analogies, permutations, and logical mutiplication.

Because the test is considered to be culture-free and even to permit learning to take place by direct exposure to certain tasks, failure on the Matrices has been accorded a much heavier weight in the assessment of innate rather than culturally determined differences in capacity. It is no wonder, then, that Jensen (1969) has pointed to the Progressive Matrices as the prototype of culture-free measures of Level II activity. However, in our experience this characteristic of the Matrices has not been supported, at least not in terms of the test being a measure of innate ability. The fact that it presents the examinee with a progressive sequence does not in itself necessarily elicit learning in the culturally deprived children with whom we have been confronted in our clinical experience. Many of these children fail to "record" and to use previous experience, for reasons discussed at length earlier. As the reader may recall, we have defined the syndrome of cultural deprivation as a low level of modifiability by direct exposure to stimuli, attributable to the lack of mediated learning experience. Therefore, the use that is made by the culturally deprived of their experience is very limited and the direct exposure to preceding tasks does not significantly affect the ability of these children to handle subsequent tasks.

In an earlier study (Feuerstein, Jeannet, and Richelle, 1954), we analyzed the errors made by children on a series of tasks taken from the Raven Matrices. We found that deficiencies of elementary functions, lack of specific concepts, attitudes, work habits, etc., determine failing behavior even on a test such as Raven's. We frequently observed errors attributable to a lack of comparative behavior. When the examinee was confronted with tasks that required him to establish a relationship among three corners of a square and to choose the fourth corner that correctly completed the square, he usually chose one of two inappropriate responses. When questioned, it became clear that he had not compared the various parts and did not see that they all were differently oriented. Subsequently, his choice of an answer was made on the assumption that what was missing was a figure identical to one of the parts of the square already given, rather than a different missing part that would complete the pattern established in the item. Another frequent error was directly determined by the lack of simultaneous use of two sources of information. For a more detailed description of the way in which the lack of appropriate exploratory and summative behaviors may detrimentally affect the functioning of children on the Matrices, the reader is referred to the section on deficient functions in Chapter 2.

In the LPAD Variations of the Matrix, these deficient functions are reflected in the incapacity of the individual to deduce the relationship in the completed part of the analogy and then to apply this relationship to the completion of the second part. The analysis of errors points to a variety of faulty strategies, the most frequent of which is the use of an *objectal* identity, instead of an identity of *relationship*. The response required in the B_8 task—the deduction and application of a relationship—cannot be achieved without first comparing the elements of the data presented and subsequently defining the relationship in terms of commonalities and differences between the terms. Similar results on the B_8 through B_{12} tasks were obtained by Raven (1965) with examinees defined as functioning on the retarded level.

In Table 6, the percentage of correct response to the B_8 to B_{12} tasks is related to the total score obtained by the examinees over the entire A, Ab, and B series. These data indicate that the B_8 to B_{12}

Table 6.   Percentages of correct answers on Raven's items B_8–B_{12}, compared with total score on Raven's Matrices A, Ab, B*

Total score	Percentage of correct answers on Raven's items				
	B_8	B_9	B_{10}	B_{11}	B_{12}
10	—	—	15	5	—
15	10	—	10	2.5	—
20	2	4	10	2.5	1
25	14	15	12	10	2
30	50	70	65	50	15
35	100	100	100	100	100

* Based on data derived from Raven (1965, p. 35, graph 3, set B).

tasks do represent a level of cognitive operation distinct from the previous tasks, which required only the completion of the Gestalt, and may explain the difficulty encountered by retarded performers in attempting to solve them.

Our interpretation of this difficulty and its significance differs, however, from that offered by Raven (1965), who described these items of his test and the difficulties they present to the retarded performer in the following way:

A high-grade intellectually defective person remains throughout life characteristically incapable of solving the more difficult problems of Set B, but is usually able to solve many of the problems of Set Ab. If he is given the Board Form of the test, he may be able with practice to select successfully the appropriately oriented parts required to complete most of the problems in Set Ab, but he still makes little progress in solving the more difficult problems in Set B. Such a person often learns to read and write, acquires a moderate vocabulary and adjusts himself not unsuccessfully to a stable environment, but he tends to be repetitive, lacks originality and finds great difficulty in meeting novel situations effectively. (p 25)

One will note Raven's pessimistic attitude and the generalization he makes from his findings to life situations. First, the population described by Raven is, in many respects, identical to the one we describe as "culturally deprived." Second, Raven claims that the incapacity of this population to deal with these tasks cannot be modified by training.

By using these particular items as a task for modifying the level of function and then measuring the modified attainment on variations of these very tasks, we have attempted to challenge the underlying basic contentions that Raven, and later Jensen (1969), derived from these results: that tasks representing Level II functioning are largely inaccessible to the retarded performer. Admittedly, the operations underlying these tasks are not present in the immediately elicitable repertoire of retarded performers, and the spontaneous response of the individual reflects this lack. However, does this, ipso facto, mean that these operations are forever inaccessible to them?

Considering the far-reaching implications the answer to this question would have on educational and socioeconomic policies for the youngsters, we decided to use these very tasks for challenging the validity of the conclusions inferred from the results obtained on them. By using these tasks with populations who, according to the described criteria and empirical data, do indeed fail to solve these problems, we attempt to prove that not only does focused learning modify the capacity to respond correctly to these problems, but, even more, that such learning enables the examinee in many instances to give proper solutions to problems representing a variety of changes in the initial task. Figure 10 in Chapter 3 illustrates our variations on the Raven's tasks B_8 to B_{12}.

Test Data   The results derived from our clinical and experimental studies have proved that not only can the B8 to B12 tasks be solved by the retarded performer after appropriate training, but, even more important, that the produced changes are stable and easily transferred to tasks of much higher complexity than the aforementioned ones.

Sixty-nine subjects, ages 13 to 16, were given the A, Ab, and B Series of Raven's Progressive Matrices in groups of 13 to 20. A mean of 22.06, and a median of 22.17 with a standard deviation of 6.50, were obtained. These results (Figure 24) placed our population among the retarded performers on this particular task. According to the table taken from Raven's data (Table 6), one should predict very poor performance on the B_8 to B_{12} tasks. Indeed this prediction became true in a way even more extreme than expected. The percentage of subjects who solved more than one out of the five B_8 to B_{12} tasks did not exceed 24.9%. The mean obtained on a maximum of five by the whole group was 1.1, with a median of 0.5. Half (50.7%) of our population did not even solve one task, and one-quarter (24.3%) solved only one of the five items.

The same population was then given training in the five original B_8 to B_{12} tasks. The training included a rather limited amount of teaching for understanding of analogical principles and for processes such as comparative behavior and systematic exploration. Following this training, the examinees were given the LPAD Variations of these five tasks. (Refer to Chapter 3 for detailed description of the test and the construction of the Variations.) It should be noted that the training received by the children was very limited compared with that given during the individualized, clinical use of the same instruments.

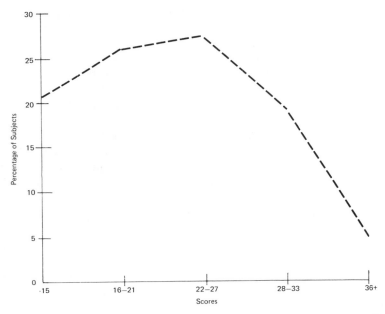

Figure 24. Distribution of total scores on Raven's Matrices, Series A, Ab, B (maximum score, 36; N = 69).

The results of the post-test are presented in Figures 24 and 25 and in Tables 7 and 8. The mean obtained on these Variations was 18.30 out of a maximum score of 30, and the median was 19.07 with a standard deviation of 7.95. In Table 7 we present the conditioned means, that is, the relationship between the total score obtained on Series A, Ab, and B and the score obtained on the LPAD Variations I. As can be seen, the responses on the LPAD Variations I indicate that even examinees who functioned very poorly on the initial test (scores of 13–18) were able to solve up to 50% (mean of 16.1; see

Table 7. Distribution of total scores on Raven's A, Ab, B series and mean scores on subsequent B_8–B_{12} Variations I

A, Ab, B score	LPAD Variation (Mean)	N
1–12	9.0	5
13–18	16.1	17
19–24	16.5	19
25–30	20.9	22
31–36	27.5	6

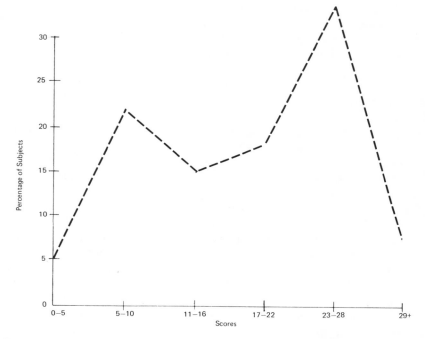

Figure 25. Distribution of total scores on LPAD Variations I (based on Raven Matrix items B_8–B_{12}) (maximum score, 35; N = 69).

Table 7) of the problems of the Variations, whereas on the basis of the scores obtained on Raven's Progressive Matrices there would have been no more than 15% to 20% probability of solving any one of these problems. Table 8 shows the relationship between the scores obtained on items B_8 to B_{12} and the total score obtained on the LPAD

Table 8. Comparison of scores obtained on Raven's items B_8–B_{12} with mean scores obtained on LPAD Variations (Var.) I (maximum score 30), frequencies, and percentages (N = 69)

N	No. of correct answers B_8–B_{12}	Percent B_8–B_{12}	Mean LPAD Var. I	Percent LPAD Var. I
35	0	0	15.1	50
17	1	20	15.4	51
6	2	40	25.0	83
3	3	60	26.0	87
4	4	80	25.5	85
4	5	100	28.5	95
Means	1.1	22.0	17.89	60

Variations I. Examinees whose results ranged between 0 and 1 correct responses on the B_8 to B_{12} tasks had a mean of 15 out of a maximum score of 30 in the LPAD Variations I. However, those who originally gave two or more correct responses rapidly approached the ceiling of the test.

How should these results be interpreted? First, we must refer back to Raven's statement and point out that in contradistinction to his findings these tasks *are* indeed accessible to the low functioning retarded performer after a rather minimal amount of investment, under group training and testing conditions that were barely adequate at best. Second, the examinees who showed a very low level of performance were still limited in their capacity to become efficient in their functioning even though they were able to grasp the underlying principle and apply it to the variety of new situations arising in the LPAD Variations I. These results, however, can no longer be interpreted as reflecting an incapacity to elaborate the task conceptually since subjects with a score of 0–1 on Raven's B_8 to B_{12} tasks have proved able to solve up to 50% of the variations based on the same tasks. Rather, the results should be viewed as an inefficiency in the subjects' use of their elaborative capacity that is attributable both to the vulnerability of recently acquired processes and the deficiencies on the input and/or output phases. As we will show in our study at the end of this chapter, the same category of children—even though known to function manifestly on a significantly lower level than the present group—attained much higher scores because of the optimal testing conditions that enabled us to control the examinee's behavior and to prevent the hampering effects of deficient functions on the input and output phases.

This interpretation receives confirmation from the results obtained in both individual and group test presentations of the LPAD Variations II. For this test, we selected six items from Raven's Adult Matrices (1974), C_7, C_8, C_{12}, D_{12}, E_{12}, and the sixth task of Raven's Advanced Matrices Set 1 (1958). We used these tasks both for testing and training, followed by variations in both the content and the form of the item, while keeping constant the rules and principles necessary for solving the problem at hand. The tasks are of considerably greater difficulty than those included in Variations I, implying a variety of operations such as logical multiplication, permutations, seriations, and the use of mathematical operations involving positive and negative numbers.

The complexity of the tasks is increased by additional units of information that must be processed both in the presentation of the problem and in the selection of alternatives. In these Matrix tasks there are nine units instead of four and there are eight alternatives instead of six. There is also an increase in the number of dimensions and attributes of each component that must be compared in order to deduce the relationship that is then applied in the progressively new situation.

For each of the previously mentioned Raven items, we have produced a number of variations, with a total number of 58 problems divided into five series, A(13), B(15), C(10), D(10), and E(10).

The results obtained on these tasks by low functioning adolescents after training range from 30% to 90% correct responses. The training for the test involves the presentation of the original task, its underlying principle, and the prerequisites for proper problem-solving behavior. In Chapter 5, we present results obtained on the LPAD Variations II in group tests.

Representational Stencil Design Test (RSDT)

Rationale   The fourth test in our clinical battery, the RSDT, was selected for a variety of reasons. The most important was the fact that, more than any other test, it permits the study of the effects of training in a structured task upon the capacity of the examinee to develop internalized problem-solving behavior. As stated earlier, we consider the lack of *representational, internalized* behavior to be the direct outcome of the interaction between the culturally deprived and his environment, such as is characterized by the lack of mediated learning experience. The frequently observed phenomenon of acting by trial and error leads to failure because it is not followed by the insightful, reflective processes required to sort out from the repertoire of behaviors used those that are more and those that are less effective for achieving the proposed goal.

Many test constructors consider trial-and-error behavior to be the royal road to the proper assessment of the disadvantaged examinee and have even built their instruments in such a way as to elicit this type of behavior. Such a test is Kohs' Block Design Test, where the examinee is confronted with a task in which he is required to rapidly manipulate the blocks in order to discover the appropriate sides necessary for composing the prescribed design. If he cannot do this or does not do it in the prescribed time, failure is inevitable, whereas it is assumed that by rapid trial and error there is at least a chance of his succeeding.

The Stencil Design Test of Grace Arthur (1930), in its conventional form, closely follows this line of thinking. The examinee is presented with a series of stencils placed before him on the table in a specified order (Figure 26). He is then presented with a model figure

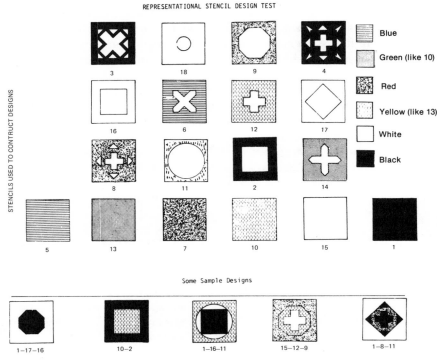

Figure 26. Representational Stencil Design Test. (Designs from Arthur, 1930. Reproduced by permission. Copyright 1947 by The Psychological Corporation. All rights reserved.)

and is asked to construct a design identical to it by superimposing the appropriate stencils one upon another. He must select from the stencils on the table those that are adequate for the given design. In the scoring of the conventional administration, *no attention is paid to the number of inappropriate stencils manipulated by the examinee during the trial-and-error search;* neither is the examinee sanctioned for one specific kind of error more than for another. He is allowed to choose and to try, without any kind of limitations, any stencil in combination with any other, with the only criterion for success being the final production of the identical design within the time limit of 4 minutes. What becomes clear is the basic contention of the test constructor that trial and error is an effective way to solve the problem at hand and that in this process there are no differences in level between various strategies used by the examinee. Thus the anticipatory and planning difficulties, reflected in the superimposition of two *solid* stencils with the top stencil obstructing the view of the bottom one, are not considered more absurd than the use of a stencil that is inappropriate only by its orientation, for example, the use of white stencil 16 in place of white stencil 17 (see Figure 26).

Our observations in comparing Afro-Asian culturally deprived children with occidental middle-class, normally functioning children have led us to the conclusion that trial-and-error strategy does not necessarily impair the final production of the middle-class examinee. However, this is strikingly different in the case of the culturally deprived child. In his case, trial-and-error behavior does not only and invariably result in failure, it also affects in a detrimental way the very learning process of the individual. This is so, even when the time factor, which is often prolonged by trial and error, is not considered as a criterion for failure. The reason for this can be found in the way in which individuals belonging to these two groups use their own acts as sources of information guiding their further behavior. The normally functioning examinee has learned to register his various steps, assigning values of efficiency to them by associating them actively and insightfully with the specific outcome. However, the culturally disadvantaged examinee is devoid of such reflective active learning processes because of his deficient functions. His behavior is marked by an episodic grasp of reality; he does not establish relationships between the experienced events because he does not compare spontaneously. He thus derives only a very limited amount of information from his trial-and-error behavior. The fact that he is given an opportunity and even encouraged to use a motor modality of search and response not only does not elicit thought processes but to a very large extent inhibits them.

We have dwelt at length on introducing this topic because it is essential in order to understand the reasons for and the meaning of the changes we have introduced in this test for the described purposes. It is our contention that when the examinee is presented with a task requiring internalized representational thinking, while being helped and oriented by the examiner acting as a mediating adult, he will show a much greater capacity to master the task than when left alone with his propensity for acting impulsively, unreflectively, and without planning. In a way, the Stencil Design Test, subsequently presented as the Representational Stencil Design Test, offers a model of the effects of mediated learning experience upon some significant behavioral patterns of the individual.

The major change we have introduced into Arthur's test structure consists of removing the opportunity for actually manipulating the stencils motorically. Even the suggestion of motor manipulation is removed by displaying the stencils on a wall poster hanging a few feet in front of the examinee. He is then presented with the prescribed design and asked to point out not only the stencils that must be used to construct the design but also the *order* in which they must be superimposed to produce the identical design. One can immediately see the difference between the task presented in this way and that presented in its conventional form. In the RSDT the examinee must keep in mind, on a representational level, the outcome of his mental acts. Thus, after selecting a stencil and mentally "superimposing" it on another, he has to represent to himself the resultant design and keep this internally constructed representation stable while proceeding with further steps. He must then change the previous representation after each new mental act. A constant internal feedback process is required in order to consider any new move. Decisions concerning correctness or incorrectness must be made by comparing a represented design with the actually perceived design (Figure 27).

3   Cut out tilted cross and triangles in black stencil

18 Cut out center circle in white stencil

1   Solid black

4   Cut out center cross and peripheral triangles and arrowheads in black stencil

2 Cut out large center square in black stencil.

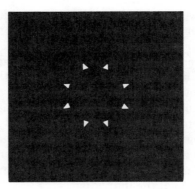

Figure 27.   Task from Representational Stencil Design Test. The circle cut out of white stencil 18 is totally unrecognizable once the black stencils 3, 4, and 2 are superimposed upon it. Only eight small triangles remain of the white circle. The only way to recognize the presence of stencil 18 is to perceive the circular ordering of the triangles.

Initially such a task seems not only inaccessible to the culturally deprived low functioning child but difficult even for the normal adolescent and intelligent adult. In fact, many of those who have actively participated and observed an LPAD session using this particular test have experienced the way in which these children, many of them labeled and dealt with as retardates, perform far above all expectation. Intelligent adults often have difficulties in following the rapidity with which some of these children solve the problems set for them in this test, during and after training.

Further confirmation of the ability of a retarded performer to perform on a representational level can be derived from the study *Problem Solving of Retarded School Children,* conducted by Ursula Neifeind and Jens-Jorg Koch (1976). In this study the authors investigated the differential effectiveness of *manipulative* vs. *conceptual* problem-solving of graphic-abstract tasks, following a period of practice. The study addressed the widespread belief that the retarded are not capable of abstract thinking and that therefore the goals set for their education and the strategies set for their attainment should be limited to concrete and motor-manual activities.

The results of the Neifeind and Koch experiment suggest that the use of motor manipulation is not advantageous for the retarded, although it is for normal children. Three groups of subjects were used in the study: older retarded, their normal functioning peers, and younger normal children. It was found that, whereas both normal groups performed better by manipulation than by conceptualization, this was not true for the retarded. The retarded also performed worse than did the normal groups for the manipulative situation in spite of their familiarity with the tasks achieved during training. But more important, the retarded group performed better than did the normal groups in the internalized anticipatory problem-solving situation.

A number of functions are involved in the appropriate performance of RSDT tasks. A first and important element is the discrimination between the various *colors* and the *forms* of both the stencils and the designs. The form is created by the cut-out part in the center and/or the periphery of the stencil. The examinee has to be able to discriminate between *form* and *background* which, in this particular task, usually have a reversed relationship; that is, what is usually the background is here perceived as the form. Thus, a cut-out cross in the green stencil (12) is perceived as a red cross surrounded by a green background when superimposed on the solid red stencil (7 on the chart). Further, the discrimination between forms will have to consider elements such as size and orientation of the various forms. Thus the white stencil with the cut-out square (16) will have to be distinguished from the white stencil with the diamond cut-out (17), and the black angles in the cut-out of stencil 3 will have to be distinguished from those of stencil 4 (Figure 28). Summative behavior will be an important component in those cases in which a specific number of angles must be used for the construction of a given design. On a more elementary level, the examinee has to learn the obstructive effect of a stencil that is not cut out and avoid using it when something should be perceived behind it.

The behavioral elements involved in this task can be divided into the three phases of the cognitive process to which we have often alluded. On the input phase, the examinee has to consider and analyze the various components of the design perceived by him and become acquainted with all of the stencils from which he has to choose the appropriate ones for the prescribed item. Here, the discrimination of color, form, size, orientation, etc., are the required cognitive steps. On the elaborational phase, the order in which each stencil has to be chosen to produce the required transformation of the

16 Large cut-out   3 Cut out tilted   18 Cut out circle in   4   Cut out center cross   15 Solid white stencil
     square in white   cross and triangles   center of white   and peripheral triangles
     stencil   in black stencil   stencil   and arrowheads in black
                                                                            stencil

Figure 28.   Task from Representational Stencil Design Test. The creation of this design requires the merger of three white stencils and the use of only parts of two black stencils.

single stencil is of prime importance. Thus the anticipation of the transformations induced by placing the white stencil with a cut-out circle (18) on a solid red stencil (7), yielding a red circle encompassed by a white square, as compared with the superimposition of stencil 18 on a solid white stencil (15) where no change occurs because the identical colors do not permit new forms to become perceptible, is a typical product of the elaboration process on a rather elementary level. The demand for internalized representational elaboration processes becomes greater not only with the increase in the number of stencils needed for the construction of the items but also with the increased complexity of their characteristics. An example is the fusion of colors from adjacent layers and the need to use an elaborate analytical system in order to sort out the various layered stencils involved in producing it.

On the output level, the response is the outcome of an anticipated transformation and therefore must be planned ahead and continuously compared with the stimulus design. The comparison of the stimulus design with a representational image as a source of information of what has to follow reminds one of the need to keep a constant flow of feedback in our speech behavior, so that what is said is determined by both what has already been said and what is still to follow. The stimulus stencil acts somewhat like the "notes" of the speaker.

In terms of the nature of the task, it is beyond doubt that what is required from the examinee is a very complex transformation process in which the acting human organism makes a significant contribution to the analysis of a complex stimulus, the breakdown into its component parts, and its reconstruction by a chain of complex comparative, discriminative, and logical steps. It is clear that we are dealing with operations pertaining to a higher level in the hierarchy of mental processes and, therefore, belonging to those operations that, according to Jensen's criteria, involve Level II behavior and presumably remain inaccessible to the retarded performer. This makes clear why we have chosen this test as a way to assess and to modify the level of functioning of the culturally disadvantaged individual.

Administration and Scoring The test consists of two phases: 1) training and 2) testing. The training is done with the help of a set of 20 simple tasks aimed at preparing the examinee for the test in several areas. First the training process helps him to become acquainted with the individual stencils printed on the chart—their location, the numbers beneath them, and their proper use. In this way, the examinee becomes familiar with the colors, forms, and other characteristics of the stencils. By inferential questioning, he is led into the understanding of the principle of the figure and background and the way by which they are combined. Finally, attention is given to a host of attitudinal and motivational aspects that were described earlier. The examinee is then presented with the 20 stimulus cards of the original Grace Arthur Tests. A parallel series is also available. The examinee is instructed to list on the recording sheet the number of each individual stencil he has selected and the order of their assembly for the construction of the specific design. In other cases, it is the examiner who records the numbers as they are given by the examinee.

The group test became possible with the printing of an enlarged chart and test booklets containing the 20 stimulus cards.

The results obtained are evaluated by applying four scoring criteria:

1. Correct: This score is assigned when the examinee has pointed out, without error, all appropriate cards in their proper order. Each correct design is given one point.
2. Spontaneous correction: This score is ascribed to the performance in which an error was made either by omitting a required stencil or by an improper ordering followed by the examinee's spontaneous correction. These types of errors are often observed with our impulsive population in the earlier stages of the test.
3. Bad-order/correct: This score is assigned whenever the examinee has chosen all the required stencils with one or more of them out of the proper order. This score is retained even if, after the inquiry and feedback process, the examinee is able to correct himself.
4. Total score: Sum of 1, 2, and 3.

In addition to this scoring system, we have another one that takes into consideration the level of difficulty of the test items. We assume that the more elements contained in each item, the more difficult is the task of identifying and arranging them in order. Therefore, the number of elements in the item is used as a criterion for difficulty and a score of $n-1$ is given to each correct answer (where n refers to the numbers of elements contained in the item). For example, if the task contains four elements and the examinee has chosen and ordered them appropriately, his score will be 3. This scoring system is applied only when all items are correct and/or spontaneously corrected. Bad-order/correct is not considered in this scoring system. The total score of the individual is the number of points he has received on all items he has completed correctly.

Our scoring procedures are rather severe compared with the scoring method in the conventional use of this test. As previously mentioned, in the conventional test there are no sanctions for inappropriate choices during the trial-and-error behavior, whereas in our approach these are all retained and recorded. The product is considered from the point of view of the process that has generated it. This allows us to distinguish between various sources of error and to assign a differential significance to mistakes. This, in turn, has important diagnostic and remediational bearings.

Numerical Progressions

In addition to the four LPAD tests detailed above, there are several others in the battery. Since they were not used in the clinical experiments discussed in the following pages, they therefore are not described here. However, Numerical Progressions, although not used in the clinical studies, was part of the battery for the group tests (Chapter 5) and is therefore presented here.

Numerical Progressions consists of a series of progressions of increasing difficulty. It focuses on the search for an extraction of the specific rule governing the relationship between numbers in a progression. Its purpose is not to test a child's arithmetic skills, although numbers are used because they require only limited verbal abilities. The major deficient function to which this test is addressed is the episodic grasp of reality that is typically encountered in culturally deprived individuals. Characteristic of this deficiency is the perception of events and objects as discrete, with little awareness of, or attention to, the relationships existing between them. Even when the relationship is grasped, nothing compels the child to search for the determinant rule governing the relationship and to apply it to new situations.

A second and more general function that this test attempts to assess is the individual's representational ability and the extent to which he is able to predict and construct relationships in new situations and tasks by means of the rules he has discovered. In order to draw the necessary conclusions, the subject must make use of comparison, inference, and deduction. Furthermore, he must be able to surmount distraction and exercise precision, discrimination, and a willingness to defer judgment until all the data have been processed. As the progressions become more complex, the subject must use several sources of information simultaneously and draw conclusions based on logical evidence, and he must find the stable, unchanging rules that serve to relate events that seem to deviate from the model of a progression with a fixed relationship between each of its members.

The test consists of two parts: six training sheets and 46 paper and pencil test items. Easy and difficult examples from the training and test sheets are provided in Figure 29. The training is mainly directed toward teaching the examinee the process of deducing a relationship, such as that found in the intervals in numerical series. This then must be followed by the application of the deduced rule to extend the progression. A great variety of training strategies may be used to produce the flexibility necessary for the discovery of the underlying rules and their application.

The test provides the examinee with opportunities to apply, in a variety of ways, the principles, skills, and strategies acquired during the training phase. In order to ensure continuous interest, the test commences with easier tasks that provide the examinee with the experience of success. The examinee is constantly provided with support to prevent him from discontinuing the test.

Because the test does not require the mastery of complex arithmetic computations, it may be used with low functioning

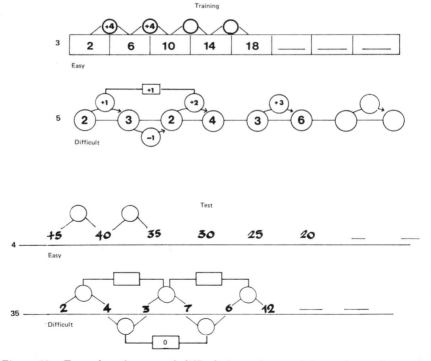

Figure 29. Examples of easy and difficult items from training and test sheets of Numerical Progressions.

children who have learning disabilities and deficiencies in this area. In addition to its use in the clinical situation, numerical progressions may also be used for group testing. The time necessary for individual testing ranges from about 30 to 45 minutes. The group test may take longer because of the necessity of ensuring mastery of the rules by all the participants. A simple scoring procedure may be adopted such that one point is given for each correctly solved progression. Another scoring procedure consists of giving a point for each of the two required numbers. If only one number is given or is correct, the subject is assigned a score of one.

A STUDY OF TWO GROUPS OF RETARDED PERFORMERS

We now present the study of two groups of retarded performers on the four tests described (Organization of Dots, Plateaux Test, LPAD Variations I, and Representational Stencil Design Test), presented to them individually, using the clinical LPAD method.

The first group was composed of 55 adolescents* referred to the Youth Aliyah Child Guidance Clinic for the assessment of their potential for modifiability as a precondition for their acceptance into the program of preparatory classes for the culturally deprived, low functioning adolescent within the Youth Aliyah framework. Preparatory classes provide a powerful educational environment specially designed to make possible the integration of culturally deprived, retarded performing adolescents into a normal school after an intervention period lasting 1 to 2 years. The strong awareness of the final goal involves both teachers and students in mobilizing adequate learning behavior and producing a high achievement motivation in the learner. The second group consisted of 36 students recruited from a special school for the educable mentally retarded (EMR).

We have four objectives in presenting the results of this study. The first is to describe the use of the LPAD clinical battery with retarded performers of differing etiologies. The second is to compare the results of the two groups on the LPAD. We were seeking the nature of the differences between the two groups of retarded performers—those who despite their low level of functioning were placed in the regular school educational framework and those who were diagnosed by conventional tests, labeled, placed, and treated as EMR in a special school. The questions we sought to answer were to what extent these two diagnostically different groups could be

---

* The number of subjects in both EMR and clinic groups vary for certain parts of the test battery.

considered to have different cognitive structures and what degree of modifiability they might show when subjected to a similar training strategy. The answer to these questions would lead us to seek the rationale for the differing placement and treatment usually considered necessary for the two groups.

As Erdman and Olson (1966) pointed out, between 80% and 90% of children diagnosed as EMR and referred to special schools belong to socioculturally disadvantaged segments of the population. This throws many doubts on the significance of the psychological label of EMR. As we have already pointed out, there is great overlap between the two classificatory systems that lead to the placement of the EMR in special schools (Mercer, 1975): the ethno-socioeconomic on the one hand, and the psychological-psychometric on the other. The classification by social criteria cannot be seriously questioned because it is based on relatively objective criteria. The question, therefore, is whether the group of children labeled and treated as EMR differ significantly from a group of culturally deprived adolescents when they are compared on measures obtained by a dynamic method of testing such as the LPAD. If differences should emerge, what is their nature, and how should they be interpreted?

Our third objective is to establish orientational criteria for the four tests to assist the clinician using the LPAD battery. Finally, our fourth objective is to obtain a measure of the nature and quantity of retention demonstrated by the EMR group and the extent to which the principles, learning sets, and work habits acquired during the first testing sessions prove to be present and effective in subsequent testing sessions. To assist in attaining this goal, the EMR group was subjected to a retest 2 months after the first testing session, with almost no teaching investment or prompting by the examiner during this retest phase.

Description of the Population

The first group, the "clinic" group, consisted of 55 adolescents referred to the Youth Aliyah Child Guidance Clinic. This group was marked by a high level of heterogeneity in a number of dimensions. The ages ranged from 12 to 16, with an average of 14 years. Only 17 children were native-born Israelis; the rest had emigrated from different countries. Among the immigrant children were adolescents from America, Eastern and Western Europe, Soviet Russia, the Far East, Pakistan, India, and Iran, and a substantial number from Morocco. The parents' occupational status and socioeconomic level were also heterogeneous. They included a few academicians and highly educated people and some people of very low and disadvantaged status. Common to all the children was an extremely low level of functioning on academically related tasks. There was a high percentage of illiteracy and impaired functioning in areas of reading comprehension, arithmetic, and general information. Many of the children were considered mentally retarded by their regular classroom teachers either on the basis of psychometric assessment or their school achievement in Israel or abroad.

The stated etiological factors were also highly heterogeneous. Certain of the children were considered to have an organic condition, either following a history of a peri- or postnatal accident or encephalitis. Others were defined as culturally deprived, in terms of extremely poor life conditions affecting their experiential backgrounds. These were children whose parents were both culturally different as compared with the Israeli culture and culturally deprived as defined by us earlier. Some of the children were referred for placement after many failures to remediate their condition through placement in remediational programs in their regular schools or in settings oriented toward prevocational training requiring a very low level of academic and intellectual achievement.

The great number of failure experiences to which this group had been exposed made many of them reluctant to enter into a new endeavor, and they openly expressed their resistance to being examined because of their expectations of still another failure. Yet, their motivation to leave home was often explained by them as their sole hope of a new start that might change the otherwise grim prospects and outlooks on life. Many expressed the feeling that the low level of intelligence ascribed to them did not reflect their true capacities.

The heterogeneity of this clinic group resided only in the *distal* etiological determinants of their conditions, such as organicity, poverty, emotional disturbance of parents, etc. In all of them, however, we were able to find signs of the same *proximal* etiology: the *lack* of mediated learning experience resulting in the syndrome of cultural deprivation, a low level of achievement, extremely low self-image, and finally, a dim perception of the existence of a higher potential that had not been realized. They differed in the amount of investment required to modify their level of functioning in one or another criterion measure of our test battery.

The second sample, the "EMR" group, was formed by a group of 36 children, ranging in age from 12 to 17, and from grades 5, 6, and 7 of a special school. Admission to this school was contingent upon an IQ ranging from 50 to 75 established with conventional tests such as the WISC and the Binet-Simon, which placed them in the EMR category. These limits were rigid, in accordance with the school's policy of not accepting children whose low level of function was allegedly because of emotional disturbance, socioeconomic disadvantage, or cultural deprivation. This gave us the opportunity to question the contention that by using static measures one can really determine precisely the diagnosis of EMR.

The group was formed of 44% boys (16), and 56% girls (20). Ninety-two percent of the children were Israeli born; however, only 16% of their parents were born in Israel, with almost 80% born either in the Middle East or in North Africa. The social and occupational levels of the parents were low. About 45% of the families had more than five children.

The children in the group all showed very poor general academic functioning, in addition to their low IQ. Many of them disclosed a low level of visual-motor performance, with a retarded performance of between 3 and 4 years on tasks such as the Bender Gestalt or the Draw-a-Man Test. At the time of their examination, their academic achievement was very impaired, with many children showing gaps of 3 to 5 years in basic school skills, despite their relatively prolonged exposure to special education. In other words, the EMR group may be considered a homogeneous group, as distinct from the clinic group, which was highly heterogeneous.

The EMR group was uniformly described by psychologists and teachers as being impaired in their capacity to grasp more complex relationships and to elaborate tasks requiring operational, conceptualized, abstract thinking. Accordingly, the educational goals set for these children were limited at best to the acquisition of the "3 R's" and training in menial work habits. To the extent that more general information was processed, it was usually simple, elementary, and concrete. This choice of restrictive goals and methods was based on the assumption that any attempt to transcend such levels of presentation would be frustrating both to the child and to the teacher, and would serve no useful purpose.

It is no wonder that the motivation of such children to academic studies proved to be low and that many tried to drop out of school at an early age to become involved in some kind of lucrative though menial job. It was only because of the devoted work of the staff that many of these children continued their education at school and did not drop out. However, what marked this population was a very low self-image, which made them refer to themselves as "defectives," using this as a defense against any attempts to confront them with tasks requiring active mental elaboration. This low level of self-expectation seemed to reflect the expectations of the teachers, as expressed in the interactive process between them and their students, the low level type of tasks offered to the students for mastery, and the protective rather than challenging approach of the school in general toward its students.

As opposed to the EMR group, the clinic group showed a much greater capacity to become involved in assessment processes in spite of their reluctance, grounded in their previous failures in test situations. The fact that they had been in direct contact with a normal environment made them more open to challenges, especially after they learned that they could succeed in the tasks offered to them in the LPAD situation and experienced the interaction between themselves and the examiner as being different from those in test situations in which they were accustomed to fail. Despite a very similar level of functioning on achievement criteria, the group was marked by heterogeneity in demographic data and in distal etiological factors.

Method

The children were tested individually by an examiner, who was usually assisted by an observer who recorded the most salient behavioral elements. The length of testing differed; some children were tested in two sessions and others in one. Total testing time varied between 3½ and 5 hours.

Results

Results are presented in the order in which the tests are usually administered: Organization of Dots, LPAD Variations, Plateaux Test, and the Representational Stencil Design Test. The usual order was changed only in cases where we felt that it might hamper the subsequent development of the examiner-examinee relationship. For example, if we felt that the child had great visual-motor difficulties, we would not start with the Organization of Dots, which requires spatial orientation and graphic skills. The order is usually preserved, however, because each test presents an opportunity for training some specific cognitive prerequisite necessary in the subsequent work of the child in other tests.

Organization of Dots Figure 30 presents the results of the two separate groups, the EMR and the clinic populations, in terms of total score, means, medians, and standard deviations. Of a total score of 40, the mean attained by each of the two groups comes very close to the ceiling of the test. One should note that scoring was stringent, since any item on which the correct answer was not produced *independent of the examiner* was not counted as correct. Therefore, the

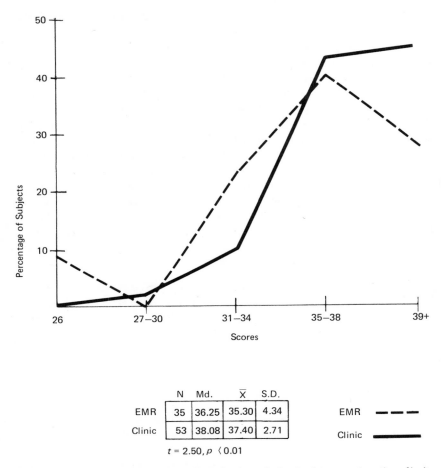

	N	Md.	$\overline{X}$	S.D.
EMR	35	36.25	35.30	4.34
Clinic	53	38.08	37.40	2.71

$t = 2.50, p \langle 0.01$

EMR ━ ━ ━

Clinic ━━━

Figure 30. Organization of Dots: Distribution of obtained scores (no time limit; maximum score, 40) by categories; comparison between EMR and clinic groups (N = 88).

levels attained by these children, many of whom manifested sizable visual-motor impairments, are very high.

However, time, which is the basis for Rey's norms, was not used in this scoring. Indeed, the time needed to attain these scores was quite prolonged, with a mean of 19.40 minutes (SD 7.5) compared with the 4-minute time limit imposed by Rey for the complete test. We are not suggesting that the scores of our groups be compared with Rey's normative data, since he usually gave the test as an aptitude test for technicians, who form his normative group. Yet, if one considers that the age of these children was lower than that of Rey's normative groups, the time should not be considered an important drawback.

It was on the Organization of Dots that we observed some significant differences between the EMR and the clinic groups, in favor of the latter. The mean total score was higher in the clinic group, significant at the .01 level. The same is true with one of the subtests, that of the two squares, with a significant difference at the .01 level. It seems to us that the reason for this difference might well be attributed to the phenomenon of impulsivity, which is by far more frequent, intense, and less accessible to change in the EMR group. The educational framework of the EMR has not been helpful in establishing internal control systems and proper regulation of their behavior. They alternate between states of extreme dependency on the adult, and requiring help from the examiner, and of total loss of control, acting erratically, impulsively, and without investment in the task they are confronted with. The modality of poorly regulated, uncontrolled, impulsive behavior, leading to a considerable increase in errors, is also a major determinant of failure in the Plateaux Test, described later.

The mean score obtained by both groups in an individual assessment situation, 35 to 37 out of 40, is high compared with results obtained by culturally deprived children in a time-free albeit group presentation: mean pretraining score of 18.06, SD of 11.07; mean post-training score of 25.47 and SD of 9.40. The task itself is a relatively difficult one and involves a variety of elaborative processes from the examinee.

The impulsivity of the EMR group, compared with the clinic group, seems to determine the difference in favor of the latter. However, this difference is eliminated at the time of retesting, despite the fact that upon retest there was no training investment.

Figure 31 shows the results obtained *without* intervention by the EMR group in the retest, 2 months later. As can be seen, the results obtained are now similar and without significant differences from those obtained initially by the clinic group. Both the numbers and means have been adjusted for attrition since only those examinees who had both the test and the retest are included. The fact that 2 months after the initial test the children were able to function at the retest on such a high level shows that the learning achieved during the initial LPAD session had a much more lasting effect than one would have expected. This supports our basic contention that reducing certain peripheral deficits responsible for failure makes later work much more successful with these children. We may consider the initial training investment in the LPAD session to have modified

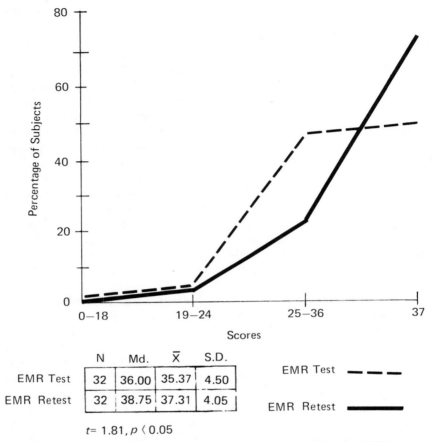

	N	Md.	$\bar{X}$	S.D.
EMR Test	32	36.00	35.37	4.50
EMR Retest	32	38.75	37.31	4.05

EMR Test   ----

EMR Retest ▬▬▬▬

$t = 1.81, p < 0.05$

Figure 31. Organization of Dots: Comparison between test and retest EMR group (N = 32); distribution of correct responses by category (no time limit; maximum score, 40).

certain structural elements of the cognitive behavior, which proved of lasting effect.

Raven Matrices   Figure 32 presents the results obtained by the two groups on the Raven Matrices, Series A, Ab, B. The mean of about 28 (out of a maximum of 36) for both the EMR and the clinic group is lower for their age group than what would be expected by Raven (1965), who cites a mean of 28 for 11-year-old normal school children; but it is significantly higher than the mean of 22, obtained by the culturally deprived group, ages 13 to 16, under the conventional test procedure.

The total score of the Raven is composed of approximately equal distribution of the three series, A, Ab, and B. This is against the expected composition of the total score in which there is usually a decrease in the number of points contributed by the later series, with the increasing complexity of the tasks for Series A, through Ab and B. The fact that the expected composition of the score is not found in our population and that the average on the three series is approximately equal, although Series B clearly entails higher mental processes, shows the effects of a learning process. Furthermore, we

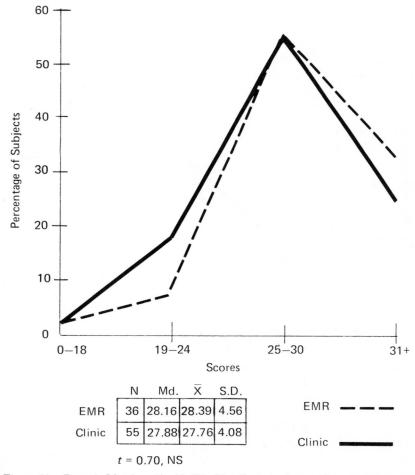

	N	Md.	$\bar{X}$	S.D.
EMR	36	28.16	28.39	4.56
Clinic	55	27.88	27.76	4.08

t = 0.70, NS

EMR   — — —

Clinic   ▬▬▬

Figure 32. Raven's Matrices (A, Ab, B): Distribution of scores by categories; comparison between EMR and clinic groups (N = 91).

are often confronted with the fact that tasks involving higher mental processes, such as in Series B, are often *more accessible* to the EMR after appropriate training. Thus, the tasks described by Raven as the more difficult ones were more positively affected by the training than the easier tasks in series A and Ab. This is in sharp contrast to the assumption made by Raven.

The differences between the EMR and the clinic groups are not statistically significant, although there is a slight tendency in favor of the EMR group. This again points out the limited value of the

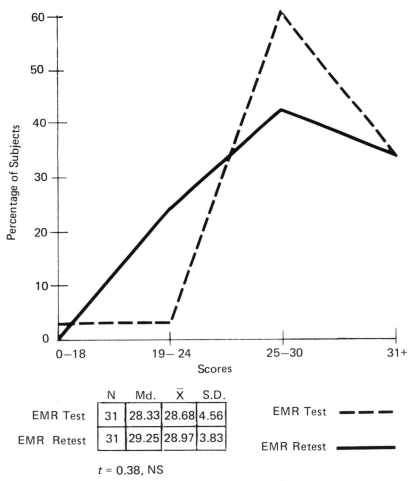

	N	Md.	$\bar{X}$	S.D.
EMR Test	31	28.33	28.68	4.56
EMR Retest	31	29.25	28.97	3.83

EMR Test ━ ━ ━ ━

EMR Retest ━━━━

$t = 0.38$, NS

Figure 33. Raven's Matrices (A, Ab, B): Comparison between test and retest EMR group; distribution by categories (N = 31).

conventional classificatory system that has channeled certain children into the stream of special education while others, similarly low functioning, were kept within the regular school system. The results obtained in the test-retest once more show no significant differences (Figure 33).

LPAD Variations I of the Matrices   Figure 34 presents the results obtained by the two groups on the LPAD Variations of the B_8 to B_{12} tasks of the Raven Matrices. The maximum score of 35 includes the five tasks of B_8 to B_{12}, which in this study are counted

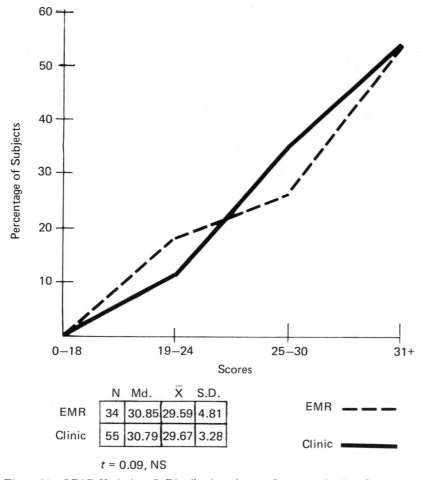

	N	Md.	$\bar{X}$	S.D.
EMR	34	30.85	29.59	4.81
Clinic	55	30.79	29.67	3.28

$t = 0.09$, NS

Figure 34.   LPAD Variations I: Distribution of scores by categories (maximum score 35); comparison between EMR and clinic groups (N = 89).

again in the LPAD Variations, of which they are an integral part. The mean total score of 29.6 is high compared to results obtained with the same test in group test situations, in which the mean is 20, and significantly better than results obtained in our large group experiment with the Analogies Test (presented in Chapter 7), which has tasks similar to those included in the LPAD Variations.

The fact that a population of retarded performers, known and proved to be unable to independently solve more than a mean of 1.1 out of the five B_8 to B_{12} tasks, is able after appropriate training to solve such a high percentage of variations of these problems once more supplies evidence of the modifiability of the level of functioning of such children, even though the amount of investment necessary may vary from one individual to another. The t test shows no significant difference between the EMR and the clinic groups. The stability of the acquired rules and the developed problem-solving strategies is clearly supported by the results obtained by the EMR group on the retest (Figure 35), where a slight increase in the mean and a reduction in the size of the standard deviation are visible. These occurred despite the fact that no further training was offered to the examinees at the retest phase.

It should be noted that, in addition to involving higher mental processes, the mode of presentation of the LPAD Variations requires a high degree of flexibility and a capacity to detach oneself from an established set by use of an analytical process and the discrimination of discrete differences between each of the seven items included in the Variations. Therefore, successful performance of these tasks should be interpreted to indicate an increased awareness on the part of the examinee that helps him to find among the otherwise similar tasks differences that he would usually tend to overlook.

Plateaux Test In Figures 36 and 37, the breakdown of various phases of the Plateaux Test shows differences in favor of the clinic group in the number of trials, with a mean of 10.18 for the EMR vs. 6.48 for the clinic group, with a t of 2.66 significant at the .01 level. The difference between the EMR and the clinic group in the mean error scores was even greater with a mean of 44.53 for EMR and 18.45 for the clinic group, significant at the .001 level (Figure 37). The great differences between the two groups in the trial and the error phases of the test, compared to the lack of differences during the schema and rotation phases (cf. Figures 43 and 44), give support to our contention that the direct determinants of failure are linked to the input and/or output phases and are heavily influenced by lack of inhibition and control over impulsive behavior.

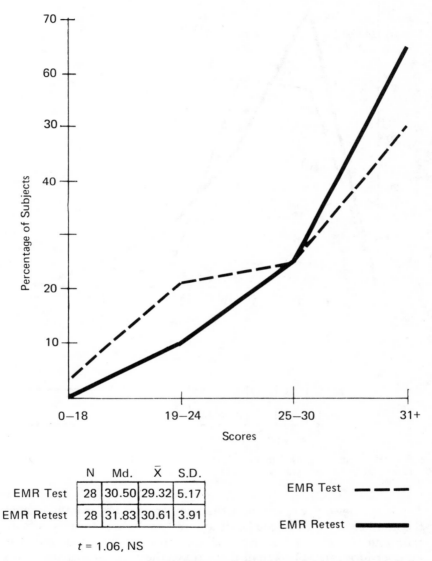

	N	Md.	X̄	S.D.
EMR Test	28	30.50	29.32	5.17
EMR Retest	28	31.83	30.61	3.91

$t = 1.06$, NS

Figure 35.   LPAD Variations I: Distribution of scores by categories (maximum score, 35); comparison between test and retest EMR group (N = 28).

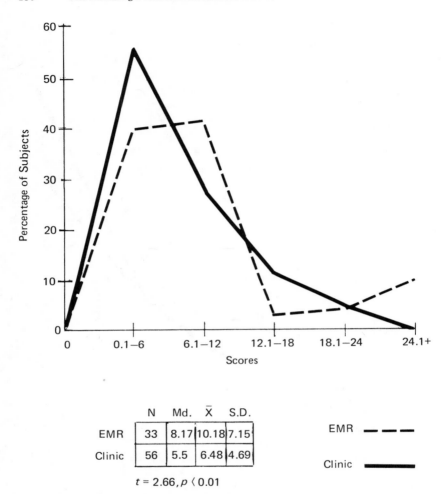

	N	Md.	X̄	S.D.
EMR	33	8.17	10.18	7.15
Clinic	56	5.5	6.48	4.69

EMR — — — —

Clinic ▬▬▬▬

$t = 2.66, p < 0.01$

Figure 36. Plateaux I: Distribution of number of trials by categories; comparison between EMR and clinic groups (N = 89).

It is noteworthy to compare the number of errors as a function of the number of trials. In the EMR group the number of errors is more than four times the number of trials, whereas in the clinic group the number of errors is less than three times the number of trials. This points to the greater impulsivity and lack of control on the part of the EMR group as a direct determinant of their failing behavior. Things change very drastically once the examinee is no longer compelled by the concrete motor nature of the task to act impulsively but is instead required to produce an internalized representation of the outcome of the transformation, imposed on the position of the buttons by rotating the stack of plates first by 90° and then by 180°. Here no differences are visible between the two groups, and in the schema phase there is even a tendency for the EMR group to give better results (see Figures 38–40).

We have already dealt with, and will return to, the meaning of the phenomenon of the better results obtained by the EMR group in a more abstract representational type of behavior than where motor manipulatory behavior is requested. One should note, however, the

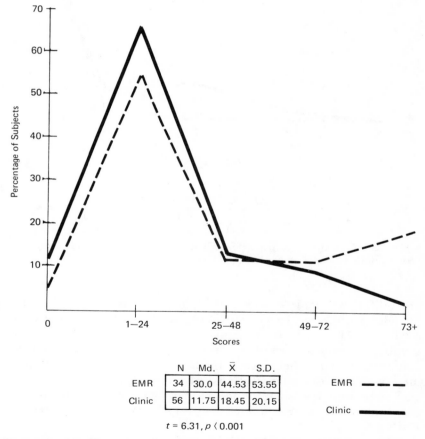

Figure 37. Plateaux I: Distribution of number of errors by categories; comparison between EMR and clinic groups (N = 90).

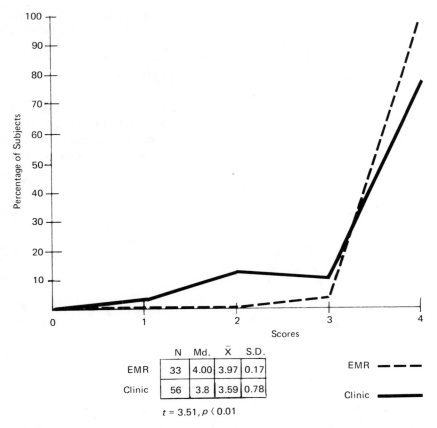

	N	Md.	X̄	S.D.
EMR	33	4.00	3.97	0.17
Clinic	56	3.8	3.59	0.78

$t = 3.51, p < 0.01$

Figure 38. Plateaux I (Schema): Distribution of correct answers; comparison between EMR and clinic groups (N = 89).

great difference depicted in Figure 37 between the mean of the errors (44.53 for EMR vs. 18.45 for clinic) and the median of the errors (30.0 for EMR vs. 11.75 for clinic). This occurs because an infinite number of errors are possible, and some EMR examinees made over 100 of them. This phenomenon is further reflected in the extremely large standard deviations (53.55 EMR and 20.15 clinic), which in each case are larger than the means. Statistically unreliable as they are, these results are of interest in comparison with the subsequent EMR retest results.

The comparison of the EMR group on test and retest shows considerable reduction in the number of trials and errors (Figures

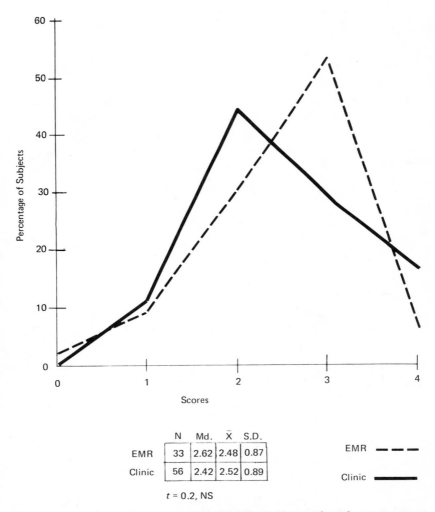

	N	Md.	X̄	S.D.
EMR	33	2.62	2.48	0.87
Clinic	56	2.42	2.52	0.89

$t = 0.2$, NS

Figure 39.   Plateaux I (Rotation I: 90°): Distribution by number of correct answers; comparison between EMR and clinic groups (N = 89).

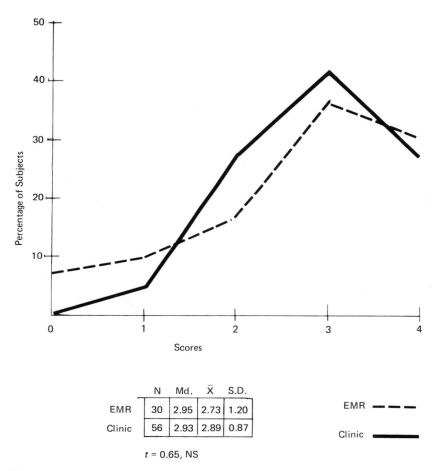

Figure 40. Plateaux I (Rotation II: 180°): Distribution of correct answers; comparison between EMR and clinic groups (N = 86).

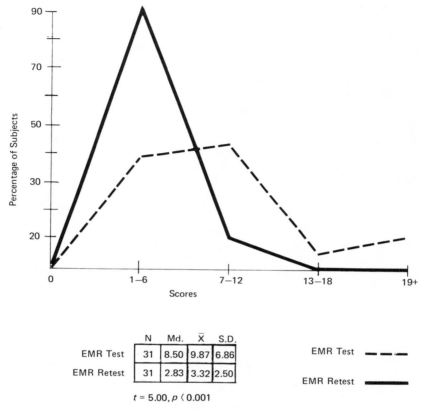

	N	Md.	X̄	S.D.
EMR Test	31	8.50	9.87	6.86
EMR Retest	31	2.83	3.32	2.50

$t = 5.00, p < 0.001$

EMR Test   ― ― ―

EMR Retest ▬▬▬

Figure 41.   Plateaux I: Distribution of number of trials by categories; comparison between test and retest EMR group (N = 31).

41–45). The mean number of trials at the retest is 3.32 (Figure 41), with less than twice the number of errors (mean of 6.58; Figure 42). The test-retest changes in the representational phases of the work, establishing the schema and rotations (Figure 43–45), are not as dramatic as the reduction of trials and errors. This is so because of a ceiling effect, but also because, in the results obtained in schema and rotation in the test phase, the elaborational capacity was already reflected in a much purer form than in the parts of the test requiring motor manipulation, in which the lack of systematic exploration and impulsive uncontrolled behavior contaminated the results. Although the improvement observed in the retest may be accounted for to a certain extent by retention, even after 2 to 3 months, the role played by the control of overimpulsivity should be considered the major

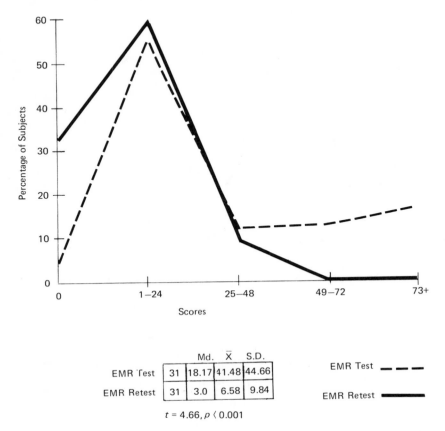

	Md.	X̄	S.D.
EMR Test	31	18.17	41.48	44.66
EMR Retest	31	3.0	6.58	9.84

EMR Test _ _ _ _

EMR Retest ▬▬▬▬

$t = 4.66, p < 0.001$

Figure 42. Plateaux I: Distribution of number of errors by categories; comparison between test and retest EMR group (N = 31).

determinant of the observed improvement. The emphasis of controlled impulsivity over pure retention draws heavy support from the results of both groups on the Plateaux II tests (Figures 46–50).

The results on the Plateaux II tests in which there are two fixed buttons per plate are presented in Figures 46–48. The means obtained by the clinic and EMR groups are 10.75 and 10.90, respectively. Compared to the means obtained by these two groups on Plateaux I (6.48 clinic and 10.18 EMR—Figure 36), they can be considered good, since one would have expected the results on the much more complex Plateaux II to be far worse. The differences between the EMR and the clinic group are completely eliminated on

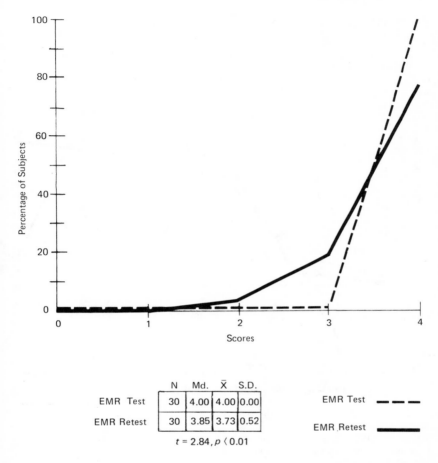

	N	Md.	X̄	S.D.
EMR Test	30	4.00	4.00	0.00
EMR Retest	30	3.85	3.73	0.52

$t = 2.84, p < 0.01$

EMR Test ‒ ‒ ‒

EMR Retest ▬▬▬

Figure 43.   Plateaux I (Schema): Distribution of correct answers; comparison between test and retest EMR group (N = 30).

Plateaux II, in both the trial and the error phases. One should also note the change in the standard deviation, which is reduced for both groups and is now suitably lower than the mean and low enough to indicate much less intragroup variability. The lack of differences between the EMR and the clinic groups throws light on the Plateaux I EMR test-retest improvement described above (Figures 41 and 42). That is, the improvement is decidedly not mere retention, but a strong demonstration of the process of learning to learn by the acquisition of problem-solving strategies accompanied by a marked improved control over impulsive response patterns.

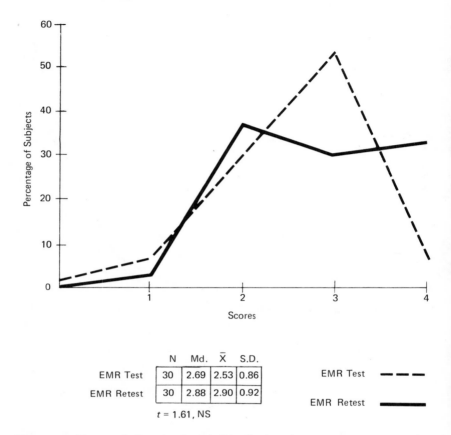

	N	Md.	X̄	S.D.		
EMR Test	30	2.69	2.53	0.86	EMR Test	– – –
EMR Retest	30	2.88	2.90	0.92	EMR Retest	▬▬▬

$t = 1.61$, NS

Figure 44.   Plateaux I (Rotation I: 90°): Distribution of correct answers; comparison between test and retest EMR group (N = 30).

Here, a word of caution should be introduced. The Plateaux II was first presented to the EMR group at the time of retesting Plateaux I. The reason was that early in our work with the EMR group we did not believe that retarded performers in general, and the EMR in particular, could possibly master a task as complex as that in the two-button Plateaux Test. It was only after we saw the great improvement in the functioning of the EMR group on the Plateaux I retest that we decided to take the risk of presenting the two groups with the more difficult test.

The comparison between the EMR and the clinic groups on the Plateaux II test is, therefore, slightly biased in favor of the EMR group because this group was exposed to the Plateaux I twice, once

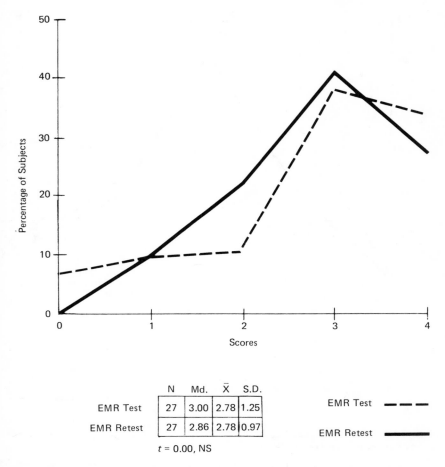

	N	Md.	X̄	S.D.
EMR Test	27	3.00	2.78	1.25
EMR Retest	27	2.86	2.78	0.97

$t = 0.00$, NS

EMR Test   ▬ ▬ ▬

EMR Retest ▬▬▬▬

Figure 45. Plateaux I (Rotation II: 180°): Distribution of correct answers; comparison between test and retest EMR group (N = 27).

during test and once during retest 2 months later, before being confronted with the Plateaux II, whereas the clinical group was exposed to Plateaux I only once. As can be seen from Figures 46–50, all the previously observed differences have disappeared with a noteworthy, even though statistically insignificant, difference in favor of the EMR group in the error score. Both groups reached a relatively high level of proficiency in all of the measured dimensions of this test. One should note especially the high results obtained in the schema and 90° rotation phases (Figures 48–50). In the latter, the

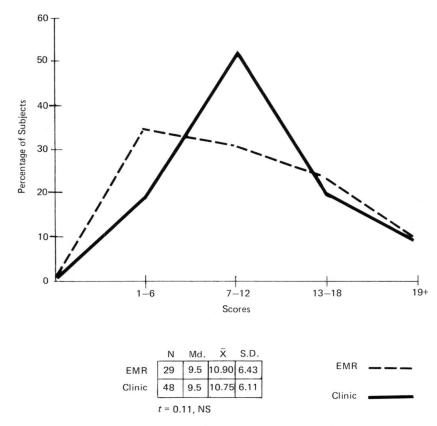

	N	Md.	X̄	S.D.
EMR	29	9.5	10.90	6.43
Clinic	48	9.5	10.75	6.11

t = 0.11, NS

EMR - - - -

Clinic ▬▬▬▬

Figure 46. Plateaux II (two-button plate): Distribution of number of trials by categories; comparison between EMR and clinic groups (N = 77).

examinees obtained an average of two plates correct out of the maximum of four possible when an all-or-none criterion of both buttons on each plate is applied (Figure 49). When, however, the criterion is the number of correct identifications of fixed buttons from a total of eight, then the examinees obtained an average of 5.28 for the EMR and 5.54 for the clinic groups (Figure 50).

Representational Stencil Design Test (RSDT) The results obtained by the EMR and clinic groups on the RSDT are presented in Figures 51 to 56, according to the following criteria described earlier: total score, which includes all correct responses, those spontaneously corrected as well as bad-order/correct (Figures 51 and 52); correct responses, which include all answers that were

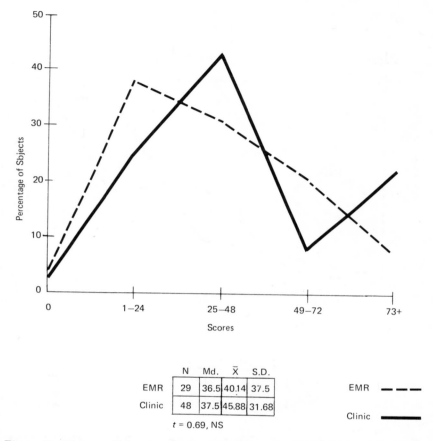

	N	Md.	X̄	S.D.
EMR	29	36.5	40.14	37.5
Clinic	48	37.5	45.88	31.68

$t = 0.69$, NS

EMR - - - -

Clinic ▬▬▬

Figure 47.   Plateaux II (two-button plate): Distribution of number of errors by categories; comparison between EMR and clinic groups (N = 77).

correct or spontaneously corrected (Figures 53 and 54); and bad-order/correct, which includes all responses in which the examinee used all the stencils required although not in the proper order (Figures 55 and 56).

Comparisons between the two groups show no differences between them on the test level or on the EMR test-retest. The results obtained on this test by the two populations can be considered relatively high as compared with the results obtained by normally functioning children, even those of approximately the same chronological age. Regular middle-class children of grades seven and eight reached averages of 11 or 12 out of 20. However, although the test was indi-

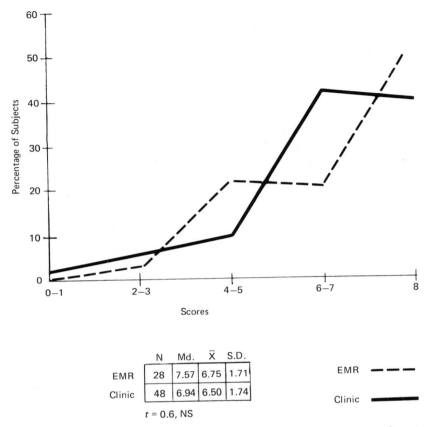

	N	Md.	$\overline{X}$	S.D.
EMR	28	7.57	6.75	1.71
Clinic	48	6.94	6.50	1.74

$t = 0.6$, NS

EMR ----

Clinic ▬▬▬

Figure 48.   Plateaux II (Schema): Distribution of number of correct answers by categories; comparison between EMR and clinic groups (N = 76).

vidually administered in our experiment, it was administered in a group setting to the regular children.

There is evidence that the conventional mode of presentation of this test, either requiring or making possible a trial-and-error approach with help of motor manipulation, makes the task much less accessible and the capacity of the culturally deprived to master it much more reduced than when the same individuals are compelled by the situation itself to use internalized, representational, and reflective thinking as the problem-solving modality. The meaning of this for educational approaches to the retarded performer is most significant.

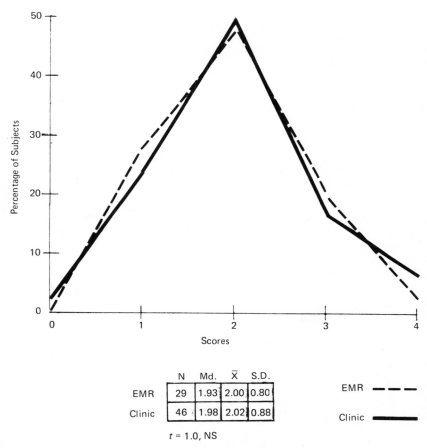

Figure 49.   Plateaux II (Rotation I: 90°): Distribution of correct plates (1–4); comparison between EMR and clinic groups (N = 75).

The difficulties and complexities of the RSDT, extensively discussed in earlier sections of this chapter, make the meaning of the results shown in Tables 9 and 10 even more significant. Tables 9 and 10 present the merged results obtained by the EMR and clinic groups, by percentiles. Merging was done wherever results showed no significant differences between the two groups. Wherever such differences were significant, however, percentiles are presented separately for each group.

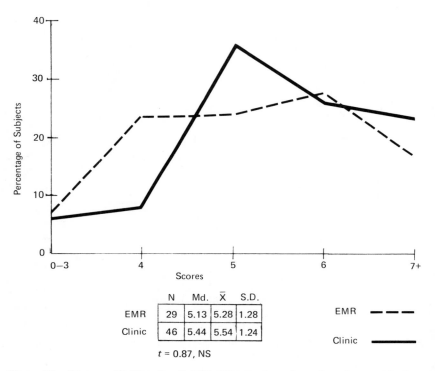

Figure 50.   Plateaux II (Rotation I: 90°): Distribution of number of correct buttons (1–8); comparison between EMR and clinic groups (N = 75).

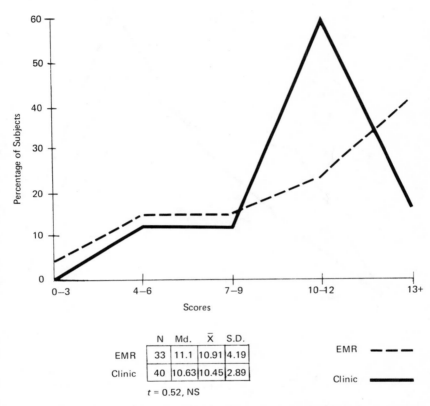

Figure 51. Representational Stencil Design Test: Distribution of total scores (maximum score, 20) by categories; comparison between EMR and clinic groups (N = 73).

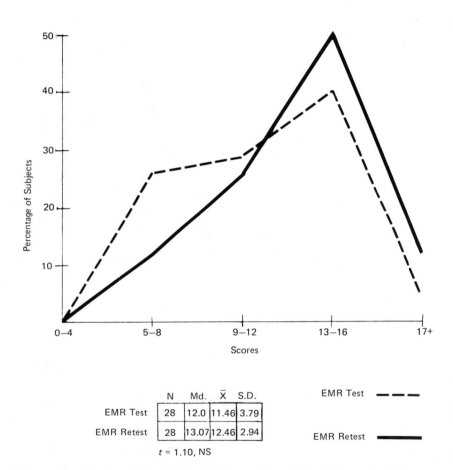

	N	Md.	X̄	S.D.
EMR Test	28	12.0	11.46	3.79
EMR Retest	28	13.07	12.46	2.94

$t = 1.10$, NS

Figure 52.   Representational Stencil Design Test: Distribution of total scores (maximum score, 20) by categories; comparison between test and retest EMR group (N = 28).

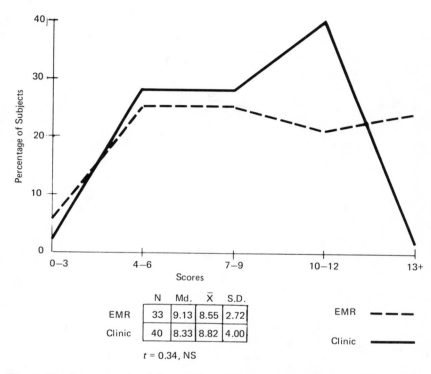

Figure 53. Representational Stencil Design Test: Distribution of correct answers by categories (maximum score, 20); comparison between EMR and clinic groups (N = 73).

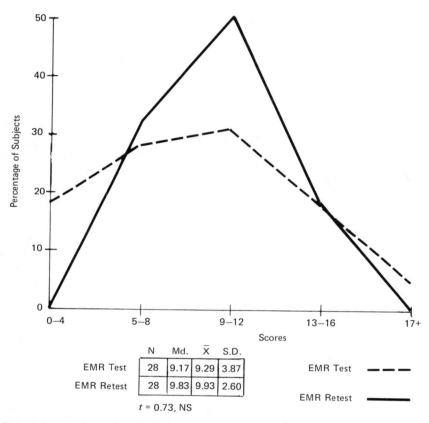

Figure 54. Representational Stencil Design Test: Distribution of correct answers (maximum score, 20) by categories; comparison between test and retest EMR group (N = 28).

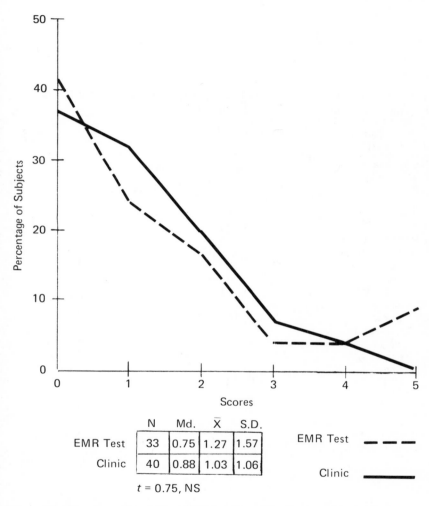

Figure 55.   Representational Stencil Design Test: Distribution of bad-order/correct (1–5); comparison between EMR and clinic groups (N = 73).

Table 9.   LPAD clinical battery: Percentiles yielded by scores based on EMR and clinic groups (combined or separate) (N = 91)

Clinical battery	Percentile					
	10	25	50	75	90	100
Raven Matrices (combined groups)						
Total	21	24	27	30	32	36
A	7	8	9	11	12	12
Ab	7	8	9	11	12	12
B	7	8	9	10	11	12
LPAD Variations I (combined groups)						
Total scores	23	26	29	32	33	35
Plateaux I						
No. of trials						
EMR	30	17	12	7	5	1
Clinic	18	10	7	4	2	1
No. of errors						
EMR	210	85	48	19	6	2
Clinic	75	34	15	5	3	1
Schema						
EMR	4	4	4	4	4	4
Clinic	2	3	4	4	4	4
Rotation I (combined groups)	1	2	2	3	3	4
Rotation II (combined groups)	2	2	3	3	4	4

Table 10.   LPAD clinical battery: Percentiles yielded by scores
based on EMR and clinic groups (combined or separate) (N = 91)

Clinical	Percentile					
battery	10	25	50	75	90	100
Plateaux II						
(combined groups)						
Trial	27	15	10	7	4	2
Error	120	69	51	28	14	3
Schema	4	6	7	8	8	8
Rotation 4/4	1	1	2	3	3	4
Rotation 8/8	4	5	5	6	7	8
RSDT						
(combined groups)						
Total (correct + spontaneous correction + BOC)	5	8	9	12	14	18
Correct	3	5	9	9	12	16
Organization of Dots						
(no time limit)						
Total	30	34	36	38	39	39
EMR	29	32	36	38	38	39
Clinic	33	36	38	38	39	39
Organization of Dots						
(within 4-minute limit)						
(clinic only)						
Total	7	9	9	12	16	24

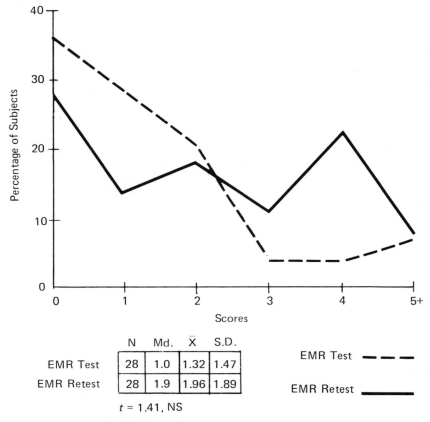

	N	Md.	X̄	S.D.
EMR Test	28	1.0	1.32	1.47
EMR Retest	28	1.9	1.96	1.89

EMR Test — — — —

EMR Retest _____

$t = 1.41$, NS

Figure 56. Representational Stencil Design Test: Distribution of bad-order/correct (1–7); comparison between test and retest EMR group (N = 28).

SUMMARY

Since the data presented in this chapter were gathered (1969–1970), hundreds of children and adolescents have undergone assessment with the clinical battery and other LPAD-oriented instruments. Scores obtained in these measures have been translated into percentiles and expressed in a profile of the individual's performance. This permits in a brief overview the perception of differences in the functioning of the individual and the interpretation of the profile in terms of relative strengths and weaknesses.

A very important source of follow-up data is the Israeli army, because it tests examinees upon their enlistment. The results of the Army's psychometric and other tests point to a high level of validity of the predicted modifiability derived from the LPAD assessment. However, it should be remembered that this validity strongly depends upon the intervening variables of educational, remediational, socializing, and therapeutic intervention that in many cases followed assessment.

The LPAD battery may be complemented by a variety of tasks, especially in nonverbal areas, in an attempt to measure modifiability. The dynamic and clinical use of basic cognitive and school tasks will be easily improvised by the clinician who has assimilated the basic principles underlying the LPAD. Such improvisation has proved necessary whenever the clinician is confronted with situations that do not permit the immediate use of the tasks contained in the battery. Rather than limiting the scope and range of functions, the LPAD battery can thus serve as a paradigm for either the construction, modification, or improvisation of tasks along with the specific needs presented by the individual child.

CHAPTER 5 **Group LPAD Tests:** *Rationale, Implementation, and Results*

The proper implementation of the Learning Potential Assessment Device (LPAD) model requires a wide range of examiner-examinee interactions. Depending on the nature of the task and the specific needs of the examinee, the interaction requires constant adaptation and adjustment. For example, attempts to modify the motivational level of the examinee require a reward system based on constant feedback by the examiner to the examinee of the results obtained and the strategies used in solving problems. Furthermore, because the training is an integral part of the assessment and is based on the specific needs of each examinee, a one-to-one relationship is necessary to reveal the nature and full extent of the examinee's difficulties. Thus, the application of the LPAD model to group testing seems almost diametrically opposed to the entire concept of dynamic assessment.

Group testing, however, has a number of obvious advantages, primarily the economy of the time invested in assessment. Additionally, because of financial, logistic, and even methodological problems, a great many children cannot be tested individually. Hence, the application of the principles of dynamic assessment to group testing is a highly desirable procedure. When concern is directed at the performance of groups, especially homogeneous ones, rather than at individuals, a group assessment technique becomes a valid proposition. In those cases where entire classes present similar problems, it would be a great advantage to use the dynamic approach for descriptive purposes and for searching for answers to educational, didactic, and organizational questions. For these purposes, the problem of standardization is of paramount importance. With a group, it is both necessary and valid to use a more rigorous standardized testing procedure than that adopted in the individual administration of the LPAD.

This chapter discusses how the LPAD has been successfully used to determine important educational policies for groups of children. Policy making was based on questions such as: Should two groups of children functioning at different levels be merged into heterogeneous classes? Is the poor performance of certain new immigrant children the result of cultural difference or cultural deprivation? As in all cases in which the LPAD is used, the criterion measure is the level of *cognitive modifiability* rather than the level of manifest functioning derived from either school performance or static psychometric measures.

CONDITIONS FOR GROUP TESTING

Confronted with the dilemma of choosing between an individual approach, which enables an examiner to identify deficient functions underlying poor performance, and the economy of the group approach with its greater methodological rigor, we have endeavored over the past 6 years to extend the LPAD model to include group administration. The group tests are in no way intended to replace individual assessment in those cases where the focus is on the difficulties experienced by a specific child. Furthermore, the group procedure may be considered complementary to the individual test, and its application is subject to three conditions.

First, the results obtained by an individual on the group test are considered valid only if they demonstrate that the examinee is able to successfully use the training provided in the test situation. In this respect, success is defined by the level of functioning achieved by an examinee on the criterion measures. A base line of the individual's actual level of performance may be established either on the criterion levels themselves or by data from other criteria and performance measures. The fact that an individual is able to achieve an adequate level of performance under the constraint of the limited interaction that occurs in the group LPAD must be regarded as a positive achievement indicative of an ability to function in situations that provide only limited personal involvement. In the school classroom, such an ability is a sine qua non for adaptation, and, hence, adequate performance on the LPAD in the group situation suggests a positive prognosis for adjustment to a school environment.

In the case of an individual who fails to perform adequately on the group LPAD, great caution must be exercised in the interpretation of the results. No decision concerning an individual's true capacity to become modified should be made until evidence based on an individual assessment is available. Poor results on the group LPAD may be because the training required by a particular individual is not provided or that the impersonal group situation, with its reduced opportunities for directed feedback, does not meet the individual's specific needs at that point in his development. Whatever the reason for failure, individual assessment is mandatory in order to identify the deficiencies responsible for poor performance and for the prescription of further teaching and training strategies and methods.

A second condition for dynamic assessment in a group situation is the use of test instruments whose structure permits the dynamic measurement of modifiability of individuals. The instrument must provide opportunities to apply the principles and skills acquired in the training phase of the testing to situations that become progressively more remote from the initial situation, more complex, more difficult, and more different in terms of modality of presentation. In this respect, the structure of the test represents a very important parameter in the use of the LPAD in both individual and group administration. The measurement of the adaptability of the individual to relatively new situations, which is the major goal of the LPAD, is best achieved by presenting the examinee with sets of tasks in which he adapts gradually and progressively to changes. The manner in which this is achieved was described in Chapter 3, where the model for constructing instruments for the LPAD was presented.

The importance of the structure of the test has been borne out by the results obtained on our Analogy tests (see Chapter 7). These tests were not constructed fully according to the model, and results obtained by the training program are significantly lower compared with those obtained by the same populations in tests which were designed in conformity with the model.

The third condition of the use of dynamic assessment in a group situation is that the training phase be presented in a manner that will ensure the maximum possible efficiency. Despite the limitations imposed by the group situation, training must still be oriented toward the correction of deficient functions that are required by the specific tasks as they are manifest in the various phases of the mental act, input, elaboration, and output. Furthermore, a number of other logistic factors will determine the procedures adopted in the test situation. For example, posters should be used to explicitly display the attributes of the sample task used in training. Scoring sheets should reduce the probability of error as a result of inappropriate marking. The presence of two or more assistants to the examiner is recommended to ensure maximum controlled intervention, when required.

Under these aforementioned conditions, we started to use the previously described clinical battery as group tests in a series of studies that aimed simultaneously at the solution of practical and applied problems and at the study of the efficacy of the LPAD in the group situation. The results obtained from these studies have proved to be highly satisfactory and useful. By using the LPAD, even in its more restricted group administration, we have been able to obtain insights into the real potential of low performing children that conventional tests—and, for that matter, conventional wisdom—did not permit.

GROUP TEST BATTERY

The battery of tests used in group testing is similar to the battery used in individual testing. It contains the following tests (described in Chapter 4): Organization of Dots, LPAD Variations I and II, Representational Stencil Design Test, and Numerical Progressions. In addition, Thurstone's Primary Mental Abilities (PMA) Test (1938; Thurstone and Thurstone, 1941) has been used to obtain a static-measure base line for comparative purposes.

The team of examiners consists of at least two people, trained in the administration of group tests, who have a thorough understanding of the LPAD model and the ability to establish a positive interaction with the examinees. Especially important is the examiners' mastery over those components of the dynamic assessment that require training in the prerequisites of cognitive processes so that they are able to transcend the written instructions whenever it becomes necessary to do so for either the group or the individual.

The team is equipped with posters that are used for training purposes and may also provide control and orientation for the individual examinee in need of intervention. Special forms are used to record the nature and quantity of intervention with particular examinees, as determined by their specific needs.

The group should be of moderate size with an optimum of 10 and a maximum of 20. Classroom teachers are encouraged to participate in the group tests but are asked not to intervene directly so that control of the administration and intervention can be exercised. For further information regarding the group test, as well as for the scoring system, the reader is referred to the LPAD manuals (in preparation).

LPAD GROUP TEST STUDIES

We now briefly present four of our studies, relevant to the present discussion: the Hodayot, Georgian and Mountain Children, Culturally Disadvantaged, and Bedouin Studies.

Hodayot

The major goal of this study was to evaluate the desirability of regrouping the ninth and tenth grades of Hodayot, a residential coeducational vocational high school in Israel. The students had been divided into two populations that were considered different on the basis of their manifest level of functioning and school achievement. Because of these differences, the educational goals and curricula for the two populations had been established in accordance with their respective performances.

Background   The lower level groups had come from preparatory classes in a residential setting that specialized in accepting culturally deprived, disadvantaged adolescents similar to those described elsewhere (Feuerstein, 1969; Feuerstein and Rand, 1977). Many of these low performing children were total or functional illiterates, with an IQ in the range of educable mentally retarded or borderline when they had been referred to the preparatory classes 2 or more years earlier. They were given special training in basic school skills, such as reading and writing, and offered some cognitive enrichment programs. Upon completion of this preparatory period, they were referred to the vocational high school with the understanding that they would continue there as a separate group for academic and vocational training, together with similarly low functioning individuals referred to and accepted in the program. However, they would be integrated into the total student body for all extracurricular activities in the life of the youth village.

The groups functioning at a regular level were referred to the residential setting from regular schools after completing eight grades. The students were admitted on the basis of average and above average levels of academic achievement and mental ability. Their referral to a vocational instead of an academic high school usually reflected a somewhat lower level of expectation on the part of the child and his parents. Because of the family's limited economic possibilities, considerable importance was attached to the child's becoming involved in a learning process that would lead to a lucrative return and self-sufficiency as soon as possible. In some cases, the decision to embark on vocational studies was made on the basis of a relatively low level of achievement in academic school subjects.

The school offered both a regular academic program culminating in the matriculation examination and an alternate program leading to certification for those students who did not wish to participate in the regular program or were unable to attain the necessary level. The different goals set for the two groups were reflected in their programs, with the higher group directed toward vocational matriculation after 4 years of study, while the low functioning group was directed towards practical work in the course of a 3-year program. During the years before our intervention, the low and regular groups had been kept apart scholastically and vocationally.

For many years, educators had complained about the very poor academic motivation of the members of the low functioning group, which contrasted with their spectacularly successful adaptation to the social life in the youth village. Their active participation in all extracurricular activities led to leadership positions in the Youth Village. The educators and teachers questioned the reasons for the disparity between the academic and social functioning of these adolescents and, consequently, for the rationale for grouping the students according to their ability. At a certain point, they even expressed their feeling that it was the ability grouping itself that was responsible for placing the low functioning students at a significant disadvantage inasmuch as it produced low expectations of their ability to achieve on the part of both the teachers and the students. In our discussion of these problems with the teachers, it became apparent that the teachers themselves refrained from presenting these adolescents with incentives for learning because they felt that this might tax the students beyond their abilities. The teachers had inferred a low capacity from the students' manifest level of functioning as well as from the fact that these students came from an institution that was known to properly handle culturally disadvantaged and low functioning children.

A decision to combine the students into heterogeneous classes required answers to two questions. The first was whether the manifest level of performance of the low functioning children was, in fact, a reflection of their true ability. Another way of posing the question was whether these children, despite their poor performance level, had the potential for modifiability. The second question concerned the problem of the possible effects of combining the students from both levels: would the two groups of students benefit from their exposure to each other or would the experience have an adverse effect on either or both of the groups? The claim has often been made that combining low and regular functioning groups is detrimental to both groups. Because of the necessity to base the final answer to this question on empirical evidence, which could only be gathered by combining the students and awaiting the outcome, a rather heavy burden of responsibility was placed on the evaluation of the potential modifiability of the low performing group.

Test Results Four groups of students were tested: two ninth-grade classes, one functioning at a regular level (9A; N = 32) and one at a low level (9B; N = 35); two tenth-grade classes, one functioning at a regular level (10A; N = 36) and one at a low level (10B; N = 23). In order to assess the modifiability of the students, three LPAD group tests were administered: LPAD Variations (Var.) II, Representational Stencil Design Test (RSDT), and Numerical Progressions (NP). In addition, students were tested on the Primary Mental Ability Test (PMA) (Thurstone, 1938; Thurstone and Thurstone, 1941) in order to obtain a static measure of their manifest performance level to supplement the impressions based upon their actual school achievements.

The means and standard deviations obtained on the various measures by the four groups, 9A, 9B, 10A, and 10B, are presented in Table 11. An analysis of variance has been performed for each of the measures, and the results are summarized in Table 12.

From these tables it is apparent that, in terms of their manifest levels of cognitive functioning as measured by the PMA, the two low functioning groups (B) were indeed significantly lower than the two regular groups (A). This finding confirmed the differences between the groups based on their school performance. However, the results for the three tests of the LPAD battery tell a somewhat different story. Only two of the six comparisons of results reported in Table 12 reveal significant differences between the regular and low groups. What this finding means is that in a test situation in which all the examinees were provided with training on a set of novel tasks, the low groups revealed that they were able to benefit from the training and reach levels of performance similar to those of the normal groups on many of the tasks. It is also necessary to point out that the LPAD tests comprise many tasks that are considerably more difficult and more complex than those in the PMA. Consequently, the conclusion was drawn that the results of the tests provided sufficient evidence of the low functioning groups' potential for modifiability to justify merging the regular and low functioning pupils. New heterogeneous

Table 11.   Hodayot Study: Means and standard deviations for the PMA, LPAD Var. I
RSDT, and NP, by classes, prior to merging of the regular group (A) with the low
functioning group (B), based upon total study population (N = 126)

Instrument	9A (N = 32)		9B (N = 35)		10A (N = 36)		10B (N = 23	
	$\overline{X}$	SD	$\overline{X}$	SD	$\overline{X}$	SD	$\overline{X}$	SD
PMA	165.9	17.8	153.8	14.7	170.28	14.9	154.3	22.6
(max. score, 220)								
LPAD Var. II	31.7	9.0	26.8	8.1	38.9	10.0	35.8	10.4
(max. score, 58)								
RSDT	11.2	3.3	10.0	3.4	13.2	3.0	9.2	4.4
(max. score, 20)								
NP	29.4	7.2	26.4	6.7	32.7	7.4	29.0	9.6
(max. score, 46)								

classes were formed, using LPAD results as the criterion for regrouping. In reality, this meant that the low functioning groups would be
given the opportunity to aspire to higher academic levels without
being restricted to educational goals determined by their low
manifest performance.

Ten of the students from the 10A group were not included in the
heterogeneous class because of the specific nature of their vocational
program. This provided us with an opportunity to also consider the
differential effects of placement in homogeneous as opposed to
heterogeneous classes. After a year spent in heterogeneous classes,
the students were retested on the same battery of tests. The means
and standard deviations for the four groups are provided in Table 13
and a summary of the significant differences between the regular and
low groups is provided in Table 14. Data comparing the students'
performance before their merging into heterogeneous classes and
after spending a year in such classes are presented in Figure 57.

The picture that emerges is clear. There is an improvement on
all the tests for all the groups after a year's participation in

Table 12.   Hodayot Study: Significant differences between
regular ninth and tenth grade groups (9A, 10A) and low
functioning ninth and tenth grade groups (9B, 10B), based upon
total study population (N = 126)

Instrument	9A vs. 9B	10A vs. 10B
PMA	$p < 0.01$ or better	$p < 0.01$ or better
LPAD Var. II	$p < 0.05$	NS
RSDT	NS	$p < 0.01$ or better
NP	NS	NS

heterogeneous classes. The significant differences that were obtained between the regular and low groups are maintained on the LPAD tests, but on the PMA the difference between the 10A and 10B groups ceases to be significant. The most interesting feature of the results is the comparison between the scores obtained by the 9B group after a year in a heterogeneous class with the scores of the two tenth-grade groups before the combining of the groups occurred. The 9B group surpassed the initial performance level of the 10B group on all the tests except on the LPAD Variations II, where the performance was the same. Even more significant is the comparison between the 9B and the 10A groups. After a year in a heterogeneous class, the 9B group surpassed the initial level of the 10A group on the PMA and reached the same level on the RSDT and Numerical Progressions test. Only on the LPAD Variations II did the 9B group remain below the initial level of the 10A group. In short, combining the groups into heterogeneous classes clearly benefited the initially low functioning B groups.

The question that arises is whether the normal groups, despite their improvement over the course of the year, were not inhibited by the presence of the initially low functioning students in the heterogeneous classes. If the performance of the 10A students who were included in the heterogeneous (H_{et}) classes is compared with that of the 10A students who remained in the homogeneous (H_{om}) class, it is clear from the graphs in Figure 57 that no meaningful differences emerged. In fact, for the PMA, the initial difference between the means of these two groups ($\overline{X}H_{et} = 167.7$; $\overline{X}H_{om} = 174.0$; diff. = 6.3 points), in favor of the homogeneous group, was reduced by nearly 50% ($\overline{X}H_{et} = 186.8$; $\overline{X}H_{om} = 190.2$; diff. = 3.4 points; $p > .05$).

Further confirmation of the positive effects of combining the regular and low groups was derived from a follow-up of the students' performance on tests administered on their induction into the army (see Table 15). The students from the original four groups were compared on the Dapar IQ test, a Hebrew language test, and the KABA (a measure used by the army that represents a combined weighted score of tests of intelligence, language, and educational achievement). Analysis of variance and t values revealed no significant differences between the groups on any of the three measures.

Discussion   Apart from the intrinsic value of the study, it serves to illustrate how the group administration of the LPAD, despite its limitations, may be applied in the solution of pressing educational problems. Even more important, its use provides answers that may not be forthcoming when conventional procedures are

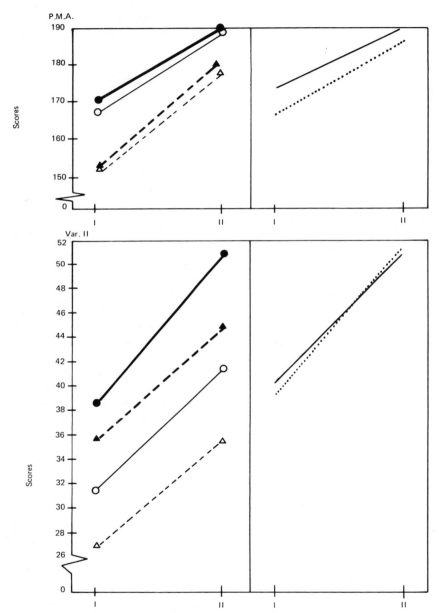

Figure 57. Graphic representation of the performance of the four groups prior to their merging (I) and after 1 year of merging (II), and of homogeneous and heterogeneous groups.

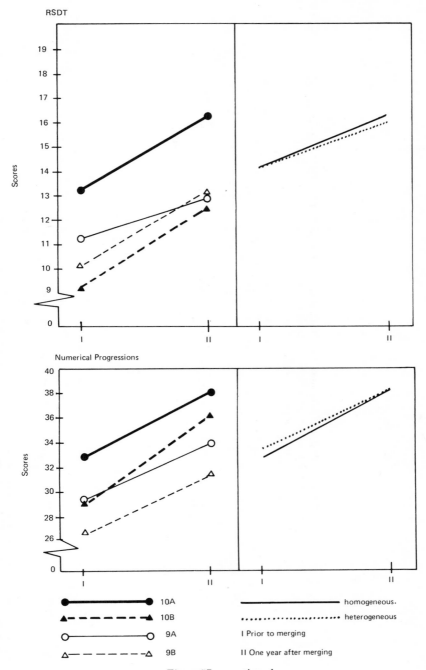

Figure 57 —*continued*

Table 13.   Hodayot Study: Means and standard deviations for the PMA, LPAD Var. II, RSDT, and NP, by classes, 1 year after merging of the regular group (A) with the low functioning group (B), based upon total study population (N = 103)

Instrument	9A (N = 28)		9B (N = 27)		10A (N = 32)		10B (N = 16)	
	$\bar{X}$	SD	$\bar{X}$	SD	$\bar{X}$	SD	$\bar{X}$	SD
PMA (max. score, 220)	189.6	12.7	179.6	13.5	190.5	11.2	183.3	20.3
LPAD Var. II (max. score, 58)	41.6	10.8	35.7	10.8	51.2	9.1	44.8	11.2
RSDT (max. Score, 20)	13.0	4.0	13.3	2.6	16.3	2.8	12.8	4.5
NP (max. score, 46)	34.1	7.8	31.7	7.8	38.3	4.4	36.1	6.2

Table 14. Hodayot Study: Significant differences between
regular ninth and tenth grade groups (9A, 10A) and low
functioning ninth and tenth grade groups (9B, 10B), based upon
total study population (N = 103)

Instrument	9A vs. 9B	10A vs. 10B
PMA	$p < 0.01$ or better	NS
LPAD Var. II	$p < 0.05$	NS
RSDT	NS	$p < 0.05$
NP	NS	NS

used. In the above study, poor students' evaluation by the teachers,
their performance at school, and their IQ scores all served to
mutually reinforce the conclusion that they should be provided with
separate educational programs and goals specially geared to their low
performance level. By introducing the LPAD a new dimension was
added: the emphasis shifted away from the students' current level of
performance as a criterion for educational placement toward an
assessment of their potential to learn and become modified. Although
some differences between the regular and low groups persisted, the
results provided sufficient evidence that the students did not differ
significantly in their ability to learn. Indeed, by the time they
entered army service, the initial differences were completely wiped
out, with all the groups attaining an average level of performance
according to the army standards. It should be recalled that many of
the children in the low performance group were total or functional
illiterates 2 years before their acceptance into the Hodayot school,
their IQs were within the borderline of educable mentally retarded
range, and the original intention was to provide them with a separate
training commensurate with their low performance level.

Georgian and Mountain Children

Background This study was initiated to provide educators
with information regarding the cognitive potential of groups of
adolescents who emigrated to Israel from the mountains of Caucasia
and Georgia in the Soviet Union. To those charged with their education and adaptation they posed a rather severe problem in the areas
of cognitive functioning, behavior, atittudes, and motivation. The
first difficulty, of course, was the language barrier that made these
children inaccessible to meaningful interaction with their teachers.
The adolescents spoke little or no Russian and had a very limited
knowledge of Hebrew. Their academic level was very limited, especially in school skills that required higher levels of functioning. This
resulted in serious doubts on the part of the teachers regarding the

Table 15. Hodayot Study: Scores obtained by population upon induction into the army—means, standard deviations, and t values for army measures DAPAR, KABA, and Hebrew by classes, based upon total study population (N = 97)

Measure	9A (N = 30)		9B (N = 25)		10A (N = 27)		10B (N = 15)		t values*	
	$\bar{X}$	SD	$\bar{X}$	SD	$\bar{X}$	SD	$\bar{X}$	SD	9A vs. 9B	10A vs. 10B
DAPAR	57.28	10.73	52.41	10.26	57.44	13.61	51.27	18.58	1.64	1.12
KABA	46.43	8.19	44.76	8.17	44.15	10.37	40.27	10.48	0.75	1.06
Hebrew	7.76	0.94	7.35	0.98	7.84	1.07	7.60	1.64	1.58	0.50

* None of the t values was significant.

students' capacity to benefit from an academic school program. The teachers questioned the level of ability that seemed to them to be low, and advocated a vocational rather than an academic educational program. This opinion was strengthened by the very low level of cognitive efficiency and motivation for academic achievement displayed by these youngsters. Their school work habits were very poor, and they showed little readiness to attend and persevere in their school work.

To what could the low manifest performance of these children be attributed? This was a crucial question since the answer would be decisive in establishing an educational policy for them. In terms of our theoretical framework, the issue involved distinguishing between whether these children should be regarded as culturally deprived or as culturally different. In both cases, performance levels at school and on conventional tests could be expected to be similar. However, according to our theory the degree of modifiability of culturally different children is considered to be greater than that of culturally deprived children, as cultural deprivation is defined as a state of reduced modifiability. Although the study has not yet been completed, the available data provide an interesting illustration of how the LPAD may be used to resolve issues of this nature in a group situation.

Five groups of Georgian and Mountain children, ranging in age from 12 to 16 years, were tested on the PMA and the LPAD Variations II tests. The children had been placed in several different villages and were in the following classes at school: two groups (1 and 2) were in grade 7, two groups (1 and 2) in grade 8, and one group was in grade 9.

Test Results The results of the five groups on the PMA and the LPAD Variations II are presented in mean scores and percentages of maximum possible score in Table 16. Also included in Table 16 are the results of the two ninth-grade groups, 9A and 9B, previously discussed in the Hodayot study. (It will be recalled that 9A comprised normally functioning and 9B low functioning, culturally deprived children.) From the mean scores on the PMA, three results—all consistent with conventional expectations—emerge. There is a steady increase in the PMA scores with age; the scores obtained by group 9 are the same as those obtained by the culturally deprived Hodayot group, 9B; there is a substantial difference of about 12 points between these two groups (Georgian and Mountain children 9, and 9B Hodayot) and the normal 9A group. These results suggest that the Georgian and Mountain subjects represent a population similar to that of culturally deprived 9B population.

Table 16.   Means scores and percentages of maximum possible scores on the PMA and LPAD Var. II, based upon total study populations (N = 111, Georgian and Mountain; N = 67, Hodayot)

Study population (grade and group)	PMA		LPAD Var. II	
	$\overline{X}$	%	$\overline{X}$	%
Georgian and Mountain				
Grade 7 (1)	125	57	32	55
Grade 7 (2)	126	57	28	48
Grade 8 (1)	142	65	32	55
Grade 8 (2)	145	66	38	65
Grade 9	154	70	36	62
Hodayot				
Grade 9A	166*	75	32*	55
Grade 9B	154	70	27*	47

* Figures rounded off.

If, however, the results obtained on the LPAD Variations II are considered, a different picture emerges, necessitating a different conclusion. In all but one of the five groups of Georgian and Mountain children, the LPAD Variations II score was either greater than or equal to that obtained by the normal 9A group. Without exception, all the Georgian and Mountain groups scored higher than the culturally deprived 9B Hodayot group, despite the differences in age and years of schooling. In effect, what this means, in terms of our approach, is that the Georgian and Mountain children exhibit high levels of modifiability and that their relatively poor PMA performance is not a function of cultural deprivation but rather of cultural difference.

The modifiability of these children is clearly demonstrated if their performance on the LPAD Variations II is compared with that on the standard Raven Matrix items upon which the Variations are based. The data in Table 17 provide a breakdown of the performance of the Georgian and Mountain children in all five merged classes in terms of the following criteria: the number of children who obtained either 0, 1 (20%), 2 (40%), 3 (60%), or 4 (80%) correct answers on the Raven Matrices; the mean score on the LPAD Variations II for the children receiving either 0, 1, 2, 3, or 4 out of five correct answers; and the mean scores expressed as a percentage of the total possible score of the LPAD Variations II. From this table, it is possible to assess the extent of modifiability of the children.

What emerges from Table 17 is that there is a very limited relationship ($r = .19$) between the children's initial performance and the LPAD Variations II of these same items. In other words, even the limited training involved in the group administration of the LPAD is sufficient to produce substantial improvement in performance. Perhaps this is borne out most strikingly by the fact that of the 111 children, 100 initially obtained scores between 0 and 2 with a mean score of 1.36 (27%) on the five standard Raven Matrix tasks. However, on LPAD Variations II, they were able, on the average, to complete 52% of the tasks. Even the 14 children who obtained scores of zero on the Raven items were able to correctly solve 43% of the LPAD Variations II.

Discussion   In short, by means of the LPAD, dimensions of ability were revealed in these children that were not reflected either in their poor school performance or their conventional psychometric scores. Indeed, the results on the PMA only served to confirm their low manifest level of performance. The implications of our findings with these particular children have had far-reaching consequences. Instead of being erroneously considered "backward" and assigned to a special training program, these children may be regarded as perfectly accessible to a normal academic curriculum on the basis of the results they obtained on the LPAD. It is, of course, necessary to ensure that appropriate steps will be taken to remove any obstacles to learning produced by cultural differences, such as the use of inadequate language for instruction.

Culturally Disadvantaged Children

Background   The subjects of this study were 34 eighth-grade boys and girls, ages 13 and 14, from a rural school, and defined by the Israeli Ministry of Education as "culturally deprived." The pur-

Table 17.   Georgian and Mountain Children Study: Comparison of scores obtained on Raven items with scores obtained on LPAD Var. II—frequencies and percentage of maximum possible scores, based upon total study population (N = 111)

Number of subjects	Raven items correct		LPAD Var. II correct	
	N	%	$\overline{X}$	%
14	0	0	25	43
36	1	20	29	49
50	2	40	33	57
100	0 + 1 + 2	27	30	52
8	3	60	30	52
3	4	80	30	52

pose of the study was to ascertain if the conventional tests given students at the end of their elementary school education, and on the basis of which they were assigned to either academic or vocational high schools, did indeed reflect the students' capacities.

The students were examined on the Adult Series of the Raven's Matrices (A–E) in a standard group test done by the school psychologist, and on the LPAD Variations I and II. The testing on the LPAD Variations was preceded by training on Raven's items B_8–B_{12}, in which the principles of the tasks were taught.

Data on the Raven's Matrices were analyzed on the total score and on the following specific tasks that ascend in their level of difficulty: Series B, 8–12; Series C, 7, 8, and 12; Series D, task 12; and Series E, task 12. It will be recalled that these items are the bases for the LPAD Variations I and II.

Test Results   Table 18 presents means and standard deviations for the total Matrix score, for items B_8–B_{12}, and for the LPAD Variations I and II. Table 19 presents an analysis of the tasks in Raven's Matrix series, which serve to establish a baseline. The data in Table 19 are presented in terms of the number correct and percentages in each category.

In discussing the results, one must consider the composition of the mean score of 29.5 out of the total score of 60, inasmuch as it is mainly formed by the results obtained on the easy tasks of A, Ab, and a very limited input from the more difficult tasks. The mean of 29.5 places the population in the category of below average and therefore not eligible for attending an academically oriented secondary school.

The mean score on the total Raven Matrices (A–E), expressed in percentages, should be compared with the mean scores expressed in

Table 18.   Disadvantaged Children Study: Means, standard deviations, and percentages correct on Raven Matrices A–E and items B_8–B_{12} and LPAD Var. I and II, based upon total study population (N = 34)

	Items correct		
Instrument	$\overline{X}$	SD	%
Raven			
B_8–B_{12} (max. score, 5)	1.09	1.50	22
A–E (max. score, 60)	29.50	8.82	49
LPAD			
Var. I (max. score, 30)	28.47	7.69	95
Var. II (max. score, 58)	41.53	8.37	72

Table 19.   Disadvantaged Children Study: Distribution of scores by frequencies and percentages for Raven's Matrices (B_8–B_{12}; C_7, C_8, C_{12}, D_{12}, and E_{12}), based upon total study population (N = 34)

Number correct	B_8–B_{12}		C_7		C_8		C_{12}		D_{12}		E_{12}	
	N	%	N	%	N	%	N	%	N	%	N	%
0	18	53	13	38	20	59	33	97	32	94	33	97
1	8	23	21	62	14	41	1	3	2	6	1	3
2	0	0										
3	3	9										
4	5	15										
5	0	0										

percentages obtained on the LPAD Variations I and II. Whereas the mean of 29.5 represents 49% of the total Raven score, the mean expressed in percentages is 95% on the Variations I and 72% on the Variations II. More important, the mean obtained on Raven's B_8–B_{12}, which is the basis for the LPAD Variations I, is only 22% whereas that on the Variations I itself is 95%.

It should also be mentioned that according to Silberzweig's data (1975) only 50% of the population answered more than 50% of the items on the total Raven Matrix items correctly. However, on both the LPAD Variations I and II, 88% of the children answered more than 50% of the items correctly, and on the LPAD Variations II, 15% of the children answered from 50% to 60% correctly.

Discussion   The results obtained in this study indicate that the capacity of these culturally disadvantaged children was far higher than that demonstrated by the standard administration of the Raven's Adult Matrices. This provides little comfort to those students who were denied admission to academic high schools on the basis of their scores on the standard Raven's Matrix test, which was successfully challenged by the LPAD.

Bedouin

Studies on Bedouin children have constantly pointed to difficulties in problem-solving behavior whenever the tasks required abstract, conceptualized, internalized mental processes. The reason for this has not yet been successfully clarified (Kugelmas and Lieblich, 1968; Wagner, 1977). The hypothesis that response style is strongly affected by cultural differences seems to be the most plausible explanation. Bedouins have shown great adaptability when confronted with modern technology such as cars, tractors, and tools. The fact that Bedouin scores on Raven's Matrices (mean = 19.2) placed them in the range of "mental defectives," despite their being scholastically capable, is tentatively explained by Shapiro et al. (1976) by their tendency to use an extreme response style, that is, to choose from a horizontally ordered set of alternative responses those that are located in the left or right extremes. However, such a style-determined choice can be partially explanatory only if the degree of cognitive oriented search is considerably lower than the style-determined orientation of the individual. Whatever the reasons for the observed deficient functions, the more essential question is to what extent does this observed phenomenon of the low level of functioning of the Bedouin children reflect immutable and stable characteristics or to what extent is their difficulty accessible to meaningful change.

Background   In a recent study of 113 Bedouin children from the sixth (N = 30), seventh (N = 28), eighth (N = 25), and ninth (N = 30) grades, we administered the following tests: LPAD Variations I, LPAD Variations II, and the Representational Stencil Design test. In the pretest phase, the tests were preceded by training on principles and basic prerequisites for their application. As usual, training for the LPAD Variations I was based on Raven's items B–8 to B–12, while Raven's five tasks—C_7, C_8, C_{12}, D_{12}, and E_{12}—were the training items for the LPAD Variations II. Training for the RSDT followed the regular administration procedure. For the posttest, the same instruments were presented again after 2 months, this time without any training. The goal of the retest was similar to that of the clinical battery: to study the long-term effects of the training, the amount of retention, and finally, the divergent effect of the training process that would be reflected in an increment in the obtained results despite the lack of immediate training and the elapsed time since the first presentation.

The expectation that such an increment would be observed is based upon the following hypothesis: That whenever investment emphasizes the acquisition of principles and strategies (Ginsburg, 1977), thereby changing cognitive behavior in a more structured way, and is not limited to sheer task-bound training, the capacity of the assessed individual to cope with new situations will increase with the amount of time that has elapsed since his exposure to the intervention (Feuerstein, 1978b).

Test Results   Table 20 presents the results obtained by the four groups on the different tests. The results presented in Table 20

Table 20. Bedouin study: Means, standard deviations, percentages correct, and t values for LPAD Var. I and II and RSDT, by classes, based upon total study population (N = 90)

Grade	Instrument	Test			Retest			t values	Significance
		$\overline{X}$	SD	%	$\overline{X}$	SD	%		
6	LPAD Var. I	15.37	8.81	44	21.07	6.99	60	4.05	0.001
(N = 21)	LPAD Var. II	18.95	6.23	33	29.95	6.64	52	8.10	0.001
	RSDT	3.77	2.28	19	5.73	2.33	29	4.10	0.001
7	LPAD Var. I	19.92	8.08	57	21.39	8.92	61	1.40	NS
(N = 22)	LPAD Var. II	18.77	10.77	32	30.69	10.60	53	5.76	0.001
	RSDT	4.96	3.04	25	6.34	3.78	32	2.94	0.01
8	LPAD Var. I	23.60	7.58	67	29.04	0.98	83	3.46	0.01
(N = 17)	LPAD Var. II	21.56	8.57	37	33.22	7.39	57	12.20	0.001
	RSDT	4.61	2.58	23	6.57	3.40	33	3.24	0.01
9	LPAD Var. I	22.18	9.05	63	20.23	9.45	58	−1.11	NS
(N = 30)	LPAD Var. II	27.90	13.76	48	41.33	11.21	71	7.06	0.001
	RSDT	4.76	2.33	24	7.82	5.19	39	2.79	0.01

* Maximum scores: LPAD Var. I, 35; LPAD Var. II, 58; and RSDT, 20.

show that all the groups show a significant increment from test to retest. Out of 12 t values only two (LPAD Variations I, seventh and ninth grades) were not statistically significant. The capacity of the population to learn and then to implement hierarchically higher mental processes is reflected in the results obtained on the various measures, especially on the LPAD Variations I at the retest stage in which scores range from 58% to 83% of the maximum possible. The results obtained on the LPAD Variations II were considerably lower, ranging from 52% to 71%, but this should not engender any surprise, considering the high level of complexity and difficulty of the items on this particular test. The greatest difficulty was experienced by the entire population on the Representational Stencil Design Test. This reflects the limited familiarity of the population not only with the content of the test but also with the modality of operating with representational material.

The results obtained by the Bedouin children, especially considering their age, were comparable to those obtained by culturally disadvantaged children (see Table 11) and by culturally different children (see Table 16) on a group test. For instance, the Bedouin eighth and ninth graders compared favorably on the retest of the LPAD Variations II with the results obtained by the tenth graders in the Hodayot study. However, in view of the limited famil-iarity of the population with the tests, it was of even greater interest to see the long-term effects of the initial training and the effects of the repeated exposure to the instruments. Unfortunately, it is not possible to attribute the observed results solely in favor of the concept of divergent effects because of the interference of the factor of familiari-zation known by itself to produce an increment in the results.

Discussion   These results, which are only part of a larger body of data gathered on the Bedouin,* point to the utility of using a dynamic assessment in cross-cultural studies. The ease with which the level of functioning of these children, considered low on the basis of other studies, was modified, points to the high modifiability of the group once they are presented with appropriate training and with tasks organized in a way that permits them to apply newly acquired principles to new situations.

SUMMARY

The group administration of the LPAD in many of the studies has proved to be of considerable value not only as a research tool but also

---

* This research is currently being prepared by R. Tahia under the author's super-vision.

as a means for solving pressing and urgent educational problems. On the basis of information yielded by the LPAD group test, decisions that would exercise a profound influence on the future lives of children could be made in the light of their potential for cognitive modifiability rather than their manifest level of performance at a given point in their development.

CHAPTER 6 Case Studies

The case studies presented in this chapter are an illustration of the meaning of the Learning Potential Assessment Device in changing the course of life of many of those referred to us for assessment. We have chosen these case studies in order to point out various conditions of retarded performance assessed by the LPAD, as well as the different etiological determinants of these conditions.

The cases, drawn from our clinical work, were referred by parents, social workers, clinics, schools, and mental hospitals. For the majority of them, we have a wealth of catamnestic data that are only partially reported here. We do not attempt to elaborate on the use of the LPAD in the specific case, nor do we try to interpret precisely and in depth the results obtained by the examinee, since this is done in the manuals (in preparation) accompanying the test material.

For some of the children described, the sole act of unraveling a hidden capacity played a decisive role in determining an improvement of their condition. This was reflected in a renewed attempt on their part to master cognitive processes, once a belief that their efforts would be rewarding was implanted. Many parents regarded the changes that occurred in their children's motivation and level of functioning as miraculous, especially since such changes appeared after only a few meetings for assessment. Some less sophisticated parents even suggested that we had treated their children with an unknown drug. We had difficulty making them understand that the very fact that the child was confronted with success and that the success and its meaning were interpreted to him were in themselves the most powerful "drug" for enhancing the child's functioning and changing his approach to himself.

Presenting parents and teachers with the results obtained by the child, and a detailed description and interpretation of the observed interactions and changes that had occurred in his level of functioning in the course of assessment, became a potent factor in changing the attitudes of these parents and teachers. In many cases, this, together with some light intervention, was sufficient to help the child integrate into a new and more challenging educational environment.

CATEGORIES OF INDIVIDUALS
FOR WHOM THE LPAD HAS AND
HAS NOT BEEN HELPFUL IN ASSESSMENT

One category of cases among those referred to us were children who did not really need a Learning Potential Assessment Device to discover the high level of their functioning. These were children who did not function appropriately for reasons totally independent of their cognitive structure. After a brief examination, we could establish that what was considered by the teacher as a lack of basic school skills and a generalized low level of functioning was not confirmed by our assessment. The conditions of a LPAD assessment made the child function in a way that was different than he did in school.

The Learning Potential Assessment Device has also proved helpful in cases in which the manifest level of functioning of the children was inadequate because of a very specific and circumscribed deficiency in one or another parameter of the cognitive process. Such difficulties were often manifested in input and/or output phases, with very limited, if any, impairment in the elaborational phase. Results obtained with such children were interpreted to the teachers and became the basis for a focused intervention in the area discovered to be the source of difficulties.

A large number of those referred to us for assessment, however, belonged to a category of children, adolescents, and young adults who demonstrated a pervasive low manifest level of functioning evidenced by their psychometric measures, by school achievement, and by their general adaptability to life situations. It is in these cases that the Learning Potential Assessment Device has been called upon to play a major role. Here the concept of modifiability transcended the limited criteria of school performance and was related to behaviors determined by cognitive functions vital to the adaptation of the individual to the requirements of the school environment and to life in general. The criteria of modifiability derived from the LPAD were not only related to the broad aspects of cognitive functioning but to changes in more elementary components of adaptive behavior.

Hundreds of cases have accumulated in our files in which the clinical individual LPAD was decisive in restreaming the child from either special schools or special classes for the educable mentally retarded, the slow learner, or the organically impaired child into the regular educational framework. Such mainstreaming has always been accompanied by preparing the child, his teachers, and his parents and by establishing a supportive system to help the child during the first period of his placement in the new academic environment. In other cases, light intervention was not sufficient to enable the child to meet the requirements of his new environment, and it was necessary to offer focused and intensive help one or two days a week for a more or less extended period of time, within the framework of our institute. For some of the children, restreaming had to be preceded by a whole year of intensive training and redevelopment with help of Instrumental Enrichment (see Feuerstein, in press) and a curriculum-oriented program.

In all of our decisions, we were guided by insights derived from the LPAD about the nature of the cognitive deficiencies responsible for the low level of functioning manifested by the child and the amount of investment necessary in order to modify him in a way meaningful for his adaptation to school. In many cases, the LPAD had to be paralleled by an assessment of the emotional structure of the child and its possible implications for the attempts to redevelop his functioning. Recommendations for therapeutic interventions were issued and implemented for the benefit of these children.

We have often been asked about the rate of failure incurred in our work. We certainly have experienced situations in which we were not able to offer help to certain children. Multihandicapped adolescents and young adults, especially those with little or no communication because of emotional disturbance, proved to be a rather difficult target for our assessment model, instruments, and technique. In certain cases, however, younger children suffering from the same conditions were more accessible to dynamic assessment although, admittedly, establishing the minimal contact necessary to affect the level of functioning in these children required a considerable amount of investment.

It has not always been possible to provide intervention for those children for whom we have been able to establish the presence of a level of modifiability that would make intervention worthwhile because of resistance from the child and/or his environment. The latter is probably responsible for the greater part of this failure. There are parents whose belief that their child is a true retardate, and whom they have treated as such, has formed the basis for the status quo and an equilibrium in the family constellation that cannot easily be renounced. In such cases, we have had to work very hard both with the parents and with the child to overcome resistance. We have not always been able to invest the amount of work required to change these deep-rooted beliefs, however; nor have we always been successful even after making the investment.

Such was the case of one our most successfully assessed children, a boy who suffered from encephalitis at the age of 6 months and who proved to be highly modifiable under specific conditions of intervention. Indeed, he succeeded in finishing the 11th grade, where he proved to excel in science and math despite his speech handicap. From the start, the parents had opposed the boy's integration into a regular school, and they finally succeeded in placing him in a sheltered workshop. The failure here was not determined by the incapacity of the boy to function, but rather by his parents' lack of readiness to accept his capacity for modifiability in spite of some limitations that were irrelevant to his adaptation.

In the majority of cases, however, after having assessed the modifiability of the area of deficiency, where we were able to invest continually in these children we have seen changes in the desired direction.

CASES REPRESENTATIVE OF THE NONORGANICALLY IMPAIRED RETARDED PERFORMER

Case 1: Abraham

The case of Abraham is presented as an illustration of the fallacious conclusions that may be reached by using conventional psychometric methods in testing culturally deprived adolescents.

Abraham was referred to our clinic when he was 13½ years old. In the records of previous testing that accompanied his referral, he was described as being able to follow instructions, although generally lacking in alertness. His attention span was noted to be limited, and he showed deficient functioning in all of the spheres of intelligence tapped by the Stanford-Binet. It was further claimed that he had no capacity for abstraction or generalization. His practical understanding, however, appeared to be somewhat more developed than his general intellectual level might have indicated.

His emotional development, the report stated, was marked by immaturity and a lack of self-criticism. The psychologists' conclusion had been that, since Abraham's IQ on the Stanford-Binet was 56, he should be removed from a normal school environment and placed in a framework with adolescents of his level where he might be trained for work requiring only a low level of intellectual functioning and no academic achievement.

It is interesting to note that even Abraham's teachers did not accept the severity of this diagnosis. In light of Abraham's emotional and behavioral difficulties, however, they tended to agree with the recommendation of placement outside of a regular educational framework.

Assessment with the LPAD revealed evidence of the syndrome of cultural deprivation. Abraham manifested, for example, a lack of spontaneous comparative behavior as indicated by his inability to formulate and express the similarities and differences between two geometric figures. He also showed marked impairment of cognitive functioning on the input level. His inaccurate visual perception was reflected in his incapacity to complete Bender-Gestalt figures and in his impaired spatial orientation.

Abraham showed a high capacity for modification after we had strengthened his input level through our strategies in the LPAD. He was able to make proper use of the concepts he acquired after only a relatively limited teaching investment by the examiner. In fact, in Raven's Progressive Matrices, Abraham went on to solve even the items of the more complex series. In the LPAD Variations I he successfully solved 25 of the 27 items he attempted. In his approach to the solution of problems, Abraham shifted from trial-and-error behavior to an internalized mode of thinking. This was especially manifest in the Raven Matrices, when he ceased to rely solely on the proposed choices but formulated the responses internally; only then did he choose the most suitable from the offered alternatives.

From our point of view, the initial diagnostic evaluation and its implied prognosis did not do justice to Abraham's actual intellectual potential. Even if we were to agree that his manifest level of functioning reflected the typical deprivational syndrome, the ease with which the effect of the impaired functions was overcome definitely indicated both a high degree of modifiability and the capacity for integration and application of new knowledge and experience for the purpose of functioning at hierarchically higher cognitive levels.

We shall not enter into an analysis of the factors responsible for Abraham's failure at school and for his being perceived as retarded. It is, nonetheless, probable that had psychological examinations revealed the existence of such potential for learning at an earlier date, the cumulative gap in Abraham's academic attainments could have been avoided, and he might have been able to become integrated into the regular school situation.

As a result of our examination, he was placed in a youth village composed of children and adolescents of normal intellectual functioning. A remedial teaching program was instituted. In a follow-up 2 years after his placement, Abraham demonstrated positive development in both social and academic activities. This development continued and resulted in Abraham's graduation from a high school in his own community, which was willing to accept him after his successful adaptation in the youth village. Abraham completed his army service and is currently a successful manager of a large business.

Case 2: Yehuda

Yehuda was referred to our psychological services at the age of 11½ by his teachers. He was an immigrant from an oriental country, and at the time of his referral he was living in a residential setting among normal youngsters.

Yehuda was considered retarded and demonstrated impaired functioning in many areas. He was apathetic, and the caregiving adults, teachers, and youth leaders in the residential setting found him largely unreachable. His sparse and impoverished verbalization made communication difficult, even with his peers in his mother tongue. He was enuretic and occasionally would lose bowel control during the day.

In our own psychological examinations, we saw many signs that explained why people referred to him as mentally retarded. His figure drawings and reproductions of Bender-Gestalt designs were typical of a child of 4 or 5. During the assessment with LPAD Variations, Organization of Dots, and other tests, he showed only limited modifiability via training. The global picture, in short, reinforced previous suspicions of true "retardation," even if the complicating effects of emotional disturbance were ignored.

The profile he presented would have led to his being perceived as functioning on the level of the severely retarded had it not been for his responses on the Plateaux Test. To our surprise, Yehuda displayed a systematic approach in his initial explorations of this material, and he reached the criterion of three errorless trials after a relatively limited number of repetitions. Moreover, during the rotation phase, he attained the maximum possible score, indicating a rather unusual capacity for internally representing the outcome of a transformation produced by a movement imposed on the Plateaux boards.

On the basis of this isolated, successful response in the context of almost complete failure on all other items, we undertook a deeper examination of this youngster. Our further evaluation disclosed a significantly higher potential for modifiability than was demonstrated in our initial sessions. However, the investment necessary in order to produce this modifiability was deemed to be considerable. Problems in the area of comprehension of instructions, on one hand, and deficiencies on the level of input, on the other, completely masked elaborational capacities that proved to be remarkable, considering Yehuda's extremely low manifest level of functioning. The area in which his capacity first manifested itself was in the Plateaux, especially when confronted with the task of operating on his internal perception of a transformation.

Yehuda was placed in one of our treatment groups, and after a short period signs of progress were discernible. Two years after his placement in the treatment group, his development was sufficient to enable placement in a regular school system at the seventh grade level, only one year behind the grade indicated by his chronological age. His strongest skills at that point were in the areas of language, including reading and writing, and in arithmetic—those areas in which he had originally shown marked impairment.

His conquest of reading provided him with such excitement that he continued to read anything he found, and for hours on end. He is fondly recalled as the "Walking Reader" by many of those who lived in the agricultural settlement where he resided with his treatment group, because he would read as he walked along the road.

Yehuda completed primary school and continued his studies in a secondary school where he specialized in horticulture. He did have difficulty in adapting to the regular school system, but this was not because of his cognitive deficiencies, which were largely overcome, but because of his emotional and behavioral problems. A particularly stubborn condition of bedwetting resisted treatment and lasted until Yehuda was 18. A considerable investment was required to make both Yehuda and his educators ready to continue his education. He completed the 11th grade and then joined a rather sophisticated pioneer group that was involved in the establishment of a new cooperative village. Given his background and his emotional condition, it was more than surprising that he became a leader in this group. He later joined the army, and because of his excellent social and intellectual adaptation, became an assistant chaplain, a position he has held for the last 6 years. Yehuda is now married and plans to continue his academic studies.

Yehuda's development was not without considerable tensions and emotional upsets. To a large extent, these tensions were related to his previous experiences and to his feelings of inadequacy during the period of his retarded functioning. Such emotional upset is often observed when a restructuring of the personality is produced through significant changes in the cognitive functioning of the individual.

The case of Yehuda illustrates how valuable a single successful response, a peak in the individual's functioning, can be for correctly indicating a potential for modifiability, thereby encouraging the examiner to probe more deeply and attempt to successfully modify the child. Yehuda himself admitted that his success, of which he became aware through the interpretation of the examiner, provided him with the positive feeling necessary to give him the desire and readiness to cooperate in the assessment. Thus, the peak of Yehuda's functioning, rather than the modal low level of his manifest behavior, was used as an indication of his potential to become modified; it oriented the search and enabled the discovery of areas of unexpected strengths.

Case 3: Eli

Eli was referred to our testing service at the age of 13½, 1½ years after his immigration to Israel. He had been examined a few months prior to our evaluation and had been diagnosed as borderline mentally retarded. The results of this examination noted "primitive and infantile functioning" as assessed on the Human Figure Drawing and Koh's Block tests. It had been noted that he was unable to follow instruction properly, could not identify colors, and lacked motor coordination. Positive signs were scarce. He could count forwards and backwards from 1 to 20 and 20 to 1, and he appeared to have made adequate contact with the previous examiner.

The examiner had concluded that it was difficult to make a differential diagnosis because of Eli's "primitive" background and "neglected" education, to which many of his cognitive deficiencies could be attributed. The suggestion for placement in a school for the retarded was made on the basis of Eli's manifest functioning and totally disregarded the highly justified reservations the examiner himself had about the ability to make a reliable diagnosis. Fortunately, Eli resisted placement in a specialized setting for the retarded. He became stubborn, acting out, and it is his aggressiveness, among other factors, that finally led to his referral to our clinic. On his own initiative, Eli had attempted to gain acceptance at a normal residential setting, one in which his younger brother was living. The director of this institution was willing to accept him but first requested a re-evaluation in the hope that Eli would demonstrate a higher IQ than that ascribed to him after his first examination.

In our assessment, we found Eli's intellectual abilities to be much above average. The investment required to demonstrate these results was minimal and almost exclusively in the induction of comparative behavior, systematic exploration, inhibition of trial-and-error behavior, and the production of a need for precision and accuracy. Eli acquired these skills with great ease and then applied them, on his own, to a variety of tasks that grew increasingly more complex in terms both of content and of the operations required to perform them.

Eli's examinations took place in three sessions. A growing security, an increased capacity, and a wider experience of success were evident from session to session. It became clear rather quickly that Eli should start his elementary education in a normal setting, despite his relatively advanced age, illiteracy, and "primitiveness."

Eli was placed in the sixth grade and successfully completed primary school. He continued his schooling in a vocational secondary school. Because he was considerably older than his classmates, he felt somewhat out of place at school. He requested an apprenticeship with a printer and proceeded to learn the trade while continuing his studies. Eli is now a skilled printer and holds a position that requires a high degree of competence in all aspects of language.

Case 4: Roger

The case of Roger illustrates cultural deprivation in an adolescent from a middle-class background. We have noted that when this phenomenon occurs in middle- and upper-class examinees, it is usually accompanied by symptoms of psychopathology. On first impression, these symptoms serve to mask the deprivational aspects. Such was the case with Roger. Ultimately, however, even in the face of his florid psychopathology, the impact of cultural deprivation on his cognitive functioning was revealed through proper assessment.

Roger was referred at age 13½ to the author by his school psychologist. It was felt that he should be withdrawn from school in order to attend a special class for the retarded. Despite his adequate command of the language and some reading skills, he showed an absolute incapacity to grasp even the most elementary concepts. In previous psychotechnical tests he had attained an IQ of 54 on a full scale WISC. On the basis of his results on the tests, it had been suggested that he be placed in some kind of menial, routine job. Furthermore, it had been recommended that he be taken out of his home environment, where he had become a severe behavioral problem to his parents. His acting out, abusive, and aggressive behavior were coupled with a variety of signs of deep emotional disturbance, with certain signs that pointed to a borderline psychotic condition. The author was asked to confirm the initial assessment of the school psychologist and to help convince the parents of the need for special placement.

On the basis of the boy's family background, and on the information that both of his parents were academically trained, the author assumed that conventional psychometric tests would be appropriate for evaluating Roger's intellectual capabilities. It was reasoned that since Roger had lived in an environment that nearly maximized his capacities, the standardized approach would serve to measure his actual abilities.

The results of the first testing session demonstrated an extremely low level of functioning on Raven's Matrices and on a variety of other tests. Roger was indeed unable to grasp even the simplest relationship and the tests had to be discontinued. His estimated level of functioning was at an IQ of approximately 45 or 50. Moreover, Roger had expressed compensatory paranoid ideas of grandiosity, infantile emotionality, incapacity for delaying gratification, a low self-esteem, and confusion in sexual identity. On the basis of the results it was assumed that Roger was a true retardate, and further, that much of the behavioral disturbance was an outcome of undue parental pressures for achievement on a boy who was incapable of meeting these pressures.

At this point, the author had not yet considered the possibility that impairments typical of the culturally disadvantaged might also characterize children from more privileged socioeconomic conditions. For advantaged youngsters, it is all too natural to dismiss a hypothesis of cultural deprivation in favor of one stressing an endogenous basis, such as mental disorder, retardation, or organicity. Therefore, the major task seemed to be to help Roger's parents to understand and accept his limitations and to decide upon the educational goals most appropriate for his condition. In other words, the most realistic solution seemed to be to induce a passive-acceptant attitude in the parents rather than press for the active-modificational approach the parents had been using. The author recalls that, following his assessment of Roger, he thought to comfort the parents by announcing to them that their son was only suffering from mental retardation and not a psychotic condition as previously thought.

Roger's behavioral difficulties at home led us to consider that placement with a foster family might be a good temporary solution and arrangements were made. While living with the foster family, Roger began job training. However, this plan soon became unworkable. He continued his acting out, aggressive behavior and resisted attending his job training or continuing school. Seven months later, he was referred again to our services.

At this time, we re-evaluated Roger's level of functioning by means of the LPAD. By inducing specified work strategies and habits, and correcting impairments at the input, elaborational, and output phases, we had some surprising results. Whereas in the first testing session Roger's responses gave evidence of a total incapacity to grasp any type of relationship or to compare data spontaneously, in the second session, after inducing modification in deficient functions, a complete about-face occurred. In the first session we were forced to discontinue the testing with Raven's Matrices after the first two series, A and Ab, where only 12 of the easier of the 24 items were completed correctly. Results of Raven's Matrices in the second session showed 10 out of 12 correct in Series A; Series Ab, 9 of 12 correct; Series B, 11 of 12 correct; Series C, 11 of 12 correct; Series D, 10 of 11 correct; and Series E, 6 of 6 correct.

After eliminating trial-and-error responses and being required to use logical explanations in response to probing with inferential questions, Roger spontaneously began to use an anticipatory approach in his problem-solving behavior. He was even able to verbalize logical relationships. Roger demonstrated improved abilities on a variety of other tests as well. In the first testing with the Porteus Maze he had reached the 6-year level; after training in appropriate exploratory techniques and strengthening input skills, he reached the maximal level of 18 years on the same test.

Roger's favorable response to the LPAD techniques gave ample evidence of a pre-existing deprivational syndrome, with all of its attendant impairments in even the most elementary levels of cognitive functioning. Another interview with the parents was scheduled to determine the extent to which this hypothesis of cultural deprivation could be substantiated by further information about the interactional process within the family. It would take us somewhat far afield to discuss the peculiar and unique facts that came to light in this interview. A special set of circumstances and a condition unique to this family had obstructed the communication patterns within the family. Communication with the children was limited to the necessary minimum, thereby circumscribing the transactional universe to the immediate here and now. Roger was highly resistant to his parents' attempts to mediate their world to him; and by association, he rejected anything concerning learning, which he perceived as pertaining to their sphere of interest. What we had originally thought to be a case of moderate mental retardation, thus, was really one of cultural deprivation. The lack of mediated learning experience was initially the result of the disruption of communicational patterns in the family and ended ultimately in Roger's unwillingness to accept the mediation offered to him.

In accordance with this new interpretation of Roger's symptoms, a combined program of intensive psychotherapy and enrichment training with a private tutor was instituted to resolve emotional conflicts and to reverse the deprivational syndrome. Within a relatively short time, much improvement was observed in Roger's cognitive functioning, although his behavioral disturbances persisted for some time. After proper preparation in a foster family, Roger was accepted at a boarding school where he began to function far above expected. He became literate in two new languages and acquired the academic skills of a 10th grader.

One of Roger's major characteristics was his anti-intellectualism, which he demonstrated ostentatiously whenever he was required to use sound cognitive, logical modalities of interaction. He would either bring inane, irrelevant support for his statements or use emotional reasons such as his likes and dislikes when more objective evidence was required. What was even more striking was his rejection of any attempt at formal teaching or training. Roger literally closed his ears at any attempt to convey information to him verbally and shut his eyes whenever something was pointed out to him. He never spontaneously asked for information, except for occasional answers to specific, immediate needs. When an attempt was made to transcend the immediate need by some additional information, he rejected it with hostility. This anti-intellectualism precluded his school activity for a long time, and even therapy and the enrichment program could not change his approach in a basic way. This is the reason that Roger only finished 10th grade.

Because Roger was older than his classmates, he was able to leave school to join the army. It was during the period of his army service that a real change occurred in his motivation. He obtained a secondary school diploma by correspondence courses and performed his army duties satisfactorily.

The true essence of Roger's modifiability is not only reflected by his capacity to learn and to become modified by life experiences, formal and informal, but even more by the considerable interest he developed for studies. In lieu of his constant argument and objection to study, Roger entered a Jewish Studies Center when he completed his army service. There he studied just for the love of study for 3 years, despite his precarious financial state. His thirst for knowledge and intellectual self-realization continued and led him to an advanced academic university degree and occupation. Fourteen years of follow-up has shown the persistence of the changes that occurred in Roger. The course of his life changed, and today he has a highly demanding managerial career.

In reviewing the results of the first testing session, it has become clear that the retardation hypothesis admitted by us was the result of a misguided use of the conventional, standard, static testing approach with this middle-class youngster. The case of Roger, and subsequently of others from similar circumstances, have led us to extend the concept of cultural deprivation to adolescents of the middle and upper classes. Their milieu is not affected by the deprivation commonly associated with the lower class but by the interactional pattern existing within a family, in which there is an obstruction of the ongoing mediational process necessary to make learning meaningful for the growing child. Roger's case, in particular, underscores the dynamics of cultural deprivation, that is, the process whereby environmentally determined interactions affect an individual's capacity to become modified by direct exposure to stimuli and life experience.

ORGANICALLY DIAGNOSED CASES

The next group of cases is of special interest since it involves diagnosed organic disorders, which are considered to affect the child's level of functioning in a variety of ways. The organicity itself can be held to directly determine the deficient functioning. One must question, however, the specific weight of this factor. It may be argued instead that organicity determines the specific deficient outcome in a more *indirect* way. For example, the mother-child relationship will be affected both quantitatively and qualitatively by the mother's belief that her organic child is inaccessible to certain types of mediated learning experiences. The parents' assumption that organicity limits the capacity of the child to properly use experiences, and their resulting low level of expectations, bring about a varied amount of cultural deprivation by placing limitations on the experiential background provided. In other cases, the organicity itself may produce limitations on the experiential background by affecting the input channels of the child. Inattentiveness produced by hyperkinesia, or by the high threshold of arousal and orienting reflexes created by a certain state of hypoactivity attributable to the organic condition, may result in reduced exposure to environmental mediation of stimuli.

It is important to distinguish in each particular case the direct *proximal* determinants of deficient cognitive behavior as contrasted with the more indirect distal determinant, the organicity. This distinction cannot be made easily in conventional testing where only a static inventory of existing functions is established. A process-oriented evaluation and measurement of modifiability are no less indicated and valuable than in the case of the culturally deprived child.

Even though the organically impaired child may originate from a culturally stimulating environment, he will still display the syndrome of cultural deprivation. Many of his deficiencies can be explained by reduced and limited mediated learning experience, either because of the lack of penetrability of the child himself, and/ or because of limited amount of mediation on the part of the parents resulting from their basic assumption of the child's incapacity, and, finally, because of the influence of a variety of emotional factors impairing the parent-child relationship. In the following, we present a few cases to illustrate this basic contention.

Case 5: Baruch

Baruch was referred to us at the age of 15. The reason for referral was an attempt to change the counseling psychologist's recommendation to place Baruch in a sheltered workshop for the trainable mental retardate.

Previous examinations by neurologists and psychiatrists indicated central nervous system determined cognitive dysfunction. One EEG-based diagnosis suggested porencephaly. This diagnosis was not accepted by another pediatric neurologist, who found no clinical signs of porencephaly but did consider Baruch to be severely retarded. The difficulties in Baruch's coordination, eye-hand and fine movements, and his impaired visual perception were coupled with states of inattentiveness, impulsivity, very poor language, and difficulties in articulation. He manifested other bizarre behaviors such as unmotivated laughter and tics.

When Baruch was first brought to our attention at the age of 12, we had recommended that the first LPAD assessment be followed by an intensive investment in reading skills and motor behavior. We considered the boy modifiable, and this investment had produced a significant change in his reading level and his writing. What surprised us even more at the time was his real propensity and need to express himself graphically. Compared to his initial difficulties, which did not enable him to make proper use of a pencil, this represented a great leap in his level of functioning; but it did not seem to impress the school authorities, who recommended his placement among the trainable mentally retarded because of his limited academic achievement and his impaired social interaction. They had come to the conclusion that Baruch needed vocational training more than he needed academic studies. It was at this point, at the age of 15, that Baruch was again referred to us for assessment.

In the first session after the new referral, Baruch manifested general dullness, a clinging behavior, and very little independence from his father, from whom he would not be separated. He manifested signs of echolalia and incoherent verbal behavior as well as uncoordinated motoricity. His level of functioning was very low, especially in arithmetic. His reading proved to be much better, though with limited comprehension because of a lack of verbal concepts and slowness. Baruch was still highly impulsive, and yet there were clear indications of his modifiability and a specific need to enhance his functioning by providing him with the prerequisites for thinking in the areas of analytic perception, precision, and the inhibition of impulsivity in the input and output phases. What was important in any attempt to enhance his functioning was the need to reinforce his purposeful behavior by providing him with feedback of his success and forging in him a sense of completion and self-reliance. Part of his extreme lack of security could be ascribed to his constant confrontation with his twin sister, who functioned normally, independently, and acted as his senior by 2 or 3 years. This state of insecurity had led Baruch to reactions that were labeled bizarre in certain stages of his life, and was pointed out as a regressive potentiality that might affect his emotional and mental conditions and his behavior.

Following our assessment, we decided to place Baruch in a treatment group among children who, despite their severe impairment, lived in an environment that provided them both with normal contacts within a foster family and with group experiences in a group care program during the day (Feuerstein and Krasilowsky, 1967; Feuerstein, Krasilowsky, and Rand, 1974; Feuerstein et al., 1976).

Baruch required a very intensive intervention program, which included cognitive enrichment, motor training, and psychotherapy. The presence of a peer group that provided pressure on him was a powerful agent in the modification of his bizarre behavior and made him give up his unmotivated smile, his hand-flipping, and his talking to himself, behaviors that had made him look exceptional even among the severely disturbed children in the group. But the greatest change in Baruch was reflected in his evergrowing capacity, interest, and gratification derived from drawing. It was his drawing, among other things, that made Baruch a recognized leader among the children and a well accepted member of the village youth movement (Figure 58).

After 3 years in the treatment group, Baruch was accepted by a vocational high school. He finished the 11th grade in 3 more years and acquired an efficient and skillful mastery of specific tasks in metal working, including welding and lathe work. He was then integrated into the army, where he is currently serving very successfully. He was recently promoted to a sergeant responsible for a shop. What is most striking in Baruch's development is the interest in plastic arts that he continues to cultivate, with hopes of following a professional artistic career.

Figure 58. Baruch's drawing.

Considering the very bad eye-hand coordination that made Baruch almost unable to handle a pencil when seen by the psychiatrist in 1970, his bizarre movements, his eye squint, his inarticulate speech, and his incapacity to handle numbers, the modifiability registered by the LPAD was a first hint and probably the sole source of information orienting the diagnosis toward a continuation and intensification of the investment in this youngster. Modifiability is reflected here in a very sharp departure in the course of life of the individual, first started by the assessment of the existence of a capacity to become involved in a process of change; changing the environment so that capacities, rather than limitations, are reinforced; and finally, actively investing in those areas in which investment was deemed both necessary and possible.

The case of Baruch, which certainly indicates an organic condition, brings further proof that organicity is not unmodifiable even in those areas in which the effects of organicity are mostly felt. For some reason, Baruch's area of performance showed this modifiability at a very early stage in our examination and was less resistant than the verbal area.

Case 6: Guy

The case of Guy illustrates very sharply the relationship between the expectations of the parents and their fear of a developmental lag produced by the initial organic condition of the child, and the lack of mediated learning experience conducive to a manifest level of mental retardation.

Immediately after Guy's birth he was recognized to be both physically and mentally impaired. Neurological examinations in the course of his first year of development pointed to a left hemiplegia, probably attributable to paranatal damage. The onset of Guy's motor behavior was delayed and deficient. He started to walk at the age of 3½, soon after he learned to stand and sit. A number of seizures were registered in early childhood but were soon controlled by anticonvulsive medication.

When referred to us at the age of 15½, Guy had a long history of hospitalization and placements in children's homes for the physically and mentally handicapped in Europe, and from the age of approximately 9 he had been living in a home for the retarded in Israel. His parents, who lived in Europe, were referred to us, paradoxically enough, for help in finding life-long custodial care for Guy in an appropriate institution, after such support was denied them by the welfare agencies who felt that the boy was able to do better than on the suggested placement.

The mother very convincingly described the boy as cognitively and linguistically retarded, socially immature, and inadequate to the extent that there was no way to keep him at home. The family was well to do, owned a factory and shop in their country of origin, but totally excluded any possibility of involving themselves directly in Guy's life except for providing him with financial support.

Guy had no part in the life of the family. During the many years he was in Israel, he had never been invited home, not even, and perhaps especially not, for events such as the marriages of his sister and brother. Furthermore, during some of the parents' visits to Israel, they avoided seeing Guy, though they conferred with the director of the residence in which the boy had been placed. They never attempted to involve other professionals either in consultation or intervention in order to improve the mental condition and social adaptability of their son. This active rejection of Guy by his parents seemed to us to be exceptional, and we tried to understand the reasons for it. The mother's major reason, which she repeatedly emphasized, was her son's very low level of functioning, falling within the range of the trainable mentally retarded, which she felt precluded any attempt to integrate him into the family.

After seeing Guy, we very quickly rejected this reason. Based on the mother's description we had expected to see a crippled, hyperkinetic, uncooperative adolescent. When he was called into the room, our first reaction was that this must be his brother. He was a red-haired, tall, slim boy, limping slightly, but extremely agile, with a normal looking face despite a divergent strabismus of the right eye. He immediately engaged in a discussion, which he initiated, in which he articulately expressed his hopes of being removed from the institution in which he was currently living inasmuch as he did not feel that he belonged with retarded children. He clearly stated his desire to live among normal youngsters in a setting where he could feel he was a part.

Recognizing that he would not be able to go back and see his parents "because they do not want me there," Guy spoke of his hopes for placement where he could become involved in work and social activities, especially among people who were as religious as he and his parents were. He showed great sensitivity and social intelligence in speaking about his mother, telling the examiner what he might and what he could not tell her of the conversation. He felt that he must make the best of it, considering the rejecting attitude his parents had toward him throughout his life. Guy did complain bitterly, however, about the fact that he had never been invited to family gatherings. In his own words, "My sister married. They sent me an invitation, but no ticket. My brother married. They sent me an invitation, but no ticket. My cousin, here in Israel, married; they didn't even send me an invitation. Her son was born; no invitation. The only time they invited me was for the ceremony a month after the birth of the first-born."*

Guy understood that the reason for keeping him so far away from home and the family was that they were ashamed of him. He had to stop rebelling, but he could not help claiming his right to be considered a part of the family, if not in the present, in a foreseeable future. Guy's language showed a great deal of eloquence. His mimicry was adaptative, rich, and vivid. His emotional level was certainly affected by the dearth of affection experienced by him throughout his life; yet, he displayed a great deal of readiness to engage in a relationship, without signs of clinging behavior or inadaptive overindulgence in possessive interaction.

When examined, Guy showed great gaps in achievement in the areas of reading and writing, limited spatial and temporal orientation, and a linguistic level that, despite its richness, showed certain agrammatisms typical of the linguistic environment in which he had been placed. Psychometrically, he fell into the area of educable rather than the trainable mentally retarded, the label that had previously been applied to him. He displayed certain low points, especially in spatial activity such as hand-eye coordination, reflected in visual-motor activities. Examined with the LPAD, he showed modifiability, particularly in conceptualized, abstract elaborative processes. Guy excelled in all the activities in which he was able to communicate his responses verbally rather than visually or, even less, motorically. His visual-motor behavior proved to be more resistant, but even it was accessible to learning processes that changed his behavior almost instantaneously. Learned behavior proved resistant to extinction, and with a progressive acquisition of the prerequisites for learning, especially in systematic exploratory behavior, need for precision, visual transport, and control of impulsivity, the acquired principles proved to be highly generalizable, pointing to his adaptability to new situations.

What marked the examiner-examinee interaction was Guy's very strong motivation and high level of coping behavior, which were probably enhanced by his awareness of the significance of this meeting for his destiny. This, in itself, threw a very different light on Guy than we had expected from his parents' description.

Guy's brother-in-law visited us together with the mother and attended part of the interview and examination. He was so shocked

---

* A special festivity for the most limited family circle.

by what he saw Guy capable of performing, responding, and reacting to, that he spontaneously concluded that Guy's place was not in custodial care. He himself offered to keep the boy in his home and to make sure that Guy underwent the development that seemed to him to be possible. When we told the mother we did not see any reason that Guy should be kept on a regimen that did not provide him with the new incentives for his growth and development, she reacted with much less enthusiasm and less readiness to accept our findings. It became apparent to us that a status quo had become established that kept Guy completely out of the family. Any attempt to change the status quo was met with a feeling of discomfort, disbelief, and outright opposition. The alienation and estrangement from this child were such that positive changes in his image did not awaken positive feelings, but were perceived as endangering the status quo, and therefore to be rejected. The mother quoted all the negative reports ever given by psychiatrists and neurologists and was able to remember all the troubles and disturbances produced by Guy's presence in the family. Finally, the true reason for the fear of making Guy a part of the family again suddenly emerged: his presence could have negatively affected the chances of two of his unmarried siblings to make suitable matches.

We understood that the integration of Guy into his family could not be the product of the sheer revelation of his potentialities and capacity for redevelopment, but would need stronger evidence and a restructuring of the total family system. We suggested to the parents that Guy be placed in a foster family. Our goal was threefold. The first was to help him become integrated within a normal environment. This became possible by placing Guy in a classroom with children who were 3 years younger than he and in which his foster father was the teacher. The second was to enrich his behavioral and cognitive repertoire by direct intervention and by exposure to cognitive and social behaviors in the family. The third was to provide a corrective object relationship (Alpert, 1959) within an emotionally warm and accepting family.

Guy's development within the foster family totally justified his placement and the investment and confirmed our prognosis of modifiability in all the described areas. Despite his relatively advanced age, he accepted his role as an adolescent 3 years younger than his chronological age and functioned among his peers in a highly adaptive way. His general repertoire of behaviors became enriched. At this time, his achievement has reached a level of a seventh or eighth grader in certain areas; while in others, a slower development is observed. He is socially active and an accepted member of a small rural community in which there are a number of residential educational settings. He is now striving for a more independent life style than that permitted by the foster family.

The death of his father affected Guy significantly. His reactions were very close to normal bereavement and mourning as he said, "It is such a pity that my father knew so little of me, and I of him."

In terms of the future, we are now starting to explore the need, the possibility, and the rationale for Guy's integration into his family. How will his long-standing feelings of being rejected and deprived affect his behavior and his relationship with his mother? How will the very long-standing image of him as retarded affect the interaction? As a possible alternative, we see having Guy learn a trade. Horticulture may be an adequate approach, with the possibility of integrating him into a semicommunal, agricultural setting.

Guy's integration into his family will be better assured, with considerably less friction, once he will be less dependent on the family, on their evaluation of him, and on their readiness to perceive him in a different light than what they are accustomed to. Therefore, we will not recommend Guy's return home, except for visits, during the continuous training period that is still before him.

Case 7: David

After their prolonged ambivalence, David was referred by his parents. The mother, a gifted sculptor, had written from abroad at least five times, asking the author to examine her son. The interview was delayed, however, despite much correspondence, by the hesitation of both parents in seeking help for their son, with whose condition they had learned to live. When they finally came to Israel the boy was 16. It became clear that their reluctance was generated by their fear that a new assessment might only exacerbate their emotional condition by reconfirming what had been stated again and again by psychologists, educators, and pediatricians: that David was unchangeable and that his status as a retarded person would become more and more salient as years passed. A part of this ambivalence also stemmed from David's reluctance to expose himself to a new assessment. Throughout his life he had been dragged from one psychologist to another, invariably leaving him with a feeling of failure and, at best, with a passive acceptance of his condition as basically unchangeable.

Despite his candid appearance, David knew a great deal about his condition and the way he was perceived by teachers, peers, and even his parents; but he covered this up very carefully by a compliant, submissive, subservient attitude that manifested itself almost as an echolalic, echopraxic behavior. Thus, he would instantly answer any encouragement, telling him how good he was, with "Yes, I know I'm a fine young man." He would repeat sentences said to him with great conformity, as if he had nothing to offer by himself. This was not caused by a deficiency of his language, which showed definite possibilities on both a receptive and expressive level. However, it was this kind of echolalic-like extreme conforming behavior that rendered many of his sayings inane. Furthermore, his obedience gave the impression of extreme suggestibility and malleability. Indeed, children had made him believe that by turning a certain key, he would cause an earthquake in Southern California. Once, having turned the key, David did not sleep for the next few nights, firmly believing that he had set an earthquake in motion. It was only later, after David was drastically modified through learning experiences, that we were able to perceive a world of hostility, resentment, and aggressiveness stored in him and ready to explode.

David was referred in order to help both him and his parents decide on his occupational orientation from among the very limited vocational possibilities considered accessible to him. It had been suggested that David be trained as a waiter because he was considered to be very complacent. It was thought that complacency alone would compensate for his extreme clumsiness and total lack of refined motor control over his body movements. It is doubtful whether those who would have received soup in their laps would have agreed with this choice of a vocation! Furthermore, knowing the social and environmental characteristics of this occupation, we deemed such an orientation to be clearly dangerous to David in terms of his being exploited by his colleagues. Such a vocation would have literally resulted in his belonging to two worlds: that of the highly cultured family environment and that of his occupational reference group. Other suggestions made by psychotechnicians and psychologists were for manual, menial types of jobs.

The parents had tended to agree with whatever was said to them, and we were merely supposed to make the final choice. One thing all of the professionals and parents had agreed upon was that formal academic training should be discontinued. His studies, even in a slow learner's class, were considered to be futile and frustrating to him, his teachers, and his parents.

David's parents immediately told us of their passive acceptance of their son and the fact that they were happy with him no matter what his academic, vocational, and behavioral attainments might be. They did state, however, that they were concerned with what might happen to him in the more remote future. For the mother, especially, David's dependent status was a very significant and highly satisfactory arrangement.

Later on, when David's mother became aware of the high modifiability revealed by her son, she burst into tears, and trembling with excitement told us that when David was born he had been considered a child with very little hopes for any significant mental development because of the many stigmata found at birth and a rather prolonged anoxia, which required intervention for his revival. The pediatrician, a very close family friend, strongly urged the parents to place the newborn infant in an appropriate institution. The mother reacted with a very deep depression, out of which she emerged only after she had made her decision to keep the baby at home with her, despite the fact that this would greatly interfere both with her handling of the other children in the family and with her career.

Upon seeing the highly significant results (Figure 59) obtained by David in the LPAD variations, and hearing our suggestion that he pursue his academic studies until he finished the 12th grade, at least, before entering into any occupation, the mother said, "I am just trembling with the idea of what would have happened, how big a loss it would have been if we had followed the pessimistic advice based on the various assessments which were done before." Asking us to forgive her for being so affected emotionally by our findings and suggestions, she said, "Consider what it means to be pulled between two poles—between seeing David as a child almost limited to a vegetative existence, and what you suggest, his finishing high school and undergoing a redevelopment which may eventuate in his being an independent, self-sufficient, assertive individual."

David himself responded in a very reserved way. For a very long period he continued to wear his mask of conformity and passivity, accepting each compliment he received as natural and not surprising. Yet very unexpected remarks broke through his complacency and permitted the perception of a turmoiled, sad, and deeply concerned existence beneath his peaceful exterior. In his Rorschach, this permeated in a very clear way. In the projective tests, David showed a high level of creativity, including a rich symbolism of internal tension and search for identity. The obsequiousness and the conformity that had marked him were subdued in psychotherapy, in which he brought to the fore his strong needs for opposition and self-assertiveness and a search for self-realization by becoming more independent of the views of others or their control over him.

NAME *David (Case VII)*

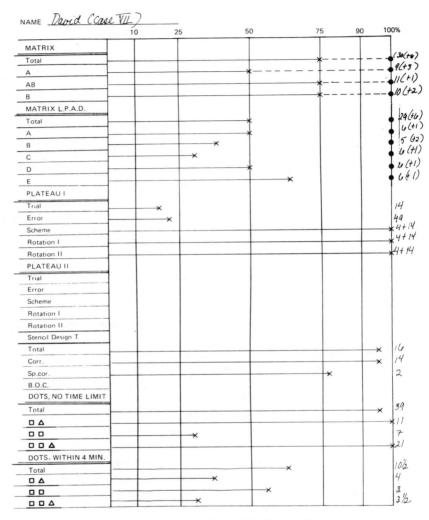

Figure 59.   LPAD profile for David (case 7).

It was only after a year of treatment that David became truly cooperative. He no longer perceived our plans and executions simply as impositions, but he adopted them, although initially they had neither been planned nor accepted by him. The idea of continuing his studies, and what is more, continuing them away from home, seemed so strange to him and his family that they did not even attempt to resist. Instead they hoped that the suggested placement in an academically oriented vocational residential high school in Israel would fail, by virtue of David's being rejected. That he was accepted was a real shock for everybody. His parents did not cease phoning, again and again, asking to be forgiven for daring to question or contradict our suggestion. By raising the most varied doubts, they repeatedly questioned both the feasibility and the rationale of David's placement outside of the family, in general, and in the vocational school in Israel, in particular.

When they were confronted with the major reason for our suggestion, the need to provide David with intellectually and socially enriching experiences, the parents were convinced—until David's strong reaction the first day after placement. He found himself suddenly uprooted from his family, lonesome and estranged. The author was telephoned in the middle of the night by the alarmed parents, who asked if they could comply with the crying boy's request that he be returned home immediately and if his being returned was not a real necessity. It became clear that the mutual interdependence between David and his parents, making detachment difficult, reflected a well established status quo that neither party wanted to relinquish. The status quo had been established by the limited expectations and reinforced by the opinions of psychologists. To use the words of David, himself, "I'm always so happy at home. Why do I have to leave it? I want to be like this always."

Once the storm had passed, David started to learn the asperities of group life while tremendously enjoying a freedom he had not learned to control. In his avidity for a relationship with his peers, he was ready for everything, including participation in raids with other children, exposing himself to pressure and punishment. He started to be rebellious and gradually gave up the conforming, subservient type of behavior, asserting himself in a childish, obstinate, and passively resistant way. During this period, limited success was observable at school. David was preoccupied with many adjustment problems. He was confronted with the semi-independent life in the group, such as getting up without the help of his parents, cleaning his room and his body without being reminded either by his mother or caregiver, going to work and keeping pace with other children, and participating actively and adequately in the discussions and free-time activities of the group.

In order to be accepted by the group and to feel he belonged, David was ready to play the clown in class, generating difficulties with his teachers. Although he had been exposed to the author's

Instrumental Enrichment program during the previous summer, when he was being prepared for better class participation at the residential school, neither it nor a tutorial program was of much help at the beginning.

Again, one had the feeling that David had to undergo a very sharp change in his approach to himself and to life before becoming able to learn and make progress. Such changes occurred progressively during the second half of the year in his residential setting.

For a long period the school itself reacted with a great deal of scepticism concerning the possibility of producing a real change in David. To prevent an overt manifestation of the staff's attitude, it was necessary to interpret not only the results of David's LPAD, which consistently showed a high level of modifiability, but also to continue during the first year to point to the clear signs of his development that were observable both in social activities and school achievement. The second year was marked by an important increase in David's capacity to cope with school, in skills required for agricultural work, and in understanding agricultural theory and practice.

David formed a good therapeutic relationship, by help of which much of his previous behavior subsided. He became free for critical, realistic, and rational thinking, accompanied by an increased awareness of his own goals as compared with those set for him by others. He not only expressed his views but became a planner and performer of the steps enabling him to reach his proposed goals. He demanded from his parents the right to present his views in family matters and was able to withstand the clashes with his father without giving in, as he previously had. David not only accepted, but actually demanded, his right to finish high school. It is only following his graduation from high school that David will return to his home.

What seemed once to be a dream has become a possibility that is arousing a good deal of anxiety and feelings of insecurity, but is considered necessary and possible. The change in the attitude of the teachers and the school staff is reflected in the fact that they felt very hurt when we and David considered his transfer to another school. A transfer was seen as a way to help David start as a more mature, coping, assertive, adequate personality in a place where his initial ineptness, candidness, suggestibility, and childish behavior were unknown. His teachers, however, rebelled against this by saying. "Now that we have discovered his real image and helped him in developing his capacity, now you want to take him away from us?"

David himself decided to remain and cope with his past in the same place where he experienced his dramatic change.

Case 8: Tamara

Tamara was referred to us at the age of 11. She had emigrated from Russia with her mother a year prior to referral, leaving the divorced father behind. Soon after her arrival, she was placed in a youth village where she attended a regular school. It was not very long, however, before it was noticed that she was functioning on a level of mental deficiency. Her condition had not been detected earlier because her lack of responsiveness had been ascribed to a language barrier. Her low scholastic achievement was especially apparent because of the optimal conditions of special help provided for the immigrant child in this particular school, and was attributed to her limited capacity to learn.

Both educators and pediatricians agreed that Tamara appeared to be mentally deficient. A very accentuated bradypsychia, bradylalia, and bradypraxia were present. Tamara seemed to perceive everything in a very cloudy way, and was little interested in what was going on around her. Her eyeglasses were always covered with mist, but she never removed them to clean them. An EEG, performed at that time, pointed to "a severe general disturbance localized in the right hemisphere with signs of paroxysmal outburst in the temporal area."

In our first encounter, Tamara showed a general state of deficient functioning, even though a certain amount of heterogeneity of results was observable. Her perceptual-motor tests showed signs of deficiency, both in terms of reproduction and organization. However, after rather limited training, a considerable amount of modifiability was observed, as is evident from a comparison between copy 1 and copy 2 of the Complex Figure Test (see Figure 60). Results on the Bender-Gestalt test were very low.

Anamnestic data revealed a history of perinatal anoxia followed by a very late appearance of speech behavior. Tamara's organized speech appeared when she was 5 to 6, with her first word, "mother," at the age of 4. The mother seemed even more concerned that the child had been born with a very peculiar skull formation and had been hairless until the age of 4. Tamara had been seen by many "defectologists" in Russia, but the mother claimed that the child had received very limited and unsatisfactory treatment. During the interview, it became clear that there was a very rejecting attitude on the part of the mother, who showed a limited readiness to interact with her child in a way that might have enhanced cognitive development.

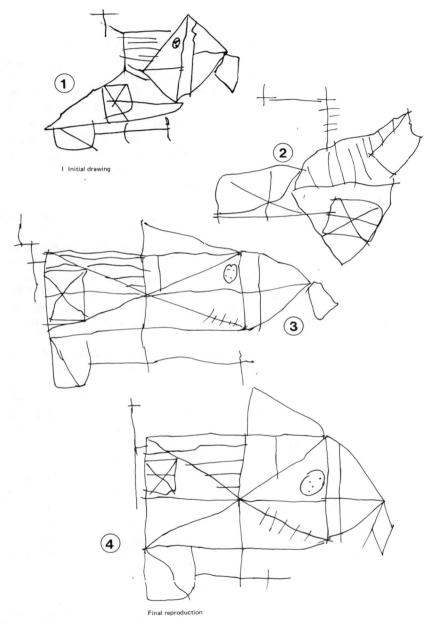

Figure 60.   Tamara's Complex Figure Tests.

The mother was ready to accept that Tamara could be a valuable person, even without knowledge and school skills, but felt that what should be offered her daughter was personality development to compensate for the girl's incapacity to accede to higher levels of intellectual functioning. However, the mother's passive acceptance of the girl's intellectual development as unmodifiable to a large extent reflected a learned behavior from contacts with "defectologists" and had clearly become the reason for the mother's "safeguarding" Tamara from certain types of stimuli. But at the time of our examination Tamara showed a level of intellectual functioning and modifiability that indicated that the mother's overprotectiveness was not only superfluous but probably noxious (Figure 61).

Tamara had far more difficulties in areas related to input processes than when internalized elaboration was required. In accordance with this formulation, her greatest difficulties were in the Plateaux II test at the trial-and-error level and in the Organization of Dots, both timed and untimed. However, on the various rotations of the Plateaux, on the RSDT (where no manual activity is required), and in certain parts of the LPAD Variations, Tamara attained maximum scores. This LPAD evaluation helped us to decide in favor of an intensive and prolonged exposure to academic study rather than an early orientation toward vocational and occupational training. Her limited capacities for motor manipulation plus the high modifiability manifested wherever internalized thought processes were required made academic study the preferred pathway to ensure Tamara's integration and adaptation to society.

Following the institution of our program, Tamara became a regular though slow student in high school. She showed a high level of motivation and adapted to group life in a way that far exceeded her otherwise generally normal level of functioning. One of the most important outcomes was the improved relationship between the mother and daughter, with the mother perceiving Tamara, to use the mother's own words, as "a newborn child, without the former defects."

When Tamara finished high school, she enlisted in the army, where she assumed a secretarial position. The degree of Tamara's success can be assessed by her current standing as a career civil servant. Today, Tamara is an executive secretary and supervisor of a secretarial pool. It is amazing that, as slow and uncoordinated as she once was, she has mastered a job requiring precision, rapidity, and efficiency.

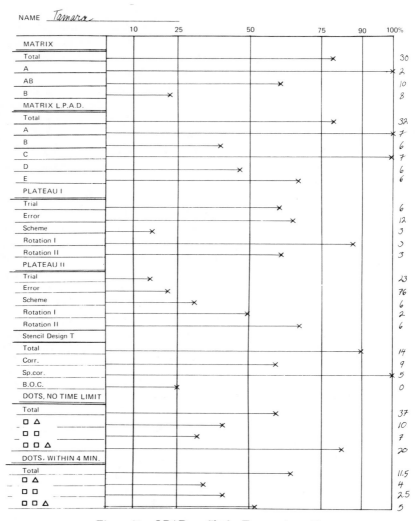

Figure 61.   LPAD profile for Tamara (case 8).

Case 9: Elisheva

The case of Elisheva illustrates the difficulties one may have, in certain instances, in conveying the findings of an LPAD and their meaning for making decisions and plans for rehabilitation to the rehabilitation field worker.

Elisheva was referred for an LPAD assessment after a long, 16-year history of difficulties. She lost both of her parents when she was

10 years old. At the age of 12, she had undergone an evaluation based on the LPAD modality. Already at the time, we had observed Elisheva's very high capacity to learn by help of insightful processes and to transfer her learning to the rather difficult new tasks with which she was confronted in the LPAD clinical battery. Her manual ability for both routine and menial work was very low.

The psychotechnical report that accompanied her referral stated, "there are some slight signs of progress capacities in certain small tasks, when she is provided with additional time for training and conditioning." The report pointed to the need for a repetitious, mechanical approach to teaching Elisheva. This contention of the psychometrist was even more clearly stated in the following paragraph:

> The girl is defective on the basis of an organic condition, is unable to function under normal conditions of the work market, needs a protective framework which will enable her gradual advancement via time and continuous training. This is so because *she is unable to transfer* the learned behavior from one task to the other, but rather fulfills short term detailed instructions repeated to her, again and again. (emphasis added)

This very pessimistic and dark prognosis was made despite the fact that earlier in the same report, the examiner had stated that the girl did not respond to and therefore could not benefit from a regular battery of tests and that her best level of functioning was in the area of verbal communication.

In our tests (see Figure 62) what was mainly perceived was the great ease with which, in contrast with the examiner's observations, Elisheva did transfer what she had previously learned, although slowly and painfully at times. Her major difficulty did not lie in the elaboration of relationships in an abstract way, but rather in her orientation and need to assemble the required data for the task at hand in an organized and systematic way. Once this method was learned and used properly, however, she proved able to reach higher levels of functioning. These findings were substantiated clearly by her learning to read and write very fluently and, what is even more important, to express herself in a rather sophisticated way.

The general feeling one had in any transaction with Elisheva was that both anxiety and reduced motivation, attributable to despair, made her function at a much lower level than that of which she was capable, even without any further investment. Unhappily, for irrelevant reasons, the girl was convinced by the rehabilitation worker against our advice that she should abandon her studies in favor of training in a manual occupation. It should be noted that Elisheva

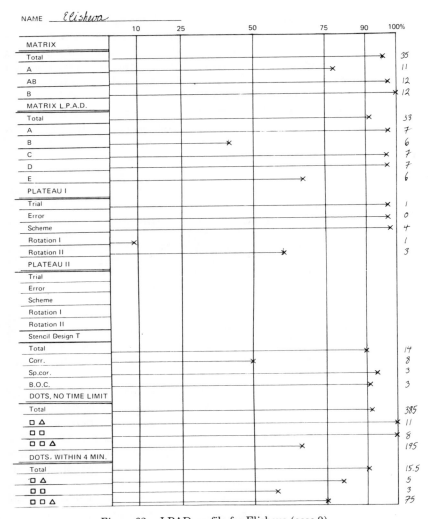

Figure 62.   LPAD profile for Elisheva (case 9).

suffered from a variety of physical handicaps in addition to her organic condition. Among these were rheumatic fever, with a slight residual heart condition, and rheumatoid arthritis, which, added to her general slowness, made physical work extremely laborious for her. The failure predicted by us came true. Her motor deficiency made manual work inefficient and therefore nonlucrative. We then encouraged Elisheva to continue her studies and to utilize her higher proficiency in the field of logico-verbal activity.

Elisheva finished high school. She then entered and completed training in a school for practical nursing. For the past 10 years Elisheva has been working in a day care clinic as a pediatric nurse.

It is unfortunate that counselors guide a child like Elisheva toward manual work. All too frequently such children have minimal motor skills and are neither suited for manual work nor find it rewarding. Instead of searching for whatever cognitive skills the child has, the counselor assumes that if the child is essentially unmodifiable, training in manual work is automatically indicated.

CASES WITH POSSIBLE DETERIORATION ATTRIBUTABLE TO PSYCHOSIS

The next two cases illustrate a special function that can be fulfilled by the LPAD. We refer here to the problem of differential diagnosis of cases in which one is confronted with cognitive manifestations that raise the suspicion of deterioration resulting from an aversive psychotic process. The question we have been confronted with is whether the observed cognitive deficiency is a concomitant phenomenon to the aversive process, which one may hope will disappear along with the other symptoms of the mental condition, or whether the signs of mental deficiency are produced by the process and are therefore to be perceived as an irreversible state of deterioration. In the past few years we have been called upon to examine and evaluate adolescents who have been hospitalized because of their deviant psychotic behavior, accompanied by a low level of cognitive functioning.

Case 10: Harry

Harry's parents had gone through all the terrors and vicissitudes of the Holocaust, and both had lost their original mates and children in concentration camps. After their marriage, three children were born to them, with Harry the eldest. The youngest sibling was considered retarded from an early age and placed in a special school.

Harry had begun his schooling in a regular class where he was said to have functioned satisfactorily until the third grade. Then he could not keep up with the work, fell behind in school activities, and began to show signs of retarded performance. He was referred for psychological evaluation. At that time, he was found to have an IQ of 70, and accordingly placement in a special school was indicated.

Harry, a rather withdrawn child, began to rebel against this placement and reacted both by truancy and aggressiveness. After a few episodes of bizarre behavior, he was referred for hospitalization. There his personality and cognitive behavior were examined. Following the manifestation of certain discrepancies and heterogeneity in his levels of performance, the hospital examiners speculated that his reduced capacity for abstract conceptual thinking, as compared with other more intact areas, was indicative of a progressive deterioration attributable to a schizophrenic psychotic process.

In our examination of Harry, we were confronted with certain bizarre behavior patterns like talking or laughing to himself. The examinations provided us with a deep insight into both the etiology of his low functioning and the precipitating cause of the psychotic breakdown that had led to his hospitalization. Harry proved to be of above average intelligence when he was given an opportunity to succeed in his work. This opportunity consisted of modifying some basic components of his cognitive behavior. It was amazing to find that when confronted with a series of stimuli he did not consider them in the sequence required for understanding the relationship between them. Instead, he looked at them randomly, demonstrating an episodic grasp of reality, devoid of comparative and summative behaviors. When presented with a stimulus situation in which counting was necessary, Harry would use a qualitative approximation rather than a precise number arrived at through an orderly quantification process. For example, he would say "a lot" when he would have to compute 3×3; or he would use inappropriate spatial concepts that made his discrimination between differently oriented objects very deficient. He spontaneously manifested very little need for marshaling logical evidence.

However, as these functions were corrected in the course of certain task performances, he used explanations and newly acquired behavior and approaches in a very precise way. It was as if one had handed him the key that opened the gate to what had previously been a mysterious world. The area of his greatest achievement proved to be just the one that had given rise to the question of the deterioration process, abstract thinking. There, not only did he prove himself a rapid learner but, even more important, his approach changed from extrinsic to a completely intrinsic motivation. Thus, after he had finished the battery of tests, the results of which are presented in his profile (see Figure 63), he asked whether he could continue on his own, at least during the time of our conference with his case worker. What resulted was a highly successful, independent performance on the more difficult tasks of the Adult Raven Matrices: he attained 11 out of 12 correct on each of series C and D; and four completely correct responses plus three spontaneous corrections on series E.

These results enabled us to reject the hypothesis of deterioration and instead to locate the major source of Harry's problems in the fact that he was a culturally deprived child. Because mediated learning experience was not offered him by his rather "primitive" and disturbed parents, Harry could not use his school experience properly despite his good intelligence. Placed in a special school, at

Figure 63.   LPAD profile for Harry (case 10).

least partly on the assumption that he was as retarded as his younger sister, he had rebelled and acted out against this placement that he felt vaguely, yet strongly, was an injustice to him, especially because he was sensitive to the condition of his sister.

Another previous finding discarded as a result of the dynamic assessment was that of a marked slowness in his ideational processes. Although this truly existed whenever the output required a verbal response, when Harry used a motor modality of response this slowness did not manifest itself. On the contrary, in many instances he showed a very quick grasp and response provided the data were made available to him. When he was first seen by us, his motor behavior was rather clumsy and unsure because of his medication regimen; however, this changed very soon after his release from the hospital.

On the basis of our findings, we were able to discard the notion of a deterioration process and recommend Harry's placement in our residential setting for the culturally deprived. Here Harry was provided with an opportunity to become involved in a process aiming at the redevelopment of his cognitive functions, and especially to acquire a better self-image by belonging to and being accepted by a normal, although deprived, adolescent peer group. For a very long period, though, Harry continued the patterns acquired during his 9-month hospitalization, as if he were afraid to relinquish those patterns before being very sure that he was an accepted member of his new peer group.

The cognitive redevelopment that took place in Harry exceeded by far what could have been measured even by our LPAD tests. He remained within the residential setting for a period of about 2 years. Then he was reintegrated into his family, who showed great eagerness in having him come home. In this case, the elicitation and subsequent measurement of modifiability required relatively little investment and provided an answer to the very difficult question of the etiology and nature of the regressive behavior observed in this youngster.

Case 11: Maimon

Maimon was referred to us by the same mental hospital that had referred Harry. Maimon had been hospitalized because of a psychotic breakdown. After a meaningful improvement in his condition, the hospital asked us to determine the feasibility of his placement within an adequate educational framework for cognitive redevelopment. The following excerpt from one of our interviews is of interest:

Q: Where did you study?

Maimon: After I was in an Amal school* for a while, I was transferred to M————.† This was a school for retardates. Before I went there I didn't know it was even worse than the first school. All the kids were disturbed and didn't learn anything, and I wanted to get ahead. We only learned agriculture and carpentry.

Q: And you didn't like it?

Maimon: Oh, no!

Q: What kind of children were there?

Maimon: At the first school, they threw chairs at the teacher. They didn't know how to read or write and just kept us from learning. I went to the municipality and I told them to transfer me. They gave me a test, but I didn't pass. I knew I didn't pass, and then they transferred me to the M———— school. There I felt I wasn't as good as other kids, and because of this they hospitalized me. But now that I was given the medication, I am completely healthy and I want to go to a kibbutz very much. I like the kibbutz very much. I've seen movies about it.

Maimon complained that he always had failed examinations and that every time he tried to improve his status by presenting himself for a test he worsened his condition instead of bettering it. No wonder he did not want to leave after being assessed by us. He was ready to continue for as long as we would let him. As he openly stated, "It's the first time I have ever succeeded in any test."

As shown in his profile (Figure 64) Maimon demonstrated a high level of modifiability, strongly contrasting with the previous diagnoses of EMR. The fact that he obtained these results during a period of hospitalization and under heavy medication promised more success under optimal conditions of functioning like those offered by the Youth Aliyah kibbutz to which we sent him. Maimon had also shown a great need for the fine arts and became an accomplished drummer, which was very helpful in his becoming an accepted member of the group despite his initial difficulties in social adaptation.

Maimon proved to be a highly ambitious, achievement-oriented youngster. This was probably one of the reasons for his breakdown, when his efforts to succeed were unsuccessful as a result of repeated diagnoses of EMR. For many children the diagnosis of EMR represents a source of pathology and emotional stress especially when

---

* The Amal school is a special education school for the EMR.

† M———— is a framework established by the Ministry of Social Welfare for school dropouts. Students are given opportunities for manual work in vocations such as carpentry, welding, machine shop, etc.

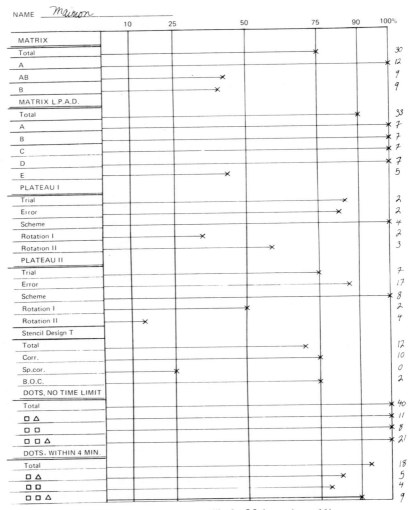

Figure 64.   LPAD profile for Maimon (case 11).

it is contrasted with their own perception of themselves as having a higher potential than that ascribed to them.

CASES REPRESENTATIVE OF
PHYSICAL AND EMOTIONAL BARRIERS

Case 12: Chaim

At the age of 14, Chaim was referred to us by the Ministry of Social Welfare for placement within one of our settings for culturally deprived children. He had initially been referred to a residential setting for retardates, but he rebelled against this placement and asked to be placed within a kibbutz.

Chaim was the third of seven children, the eldest of whom was 18 and the youngest, 6. Chaim's mother had died of cancer when he was 12. When we first saw Chaim, he was illiterate and showed a very marked retarded performance. He was unable to do any kind of written work. In arithemetic, he knew only very simple addition, almost no subtraction, and no multiplication or division. The report of a previous psychological examination described him as having a very limited intellectual capacity. The examiner's report follows:

> Chaim is a nice boy, enters the room without hesitation, carries with him his hearing aid (which includes a huge transistor battery to be kept in the pocket), but he did not employ it despite his difficulties in communication. When asked to put it on, he did so but soon removed it, claiming that the noise of the apparatus disturbed him. His articulation is relatively correct. The intonation is monotonous, however, and uncontrolled because of his hearing deficit. He behaved quietly, with a certain passivity, during the session. Chaim did not express any aspirations concerning his future. He manifested a great deal of apathy and limited attachment. The results of the examination point to a very limited intellectual capacity. This limitation is visible in all areas of intelligence, but is particularly marked in the logico-verbal field. Thus, Chaim is unable to solve routine and daily problems, has no command of the four arithmetical operations, reads very little and expresses himself very primitively in writing. Despite the fact that his deficiencies in practical performance do not seem to be as great, he has definite difficulties in tasks requiring analytic and synthetic functions.

The psychologist recommended that Chaim be placed in a residential setting where the boy could be helped to develop a better command of basic school skills, but where the major activity and training would be for a menial, manual-type occupation.

Our examination supplied evidence of a culturally deprived youngster whose modifiability was not only easily achieved with a limited amount of investment, but, even more important, whose capacity for generalizing what was learned was considerable. His redevelopment required temporary placement in a treatment group in a foster home–group care program. There he learned to read and write. He started to relate to his peers and, later, to adults. His foster parents became strongly attached to the boy, despite his limited readiness to engage in verbal communication. However, his work on the foster family's farm made his growing attachment and commitment to the family evident.

After 2 years of intensive training in the treatment group a dramatic change became evident in his level of functioning. Despite the limitations imposed by his hearing deficiency, Chaim was integrated into a vocational high school, where he showed high technical and scholastic skills. When he was graduated from the vocational high school he was exempt from military service because of his hearing deficit, which became progressively worse. He was accepted for a postgraduate year in a vocational high school for qualified technicians. He started to work as a foreman of a work crew and later became a qualified technician in a ship construction company.

Chaim continues to maintain a strong relationship with his foster parents and spends his vacations working on the farm. He is of great help to them whenever there is a need for assistance and recently took over the responsibility of the farm temporarily, when his foster father became disabled by a severe stroke.

In reviewing the case of Chaim, one must sharply distinguish between manifest level of functioning and modifiability. When we first examined the boy, he had no accurate concept of numbers and no concept of verticality, for which he used the term "long," or horizontality, which he called "fat." He could not supply missing vertical and horizontal lines simultaneously because he used only one source of information at a time. However, when he came to more difficult problems he was able to use all that had been taught him during a short span of an hour or so. This application of acquired processes was the first accurate measure of his real potential.

The concept of cultural deprivation that must be considered here is one of a limitation imposed by physical-sensory barriers upon the quantity and quality of mediated learning experience. Chaim's hearing deficiency caused an incapacity to attend to cues mediated to him and at the time discouraged and strongly limited the attempts of the parental figures to communicate with him and mediate the world to him. Since his deficiency was selective rather than complete, no real intervention was introduced, and he was left at the mercy of fragmented, and therefore deceptive, attempts to communicate. The strong feeling of insufficiency and incapacity that followed his failures reflected itself in two ways. First, there was his lack of eagerness to clarify the auditory cues by amplifying them. He gave up wearing his hearing aid and resisted all attempts to compel him to do so even after the aid was changed to an inobtrusive one, as if to say, "It doesn't matter to me what you all talk about." Then, any confrontation with a task resulted in a reaction of futility. At the beginning of any task, Chaim's own words were, "I won't be able to do it. I never did it and will never be able to do it," despite the fact that he was easily and unhesitantly able to solve the task immediately afterwards.

In the case of Chaim, the LPAD assessment was crucial for uncovering hidden potential, both cognitive and emotional, and for orienting those who dealt with him toward the areas in which he could best be redeveloped.

Case 13: Ruthy

Ruthy was referred to us for assessment of her true potential by a residential setting in which she had been placed a year earlier. She had come to the setting as an illiterate, and despite an IQ of 80 and a great amount of help and investment, she had not made any progress during the year. The educators doubted whether there was any way at all to make her progress.

Ruthy was an offspring of a very disturbed family. Her father, an alcoholic and drug addict, was unemployed. He showed no understanding of the needs of his children, nor did he supply the money necessary for their upkeep. Her mother, a very tired looking yet beautiful woman, worked very hard to nourish her eight children; however, she showed variability in her relationship with them. In her own words, "I know that there are times that I can't stand it anymore, and I run away from my home, husband, and children. All I want then is to forget."

Our first attempts with Ruthy were not very successful. She kept claiming constantly that she did not understand and did not know what she was being asked to do. Ruthy's behavior was affected by a combination of a lack of motivation and feelings of insufficiency and low self-esteem. When she was confronted with a task, she would use a very primitive way of exploring its elements and selecting the appropriate answer. Even when she was willing to respond, she showed great dependency. Instead of looking at the task at hand she would constantly look into the eyes of the examiner in order to determine the nature of the required response. She would point blindly to one of the choices and await the "yes" or "no" of the examiner.

It was first necessary to discourage this kind of approach by restricting Ruthy's field of search and making her focus on the problem. She was slowly initiated into an appropriate exploration of the data by pointing to each choice in the Raven's Matrices and helping her to elaborate the reasons why five answers were wrong and only the sixth was correct. By this, we immediately induced a series of functions that Ruthy had not initially possessed in her repertoire. She was taught to compare not only the possible solution with the problem, but also the various alternatives with one another using such dimensions as color, size, and orientation. She then applied this comparative behavior throughout the test. Later, when she saw a task including a cloud of dots into which she had to project a square and triangle, she spontaneously pointed out the constancy of size and form of a square across the variations in its orientation or in its relationship to other figures in the task. The need for logical evidence in communication was induced through inferential questioning such as, "What would be the solution if the tasks had been changed in this way or another?" Very soon she proved able to bring real support to her contentions, which were proper internalized anticipations of a solution, by pointing to the adequate source of evidence such as the relationship in the upper row which had to be applied in the second row of an analogy task (Figure 65).

Ruthy proved to be a very deprived, emotionally distressed, and strained little girl. Her incapacity to function in the school situation and her limited capacity to use individual tutoring were attributable to a combination of the lack of basic strategies and cognitive working habits and a mild state of depression, resulting in a complete lack of motivation. In the words of her teacher, "She stayed passive and completely impenetrable to any attempts to break through her system." However, after providing her with the elementary prerequisites for cognitive functioning, she manifested slow but very steady and meaningful modifiability.

Ruthy's major area of success was in the field of analogical thinking, required in the LPAD Variations. The lowest functioning was in tasks in which she had to use a more complex set of data and in which she was given the opportunity to act out her impulsive behavior, as can be seen from the results of her Plateaux test (Figure 65). However, each time she was requested to use an internalized anticipatory, elaborative type of behavior she succeeded after training. Her attainment of 8 out of 12 on the B series of the Raven Matrices (24th percentile), during training, was followed by her subsequent outstanding performance on LPAD Variations, where she reached the 90th percentile on the total score.

Having been able to prove the modifiability of the child, despite the difficulties encountered in initial attempts, we recommended a continuation of the previous efforts with a more planned program for remedial teaching. However, this was not accepted easily either by the child, who had already experienced failure, or by the teachers. Because of this and other considerations, we decided to remove Ruthy from the residential setting to one of our treatment groups, where she was placed with a foster family and attended our special school. The 2 years she spent there proved to be highly beneficial and she gained total command of school skills. This was coupled with a noteworthy change in other areas of behavior.

Following the treatment group, Ruthy was placed in a regular residential setting where academic studies were combined with vocational training. With the proper investment required by the goals set for her in her new school, Ruthy was able to finish high school. Her school recommended her acceptance by a teachers' seminary for training as a teacher of handicrafts because of her great proficiency in needlework.

Ruthy is now married and has three children. She continues to work as a highly successful teacher. The author has subsequently referred children to her for training and special care at her school.

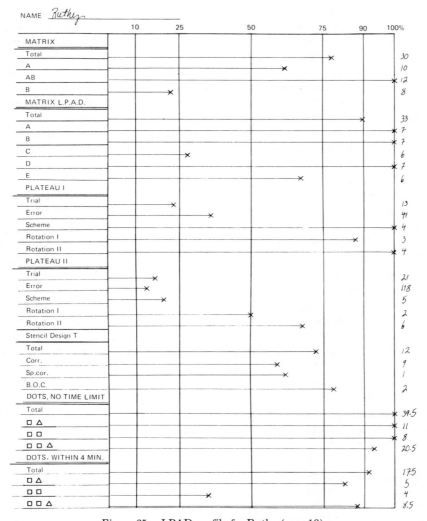

Figure 65.   LPAD profile for Ruthy (case 13).

Ruthy responds most enthusiastically to our calls for assistance, constantly reminding us of her despair many years ago.

CONCLUDING REMARKS ABOUT THE CASES

In presenting these cases, we did not attempt to exhaustively describe all of our experience in using the LPAD battery with them. The reader should be cautioned against misinterpreting our presentations as either all inclusive or thoroughly representative of our findings. The score distributions indicate that some of the children experienced great difficulties and did not show much improvement as a result of the amount of intervention given to them in this experimental situation. When brought back for further individualized testing, some of these children functioned better after additional training investment. Some, however, were still very resistive.

We deliberately selected cases for presentation that would demonstrate the effectiveness of the LPAD method in solving different types of commonly encountered though puzzling cases for rehabilitation that are often mishandled as a result of traditional evaluative procedures. It should be stressed, however, that there are certain cases in which attempts to demonstrate and assess the degree of modifiabililty meet with considerable difficulty. Sometimes it is merely a matter of adjusting the quantity and quality of the investment in order to produce a given change in the level of functioning. In other cases, only very slight changes are achieved even with maximal investment. However, the latter are rare, and the difficulty is usually determined by deep communicational deficits or by a complete lack of motivation displayed as intense negativism. Children who fall in the range of severe retardation are not usually referred to us; when they are referred, they are not easily helped because our instruments operate on a level above that of the repertoires accessible to them. For such children, training and assessment techniques employed by Schucman (1968), Haeussermann (1958), and Clarke, Clarke, and Cooper (1970) are more appropriate.

Another point we should like to make concerns the kind of intervention strategies we suggest as a result of LPAD assessments. A process-oriented approach to the child's LPAD results enables us to distinguish the locus of the child's deficiencies in one or more phases of the mental act (input, elaboration, and/or output) or in one of the specific parameters of the mental act, such as its content, the language of its presentation, its level of complexity, its operations, or its level of abstraction (Feuerstein, in press). A process-oriented approach enables us to point to the specific area in which the investment is mainly necessary and allows us to derive specific prescriptions of a didactic nature in order to remedy the difficulty which has been disclosed.

In certain cases, results of the LPAD indicate the need for a broad spectrum approach in order to raise the child's level of functioning. An example of such a pervasive prescription is the placement of the child in an enriched environment, outside of his family; the use of intensive individual and group care approaches; and finally, the use of our Instrumental Enrichment program (Feuerstein, 1969, in press), which was generated by our experience in developing the Learning Potential Assessment Device.

In other cases, the major remedy is in conveying the results of the LPAD to all those concerned and conclusively showing the existent gap between the capacity demonstrated in the LPAD and the manifest function of the child. Vital changes in the child's future functioning are set into motion by one or more of the following factors:

1. The child's self-concept and his future expectations are greatly enhanced by his discovery of how capable he was during the course of the LPAD.
2. Teachers are able to work far more effectively with children once they are informed of the nature of the problems that the child was able to solve in the LPAD assessment—abilities that the child had never demonstrated in the classroom.
3. Parents, guardians, teachers, youth leaders, etc., change their expectations and their attitudes toward such children when they become convinced that the children have potentials that are far higher than they ever imagined. Interactive patterns between the child and the "significant others" change, permitting a different communication to take place between them.
4. Prescriptive remediational programs are instituted, aiming at long-term changes in areas proved to be modifiable within the dynamic assessment situation.

In a great number of cases, of which the presented studies are an illustration, the Learning Potential Assessment Device had demonstrated its value in formulating the discrepancy between the manifest level of functioning of the child and his true capacity, as reflected in the dynamic assessment situation. The modifiability achieved in the Learning Potential Assessment Device has become a source of change in the educational policy, goals, methods, and expectations set for the culturally deprived child.

CHAPTER 7 **Testing the LPAD Model:** *Methodology for Research on Cognitive Modifiability*

The previous chapters have been concerned with describing the Learning Potential Assessment Device (LPAD) model and its application to individual and group assessment of low cognitive functioning. In this chapter, we return to the model upon which the LPAD is based to illustrate how its various parameters may be manipulated to render a more accurate assessment of cognitive modifiability and to provide the information necessary to bring about changes in the cognitive functioning of the retarded performer.

It will be recalled from Chapter 2 that the LPAD model differs from conventional psychometric tests along four dimensions: the structure of the test instruments, the nature of the test situation and procedures, the process as opposed to product orientation, and the interpretation of results. The model itself allows for variation in terms of modalities of presentation, different kinds of operations, and levels of complexity.

Apart from its purely clinical application, the LPAD model also can be used to generate many research hypotheses. We are currently involved in exploring some of the issues provoked by the model. This chapter does not present final answers to any questions but rather describes the kinds of questions to which answers are needed if the LPAD model is to be exploited to its full potential. Although the research described here is still at a preliminary stage, it is important to present to the reader our basic research paradigm. In this way, it should become clear that many issues require investigation and that considerable research is required to answer the question of how we can most efficiently produce and measure cognitive modifiability. To this end we are concerned with investigating the following issues:

The extent to which the low performer is able to solve a given problem and grasp the underlying principles governing its solution

Identifying the locus of difficulty in terms of input, elaboration, and output processes

The impact of modalities of presentation on performance

Determining the preferential training strategies for the remediation of specific difficulties

Assessing the extent of investment necessary to produce meaningful change

The differential effects of training on individuals performing at different levels and manifesting various kinds of difficulties

The extent to which newly acquired principles are successfully applied in solving problems that become progressively more different from the initial one

In general, our ongoing research paradigm is intended to provide refinements in our assessment techniques, a reliable means of measuring cognitive modifiability, and information upon which prescriptive training strategies may be designed that will provide the structural changes necessary to produce a permanent state of cognitive modifiability.

All our research and clinical work has indicated that, with very few exceptions, children who for a variety of reasons are classified as retarded or low performers are able to become modified and improve their current levels of functioning. The major question guiding our research is how to increase the level of functioning. In terms of our process-oriented approach, this means that attempts must be made to establish the nature of the difficulty. The LPAD model distinguishes between difficulties on the periphery of the mental act, that is, at the input and output phases, and those involving the elaborational processes. Thus, it is necessary to investigate whether a resistance to learning may be differentially related to difficulties at the peripheral rather than at the central elaborative phase. On the basis of our experience, we have hypothesized that the major resistance to learning occurs at the input and output phases. Once these difficulties are overcome, problems of elaboration, such as the proper execution of logical operations, are far less resistant to change.

This hypothesis was one of the major considerations in the initial design of our research and construction of materials.

Another major consideration implicit in the LPAD model concerns the modality of presentation of a given task. Thus, for tasks involving the same operation, differential performance may result, depending on whether a verbal, figural, numerical or other modality of presentation is used. This is a particularly important issue because it has implications not only from a diagnostic point of view but also with regard to prescriptive teaching. Individuals may respond better to one modality than another and may require more investment in certain kinds of modalities. In designing our research we were concerned with whether or not different modalities produce differential performance. Consequently, provision was made for the assessment of possible differential performance on similar tasks presented in different modalities.

Of particular importance in the planning of remedial strategies is the relative efficiency of different training techniques. The basic question in this regard is whether or not training as such produces beneficial effects. This question cannot be divorced from the issue of whether different kinds of training are superior to a condition of no training. It is possible that certain kinds of training may not only fail to prove beneficial but may even prove detrimental to improving performance. For example, children with poor verbal skills may become more confused when trained exclusively by verbal techniques. Following this question, it is of course of the greatest importance to attempt to determine which kinds of training are likely to prove most successful. This is a complex question inasmuch as many factors are likely to interact with a given training strategy. For example, a particular task or operation may respond better to specific kinds of training. The modality, extent, and quality of investment and the level of functioning of the individual may all influence the outcome of specific training strategies, either independently but more likely in interaction with one another. Despite the complexity of a given task, it is important to identify those factors associated with successful training so that prescriptive instructional techniques may be developed.

Although we hope eventually to be able to provide answers to the problem of preferential training, our initial research was less ambitious. Clearly, to test the efficiency of different training strategies, not only are the qualitative differences among the strategies important but the amount of time necessary to produce change must also be considered. As an initial probe, we decided to limit the quantity of training to a minimum and to focus on the more general issue of whether different training strategies yield different results, given the constraints of time and the group testing procedure. In this context, we were less concerned with the specific effect of a particular strategy than with establishing a kind of base line of differential performance given a minimum of training.

As is evident from the above discussion, the research effort necessary to provide answers to the questions raised is considerable. Our research to date has been largely devoted to some of the more basic issues previously discussed. However, our main concern has been to identify the issues and to develop a long-range research plan. This chapter reports some of the methods we have used and any appropriate results obtained. It must be emphasized, however, that our results at this stage are tentative. Any conclusion that may be drawn is intended to guide future research, and in this sense our research should be interpreted as a pilot stage.

The first step in our research program involved the construction of a suitable instrument with which to test our hypotheses. Account had to be taken of the fact that tests appropriate for individual administration would not necessarily be suitable for the self-administered group testing necessitated by large-scale research methods. The operation of analogical thinking was selected as a criterion measure because it is basic to cognitive functioning and is involved in the B_8–B_{12} tasks of Raven's Matrices, upon which the LPAD Variations I are based (see Chapter 3). In addition, analogical thinking plays a major role in many other tests of intelligence.

The instrument we designed is called the Analogies Test, and its items are presented to the examinee in two languages, verbal and figural. A description of this test and the theoretical considerations underlying its construction is followed by a presentation of first a pilot study and then a more in-depth experiment exploring how we used the Analogies Test to answer some of the issues outlined above.

RESEARCH CONSIDERATIONS

True Analogies vs. Quasi-Analogies

In any discussion of analogical thinking, a distinction must be made between true analogies and quasi-analogies. True analogical reasoning requires the extraction of a relationship in one realm, construction of a closely equivalent relationship in another realm, and a careful inspection to see that both relationships are closely matched (Willner, 1964). In addition to the inference of a relationship that exists between an ordered pair of terms and its application to another ordered pair, Levinson and Carpenter (1974) noted that the logical structure of true analogies parallels that of a statement of proportionality. They cited Lunzer's (1965) example, "Bird is to air as fish is to _____ (water)," to show that the "words are united by appropriate relationships in two directions, bird:air = fish:water, and bird:fish = air:water. This structure parallels a mathematical proportion such as $3:4 = 15:20$ and $3:15 = 4:20$." (p. 857).

True analogies differ from quasi-analogies in three respects. "Quasi-analogies"[1] have a grammatic structure that is absent in true analogies, and [2] they do not have the characteristics of a statement of proportion. For example, in the analogy 'a bird uses air; a fish uses _____ (water)', the order of the words is fixed. The problem cannot be presented as: 'a bird uses fish; air uses _____ (water)'. In addition, [3] the quasi-analogy appears to reveal the relationship between the first two stimulus words, thus eliminating the necessity for deducing the relationship" (Levinson and Carpenter, 1974, p. 857). Thus, an example of a quasi-analogy item would be, "On my head, I wear a hat. On my hand I wear a _____ (glove)."

The distinctions between a true analogy and a quasi-analogy become important in light of the basic assumption that children below the age of 12 are capable neither of true analogical reasoning nor of understanding proportionality (Inhelder and Piaget, 1958; Lunzer, 1965; Lovell and Butterworth, 1966; Chapman, 1975). It has been postulated that the analogy items in psychometric tests (Wechsler, 1949; Terman and Merrill, 1937, 1960; McCarthy and Kirk, 1961) used with children below the age of 12 are actually quasi-analogies in which the child does not have to infer the relationship but merely to apply it.

Finding the relationship between the terms is a psychological process and implies forming a connecting formula (CF) or a rule that connects items. Obviously, there may be more than one connecting formula that is appropriate for describing relationships. Shalom and Schlesinger (1972), for example, suggest that the connecting formula between tree and fruit differs in each of the following analogies:

(1) tree:fruit = cow:____(milk)   The CF may be expressed as "belongs to and is its natural product"

(2) tree:fruit = cow:____(tail)   The CF is merely "belongs to"

(3) tree:fruit = investment:____(dividend)   The CF is "yields"

A distinction therefore must be made between a tentative connecting formula and the final one that is correct and becomes the selection rule of the analogy. The selection rule reflects the logical structure of the analogy and therefore is synonymous with the final connecting formula. The difficulty finding the selection rule lies first in the distance between the initial connecting formula that is considered and the final one, and second, in the number and nature of the steps involved in arriving at the correct selection rule.

There are difficulties involved in the application of the relationship as well, for any given selection rule may have a large number of ordered pairs, and, therefore, many different ordered pairs can be constructed for which the same selection rule is applicable. In the construction of an analogy task, the usually followed format is that the left side of the ordered pairs suggests a set of some kind, called a "domain," and the right side of the analogy expresses "the range," or the items to which the rule governing the analogy may be applied.

Modalities of Presentation

As modalities for the group analogies test, we selected two of those presented in the LPAD model, the verbal and the figural. These two languages of presentation are not definitive or exhaustive, but they were selected for two reasons.

First, the verbal factor is commonly considered to be the major locus of deficiency in both of our target populations: the culturally deprived retarded performer and the educable mentally retarded. The literature describing this deficiency and its determining role in retarded performance is extensive and supported by experimental data (see Bernstein, 1960, 1961, 1971; John, 1963; Engelmann and Bereiter, 1966; Whiteman and Deutsch, 1968; Schiefelbusch and Lloyd, 1974; Anastasiow and Haynes, 1976). The use of a verbal task as a vehicle for training and measuring change in the verbal area seemed important despite the inadequate language skills of our populations. It should be remembered, however, that in devising a verbal analogies test, the comprehension and application of relationships, not the extent of vocabulary or reading level, should play the crucial role in determining the test performance of the examinee.

Second, the figural modality is of interest because of the variety of factors that influence the discrimination of figural elements. Many of these, such as spatial orientation, evaluation of size, closure, and visual transport, are known to cause difficulties in the performance of these populations and were of particular interest in our attempt to measure the modifiability of cognitive structures in our culturally deprived retarded performers.

The inventory of deficient functions, described in Chapter 2, served as building blocks for the construction of items in the figural modality and, to a lesser extent, in the verbal modality. The figural modality was, and still is, widely used in the LPAD clinical battery and, incidentally, has been a major source of data and clinical observations on the study populations described in Chapters 4 and 6.

One of the first problems with which we were confronted was the relative difficulty of the two modalities. Shalom and Schlesinger (1972) assert that verbal analogies are more difficult to solve than figural ones. To find the connecting formula of a verbal analogy involves a search through the network of semantic relationships. For figural analogies, they claim, all the required information is given in the task, and one merely has to determine what operation has been performed to turn one item into another. Shalom and Schlesinger contend that, even when words are within the vocabulary, verbal items are more dependent on cultural background than is the case for figural items, because with verbal tasks the relation has to be established between concepts already existing within a network.

Two parallel sets of analogies were produced, each using both verbal and figural modalities. In order to prevent too great a habituation to one modality of presentation, and to avoid boredom, verbal and figural items were alternated in each test. By this procedure, examinees were kept in a state of arousal and increased task-intrinsic motivation.

In accordance with the LPAD model our major interest in using the analogical operation was to isolate, as much as possible within the limits imposed by the group test situation, the elaborational dimension from other factors involved in the appropriate solution of the analogical task. As has been stated, in each mental act we can distinguish an input phase, which, in the case of verbal analogies, can be equated with decoding a written symbol and with understanding the specific meaning assigned to it within the given context. We can also distinguish an output phase, which implies the construction of a new task with the help of relationships among the data gathered at the input phase. Our goal of giving a central position to the elaboration processes was achieved by controlling for the degree of linguistic complexity on both input and output phases and the optimalization of the process of deduction of relationships and their application to other situations (see Chapter 3).

In a similar way, the figural items were constructed to optimize the possibilities of locating the success or failure in one of the three phases of the mental act through an analysis of the obtained results. Examples of figural and verbal items from the Analogies Test are provided in the Appendix.

It should be stressed, however, that the structure of the Analogies Test conforms more closely to that of the conventional psychometric test in several respects. The tasks do not represent progressive changes in the parameters of the problem. Each task differs from the other in its content and the specific rule by which it is solved. There is an alternation of verbal and figural items as opposed to the model used in constructing the LPAD variations of the matrices and other tests presented in the clinical battery. The format of the items does not vary: the domain is always given on the left, and the range, containing the missing term, is given on the right. To test whether principles acquired in the course of training and practice would be successfully applied in solving problems that are progressively different from those used in the initial testing and training, another test, the Shift, was constructed more along the lines of the LPAD model.

The Shift Test items had an analogy format different from the one followed in the Analogies Test. Some of the verbal and figural analogy "shift" items were constructed by varying the position of the missing term. In other items, more than one term was omitted, so that the examinee was required to deduce a relationship from one statement and apply it by constructing a second or third statement. A third type of item necessitated the examinee's independent construction of an analogy from a universe of alternative stimuli. Another type employed a four-sentence format: first, the completion of an analogy was required; then, the completion of this same analogy with its term changed to different positions; and finally, the construction of a new analogy based upon the relationship deduced from the initial completed statement. The examinee was also asked to use his critical skills in correcting completed analogy items, which were purposely inappropriately constructed. There is obviously a need for flexibility and generalization in the use of previously learned or experienced principles and techniques in the Shift Test items (figural and verbal examples are given in the Appendix).

Remediational Strategies

Testing the analogical operation within the LPAD dynamic model requires the introduction of remediational or instructional strategies aimed at correcting those cognitive functions that are prerequisite for the solution of analogies or proportions. It is this attempt to modify the functioning of the individual that provides information concerning the *learning potential* of the examinee. Thus, we set out to devise *both* testing and training procedures.

We constructed instructional strategies to accompany each of the two languages of presentation in an attempt to study cross-sectionally the optimal differential effectiveness of each one of the strategies in interaction with each modality. Thus, the effectiveness of a verbal learning strategy could be compared not only against the verbal post-test, but also for its effect on the figural posttest.

We also sought to determine the differential effects of various training strategies in relation to some specific characteristics of the examinee, such as level of functioning in areas related to the task or demographic characteristics. The two major instructional strategies we considered important to investigate were direct training (hereafter simply called *training*) and the teaching of some cognitive prerequisites we consider essential for proper cognitive functioning (hereafter referred to as *mediated learning*).

Training is conceived of as being limited to demonstrating directly the properties of the problem-task and the technique for its solution. By *mediated learning,* we refer to an intervention by means of which the prerequisites of learning necessary for adequate problem-solving behavior—such as rules and strategies at the elaboration phase and functions at the input and output phases of the mental act—become instrumental in modifying the level of functioning of an individual. Such modification is conceived of as having more pervasive effects on the individual's performance than sheer task-bound training. Mediated learning focuses on correcting deficient functions such as blurred sweeping perception, lack of stable systems of spatial and temporal reference, an inability to use two sources of information concomitantly, a lack of spontaneous comparative behavior, an inability to project relationships, and impulsivity in both the input and the output phases. It encourages the establishment of proper attitudes and reinforces motivation by interpreting the meaning of his success to the examinee. (For a more detailed explanation of mediated learning, see Feuerstein and Rand, 1973; Feuerstein, in press.)

A comparison between these two remediational strategies allows us to ask and, hopefully, to answer some important questions about the relative effectiveness of training children in a direct way to solve a certain type of problem as opposed to teaching them *general strategies of thinking* that might prove to be even more useful in solving analogies, as well as being applicable to all problem solving and to orderly thinking, in general. (Examples of both training and mediated learning are given in the Appendix.)

Our preliminary research was guided by three broad questions:

1. To what extent can retarded performing adolescents solve "true" analogical problems presented in verbal and figural modalities?
2. To what extent can one modify, by remedial investment, a low level of functioning in the area of analogical thinking?

3. To what extent are the results obtained after instruction influenced by the specific nature of the training strategies?

THE PILOT STUDY

Test Construction

We set out to construct two parallel group tests of verbal and figural analogies that would yield reliable measures of analogical thinking. About 100 verbal analogy items of the form "A:B = C:?" were produced by six researchers. To meet the criterion that the vocabulary used in the items should be basic to a child's language, high frequency words were selected from Balgur's frequency list of words in children's fiction (Balgur, 1968). These analogies were grouped into categories of relationship such as synonyms, antonyms, locations, whole-part, and function. They were then divided into 10 sets of 10 items each and matched in difficulty as judged by the vote of the six item-constructors. Several types of analogical relationships of increasing levels of difficulty were included in each set. Six booklets, each containing two sets of items, were compiled, with two of the sets repeated, each in a different booklet.

Each item was made up of a four-term analogical statement, with the fourth term to be selected by the examinee from six possible responses that included the correct completion term and five distractors (see Guttman and Schlesinger, 1967). The distractors included two responses that were nearly correct, employing the appropriate relationship that did not completely conform to the constraints of the given analogy item; one that related to term B of the analogy; another that related to term C of the analogy; and one that related in some way to all three given terms of the analogy item (Figure 66).

Similarly, 100 figural analogy items were devised and divided into 20 sets of five items each. Each set was homogeneous in that it dealt with the same two spatial figural relationships. The items within each set were arranged, insofar as possible, to provide a parallel increase in complexity over the five items. The figural items each included a four-term analogical statement similar to the verbal items. The five distractors included one response close to correct, two that had the same elements within an inappropriate relationship, a fourth that related to term B of the analogical statement, and finally one that was made up of a combination of elements from both rows of the task. This system for devising figural distractors was approximately the same as that for devising verbal distractors (Figure 67).

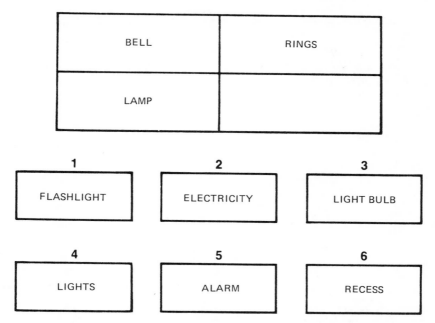

Figure 66.   Sample verbal analogy.

Six test booklets, each containing 20 verbal and 20 figural items, were assembled from the 100 verbal and figural analogies. The verbal and figural items were alternated in each booklet. Half the booklets started with verbal items and half with figural items.

The Shift Test had a total of 50 items, with verbal and figural items alternated in sets of three. The administration of the Shift Test to the study population enabled us to determine whether any of our treatments differentially affected flexibility and generalization. The Shift Test did not include items used in any of the previous tests. It was presented to the examinees immediately after they completed the Analogies posttest for the purpose of assessing the use of pre-requisite cognitive functions (for example, comparison, categorization, summation, deduction of relationships) learned and practiced during the previous training and testing.

Test Population

The subjects for the pilot evaluation of the analogy tests were drawn from the sixth grades of all the elementary schools in an Israeli development town. The town schools contained mainly native-born Israelis or immigrant children who were totally educated in Israel. This community was considered representative of the populations of

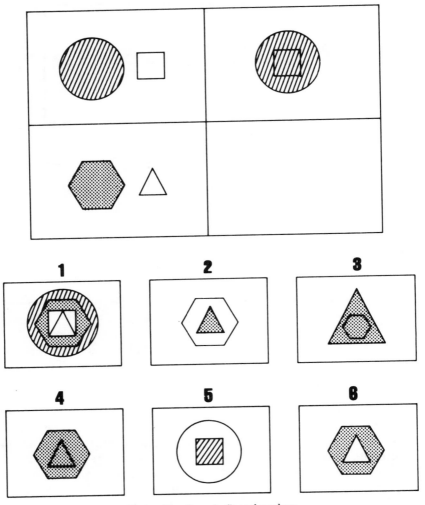

Figure 67.   Sample figural analogy.

development towns that contain a large number of culturally deprived children.

We selected sixth graders for our population as Piagetian theory suggests that normal 11- to 12-year-olds should be at the stage of cognitive development that we felt would be similar to that of the culturally deprived 14- to 16-year-olds with whom we customarily work. In all, 386 students served as subjects in the pilot study, with each subject completing two of the six forms of the pilot test. Thus, each form was completed by 113–147 students.

Test Items

Selection   The reuse of 20 verbal and 20 figural items in the pilot testing allowed us to determine that the level of difficulty for the 40 items was highly stable ($r = .94$). It was also found that the order of presentation, with either verbal or figural items first, did not affect performance.

The data from the pilot study underwent an item analysis by both small space analysis and multidimensional scalogram analysis (Lingoes, 1965, 1968). These analyses were used to select 40 verbal and 40 figural items out of a total of 200.

A difficulty level score was obtained by computing the percentage of correct answers for each item. Test booklets in the pilot study had a mean difficulty score of 60% (that is, on the average, 60% of the population did not solve the test items) with a standard deviation of 20%. The criterion for scoring was based upon the number of correct answers obtained by the examinee without a time limit. We had two major reasons for selecting a power rather than time criterion.

First, culturally deprived children have an approach to time that is different from that of typical middle-class children. Therefore, a speed test would have impeded the attainment of our major goal, the assessment of the *full* potential of the examinee. A time limitation has an even more deleterious effect upon the motivation and composure of the disadvantaged child, who rapidly becomes frustrated when he cannot complete a given task. Our second reason for rejecting a time criterion was to enable the examinee to become familiar with the test tasks, which are usually strange to him and only slowly understood. Disregarding the time factor is vital to the elimination of irrelevant difficulties. This is essential for a complete assessment of each child's elaborative capacities.

The examiners therefore were instructed to give the examinee all the time he needed and to encourage him to slow down and to invest the time and effort necessary to solve the problems. We anticipated that this approach would relax the children and encourage them to adopt a more thoughtful approach to the tasks.

Difficulty   In constructing the final versions of the test, we included some easier items to promote an initial feeling of success. This was especially necessary for the low functioning subjects who were concerned about their possible failure. On the other hand, it was necessary to have sufficient variation to permit gains on the posttest to prevent the occurrence of a ceiling effect. Therefore, we decided to construct the final test booklets so that the average difficulty score would be about 50%, with a standard deviation of about 20%.

Order   In the majority of psychometric tests, items are arranged in ascending order of difficulty. There are a number of reasons for this, the most important of which is the convention of terminating the test after the examinee has failed a certain number of items. The assumption is, of course, that because the items are arranged in a hierarchy, future success is highly unlikely after a certain number of failures, particularly when time is limited. However, as we have already pointed out, the performance of our study population is very unpredictable and the examinee may often solve difficult problems after failing much easier ones. This is especially true when the various sources of failure are located in the input or output phases, rather than the elaboration phase, or when the examinee is unfamiliar with the content. We decided, therefore, to distribute the difficult items among the easier ones throughout the test and, by so doing, to avoid the deleterious effects of continuous failure during any part of the test, even at its end.

Test Subscales

The total score reflects the manifest level of functioning of the examinee. Items also can be broken down into a number of subscales, each of which reflects a particular category of analogical relationships. Each subscale has five items, differing in degree of complexity. Qualitative characteristics, such as complexity or the type of operation required for the appropriate solution of an item, are also noted. This type of qualitative analysis is mainly used for clinical purposes in individual and group assessment.

Parallel Forms

Because the research design required a pre- and a posttest, two parallel forms were produced. In the posttest, each child was given the parallel form of the test to which he had been previously exposed, thus reducing the effects of practice. In addition, to prevent copying in the crowded classroom during testing, the two forms were distributed alternately to neighboring children. In the pilot study, the correlation between the two parallel forms was .86.

THE EXPERIMENT

Demographic Data

During the pretest stage, descriptive demographic data were gathered by questionnaire, and a base line of the manifest cognitive performance of the study population was established using the MILTA Verbal Intelligence Test (Ortar, 1966) and the verbal and figural Analogies Test.

We examined 856 students from 56 classes drawn from 12 schools in different areas of the country. Forty-three classes were taken from 10 day centers, and the remaining 13 classes came from two residential settings for low functioning, culturally deprived adolescents. The students at the day centers were mainly drop-outs from regular schools, and their study program was essentially geared to prevocational training. In the residential settings, a 2-year special program was designed to prepare students for reintegration into normal and vocationally oriented high schools.

In the course of the experiment, which lasted nearly 3 months, new students joined the classes and others were absent during one of the stages. For research purposes, only the 551 students who participated in the pretest, treatment, and posttest stages were considered. The scores of the final sample were slightly higher than those of the original larger population, but not significantly so. The attrition rate was more or less evenly distributed across treatment groups.

The total study population was composed of 78% boys and 22% girls, and the control group contained 88% boys and 12% girls. There were slight differences in the male-female ratio between treatment groups. The average age of the study population was 15 years, 3 months (S.D. = .94). Despite the large age span between individuals (13–17 years), there were only minor age differences between groups, with the highest deviation from the average for the whole study population not exceeding 5 months.

Number of Children per Family   At the time of the study the number of children per family for the entire population was 5.2. The birth rate of the study population was higher by far than the average birth rate in Israel. No significant differences were found between groups, and the distributions around the mean were also similar for all groups.

Ethnic Background and Year of Immigration   The study population was composed of 52% native-born Israelis and 48% immigrants (N = 266). Of the latter, 67% were of North African origin, 16% emigrated from Asian countries, and 17% were from European countries and North America.

Immigration occurred on the average 4 years, 10 months prior to the study. There was no significant intergroup difference in the average year of immigration. The highest difference from the mean was 7 months. We may assume, therefore, that the great majority of the study population was mainly educated in the Israeli school system and exposed to its methods and educational atmosphere.

Housing Density   Housing density of the study population was relatively high, with a mean of 2.67 persons per room compared to 1.58 for the total Jewish population in Israel and 1.93 for the total Jewish population born in Asian or African countries (Statistical Abstract of Israel, 1971, p. 300).

Family Intactness   The data on family intactness are incomplete and refer only to about 80% of the total study population (N = 446). The distribution shows that 363 subjects (81%) reported some degree of family stress attributable to illness, death, divorce, chronic belligerence between parents, etc. This rate is very high and underscores the intensity of social stress characteristic of our study population.

The MILTA Verbal Intelligence Test   The MILTA Verbal Intelligence Test (Ortar, 1966) was administered to all of the subjects and provided a general description of the population. This test is composed of four subtests: vocabulary, sentence completion, arithmetic, and concept formation. From the raw scores of subtests, an IQ score is computed on the basis of Israeli norms.

Table 21 presents the results obtained by the study population and each treatment group on the subtests of the MILTA, expressed in means and in percentages of the maximum possible score. The subjects scored best on the arithmetic subtest and worst on the concept formation subtest, which is most similar to the tasks involved in the Analogies Test. In terms of the demographic information and performance on the MILTA IQ test, the study population could be described as high risk.

To determine the position of the study population in terms of its level of performance on the Analogies Test, it was compared with two other populations whose level of functioning was empirically defined through diagnostic and/or school achievement criteria. The first comparison population was an upper-middle class urban group in which we examined all the children in grades two through eight. A second comparison population consisted of an urban lower-class group of grade three children. A third comparison population was formed by children in the seventh and eighth grades in special schools for those diagnosed as educable mentally retarded (EMR).

The results obtained by the different populations are presented in the Table 22. The performance of the urban upper-middle class children improves with age, reaching a plateau at about the sixth grade. The test proved difficult for grade two, ages 7–8, a result that conforms with the finding that at this development stage analogical

Table 21.   MILTA Verbal Intelligence Test scores on subtests and IQ by treatment groups: Means, mean percentage correct, and standard deviations (N = 498)

Test	Max. score	VTM (N = 49)	VM (N = 43)	VT (N = 78)	FTM (N = 62)	FM (N = 62)	FT (N = 62)	VFTM (N = 64)	C (N = 78)	Total (N = 498)
Vocabulary										
$\bar{X}$	25	10.96	9.02	8.42	8.71	7.84	8.71	8.08	8.30	8.66
%		43.84	36.08	33.68	34.84	31.36	34.84	32.32	33.20	34.64
SD		4.54	4.71	4.45	4.93	4.04	5.21	4.83	4.23	4.65
Sentence completion										
$\bar{X}$	15	6.04	4.98	5.12	5.07	4.68	4.60	4.49	4.03	4.82
%		40.27	33.20	34.13	33.80	31.20	30.67	29.93	26.87	32.13
SD		2.86	2.72	2.92	3.01	2.69	2.85	2.88	2.43	2.83
Arithmetic										
$\bar{X}$	15	8.27	8.25	7.21	7.75	7.69	7.18	6.52	7.23	7.35
%		55.13	55.00	48.07	51.67	51.27	47.87	43.47	48.20	46.67
SD		2.78	2.82	2.85	3.09	3.08	2.68	2.85	2.86	2.90
Concept formation										
$\bar{X}$	15	5.29	4.14	4.01	4.83	4.00	4.07	3.80	3.77	4.18
%		35.27	27.60	26.73	32.20	26.67	27.13	25.33	25.13	27.87
SD		2.81	2.39	2.49	2.41	2.06	2.79	2.32	2.65	2.53
IQ										
$\bar{X}$		70.12	67.76	68.37	68.12	65.92	68.15	66.45	64.51	67.27
SD		11.20	12.59	11.24	11.21	8.52	12.53	11.55	11.41	11.33

* VTM, verbal training and mediation; VM, verbal mediation; VT, verbal training; FTM, figural training and mediation; FM, figural mediation; FT, figural training; VFTM, verbal and figural training and mediation; and C, control.

operations have not been consolidated and are not stable (Inhelder and Piaget, 1958). The test discriminated efficiently among individuals in the age range of 8 or 9 to 12. Beyond this age, the test items seemed too easy for this population, and therefore a ceiling effect limited the discriminative power of the test for these subjects. The comparison between the results of the study population and those obtained by the urban middle-class group underscores the low manifest level of functioning of the study population, whose ages ranged from 13 to 17 and whose results are comparable to those of middle-class third graders, age 9.

The magnitude of the gap in the manifest functioning between the two groups strongly confirms our findings in previous studies (Feuerstein and Richelle, 1957; Feuerstein, 1970b), and those of other researchers in this field (e.g., Ortar, 1960). This gap is also reflected in the low average IQ ($\bar{X}$ = 67) found in the study population by the MILTA Verbal Intelligence Test. It is opportune to remind the reader that we consider these data to reflect only the

Table 22. Pretest scores on Analogies Test (verbal, figural): Means and standard deviations for the study population (N = 551) compared with urban, middle, and low classes and urban special schools (N = 406)

Population	Grade	Age	N	Verbal (max. score, 20)		Figural (max. score, 20)		Total (V+F) (max. score, 40)	
				X̄	SD	X̄	SD	X̄	SD
Experimental (treatment and control groups)		13–17	551	11.47	4.52	10.88	4.73	22.35	6.50
Urban, upper-	2	8	35	4.5	3.79	4.8	3.07	9.30	4.88
middle class	3	9	36	11.9	4.40	10.3	4.3	22.20	6.13
school	4	10	40	14.4	3.39	12.3	3.64	26.70	4.97
	5	11	30	14.9	4.1	13.3	4.2	28.20	5.87
	6	12	34	17.4	2.3	15.9	2.3	33.30	3.40
	7	13	42	17.7	1.9	15.2	2.7	32.90	3.30
	8	14	36	18.2	1.9	15.6	1.9	33.80	3.04
Urban lower- class school	3	9	62	6.92	3.24	5.31	3.65	12.23	4.88
EMR special	7	13	41	7.90	3.46	6.46	3.92	14.36	5.25
school	8	14	50	9.34	4.51	8.38	4.31	17.72	6.24

manifest level of functioning of the children in this particular testing situation and that one cannot infer from this their true potential to become modified by proper strategies.

A further comparison can be made on the basis of Table 22 between third-grade children of an urban lower-class school who, though younger, are essentially similar in demographic and achievement characteristics to our study population and their middle-class peers. Their level of functioning, though meaningfully higher than the results obtained by younger, more advantaged second-grade students, is considerably lower than that of their third-grade advantaged peers.

A comparison between the EMR population of seventh and eighth graders drawn from a special school and their urban and middle-class peers shows an increase by age for the EMR population as contrasted with the results obtained by the regular group of the same ages and grades, in which the change was negligible.

The difference between our experimental population and the EMR children reflects the wider range of deficiencies found in children placed in special schools for the EMR where lower educational goals are set.

Assignment to Levels and Treatments On the basis of the mean scores obtained on the Analogies pretest, levels were created by ranking the classroom means of performance and dividing them into six groups ranging from a high of 1 to a low of 6. Using a table of random numbers, classrooms of any given level were assigned to treatment groups so that in each treatment group all levels of initial functioning were represented. This procedure seemed the most appropriate, given the necessity of implementing the different treatments into already existing classrooms (Lindquist, 1953).

The research design included a study of the differential effects of various training strategies. Seven different kinds of training were provided, and a condition of no training was included to serve as a control. A description of the various kinds of training is provided in the Appendix. All the students in a given class received the same kind of training. The design provided for eight different treatment groups as follows:

1. Verbal training (VT)
2. Verbal mediated learning (VM)
3. Verbal training and mediated learning (VTM)
4. Figural training (FT)
5. Figural mediated learning (FM)
6. Figural training and mediated learning (FTM)
7. Verbal and figural training and mediated learning (VFTM)
8. Controls (CN)

Two months after the pretest, all of the groups, except the controls, were exposed to their assigned treatment in a session lasting from one to two school class periods. For a full description of the different treatments, see the Appendix.

The Posttest Stage   Two to three weeks after the treatment session, posttests were administered. The testing included the verbal and figural Analogies Test and the Shift Test. Each subject was tested on a version parallel to that to which he was exposed on the pretest. The Shift Test was administered only at the posttest stage and only after the other measures had been completed.

Results and Discussion

The means and standard deviations obtained by the different treatment groups for the verbal and figural Analogies Test and verbal and figural Shift Test are provided in Tables 23 and 24. No significant differences were found between the control and combined treatment groups for the Analogies pretest. For the Analogies posttest significant differences were obtained between the control and combined treatment groups (verbal, $t = 2.81$, $p < .01$; figural, $t = 3.1$, $p < .01$), and for the Shift Test a significant difference was obtained for the figural subtest ($t = 2.58$, $p < .01$) but not for the verbal subtest.

In order to assess the contribution of demographic variables, intelligence subtest scores, and pretest scores on the Analogies posttest, stepwise multiple regression analyses were conducted. The

Table 23. Analogies Test (verbal, figural, and total): Means and standard deviations, pre and post, by treatment groups based upon total study population (N = 551)

Treatments*	N	Verbal (max. score, 20)				Figural (max. score, 20)				Total (V+F)			
		Pre		Post		Pre		Post		Pre		Post	
		$\bar{X}$	SD	$\bar{X}$	SD	$\bar{X}$	SD	$\bar{X}$	SD	$\bar{X}$	SD	$\bar{X}$	SD
VTM	63	11.77	4.63	13.39	4.42	11.70	4.76	13.44	4.58	23.47	6.64	26.83	6.36
VM	51	11.31	4.29	12.74	4.17	9.88	4.25	12.11	4.68	21.19	6.04	24.85	6.27
VT	81	11.74	4.63	12.78	4.66	11.05	4.70	12.50	4.78	22.79	4.85	25.38	6.68
FTM	62	12.35	4.64	14.00	4.07	11.56	5.26	13.27	4.56	23.91	7.01	27.27	6.11
FM	68	11.25	4.11	12.55	4.08	10.82	4.77	11.80	3.96	22.07	6.30	23.35	5.69
FT	69	11.34	4.71	12.42	4.57	10.78	4.87	12.82	4.83	22.12	6.77	25.24	6.65
VFTM	64	11.06	4.82	12.90	3.92	10.89	4.53	12.85	4.68	21.95	6.61	25.75	6.10
Total treatment	458	11.55	4.55	12.95	4.30	10.98	4.75	12.68	4.59	22.53	6.58	25.36	6.29
C	93	11.05	4.32	11.63	4.14	10.34	4.61	11.07	4.51	21.39	6.32	22.70	6.12

* VTM, verbal training and mediation; VM, verbal mediation; VT, verbal training; FTM, figural training and mediation; FM, figural mediation; FT, figural training; VFTM, verbal and figural training and mediation; and C, control.

Table 24.   Shift Test verbal, figural, and total: Means and standard deviations, post testing by treatment groups based upon total study population (N = 520)

Treatment*	N	Verbal (max. score, 25)		Figural (max. score, 25)		Total	
		X̄	SD	X̄	SD	X̄	SD
VTM	59	19.57	7.42	21.84	7.64	41.41	10.65
VM	51	18.41	6.92	18.64	8.56	37.05	11.01
VT	70	19.12	6.35	19.87	7.29	38.99	9.67
FTM	61	18.88	7.43	20.49	8.37	39.37	11.19
FM	68	17.32	6.26	16.89	7.95	34.21	10.12
FT	60	17.60	7.45	19.16	7.68	36.76	10.70
VFTM	60	17.76	7.87	18.65	7.19	36.41	10.65
Total treatment	429	18.37	7.07	19.34	7.79	37.71	10.49
C	91	16.94	6.77	16.97	8.51	33.91	10.87

* VTM, verbal training and mediation; VM, verbal mediation; VT, verbal training; FTM, figural training and mediation; FM, figural mediation; FT, figural training; VFTM, verbal and figural training and mediation; and C, control.

results for the verbal and figural Analogies Test, provided in Tables 25 and 26, indicate that more than 50% of the posttest variance is accounted for by the Analogies pretest scores themselves. None of the intelligence measures or demographic variables appear to contribute meaningfully to the multiple correlation coefficient.

The posttest scores were analyzed by means of analysis of variance tests using a randomized block design in which the

Table 25.   Multiple regression analysis: Controlled variables contributing significantly to posttest variance on verbal Analogies Test (study population, N = 551)

Step	Controlled variable	Accum. R^2	F for each separate step
1	Pre: Verbal Analogies	0.459	466.12*
2	Pre: Figural Analogies	0.546	104.42*
3	Milta: Sentence completion	0.569	30.16*
4	Milta: Arithmetic	0.582	16.17*
5	Sex	0.590	10.72*
6	Milta: Vocabulary	0.596	7.97*
7	Milta: Similarities (dummy)	0.601	6.36†
8	Family intactness (dummy)	0.604	4.94†
9	Family intactness	0.607	4.48†
10	Test form	0.610	4.18†
11	Placement (residential vs. nonresidential)	0.613	3.93†
12	Others	0.619	

* Significant at the 0.01 level or better.

† Significant at the 0.05 level.

Table 26.   Multiple regression analysis: Controlled variables contributing significantly to posttest variance on figural Analogies Test (study population, N = 551)

Step	Controlled variable	Accum. R^2	F for each separate step
1	Pre: Figural	0.521	597.71*
2	Pre: Verbal	0.575	69.06*
3	Test form	0.591	21.37*
4	Milta: Vocabulary (dummy)	0.596	7.42*
5	Milta: Similiarities	0.602	7.73*
6	Family intactness	0.605	3.95†
7	Number of children (dummy)	0.608	4.78†
8	Others	0.615	—

* Significant at the 0.01 level or better.

† Significant at the 0.05 level.

classroom mean serves as the unit of analysis (Lindquist, 1953; Edwards, 1965). Because each class had been assigned to a treatment and level, the resulting analyses comprised eight treatments and six levels, with the mean score for each class entered in each cell. The error term in this design is the level × treatment interaction, and its use is based on the assumption that the interaction will not be significant. Despite the fact that our pretest evaluation indicated differently, we nevertheless pursued the analysis because the significance of the interaction would only influence the results in the direction of the null hypothesis; consequently, our analyses are more conservative than they otherwise might be. The mean scores by treatment and levels are provided in Tables 27 and 28 for the verbal and

Table 27.   Analogies Test: Posttest class means by treatments

Verbal		Figural	
Treatment*	$\bar{X}$	Treatment*	$\bar{X}$
FTM	13.64	FTM	13.35
VT	13.18	VTM	12.77
VTM	13.04	VFTM	12.70
VFTM	12.71	VT	12.45
VM	12.53	FT	12.15
FM	12.41	FM	11.62
FT	12.10	VM	11.49
C	11.17	C	10.62

* FTM, figural training and mediation; VT, verbal training; VTM, verbal training and mediation; VFTM, verbal and figural training and mediation; VM, verbal mediation; FM, figural mediation; FT, figural training; and C, control.

Table 28. Analogies Test: Posttest class
means by levels

Level	Verbal	Figural
1 (high)	15.20	14.95
2	14.55	13.65
3	12.39	12.46
4	12.82	11.96
5	11.46	11.42
6 (low)	9.15	8.43

figural Analogies subtests. The results of separate analyses of variance tests for the verbal and figural Analogies posttest scores are presented in Tables 29 and 30. In both cases the levels and treatment effects yielded significant differences beyond the .05 level.

Further analyses were conducted to establish individual differences between the treatments by means of t tests using the treatment $\times$ levels-mean-square as the unbiased estimate of the common variance. The results of these analyses are presented in Table 31. For the verbal analogies, four significant differences between treatments emerged, three of them between the control group and other specific treatment groups. For the figural analogies, seven differences proved significant, five of which were between the control and the treatment groups. The most striking feature of the results in Table 31 was the fact that most of the significant differences between the treatment groups involved the superior performance of combined training, that is, treatments in which both direct and mediated learning were used. Given the rather severe time limitations of the training, these results are not altogether unexpected. What is more surprising is that only one period of training produced significantly better results in some cases than did the control condition of no specific training at all.

The mean scores on the verbal and figural Shift subtests for each treatment group are provided in Table 32, and the results of analyses of variance using the classroom mean as the unit of analysis are reported in Tables 33 and 34. Although significant differences between levels were obtained for both subtests, no differences emerged between the treatment groups.

Table 29. Verbal Analogies Test: Analysis of variance of
posttest scores (class mean as unit)

Source	Sum of squares	df	Mean square	F	Sig.
Levels (L)	190.48	5	38.10	38.94	$p < 0.001$
Treatment (T)	23.63	7	3.38	3.45	$p < 0.01$
L $\times$ T (E)	34.24	35	0.98		
Total	248.35	47			

Table 30.   Figural Analogies Test: Analysis of variance of
posttest scores (class mean as unit)

Source	Sum of squares	df	Mean square	F	Sig.
Levels (L)	196.37	5	39.27	22.80	$p < 0.001$
Treatment (T)	31.51	7	4.50	2.61	$p < 0.05$
L × R (E)	60.29	35	1.72		
Total	288.16	47			

As the reader compares results for the Analogies and the Shift
Tests, he should recall that the maximum score for the verbal and
figural Analogies subtests is 20 and for the Shift, 25. To facilitate
comparison of the performance on the Analogies and Shift Tests, the
total mean percentage of correct answers is provided in Table 35.
From the table it is evident that the subjects' performance on the
Shift Test was considerably better than on the Analogies Test. This
result, however, needs to be interpreted with caution. Although none
of the specific training techniques appeared to significantly influence
performance on the Shift Test, two factors should be taken into
consideration. First, the Shift Test was administered after the pre-
and postadministration of the Analogies Test. Consequently,
considerable learning may have taken place simply as a result of
doing the Analogies Test. A second and related point is that the Shift
Test is deliberately constructed to promote training by emphasizing
the common operation of analogical thinking while varying the
format of each item. Taken together, these two factors may well have
blurred the effects of any specific training, given the short exposure
to the different training techniques. Clearly, before any conclusion
may be drawn regarding the influence of the structure of the test on

Table 31.   Analogies Test: Significant differences between
treatment groups

Verbal		Figural	
Treatment*	Sig.	Treatment*	Sig.
VTM > C	$(p < 0.01)$	VTM > C	$(p < 0.01)$
FTM > C	$(p < 0.01)$	FTM > C	$(p < 0.01)$
FTM > FT	$(p < 0.05)$	FTM > VM	$(p < 0.05)$
VT > C	$(p < 0.01)$	FTM > FM	$(p < 0.05)$
		VT > C	$(p < 0.05)$
		FT > C	$(p < 0.05)$
		VFTM > C	$(p < 0.05)$

* VTM, verbal training and mediation; FTM, figural training and
mediation; FT, figural training; VT, verbal training; VFTM, verbal and
figural training and mediation; and C, control.

Table 32. Shift Test: Posttest class means by treatments

Verbal		Figural	
Treatment*	$\bar{\text{X}}$	Treatment*	$\bar{\text{X}}$
FTM	18.73	FTM	20.84
VTM	18.67	VTM	19.61
VT	18.60	VT	19.50
FM	18.48	VM	18.44
VM	18.19	VFTM	18.44
VFTM	17.89	FT	18.22
C	16.78	FM	17.24
FT	16.75	C	16.96

* FTM, figural training and mediation; VTM, verbal training and mediation; VT, verbal training; FM, figural mediation; VM, verbal mediation; VFTM, verbal and figural training and mediation; and C, control.

performance, additional control groups will have to be introduced into the design to eliminate the effects of prior experience.

The above results must be interpreted in the light of the limited training provided to the subjects. As stated previously, the amount of training necessary to produce changes, especially of a differential nature, is an important variable. For this reason we felt constrained to initiate our research program by providing only a minimum of training. On this basis, our results suggest the following tentative conclusions.

First, low performing individuals are able to grasp the underlying principles governing analogical thinking, and even very limited training produces an improvement in performance. Second, it would appear that the acquired principles are successfully applied to the solution of problems that are progressively different from those used in the initial testing and training. Third, different training strategies do produce differential performance. In this respect, given the limited exposure to different training strategies the combined treatment groups appear more successful than either the direct or mediated strategies on their own. It is more than likely that different

Table 33. Verbal Shift Test: Analysis of variance (class mean as unit)

Source	Sum of squares	df	Mean square	F	Sig.
Levels (L)	444.10	5	88.82	13.59	$p < 0.01$
Treatment (T)	29.59	7	4.23	0.65	NS
L × T (E)	228.80	35	6.54		
Total	702.47	47			

Table 34. Figural Shift Test: Analysis of variance (class mean as unit)

Source	Sum of squares	df	Mean square	F	Sig.
Levels (L)	605.41	5	121.08	16.44	$p < 0.01$
Treatment (T)	69.28	7	9.90	1.34	NS
L × T (E)	257.83	35	7.37		
Total	932.51	47			

kinds of training will interact with the amount of such training. In addition, it is likely that individuals performing at different levels and manifesting various kinds of difficulties will respond differently to specific training techniques. For all these reasons, judgment should be deferred concerning the influence of training strategies on performance until the necessary research has been completed.

EXTENDING THE EXPERIMENT

One immediate outgrowth of the above findings was to extend our baseline data to include an age dimension. We were interested in investigating the effects of training on third-grade culturally deprived children. On the basis of our results for the upper-middle class second to eight grade children (see Table 36), it was apparent that the Analogies Test was able to discriminate among third graders. We selected a group of 56 children functioning at very low levels of performance from the third grade of a school serving a community with demographic characteristics similar to those described above for the preceding study. After the pretest administration of the Analogies Test, the children received three to four class periods of training, substantially more than provided in the earlier experiment. Because our preliminary findings indicated that combined training was most effective, we selected the verbal and figural training and mediated procedure (VFTM), as described in the Appendix. After the completion of the training, the subjects were retested, and 2 months later a further retest ("post-post" test) was carried out to assess the stability of any training effects.

Table 35. Total mean percentage of correct answers for verbal and figural subtests of the Analogies and Shift Tests

Test	Analogies		Shift	
	Verbal	Figural	Verbal	Figural
Pre	57.3	54.4	—	—
Post	63.6	62.1	72.5	75.7

Table 36.   Analogies Test: Comparison of the
performance (means and standard deviations)
of middle-class (MC) and culturally deprived
(CD) third-grade children

Subjects	N	$\bar{\text{X}}$	SD
MC	36	21.6	8.1
CD pretest	56	12.8	5.9
CD posttest	56	19.0	8.6
CD post-posttest	56	20.0	8.2

The results of the study are provided in Table 36. On the pretest, the culturally deprived group performed well below their middle-class age peers ($\bar{\text{X}}$ = 12.8 vs. $\bar{\text{X}}$ 21.6; t = 14.92, p < .001). After training, the posttest scores ($\bar{\text{X}}$ = 19.0) revealed a dramatic and significant improvement (t = 4.19, p < .001). The initial gap between the culturally deprived and middle-class groups was virtually closed, and the post-post scores indicate that the improvement appeared to persist although the further increase in performance was not statistically significant.

These results provide three interesting observations. First, even as early as the third grade rather moderate intervention appears to reverse the typical poor performance levels of the culturally deprived children to a point at which they are virtually indistinguishable from their middle-class peers. This finding should be viewed in the context of the nature of the analogy tasks, which, as pointed out, provide the basis for many cognitive operations. Second, the group administration and training, despite its diminished potency as compared with individual testing, nevertheless is an effective means of producing change. Third, the Analogies Test may be used as an effective means to discriminate manifest performance across a fairly wide ability and age range and to assess the extent of cognitive modifiability and the influence of preferential training strategies.

In addition to the above analyses, a more qualitative evaluation was undertaken with a view to better understanding some of the processes involved in the solution of analogy tests.

QUALITATIVE EVALUATIONS: EXTENSIONS AND APPLICATIONS OF THE RESEARCH

Determining Deficient Processes

One must remember that many authors have pointed out that an individual functioning at the level of 60–70 IQ will not be able to deduce the relationship between two concepts and then apply this relationship to another pair of concepts. It is our contention (see Chapter 2 on the deficient functions) that the factors responsible for this manifest low level of functioning are a series of deficient functions that do not reflect the true capacities of the individual but prevent them from displaying appropriate problem-solving behavior. Thus, a lack of appropriate exploratory behavior, a lack of need for logical evidence, and a lack of need for precision obscure an existent capacity for thought and elaborative processes. In other words, in many cases the factor determining failure in the test response is not necessarily a low level of elaboration, but the deficiencies and difficulties on the input phase that involve the processing of data required for problem solution (see Gordon and Haywood, 1969; Schwebel, and Bernstein, 1970). In order to test these hypotheses, we had to carry our analyses beyond the quantitative aspect of our results and attempt to analyze the results given and the nature of the performed errors. This may be demonstrated by one figural and one verbal item.

Figure 68 is composed of two parts. The relationship between the two figures in the upper row is one of increase in size from the first item to the second. Therefore, alternative 2 is the correct response and reflects the examinee's ability to conceptualize an existing relationship and apply it correctly to complete the analogy. The deduction of such a relationship is considered evidence of the ability for abstract thinking at the level required by the immediate task. Usually no credit is assigned for any other response, which, were it given, would be interpreted as indicating an inability of the examinee to deduce the relationship, to apply it, or to think abstractly on the level required by the item. We have found, however, that the selection of another alternative as a response may indicate that the examinee is capable of exercising adequate processes of elaboration.

In Figure 68, by choosing 6 as the response, the examinee demonstrates that he has found the relationship of transformation of size and applied it. Despite his appropriate elaboration, his failure may be attributable to one or more deficient functions affecting his mental processes. The examinee may not have paid attention to the second of the two sources of information, or he may not have magnified both components of the figure to the same extent because of the lack of need for precision. In the clinical one-to-one situation, it is only after the examiner points to response 2 and asks why 6 is not correct, and thereby directs the child's attention to a comparison of both responses (2 and 6), that the examinee is able to discover and correct his error. Thus, it emerges that failure is not in the deduction of a relationship or rule and its application in a different situation,

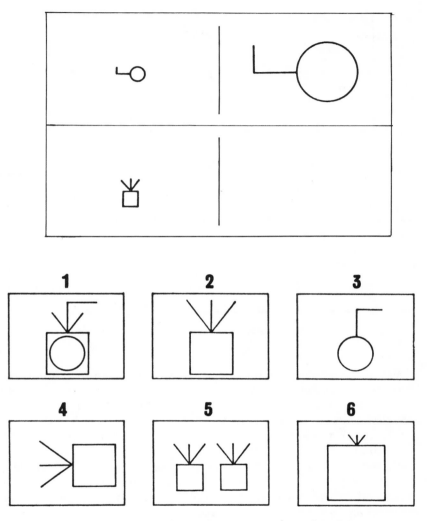

Figure 68.   Figural analogy with underlying relationship of size.

but in a specific quality of an examinee's approach to the data required for this operation.

A similar example is illustrated in the verbal modality in Figure 69. The underlying relationship can be expressed: "How do we travel on the ocean?" "By ship." The appropriate response to "How do we travel over the desert?" is, therefore, "by camel." Further scrutiny of the alternatives reveals, however, that 2, "caravan," satisfactorily fulfills the relationship. Its choice demonstrates an appropriate ana-

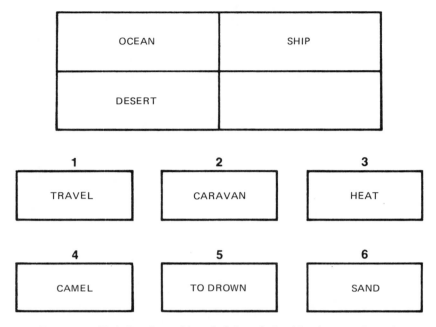

Figure 69.   Verbal analogy with underlying relationship of means of travel.

logical thought process as reflected by the deduction of a relationship between concepts and its generalization by application to another set. The choice of 2 indicates clearly that the respondent has not considered all of the components of the concept and has not discriminated between the singular of "ship" and the plurality of "caravan."

In clinical examinations, certain examinees have explained their selection of 6, "sand," by saying, "In the ocean, there are lots of ships, and in the desert there is lots of sand." Undoubtedly, even such an answer testifies to a certain level of analogical thinking. What makes this response erroneous is that the examinee has not deduced the specific relationship of a "means of travel" as distinct from any more general relationship that may exist between the two concepts.

As indicated earlier, each set of alternative responses to a given item includes one correct answer and five distractors. One of the distractors is always very nearly correct, entailing a connecting formula but lacking some detail in order to make it the sought response on the basis of the selection rule. We believe that the choice of this second-best alternative does not result from deficient elaboration but from failure at either the input or the output phases. Therefore, we developed and used two scoring procedures to take this into account.

The first score, the simple raw score (SRS), is given in the usual way of one score point for the correct answer only. The second score, the adjusted raw score (ARS), accords one score point to either of the two best answers in each task. The ARS thus should yield a higher mean score than the SRS. By means of the following formula, it is possible to calculate the percentage of incorrect responses that may be regarded as almost correct:

$$\frac{ARS - SRS \times 100}{Maximum - SRS}$$

Thus, it is apparent that more than one-third of the inadequate responses can be classified as almost correct. More precisely, 39% of the verbal Analogies Subtest and 34% of the figural Analogies subtest are almost correct answers. The difference between the two scores indicates the extent to which appropriate elaborational processes were operating together with inappropriate input and output processes. A measure of the modification of the peripheral deficient functions as a result of treatment may be expressed by the formula:

$$\frac{SRS_{post} - SRS_{pre}}{ARS_{pre} - SRS_{pre}} \times 100$$

This formula reflects the amount of correction, in percentages, of answers that were almost correct. Any score derived by this formula that is higher than 1.00 shows that there has been a full correction of the almost correct answers and additional gains by the individual.

The results for both the verbal and figural Analogies subtests by our study population are presented in Tables 37 and 38. The difference ratios of 43% for the verbal Analogies subtest and 56% for the figural Analogies subtest show that even a minimum of treatment can convert about half of the almost correct responses on the pretest into fully correct answers. This finding supports our general

Table 37. Verbal Analogies Test: Means of simple and adjusted raw scores (SRS, ARS) in pretest and posttest, treatment groups only (N = 458)

Score	Pretest	Posttest	Difference pre-post
Simple raw score	11.56	12.96	1.40
Adjusted raw score	14.84	16.02	1.18
Difference (ARS − SRS)	3.28	3.06	
Difference Ratio: $\frac{Post - Pre \ (SRS)}{ARS - SRS \ (Pre)} \frac{1.40}{3.28} = 43\%$			

Table 38.   Figural Analogies Test: Means of simple and adjusted raw scores (SRS, ARS) in pretest and posttest, treatment groups only (N = 458)

Score	Pretest	Posttest	Difference pre-post
Simple raw score	10.99	12.69	1.70
Adjusted raw score	14.04	15.48	1.44
Difference (ARS − SRS)	3.05	2.79	
Difference ratio: $\dfrac{\text{Post} - \text{Pre (SRS)}}{\text{ARS} - \text{SRS (Pre)}}$ $\dfrac{1.70}{3.05} = 56\%$			

assumption that a great part of the low performance manifested by disadvantaged populations does not reflect poor elaborative thought processes but is determined by other variables such as deficient functioning at the input or output phases.

As already pointed out, our target populations originally attained a level of functioning comparable to the third-grade children of the middle-class population. However, after treatment, on the posttest they demonstrated fourth-grade capability. Thus, we were interested to see what the relationship between the two populations would be if we compared their *ARSs instead of their SRSs*. The mean ARS pretest score was 14.48 on the verbal and 14.04 on the figural. This is comparable to the SRS of the fifth grade of the normative population. On the posttest, the ARS scores obtained by our population were 16.02 on the verbal and 15.48 on the figural, results that come very close to the average SRS obtained by the sixth graders, beyond which no differentiation occurs because of the ceiling effect of the test. This finding again reinforces our view that the elaborative ability of our population, as reflected in the thought processes required in the solution of analogical problems, is not essentially different from the advantaged group. This finding is at variance with the views of Jensen (1969) that disadvantaged groups are differentiated primarily by their deficiency in the conceptual elaborative processes, whereas simple tasks requiring only appropriate input and output (Level I type) show no differences between disadvantaged and normal populations. In order to further probe the qualitative aspects of the retarded performer's thought processes, we attempted to devise a means of comparing the differential functioning of our culturally deprived population with a normative middle-class sample.

The results obtained on the pretest have shown that the target population functioned at the same level as third graders of the urban middle-class population. This result approximated the results obtained on the MILTA verbal intelligence test. The mean IQ of 67 could be equated with a mental age of 10 years. Usually, one considers that there is still a qualitative difference between individuals of different chronological ages who have the same mental age. The older individual is considered to be of lower intelligence, even retarded, whereas the younger is of normal, average intelligence. The question raised is whether one might distinguish qualitative differences in the thought process required for solving analogical problems between the two populations, of different chronological ages and matched for their average score obtained on the analogies. Could one find in our results differences in the *structure* of their thought processes that would enable us to better understand the characteristics and the qualities of these two groups and any differences between them? It goes without saying that findings obtained by such an analysis may prove to be very important in understanding the particular deficiencies and their development in the disadvantaged group.

Determining Preferred Training Modalities

Many students in the field have pointed to the decisive role played by language in the cognitive development of the child and the role played by impaired linguistic development in the evolution of the phenomenon of retarded performance in disadvantaged populations (e.g., see Bernstein, 1961; Whiteman and Deutsch, 1968; Schiefelbusch and Lloyd, 1974). Therefore, it would not be surprising to find that the different modalities of presentation, verbal and figural, affect an examinee's level of functioning. We might assume that the advantaged child would perform better than the disadvantaged child on the verbal modality.

We might also assume that any difference that exists between the two modalities does not relate to the underlying thought process required for the solution to the analogy. In either modality the analogy might be solved with or without the help of linguistic mediators. The only difference between the two modalities, therefore, is the nature of the cue provided: in one modality, the problem is presented through verbal cues, and, in the other, through figural ones. In the first case, the examinee has to find a relationship between verbal concepts and to use their semantic space, and in the second case he has to deduce the relationship between figures by considering changes that occur in their form, orientation, number, and so forth. Common to the two modalities is the formal mental operation, that is, the deduction of a relationship and its application to the completion of the task. It is of interest, therefore, to compare the disadvantaged and the normal populations in regard to the difficulties each encounters in attempting to solve verbal and figural analogies.

The population used for this analysis was eight third- and fourth-grade classes from an urban middle-class school. The students were evaluated by the educational supervisor as functioning between the "average" and "good" level by general school standards. In this framework, we examined 138 children on one test form and 134 children on the parallel test form. This population then served as a comparison group for 551 culturally deprived adolescents in the target population.

In order to contrast the performance of the two populations on the verbal and figural tasks, it was necessary to control the level of difficulty of each test. It appeared to us that the verbal Analogies subtest was considerably easier than the figural and that this may account for the higher performance scores on it (see Table 23), and so we embarked upon the following procedures.

The percentage of correct responses for each item of the test was computed. This percentage was used to assign a difficulty level to each item. An item solved by all examinees received a difficulty level of 100%. Thus, relatively easy items were assigned a level ranging from 80% to 90%. Difficult items were assigned levels from 10% to 30%. An item unsolved by anyone received the score of 0%. Thus, an item assigned a 75% difficulty level should be understood to have been solved correctly by 75% of the population. The difficulty level of each item for each of the two populations was calculated. For example, the level of difficulty of item A-5 in the normative group was 78% and in the target population it was 71%. The difference between the two was $+7$ in favor of the normative group. The mean difference between the two groups on both the verbal and the figural subtests was calculated. The results for the pre- and posttests are presented in Tables 39 and 40, respectively.

For the pretest, the mean difference in the level of difficulty between the two populations was 9.1 for the verbal and 3.68 for the

Table 39. Comparison between culturally deprived (CD) and middle-class (MC) populations: Item difficulty for verbal and figural pretest

Item	N	Item difficulty: Difference between MC and CD pretest		t test for difference between means		
		$\bar{X}$	SD	t	df	p
Verbal	20	9.100	9.519	2.75	78	<0.01
Figural	20	3.68	7.820			

Table 40.   Comparison between culturally deprived and middle-class populations: Item difficulty for verbal and figural posttest (control group omitted)

Item	N	Item difficulty: Difference between MC and CD posttest		t test for difference between means		
		$\bar{X}$	SD	t	df	p
Verbal	20	1.33	8.720	3.09	78	<0.01
Figural	20	−4.38	7.540			

figural modality. A t test revealed that the difference between the two mean scores was significant beyond the .01 level ($t = 2.75$). For the posttest, the mean difference in the level of difficulty between the two populations was 1.33 for the verbal and −4.34 for the figural modality. Again, a t test confirmed that the two mean scores were significantly different at the .01 level ($t = 3.09$) although in this case the disadvantaged group scored higher on the figural test than the middle-class control group.

These results present an interesting picture. Initially, the middle-class group is superior to the disadvantaged group on both the verbal and figural subtests. This finding of course tells us nothing new. On the posttest, however, after only a minimum of training, the mean difference between the groups on the verbal tests is considerably reduced, from 9.1 to 1.33, and for the figural test a reversal occurs with the disadvantaged group out-performing the middle-class control group. Nevertheless, the most revealing aspect of the results is that, despite the improvement of the disadvantaged group, the gap in their functioning on the verbal and figural subtests remains virtually constant between the pre- and posttest. Although the difference in the level of functioning between the two groups appears to have disappeared, the relationship between the verbal and figural modalities of functioning for the culturally deprived group has not changed. It may be concluded that, although the treatment was effective in raising the general level of functioning, it did not produce changes in the relative preference of the target population for figural as opposed to verbal modes of functioning.

Determining an Index of Modifiability

Another potentially useful application of our research paradigm concerns the production of an index of modifiability. Using the regression equations derived from the multiple regression analyses, pretest scores on the verbal and figural analogy tests may be used to predict posttest performance. This procedure is described graphically in Figure 70. The vertical axis indicates scores obtained on the figural pretest while the horizontal axis shows verbal pretest scores. The intersect between the two scores yields a predicted posttest score. The predicted posttest score is then compared with the score obtained, and a difference score between the two ("obtained" minus "predicted") is derived. The difference is then divided by the standard error of estimate for the whole group. We thus obtain a measure of individual change as compared to the group change as follows:

$$\frac{PrPTS - PTS}{SE}$$

where PrPTS is the predicted post total score, PTS is the post total score, and SE is the standard error of estimate.

Verbal Pretest Scores

Figural \ Verbal	0	1	2	3	4	5	6	7	8	9	10	11	12	13	14	15	16	17	18	19	20
0									13	14	15	15	16	17	17	18	19	19	20	21	21
1	INDIVIDUAL	TESTING						14	14	15	16	16	17	18	18	19	20	20	21	22	22
2							14	14	15	16	16	17	18	18	19	20	20	21	22	22	23
3						14	15	15	16	17	17	18	19	19	20	21	21	22	23	23	24
4					14	15	16	16	17	18	18	19	20	20	21	22	22	23	24	24	25
5				14	15	16	16	17	18	18	19	20	20	21	22	22	23	24	24	25	26
6			15	15	16	17	17	18	19	19	20	21	21	22	23	23	24	25	25	26	27
7		15	15	16	17	17	18	19	19	20	21	21	22	23	23	24	25	25	26	27	27
8	15	16	16	17	18	18	19	20	20	21	22	22	23	24	24	25	26	26	27	28	28
9	16	16	17	18	18	19	20	21	21	22	23	23	24	25	25	26	27	27	28	29	29
10	17	17	18	19	19	20	21	21	22	23	23	24	25	25	26	27	27	28	29	29	30
11	18	18	19	20	20	21	22	22	23	24	24	25	26	26	27	28	28	29	30	30	
12	18	19	20	20	21	22	22	23	24	24	25	26	26	27	28	28	29	30	30		
13	19	20	21	21	22	23	23	24	25	25	26	27	27	28	29	29	30	31			
14	20	21	21	22	23	23	24	25	25	26	27	27	28	29	29	30	31				
15	21	22	22	23	24	24	25	26	26	27	28	28	29	30	30	31					
16	22	23	23	24	25	25	26	27	27	28	29	29	30	31	31						
17	23	23	24	25	25	26	27	27	28	29	29	30	31	31							
18	24	24	25	26	26	27	28	28	29	30	30	31	32								
19	24	25	26	26	27	28	28	29	30	30	31	32		OTHER	TESTING	REQUIRED					
20	25	26	27	27	28	29	29	30	31	31	32										

Figural Pretest Scores (vertical axis label)

Figure 70. Predicted posttest total score on the basis of verbal and figural analogies pretest scores. (Regression equation: $.67x + .86y + 8.07$, where x = verbal pretest score and y = figural pretest score.)

Table 41. Illustration of change scores (three subjects)

Score	Subject		
	1	2	3
Pre total score	20	19	25
Predicted post total score	24	23	27
Obtained post total score	28	30	21
Difference score	4	7	−6
Standard error of estimate	4.62	4.62	4.62
Change score	.87	1.52	−1.30

Three examples taken from our population illustrate the way in which this procedure may be used. From Table 41 it may be observed that subjects 1 and 2 have obtained positive change scores. Although the change score of subject 1 represents only 87% of the standard error, subject 2 considerably exceeds the standard error of estimate (1.52). We may conclude that the modifiability of subject 2 is much higher than that of subject 1. The performance of subject 3 in the posttest is lower than that predicted so that he obtains a negative change score (−1.3). This finding suggests that some interfering variable has impeded the adequate performance of the subject on the posttest. Additional and more refined testing is required to discover the specific reason for this inadequacy and the most desirable procedures for modifying his level of performance.

This methodology for predicting and assessing change may be used with any assessment device where training intervenes between a pre- and a posttest and may be viewed as a precursor of the establishment of an index of modifiability.

Conclusions

As we have stated, our intent in this chapter is to acquaint the reader with our general research paradigm. In this respect, the purpose is to illustrate the kinds of problems we are currently investigating rather than to offer conclusive answers. Needless to say, research of this nature is beset by many problems, and we are constantly aware of the limitations both of our methods and our results. For this reason, we regard our present findings as tentative and as useful pointers to further and more detailed research efforts. Given the above qualifications our findings suggest the following:

1. True analogical thinking appears to be present in the active repertoire of cognitive operations of individuals functioning on the EMR level. This operation was found in both the verbal and figural modalities, although the level of efficiency, as defined by the percentage of correct answers, is low. Considering the important role played by analogical thinking in cognitive behavior, the existence of this operation in the retarded performer and the fact that efficiency in its use can be improved by appropriate training strategies call into question the assumptions of many authors. Many psychologists (Jensen, 1963; Raven, 1965) consider this operation inaccessible to individuals functioning at retarded levels and maintain that training is not likely to prove effective in improving performance. Our results challenge these assumptions, and our findings confirm our clinical experience in which many different tasks and modalities of presentation have been used to redevelop cognitive performance.

2. Analogical thinking, as measured by our assessment instruments, displays developmental characteristics, with significant age differences in middle-class children from the third to the sixth grades, after which they approach the ceiling of the test. Second-grade, middle-class children do not score above chance expectations, suggesting that analogical thinking is still inaccessible to children at the age of 7 or 8, under the specific test situation used.

3. Retarded performers do not manifest a rate of growth similar to that of middle-class children, and they approach a ceiling at a much later stage in their development. Our study population, with an average age of 15.3 years, manifested a pretest level of functioning comparable to that of 8- or 9-year-old, middle-class children in the third grade. However, this should not be interpreted, as is all too often the case, as a reflection of an elaborational incapacity, but rather the reasons for this behavior should be sought in the deficient cognitive functions that operate at the peripheral phases of input and output.

4. The significant gains of the treatment groups from pretest to posttest demonstrate the effectiveness of the treatment as compared with the results obtained by the control group, for which no significant differences were found. Most of the significant differences between the treatment groups involved comparisons with the control group. Although it is premature to draw firm conclusions concerning the efficacy of the various training strategies, the results do suggest two things. First, even very short

exposure to training may produce a significant improvement in performance. Second, under conditions of limited training, the mixed strategy in which both training and mediation was used appears to be most successful.

5. Although all the groups appear to score higher on the Shift Test than on the Analogies Test, the results did not reveal any significant differences between the various treatment groups. The apparent improvement on the Shift Test may be attributable to a number of factors, all of which require further investigation. The Shift Test was designed to provide a certain amount of training by varying the tasks while retaining a common underlying analogical operation. Consequently, it is possible that the training inherent in the test itself may neutralize the effects of specific brief training strategies. Another closely related factor is that the subjects had previously received an Analogies pretest and posttest, which no doubt also served to familiarize them with the test situation and the analogical operations common to all the tests. None of these factors need be regarded negatively, as the overriding point is that training will enable an individual to apply an acquired principle to the solution of tasks that are progressively different from the initial training. Nevertheless, it is necessary to separate out and identify the factors responsible for success on the Shift Test. The only negative factor is the possibility that, contrary to our intention, the Shift Test is simply easier than the Analogies Test. We hope these issues will be resolved by future research.

6. An interesting finding that confirms our clinical experience is the relative difficulty experienced by our subjects in working with the verbal as opposed to the figural modality. Despite the gains made between the pre- and posttests, the gap between performance on the verbal and figural subtests remained remarkably constant. It would appear that verbal behavior requires more intensive and prolonged intervention in order to produce meaningful changes. The question of preferential modalities of task presentation, and, more important, of training, remains a central issue. In concrete terms we need to establish how specific training strategies may interact with preferential modalities of presentation. Ideally, it should be possible to predict on the basis of an initial screening the kind and extent of training that are likely to produce the best results for a given individual. Using the Analogies Test it is possible to obtain three kinds of poor performance: low verbal and low figural, low verbal and high figural, and high verbal and low figural. Each of these

three conditions may require different training strategies, and future research must guide our approach to the development of the most efficient and effective means of producing change in the cognitive functioning of the retarded performer.

7. Although in the individual clinical LPAD situation it is standard practice to analyze the examinee's errors, this same principle may also be applied in large-scale research. The analysis of the subjects' errors in terms of nearly correct answers yielded interesting results. One of the major effects of training appears to be that subjects are able to move from nearly correct to completely correct responses. This tends to confirm our conviction that many of the difficulties encountered by the retarded performer concern his functioning at the peripheral phases of input and output rather than an inability to execute operations at the elaboration phase. This is a crucial issue affecting both assessment and treatment. Taking the Analogies Test at its face value and drawing conclusions about analogical operations based only on a score of correctly answered items are likely to prove misleading and, indeed, counterproductive to redevelopment efforts. If an individual's low score is, nevertheless, accompanied by a number of nearly correct answers, it would be erroneous to conclude that an inability to perform analogical operations is the core of the problem. Rather than focusing on the training of analogical thinking, it would be more beneficial to attack the deficient functions operating at the input and output phases.

We are currently engaged in planning and executing research concerning many of the issues enumerated above. Although our present findings do not allow us to draw any final conclusions, they do serve to generate working hypotheses to guide our own research and, we hope, that of others. This chapter illustrates how the LPAD may be used as a research tool and demonstrates a research model that we hope will provide the knowledge to render cognitive modifiability accessible to increasingly large numbers of retarded performers.

CHAPTER 8 **General Summary, Conclusions, and Suggestions for Future Development of the LPAD**

In the previous chapters we have extensively reviewed the problems inherent in conventional testing. We indicated the need for a radical change in the orientation of current psychometric procedures. Accordingly, we suggested a theoretical framework for the dynamic assessment of retarded performers and a model for the construction of instruments to implement this approach. As a paradigm for dynamic assessment, we presented the Learning Potential Assessment Device and described the required modifications of test instruments and the appropriate changes in examination procedures, examiner-examinee interactions, process orientation, and interpretation of results. The efficacy of the LPAD in revealing the hidden capacities of retarded performers of various etiologies was reflected in data from both clinical individualized and group assessment. We then presented a paradigm of research methodology in accordance with the LPAD model and preliminary experimental findings using analogical tasks with a large population of retarded performers. In the following pages we summarize the various topics with which we have dealt in this book and point to present and future implications in both theoretical and applied areas.

INADEQUACY OF
CONVENTIONAL PSYCHOMETRIC PRACTICE

The disenchantment with conventional psychometric theory, instruments, and methodology has been well documented. In this volume, the inadequacy of this approach was contrasted with the contribution that appropriate assessment can make in the integration of the culturally different individual and/or the redevelopment of the culturally deprived retarded performer. There is little doubt that conventional psychometry tends to disfavor those who belong to disadvantaged ethnic, social, and economic subgroups. Examiners do not limit themselves to describing the observed gap between the advantaged and disadvantaged groups, but often interpret it as the result of stable, immutable characteristics. This interpretation is then turned into a powerful predictor for the future development of the tested individual.

Thus, results obtained by a performance on a *specific set of tasks,* under a *given condition of examination,* in a *delimited period of time,* and *within a certain phase of the individual's development* are generalized into a *whole universe of behaviors* that will be produced in *very different conditions* and *stages of the individual's life.* This prediction generates negative stereotyped attitudes that inevitably turn noxious for the retarded performer because the educational goals set for him are based on the pessimistic prognosis for his future development and are subsequently drastically curtailed.

The use of conventional psychometric measures in individual, group, and cross-cultural studies does little beyond making a statement about observed differences from a statistically derived norm. Their static nature and orientation to product contribute little to our understanding of the cognitive processes. By basing conclusions regarding the individual's level on his performance, the conventional psychometric approach confounds the precision-rapidity complex equating efficiency of manifest functioning with capacity. It is only by monitoring the changes that occur in the course of a dynamic evaluation procedure that capacity, manifest functioning, and efficiency can be distinguished and assessed.

The Learning Potential Assessment Device has proved its efficacy in assessing diverse populations. The value of the concept of modifiability as the criterion for true capacity for the individual has been demonstrated throughout the years of our clinical work, and for the group has been demonstrated through the results obtained in a fairly standardized way for the clinic and the educable mentally retarded (EMR) populations on whom we have reported (see Chapter 4).

In assessing the retarded performer, the dynamic approach does not deny the low level of functioning reported by static measures. It uses the low manifest level, however, as the background against which modifiability is assessed. It also differs in its interpretation of the etiology, the meaning, and the prognosis of the retarded performance. The etiology of the syndrome of cultural deprivation as defined by us in our theoretical framework (see Chapter 1) appears to be directly linked to the quantity and quality of mediated learning the individual has experienced, irrespective of the distal etiological determinants of his condition. We find that the nature of the difficulties experienced by the individual and leading to retarded performance is often peripheral rather than central. Since it is related to input and output deficiencies, rather than to problems in elaboration, the prognosis for modifiability is far more favorable than traditionally argued. This assumption is strongly supported by our data. What can be derived from this is the concept of the human organism as an open system whose cognitive structure is subject to meaningful change under specified conditions of intervention. The LPAD is based upon this assumption and attempts to measure the modifiability elicited during the dynamic assessment.

The relationship between the results obtained by the EMR and the culturally deprived group of retarded performers, referred to in our study as the clinic group, supports our definition of retarded performance. The fact that no differences were found between the performances of these groups on the majority of the measured variables confirms both our contention and the findings of other researchers that the category of EMR is essentially composed of socioculturally disadvantaged and culturally deprived children. The diagnostic labeling of EMR, rendering it critically different, is questionable. Our findings clearly suggest that many of the EMR children, placed in special schools and treated as "truly retarded," are hampered in their development by the reduced regimen of intellectual stimulation engendered by the assumption that such children have limited access to abstract and representational thinking. Our follow-up data, illustrated only briefly by the case histories and the follow-up study on the group test, show that whenever this contention is challenged in a particular case, and the retarded performer is placed within an environment that involves him in higher intellectual pocesses under appropriate enriching conditions, the development that takes place is likely to follow a course that leads to and even reaches normalcy. It should not be necessary to point out that this is not often likely to occur when the child is placed and treated as mentally retarded, even if only EMR.

The fact that our EMR group in this particular study, and other groups as well, had not lost their gains, and in certain cases had even improved their performance when they were retested 2 months after the initial test despite the lack of intervention during that period, provides evidence for the stability of changes produced by the LPAD training technique. It forecasts the potential effects of a more systematic and prolonged intervention on the future successful cognitive redevelopment of the retarded performer.

LPAD CLINICAL BATTERY

Examples from the clinical battery provided in the text illustrate the changes in test instruments required by dynamic assessment. The LPAD battery permits the measurement of a variety of mental operations and cognitive functions and is therefore helpful in uncovering the intraindividual differences in levels of functioning and the preferential areas of learning critical for the modifiability of the individual. These findings of a dynamic assessment can be used for outlining strategies of remediation and prescriptive teaching.

It is the author's contention that some conventional psychometric instruments may be administered dynamically by incorporating the required changes in examiner-examinee interactions, in a shift from product to process orientation, and in the interpretation of results. To be compatible with the LPAD model, the conventional test must be so constructed as to systematically keep some of its items constant while others are varied in an equally systematic fashion.

Changes in the Testing Situation

The examiner must be able to transcend the level of pure objectivity and become sincerely involved with the examinee. Unless there is this active involvement, there is no guarantee that either the examinee's responses will receive an adequate amount of reinforcement or that the feedback that is so important for the culturally deprived child's further motivation and achievement will be supplied.

However, rendering the method less dependent upon the clinical skills of the examiner is a desirable goal, and its attainment would deal with the frequently voiced criticism that the outcome of LPAD testing is crucially determined by the personality of the examiner. In line with this criticism, positive results are often denigrated by claiming that they were determined by the interaction between the examiner and the examinee. This may certainly be true, but in no way does it detract from or deny the fact that the examinee has proved able to accede to higher levels of performance. Demonstrating that a special interactive process is able to activate the cognitive potential of an examinee does not negate the existence of the potential but points toward the kind of interpersonal conditions under which such potential can become manifest. Unfortunately, the reverse effect is not considered frequently enough. That is, the presence of negative examiner-examinee interactions that contribute to the masking of potentiality is usually ignored, and failure is attributed to the child's lack of capacity.

The personal interaction enables the examiner to analyze the cognitive behavior of the examinee according to the parameters of the cognitive map and to provide the intervention indicated. It also allows the examiner to help the examinee to restrain his impulsivity, which, in the author's opinion, is responsible for a great number of the faulty test responses of the culturally deprived.

Individual administration of the clinical battery permits a much more intensive investment aimed at modifying precisely those functions that are seen to be deficient in the examinee. This is not only based upon the greater quantity of time and effort expended in one-to-one testing; there is also an inevitable qualitative difference in the relationship. The individualized testing situation provides the opportunity for an interactive process that permits the establishment of a sensitive two-way feedback flow between the examiner and the examinee. This, in turn, helps focus intervention on relevant problems, thereby leading to a greater efficiency in producing, rewarding, and consolidating the desired changes and eliciting a high level of adequate responses from the examinee in many areas of functioning.

The experimental work completed indicates that individual administration of the LPAD clinical battery has substantial advantages over group testing. In evolving the group test procedures clearly some of the benefits accruing from the one-to-one interaction are attenuated. Standardized instructional procedures inevitably create distance between the examiner and the examinees. Nevertheless, in the interest of economy of time and effort, it has been felt that a group testing procedure is necessary.

Efforts have been made to mitigate the foreseen difficulties of group testing in several ways. The first is to structure the testing instruments according to the model that permits the examinee to demonstrate his ability to use acquired principles in situations becoming progressively more complex and more remote from the task in which he was trained. The second is to build into the group testing situation those training elements that have been clinically determined to be significant in modifying cognitive behavior. The third is to use the results of group testing as a screening process that may either sufficiently attest to the modifiability of some examinees or indicate that an individualized, clinical procedure is necessary for those who have not succeeded. The fourth is to test in small groups with enough staff to answer questions that may arise. The fifth is to maintain the same warm, caring atmosphere that is present in the clinical situation. The sixth is to note specific difficulties expressed by individuals within the group on a specially constructed recording sheet, so as to adhere to the process orientation as closely as possible, even in a group situation.

As we indicated in Chapter 5, the group test is being increasingly requested by school administrators and teachers to determine academic policy and set educational goals. Because the group test also furnishes information about an individual's behavior as part of a group and his ability to respond to directions that are impersonal, it more closely is associated with the functioning of the individual in the classroom.

Process-Oriented Approach

The process-oriented approach has resulted in data that confirm our assumption regarding the basic determinants of failure in both test situations and classrooms. Again we assert that the determinants of success or failure are not necessarily or always in the elaboration phase but are largely located in the input and output phases of the mental act. The fact that complex tasks such as those contained in our instruments are mastered successfully by individuals who were considered and manifestly functioned as educable mentally retarded or culturally deprived retarded performers is a rather strong challenge to the accepted contentions of developmental and differential psychologists concerning the hierarchical organization of mental operations and the predictability of potential functioning, which have been derived from samples of current cognitive behavior in such populations. Indeed, many of our children who experienced great difficulty in learning rather simple elements showed much greater capacity when confronted with tasks requiring internalized abstract thinking. This finding is strongly supported by the findings on the Representational Stencil Design Test, Plateaux I and II Rotations, and the LPAD Variations I and II, and has been confirmed by other studies.

The meaning of these findings should have broad implications for educational policy, especially for the strategy of teaching retarded performers. One may question whether the use of the concrete and familiar is really the best way to teach the retarded performer. One may ask if sheer exposure to simple and elementary stimuli is the way to positively affect a low level of functioning.

CURRENT AND FUTURE PROBLEMS FOR STUDY

Our work, clinically useful as it has proved to be, still requires some very important elaborations and development. Among them are: 1) the establishment of a base line, the creation of norms for evaluating modifiability, and an Index of Modifiability; 2) the expansion of the battery of individualized and group instruments; 3) the testing of a broader segment of the population by LPAD procedures; 4) the development of techniques for assessing potential modifiability in areas of specific learning disabilities; 5) the expansion of methods of identifying individual preferential language and modalities of learning; and 6) a clarification of the nonintellective factors critical to specific and individual levels of modifiability.

Establishment of a Base Line

The reader may be aware that with the individually studied population we did not always establish a base line on the measured variables. This is because our experience indicates that the attempt to modify the behavior of children on a test in which they have already experienced failure is, in many instances, a Sisyphean task. The child often tends to perseverate in his failing responses, and any attempt to change this propensity for perseveration is met with great resistance. What is even more important, once an examiner has allowed the child to function in an indiscriminate way, without providing the help entailed in the LPAD technique, this child will show little if any readiness to enter into the examiner-examinee relationship necessary for the evaluation of cognitive modifiability.

Another reason we did not always attempt to establish a base line on our measures, especially in the clinical battery, is the complexity of our tasks relative to those presented to such children in current generally accepted practice. As we pointed out earlier, the LPAD battery uses tasks requiring higher mental processes—tasks rarely used with a retarded performer. Even understanding the instructions requires mobilizing and training a higher level of knowledge and cognitive skill than that usually present in the repertoire of spontaneous responses of our target population. If the tasks of Organization of Dots, the Representational Stencil Design Test, the LPAD Variations, and the representational phase of the Plateaux Test are analyzed and considered against the background of the tasks usually used to measure the level of functioning of the retarded performer, our reason for not attempting to establish a base line for these tasks becomes apparent.

Any attempt to require the retarded performer to fulfill such tasks without first providing him with the prerequisites of functioning through the reinforced instructions and training necessary to make him grasp even the basic requirement is doomed to fail. Indeed, this was our constant experience. Our reluctance to present children with a task in which failure is inevitable is also based on ethical grounds. We have therefore decided that, wherever possible and necessary, we will use as a quantitatively comparable base line the level of functioning of the individual in the areas of general cognitive behavior and school achievement or his established level of intelligence as ascertained on a conventional test such as the Weschler Intelligence Scale for Children or the Stanford-Binet, administered to many of the children prior to referral to us.

Establishment of a Quantified Index of Modifiability

Another aspect with which we have not dealt in the clinical phase of our research is the establishment of an Index of Modifiability. To produce such an index, we would have to quantify the obtained change and express it as a relation between a given base line level of functioning and the results attained following intervention. The measurement of such a change is known to be a relatively difficult area in psychometric theory and practice (Cronbach and Furby, 1970). However, theoretically the establishment of an Index of Modifiability within the LPAD model requires an assessment of the nature and amount of investment needed by the examinee to reach a given level of functioning starting from a registered base line level. That is, we must find and then use measures of change. Thus, not only must the base line level of functioning be established, with all the difficulties alluded to above in doing so, but the nature of input must be categorized and ascribed a certain value; then the amount of this investment must be quantified and used as a control variable in assigning a quantitative weight to the achieved modification.

Modifiability within the assessment is currently inferred by us in a direct way from the observed behavior. Thus, for instance, the emergence of spontaneous comparative behavior, the use of an acquired operation, and the progressive and autonomous regulation of behavior, such as the control of impulsivity, are carefully registered and evaluated against initial behaviors. The meaning of these qualitative changes in the cognitive behavior is inferred from the efficiency with which the examinee solves the problems presented to him in the course of the assessment. This leads to a score of correct answers that is then compared with other data on the examinee derived from his school achievement, previous measures of intelligence, and general criteria of adaptive behavior.

One can immediately be aware of the contradiction *in sensu* between a goal of establishing an Index of Modifiability and the clinical nature of our method of assessment. In order to establish an exact measure of investment, the interventional strategies would have to be standardized to such an extent that the effectiveness of the clinical method would be greatly reduced. The differences inherent in the individuals assessed under this method could no longer be handled flexibly; they would have to follow a rigid, confining prescription.

In a 1968 discussion of the LPAD method at George Peabody College in Nashville, Tennessee, Lloyd Dunn, a specialist in the field of the exceptional child, pointed to the inappropriateness of seeking to reconcile conventional psychometric rules with the dynamic LPAD assessment procedure.

Notwithstanding the above rationale and difficulties to be overcome, we still considered an attempt to create an Index of Modifiability sufficiently important to set it as one of the first steps in our research. We have begun by the preparation of a list of the categories of investment commonly used in LPAD sessions as compared with those used only in specific cases. With this list, we have distinguished between interventional strategies that are used with every one of the assessed subjects in a more routine and generalized way and those required only in those cases that disclose more particular difficulties. A current area of research is the conceptualization of the interactive processes involved in the LPAD session.

An alternate step leading to an Index of Modifiability is the use of the group mode of presentation, permitting a much higher degree of standardized procedure in establishing a base line, in quantifying the intervention, and in measuring the change by a post-test. (A comparison of the individual mode of assessment and the use of the LPAD in group settings is presented in Chapter 5. The methodology of group testing is discussed in Chapters 5 and 7.)

Expansion of the Battery

The development of individual and group instruments for assessing additional cognitive functions and operations will make possible the broader and more precise assessment of cognitive modifiability and the improved prescription of remedial strategies. We are developing instruments in the logico-verbal and numerical modalities, using a variety of operations, in accordance with the LPAD model (see Figure 9, Chapter 3).

Use of the LPAD with Other Populations

Our current instruments and modification techniques were designed for use with culturally deprived adolescents in their early and mid teens, regardless of the distal etiology for their manifest level of functioning. They are not suitable, however, for multihandicapped with extreme communication problems, for the blind, or for young children. Yet, questions regarding the existence of higher cognitive potential are raised and are crucial to adequate assessment of these populations as well. The theoretical framework and model we have presented can be expanded for the construction of specific instruments and procedures that will permit the assessment of these additional populations.

Specific Learning Disabilities

An area for additional investigation is the focused assessment of modifiability in specific deficient functioning, such as psychomotor, lexical, and mathematical difficulties. A first step toward the development of such assessment methods for psychomotor deficit, following the LPAD model, has already been initiated (Feldman, 1970).

Preferential Modalities

Still another area requiring research is the determination of individual preferences for learning through specific modalities. That individuals differ in their optimal use of specific modalities of information processing is well documented (Deutsch, 1964; Lesser, Fifer, and Clark, 1966; see also Chapter 7).

Our research program calls for the expansion of profiles drawn for each examinee so that the hierarchy of preferential modalities used in attempts at modification can be determined. Such a profile would be instrumental in underlining the most effective remediation approaches to undertake. Information gained about the individual preferential modality, as well as the grouping of similar profiles to ascertain the most effective instructional modality for differing types of profiles, should provide guidelines for the construction of further diagnostic instruments and the future development of additional instructional devices.

Diagnosis is significant only insofar as it forms the basis for a treatment program. Diagnosis in and of itself only allows insight into those factors responsible for the child's learning difficulty. For example, if for a given examinee the probability of transfer from a pictorial to a verbal modality is found to be high, it would be reasonable to invest effort in the construction of teaching material in pictorial form. On the other hand, should such transfer prove to be minimal, it would be more strategic to aim directly at improvement of functioning within the verbal modality itself. Although our clinical individualized approach gives us insight into the problem, a standardized method would be desirable. This would allow the possibility of sensitively including knowledge of each individual's cognitive preference in the remediational strategies we prescribe.

The experiment described in Chapter 7 on the differential effects of two modalities of presentation and two different styles of treatment is part of ongoing research into this complex problem. Although the results obtained in this study were not conclusive, they indicate significant differences and delineate areas for continued exploration.

Nonintellective Factors

We seek clarification of the nonintellective factors that are critically related to the specific levels of modifiability manifested by given individuals. Although our emphasis is on the study of the cognitive structure and functions, we in no way neglect the interaction between affective and cognitive elements in the behavior of the individual. An appreciation of how self-image and affective, motivational, and other factors interact with cognitive behavior is necessary in order to achieve a more precise prescription of remedial strategies. As an outgrowth of assessing the specific weight of such factors, our attempts to validate the LPAD can be far better developed.

Validity Studies

One particular cluster for further study is that of in vitro vs. in vivo validity. During the testing sessions, there is no question that changes occur under the prescribed strategies. Examinees who have become modified within the test situation quite obviously leave the concrete and task-bound level and are able to function with an abstract, internalized conceptual thinking that was unjustly considered inaccessible to them previously. But to what extent and under what conditions will modification achieved within the test situation predict later performance in academic and real-life settings?

The conventional assessment procedure, be it in the realm of IQ or other ability testing, has shown statistically high reliability and validity values. The question of whether our Learning Potential Assessment Device procedure can attain such degrees of reliability and validity might be answered by another question: Under what conditions can and should one test for validity? It is appropriate to quote from a review of research on ability grouping (Findley and Bryan, 1971) in which the meager outcome of efforts made by test publishers to meet the problem of assessing the capabilities of disadvantaged children is discussed. Findley and Bryan say:

> The negative evidence that tests standardized on other populations tend to over-predict the subsequent performance of disadvantaged individuals, hence, are not unfair to them, is cold comfort. The challenge is to mount a campaign of innovative teaching and evaluative research, rather than to settle for procedures that are fair only in the sense that they reflect fairly the current unmitigated disadvantages. (pp. 68–69)

Our interpretation of the low test-retest correlations, wherever they appear, is that the more powerful an interventional strategy may be, the less the product of intervention will be related to the initial level of functioning of the individual. The validity of a test can only be a reflection of the stability and fixity of the cognitive behavior of the individual subjected to it. Once a change is induced in the individual by a specific intervention, thereby disrupting the stability, one can expect a low correlation with the initial results.

Validity values of static tests will necessarily be high wherever conditions for producing change in the level of the examinee have not been instituted. Since the "expectations for low achievement" receive no treatment that might counteract them, one cannot but expect the fulfillment of the anticipated. The search for validity of the LPAD is therefore not to be centered on the instruments of assessment but on the changes in the functioning of the individual following the intervention characteristic of the dynamic assessment. Extrinsic criteria can be used as a source of validation of the LPAD only in those cases in which the subsequently prescribed remedial strategies, resulting from the LPAD assessment, have been used. For those children for whose development we were directly responsible, a great amount of clinical follow-up data were gathered that provided ample support for the value of the LPAD in the course of more than 25 years of use of the theory and technique.

A basic reason for not attempting to present the validity of the LPAD in a quantified way is that we think it far more important that modifiability be demonstrated according to intrinsic criteria than by any extrinsic criteria we might attempt to use. The fact that a child diagnosed and known to function as retarded is able to accede to levels of functioning that are known to have been previously inaccessible to him should be considered valid enough evidence of his modifiability. Whether or not this basic potential for change will be materialized depends on factors that are not always under control. To make the validity of estimated potential contingent upon the extent of its realization is like denying the wealth of a miser because he never spends his money.

The clarity of the concept of capacity indeed depends on the crucial difference between potential and actualized achievement levels, for if capacity for achievement did not require special conditions for its actualization, what difference would there be between capacity and manifest level of function? Capacity for change requires intervention in order to become realized.

Economic considerations demand that we be able to predict where intervention efforts will prove worthwhile in order to permit the best possible practical decisions. However, it has been enough for us at this point to assess modifiability on the basis of intrinsic criteria, behavior change within the test itself, which we feel demonstrates that capacity for change truly exists in the individual, and that appropriate investment is pertinent and will be effective.

More recent studies derived from both clinical and group tests have been germane in producing the evidence of the validity of the LPAD approach. Crucial evidence lies in the fact that, with this method, we were able to return masses of adolescents previously placed in special schools, classes, and institutions for the retarded into Youth Aliya preparatory classes and then into the regular educational framework, in agricultural, vocational, and academically oriented high schools.

PLANNED INTERVENTION

The utility of the LPAD approach is not always contingent upon instituting specialized remedial techniques. In many cases, the new awareness of existent and/or potential skills brings about the desired change. In other cases, there is no alternative but to institute a special program. Indeed, the development of Instrumental Enrichment theory and technique is largely based on the LPAD and the findings produced by it (see Feuerstein, in press). Instrumental Enrichment is an illustration of the way in which remediational strategies can be generated in order to bring about the modification that was first elicited and then measured by the LPAD.

Instrumental Enrichment is an intervention program that aims at the cognitive redevelopment of the retarded performing adolescent. Its goal is to enable the retarded performer to use formal instruction and general life experience for learning. It is a phase-specific substitute for mediated learning experience and provides a direct and focused attack on those deficient cognitive functions that are considered responsible for retarded performance, irrespective of their distal etiology. Through more than 400 pages of paper and pencil noncontent exercises, Instrumental Enrichment also aims to assist the child in the acquisition of concepts, operations, and strategies; to encourage intrinsic motivation; to provide insight into the causes of success and failure; and to transform the individual from a passive recipient of information into an active generator and extrapolator of new ideas. Through varied repetition, the program helps the individual automatize and crystallize behaviors that will assist him in coping with and solving new problems. Instrumental Enrichment currently consists of fifteen instruments, each of which focuses on a specific deficient cognitive function but simultaneously addresses itself to many of the others. It can be taught as a total program of a 2- to 3-year duration, concurrent with the regular school curriculum, or as an individualized remedial program with the selection of instruments determined by the deficiencies revealed in the LPAD assessment. The instruments, so-called because they serve as a vehicle by means of which the prerequisites of thinking may be developed and refined, equip the individual for representational, symbolic, and operational thinking.

IMPLICATIONS FOR IMPLEMENTATION

The described philosophy, theory, model, and clinical technique underlying the Learning Potential Assessment Device do not simplify the task of the examiner, nor do they necessarily render the assessment of the retarded performer more economical. The practitioner involved in dynamic assessment is required to invest in the study and understanding of intimate cognitive processes, their development, structure, and meaning, and the very intricate way in which they converge into the end product, that is, the score obtained by the examinee on the tasks. Furthermore, the assessment that is constantly associated with a training process requires time and effort from both the examiner and the examinee. The interpretation of results will never be a matter of an automatic mechanical computation of scores and their transformation into an index, as is often the case with conventional static measures. In the LPAD, it is each single response and the understanding of the processes that have produced it that will be the object of scrutiny and the source of a deeper understanding of the examinee's cognitive structure and the changes occurring in the course of assessment.

In addition to the intellectual cognitive elements, the nature of the interaction in the dynamic assessment requires that the examiner create a rapport marked by personal warmth, sincere interest in the success of the examinee, and a readiness to communicate and even amplify feelings of pleasure whenever the examinee succeeds. The examiner must be constantly alert to those characteristics in the examinee's functioning that require intervention to prevent failure and to enhance success.

Considering the quantity and quality of investment and the required special personal characteristics of the practitioner, one may legitimately question the feasibility of such a diagnostic procedure and the extent to which it can be made accessible to a wider audience of practitioners. There are some who have directly observed the author assessing children with the LPAD who have tended to attribute his success to what they have labeled his "personal charisma." They have honestly questioned whether the skill in dynamic assessment does not border on an art and therefore be limited to a chosen few. The question seems to be to what extent is the LPAD transmissible as a method to all those who may be called upon to assess the child.

It is our experience that the behavior of the practitioner involved in the LPAD assessment is usually shaped by the constraints created by the dynamic assessment situation. The fact that the examiner must interact with the examinee by assuming the role of teacher-trainer in order to produce the desired changes in the examinee has a very deep effect on the examiner's attitude, the degree of his scientific curiosity, his clinical orientation, and his emotional involvement. Rather than taking the given response for granted as correct or incorrect, the LPAD examiner will question its true meaning and transcend the established norm-referenced evaluation by searching for the process that engendered the response as a valuable criterion for its significance. It has been our recurrent experience that examiners who were known to appear neutral, cold, and even disinterested when administering static tests became intensely involved, interested, and vigilant when they were called upon to interact in the role of dynamic assessors. One may therefore consider the clinical capacities of the examiner to depend largely on the nature of his interaction and the role assigned to him. Offering the LPAD as an alternate way of assessment may increase the readiness of many psychologists to again become interested in the art of testing.

The second question is one of the cost effectiveness of the LPAD. It is clear that the LPAD may be an expensive and lengthy process.

It should therefore not be considered for universal application, but for selective use. The LPAD will become necessary whenever the manifest level of functioning of an individual is so low that it may have a hampering effect on his future development, on his integration among his normal peers, and on the establishment of educational, vocational, and social goals for him. Whenever critical decisions are to be based on the cognitive structure of the individual, reflected in his achievement or in results obtained by static measures, it is the LPAD assessment that may help transcend the immediate manifest level of functioning of the individual by producing evidence of his modifiability and by specifying the conditions under which changes may be best produced.

This shift in the orientation from the use of a low manifest level of functioning to an anticipated redevelopment may result in decisions of an educational, remediational nature that will be critical in determining a change in the course of the individual's life. In such cases, cognitive assessment may become the fountainhead for processes involving the total personality of the individual. As shown in the case studies (see Chapter 6), such changes closely resemble a true renascence, with the joy of rediscovering one's emotional, motivational, and behavioral patterns. Social positions, even though they are the last to change because of prior stigmatization, may undergo a real process of betterment and an increased confidence in the individual's own judgment and self-evaluation. Can one consider any investment too costly against the backdrop of such potential changes?

CONCLUSION

It seems that dynamic assessment, its philosophy, methodology, instruments, and techniques, of which LPAD is only a modest beginning, can be a meaningful approach to three broad areas of psychological study, with implications for wide social, economic, and cultural betterment.

The first area that may benefit from a dynamic assessment of cognitive functions is the study and deeper understanding of widely used constructs such as intelligence and capacity. The nature of these constructs, in dispute today, may gain in clarity when viewed from the angle of changes that may be produced in the nature, quality, and quantity of mental processes under specific conditions of manipulations and intervention. It is under such search and scrutiny that the components of the mental act and their prerequisites for mastery may become evident. The limits imposed by age, structure, and the state of the human organism may be better understood as to their central or peripheral nature. Such a philosophy will dispute many of the established conceptions and permit the dissipation of many stereotypes prevalent today in developmental and differential psychology.

The second area is a better understanding of culturally determined differences between groups such as are revealed by cross-cultural studies. These studies, which mainly use static measures for the description of differences, may bring more relevant information once they add a dynamic dimension, focusing on the problem of how such differences should and could be limited by a process of modification. This is especially necessary considering the rapid changes occurring in societies where development requires adaptation to modalities of functioning that are uniformly based on conceptualized, abstract, and efficient operational thinking. Dynamic assessment could provide information regarding the extent to which changes are necessary or desirable, the preferential modalities by which a given cultural subgroup may best be modified, and the amount and kind of investment necessary to attain this goal. A most desirable product of such an approach would be how such changes could take place without altering dimensions, attributes, and characteristics vital for and inherent to the cultural identity of the subgroup.

Finally, dynamic assessment, such as the Learning Potential Assessment Device presented in this book, is the source of direct and immediate help for all individuals whose current level of functioning may become the source of decisions whose far-reaching effects may be crucial for their destiny. It is here that dynamic assessment, and all that it entails, has contributed and may continue to contribute even more when it is developed further, rendered more efficient, and properly disseminated.

The harmful effects of conventional static measures may be avoided by using the dynamic assessment. The practitioner often finds himself in a role similar to that of a witness on whose testimony far-reaching decisions depend. The use of approximate and norm-based data, rather than directly observed evidence of modifiability, may prove to be an illicit and unwarranted act. It is for the practitioner that the alternative of a dynamic assessment should have its greatest appeal.

The true and all too often hidden capacities of individuals and their modifiability cannot be revealed except by an appreciable and costly investment on the part of the practitioner. This is even more evident once the materialization of potential becomes the target of the caregiving environment, parent, teacher, and psychologist.

The uniqueness of each individual turns his fate into the fate of the world—his world. According to the Sages:

> Why was Adam created alone and unique? To teach us that he who brings about the loss of one soul is as if he has annihilated a whole world; while he who saves a soul is as if he has rescued a whole world.
> —Talmud Sanhedrin 37a

REFERENCES

Abel, T. H. Psychological Testing in Cultural Contexts. New Haven: University Press, 1973.

Abrahamson, T. The influence of examiner race on first grade and kindergarten subjects: Peabody Picture Vocabulary Test Scores. Journal of Educational Measurement, 1969, 6:241–246.

Adams, J. Adaptive behavior and measured intelligence in the classification of mental retardation. American Journal of Mental Deficiency, 1973, 78:77–81.

Alpert, A. Reversibility of pathological fixations associated with maternal deprivation in infancy. Psychoanalytic Study of the Child, 1959, XIV.

Ammons, R. B., and Aguero, A. The full-range picture vocabulary test VII, results for school age Spanish American population. Journal of Social Psychology, 1950, 32:3–10.

Anastasi, A. Some implications of cultural factors for test construction. Proceedings of the 1949 Invitational Conference on Test Problems. Princeton, N.J.: Educational Testing Service, 1950, 13–17.

Anastasi, A. Psychological Testing. New York: Macmillan, 1954.

Anastasi, A. Differential Psychology. 3rd Ed. New York: Macmillan, 1958.

Anastasi, A. Psychological Testing. New York: Macmillan, 1961.

Anastasi, A. Culture-fair testing. Educational Digest, 1965, 30:9–11.

Anastasi, A. Psychological Testing. 4th Ed. New York: Macmillan, 1976.

Anastasiow, N. J., and Haynes, M. L. Language Patterns of Poverty Children. Springfield, Ill.: Charles C Thomas, 1976.

Ansbacher, H. L. The Goodenough Draw-a-Man test and primary mental abilities. Journal of Consulting Psychology, 1952, 16:176–180.

Arthur, G. A. A Point Scale of Performance Tests: Clinical Manual. Vol. 1. New York: Commonwealth Fund, 1930.

Avery, C. D. A psychologist looks at the issue of public vs. residential school placement of the blind. In R. L. Jones (ed.), Problems and Issues in the Education of Exeptional Children. Boston: Houghton Mifflin, 1971.

Backman, M. E. Patterns of mental abilities: Ethnic, socioeconomic and sex differences. American Educational Research Journal, 1972, 9:1–12.

Baer, D. M., Wolf, M. M., and Risley, T. R. Some current dimensions of applied behavior analysis. Journal of Applied Behavior Analysis, 1968, 1:91–97.

Balgur, R. The Basic Word List for Elementary Schools. Israel: Otsar Hamoreh, 1968.

Baller, W. R., Charles, D. C., and Miller, E. D. Mid-life attainment of the mentally retarded: A longitudinal study. Genetic Psychology Monographs, 1967, 75:235–329.

Baratz S., and Baratz, J. C. Negro ghetto children and urban education: A cultural solution. Special Education 1969, 33:401–405.

Beeman, N. P. (ed.). Assessing Minority Group Children: A Special Edition of the Journal of School Psychology. New York: Behavioral Publications, 1974.

Beez, W. V. Influence of biased psychological reports on teacher behavior and pupil performance. Proceedings of the 76th Annual Convention of the American Psychological Association, 1968, 3:605–606.

Belmont, J. M. Long-term memory in mental retardation. In N. R. Ellis (ed.), International Review of Research in Mental Retardation. Vol. 1. New York: Academic Press, 1966, 219–255.

Bender, L. A visual-motor Gestalt test and its clinical use. American Orthopsychiatric Association Research Monograph, 1938, No. 3., xi–176.

Bennet, G. L. Response to Robert William. Counselling Psychologist, 1970, 2:88–89.

Bereiter, C. Using tests to measure change. Personnel and Guidance Journal, 1962, 41(1):6–11.

Bereiter, C. Genetics and educability: Educational implications of the Jensen debate. In J. Hellmuth (ed.), Disadvantaged Child: Compensatory Education: A National Debate. Vol. 3. New York: Brunner-Mazel, 1970, 279–299.

Bernstein, B. Language and social class. British Journal of Sociology, 1960, 11:271–276.

Bernstein, B. Social structure, language, and learning. Educational Research, 1961, 3:163–176.

Bernstein, B. Class, Codes and Control. London: Routledge and Kegan Paul, 1971.

Berry, J. W. Radical cultural relativism and the concept of intelligence. Paper distributed at the NATO Conference on Cultural Factors in Mental Test Development, Turkey, 1971.

Bersoff, D. N. Silk purses into sows' ears: The decline of psychological testing and a suggestion for its redemption. American Psychologist, 1973, 28:892–899.

Biesheuvel, S. (ed.). Methods for the Measurement of Psychological Performance. Handbook No. 10. Oxford: Blackwell Scientific Publications, 1969.

Biesheuvel, S. The measurement of adaptability and its determinants. Paper distributed at the NATO Conference on the Cultural Factors in Mental Test Development, Turkey, 1971.

Black, H. They Shall Not Pass. New York: Morrow, 1963.

Blatt, B. Public policy and the education of children with special needs. Exceptional Children, 1972, 38:537–545.

Block, N. J., and Dworkin, G. (eds.). The IQ Controversy. New York: Pantheon, 1976.

Bloom, B. S. Stability and Change in Human Characteristics. New York: John Wiley and Sons, 1964.

Bortner, M., and Birch, H. G. Cognitive capacity and cognitive competence. American Journal of Mental Deficiency, 1970, 74:735–744.

Bourdieu, P., and Passeron, J. C. Les Héritiers: Les Étudiants et la Culture. Paris: Les Éditions de Minuit, 1964.

Brazziel, W. F. Foreword. In LaMar P. Miller (ed.), The Testing of Black Students. Prentice-Hall: Englewood Cliffs, N.J., 1974, 9–10.

Bricker, D. D. A rationale for the integration of handicapped and non-handicapped preschool children. In M. J. Guralnick (ed.), Early Intervention and the Integration of Handicapped and Non-handicapped Children. Baltimore: University Park Press, 1978, 3–26.

Bricker, W. A. Identifying and modifying behavioral deficits. American Journal of Mental Deficiency, 1970, 75:16–21.

Bricker, W. A. A constructive interaction adaptation system: A new approach to the education of young children. Colloquium presented at University of Wisconsin, Madison, Wis., 1973.

Bricker, W. A., and Bricker, D. D. Early language intervention. Invited Address at the NICHD Conference on Language Intervention with the Mentally Retarded, Wisconsin Dells, 1973.

Bryant, P. E. Perception and Understanding in Young Children. London: Methuen, 1974.

Bryant, P. E., and Trabasso, T. Transitive inferences and memory in young children, Nature, 1971, 232:456–458.

Budoff, M. A learning potential assessment procedure: Rationale and supporting data. In B. W. Richards (ed.), Proceedings of the 1st Congress of the International Association for the Scientific Study of Mental Deficiency. Reigate (Surrey): M. Jackson, 1968.

Budoff, M. Learning potential and educability among the educable mentally retarded. Progress Report, Grant No. OEG-0-8-080506-4597, National Institute of Education, HEW. Cambridge, Mass.: Research Institute for Educational Problems, 1973.

Budoff, M., and Hamilton, J. L. Optimizing test performance of moderately and severely retarded adolescents and adults. American Journal of Mental Deficiency, 1976, 81:49–57.

Burt, C. The genetic determination of differences in intelligence; A study of monozygotic twins reared together and apart. British Journal of Psychology, 1966, 57:137–153.

Butcher, H. J. Human Intelligence, Its Nature, and Assessment. London: Methuen, 1968.

Caldwell, M. B., and Knight, D. The effect of Negro and white examiners on Negro intelligence test performance. Journal of Negro Education, 1970, 39:177–179.

Call, R. Verbal abstracting performance of low SES children: An exploration of Jensen's theory of mental retardation. Unpublished doctoral dissertation. George Peabody College, Nashville, Tenn., 1973.

Cattell, R. B. A culture-free test of intelligence. Journal of Educational Psychology, 1940, 3:161–179.

Cattell, R. B. A Culture-Free Test: Manual of Directions. New York: Psychological Corporation, 1944.

Chapman, R. H. The development of children's understanding of proportions. Child Development, 1975, 46:141–148.

Clark, K. B. Dark Ghetto. New York: Harper and Row, 1965.

Clarke, A. D. B., and Clarke, A. M. Early Experience: Myth and Evidence. London: Open Books, 1976.

Clarke, A. D. B., and Cooper, G. M. Age and perceptual-motor transfer in imbeciles: Task complexity as a variable. British Journal of Psychology, 1966, 57:113–119.

Clarke, A. M., and Clarke, A. D. B. Learning transfer and cognitive development. In J. Zubin and G. Jervis (eds.), Psychopathology of Mental Development. New York: Grune and Stratton, 1967, 105–139.

Clarke, A. M., and Clarke, A. D. B. What are the problems? An evaluation of recent research relating to theory. In A. D. B. Clarke and A. M. Clarke (eds). Mental Retardation and Behavioral Theory. Edinburgh: Church and Livingstone, 1973, 3–22.

Clarke, A. M., and Clarke, A. D. B. Mental Deficiency: The Changing Outlook. 3rd Ed. New York: Free Press, 1975.

Clarke, A. M., Clarke, A. D. B., and Cooper, G. M. The development of a set to perceive categorical relations. In H. C. Haywood (ed.), Sociocultural Aspects of Mental Retardation. New York: Appleton-Century-Crofts, 1970, 433–447.

Clarke, A. M., and Cooper, G. M. Transfer in category learning of young children: Its relation to task complexity and overlearning. British Journal of Psychology, 1966, 57:361–373.

Clarke, A. M., Cooper, G. M., and Clarke, A. D. B. Task complexity and transfer in the development of cognitive structures. Journal of Experimental Child Psychology, 1967, 5:562–576.

Clarke, A. M., Cooper, G. M., and Henney, A. S. Width of transfer and task complexity in the conceptual learning of imbeciles. British Journal of Psychology, 1966, 57:121–128.

Cleary, T. A., Humphreys, L. G., Kendrick, S. A., and Wesman, A. Educational uses of tests with disadvantaged students. American Psychologist, 1975, 30:15–40.

Cleveland, S. D. Reflections on the rise and fall of psychodiagnosis. Professional Psychology, 1976, 44:54–60.

Cobb, H. V. The Forecast of Fulfillment. New York: Teachers' College Press, 1972.

Cohen, E. C., and Roper, S. S. Modification of interracial interaction disability: A modification of status characteristic theory. American Sociological Review, 1972, 37:643–657.

Cronbach, L. J. Beyond the two disciplines of scientific psychology. American Psychologist, 1957, 12:671–684.

Cronbach, L. J. Essentials of Psychological Testing. 3rd Ed. New York: Harper and Row, 1970.

Cronbach, L. J. Judging how well a test measures: New concepts, new analyses. Paper distributed at the NATO Conference on Cultural Factors in Mental Test Development, Turkey, July, 1971.

Cronbach, L. J. Five decades of public controversy over mental testing. American Psychologist, 1975, 30:1–14.

Cronbach, L. J., and Drenth, P. J. D. (eds.). Mental Tests and Cultural Adaptation. The Hague: Mouton, 1973.

Cronbach, L. J., and Furby, L. How we should measure "change"—Or should we? Psychological Bulletin, 1970, 74:68–80.

Davis, A., and Eells, K. Davis-Eells Games: Davis-Eells Test of General Intelligence or Problem-solving Ability. Manual. New York: Yonkers and Hudson, World Book, 1953.

De Avila, E. A., Havassay, B., and Pascual-Leone, J. Mexican-American School Children: A Neo-Piagetian Analysis. Washington: Georgetown University Press, 1976.

Deutsch, C. Auditory discrimination and learning: Social factors. Merrill-Palmer Quarterly, 1964, 10:277–296.

Deutsch, J. A., Fishman, A., Kogan L., North, R., and Whiteman, M. Guidelines for testing minority group children. Journal of Social Issues, 1964, 20:127–145.

Dewey, J. How We Think. Boston: Heath, 1933.

Dubin, J. A., Osburn, H., and Winick, D. M. Speed and practice: Effects on Negro and white performance. Journal of Applied Psychology, 1969, 53:19–23.

Dunn, L. Special education for the mildly retarded—Is much of it justifiable? Exceptional Children, 1968, 34:5–21.

Edgerton, R. B., and Bercovici, S. M. The cloak of competence: Years later. American Journal of Mental Deficiency, 1976, 80:485–497.

Edwards, A. L. Experimental Design in Psychological Research. Rev. Ed. New York: Prentice-Hall, 1965.

Eells, K., Davis, A., Havighurst, R. J., Herrick, V. E., and Tyler, R. M. Intelligence and Cultural Differences. Chicago: University of Chicago Press: 1951.

Engelmann, S. The effectiveness of direct instruction on IQ performance and achievement in reading and arithmetic. In J. Hellmuth (ed.), Disadvantaged Child. Compensatory Education: A National Debate. Vol. 3. New York: Brunner-Mazel, 1970, 339–361.

Engelmann, S., and Bereiter, C. Teaching Disadvantaged Children in the Preschool. Englewood Cliffs, N.J.: Prentice-Hall, 1966.

Epps, E. G. Family and achievement: A study of the relation of family background to achievement orientation and performance among urban Negro high school students. Final Report of USOE Project No. 5-1006, Contract No. 0E6-85-017 (ERIC Microfilm No. Ed. 027 592), 1969.

Epps, E. G. Situational effects in testing. In LaMar P. Miller (ed.), The Testing of Black Students. Englewood Cliffs, N.J.: Prentice-Hall, 1974, 41–51.

Epps, E. G., Katz, I., Perry, A., and Runyon, E. Effects of race comparison referent and motives on Negro cognitive performance. Journal of Educational Psychology, 1971, 62:201–208.

Erdman, R. L., and Olson, J. L. Relationships between educational programs for the mentally retarded and the culturally deprived. Mental Retardation Abstracts, 1966, 3:311–318.

Eysenck, H. J. Race, Intelligence and Education. London: Temple Smith, 1971.

Feldman, H. Une mesure dynamique de la psychomotoricité. Unpublished report, Geneva, 1970.

Ferguson, J. D. On transfer and the abilities of man. In P. F. Grose and R. C. Birney (eds.), Transfer of Learning. Princeton, N.J.: D. van Nostrand, 1963, 181–194.

Ferron, O. The test performance of "colored" children. Educational Research, 1965, 8(1):42–57.

Ferster, C. B. Classification of behavior pathology. In L. Krasner and L. P. Ullman, (eds.), Research in Behavior Modification. New York: Holt, Rinehart and Winston, 1965.

Feuerstein, R. The learning potential assessment device. In B. W. Richards (ed.), Proceedings of the 1st Congress of the International Association for the Scientific Study of Mental Deficiency. Reigate (Surrey): M. Jackson, 1968, 562–565.

Feuerstein, R. The Instrumental Enrichment Method: An Outline of Theory and Technique. Jerusalem: Hadassah-Wizo-Canada Research Institute, 1969.

Feuerstein, R. A dynamic approach to the causation, prevention and alleviation of retarded performance. In H. C. Haywood (ed.), Socio-cultural Aspects of Mental Retardation. Appleton-Century-Crofts: New York, 1970a, 341–377.

Feuerstein, R. Les Differences de fonctionnement cognitif dans des groupes socio-ethniques differents: Leur nature, leur etiologie et les prognostics de modifiabilite. Paris: Dactylo-Sorbonne, 1970b.

Feuerstein, R. Low functioning children in residential and day settings for the deprived. In M. Wolins and M. Gottesman (eds.), Group Care: The Israeli Approach. London: Gordon and Breach, 1971, 224–231.

Feuerstein, R. Cognitive assessment of the socioculturally deprived child and adolescent. In L. J. Cronbach and P. Drenth (eds.), Mental Tests and Cultural Adaptation. The Hague: Mouton, 1973a, 265–275.

Feuerstein, R. The role of cultural transmission in the development of intelligence. Allan Bronfman Lecture, Quebec, September, 1973b.

Feuerstein, R. Mediated learning experience: A theoretical basis for cognitive human modifiability during adolescence. In P. Mittler (ed.), Research to Practice in Mental Retardation. Vol. 2. Baltimore: University Park Press, 1977.

Feuerstein, R. L'attitude active modifiante envers des difficultés d'apprentissage par l'integration et l'innovation. L'association Quebecoise pour les Enfants ayant des Troubles d'Apprentissage. Montreal: Mars, 1978a.

Feuerstein, R. Ontogeny of learning. In M. Brazier (ed.), Brain Mechanisms in Memory and Learning. New York: Raven Press, 1978b.

Feuerstein, R. Instrumental Enrichment. Baltimore: University Park Press, in press.

Feuerstein, R., Jeannet, M., and Richelle, M. Some Aspects of Intellectual Development in Young North African Jews (in French). Geneva: University of Geneva, 1954.

Feuerstein, R., and Krasilowsky, D. The treatment group technique. The Israel Annals of Psychiatric and Related Disciplines, 1967, 5(1):69–90.

Feuerstein, R., Krasilowsky, D., and Rand, Y. Innovative educational strategies for the integration of high-risk adolescents in Israel. Phi Delta Kappan, April, 1974, LV, 8:1–6.

Feuerstein, R., Narrol, H., Schacter, E., Schlesinger, I. M., and Shalom, H. Studies in Cognitive Modifiability: The Dynamic Assessment of Retarded Performer. Clinical LPAD Battery. Vol. 1 and 2. Jerusalem: Hadassah-Wizo-Canada Research Institute, 1972.

Feuerstein, R., and Rand, Y. Mediated learning experiences: An outline of the proximal etiology for differential development of cognitive functions. In L. Gold Fein (ed.), International Understanding: Cultural Differences in the Development of Cognitive Processes, 1974, 7–37.

Feuerstein, R., and Rand, Y. Studies in Cognitive Modifiability: Redevelopment of Cognitive Functions of Retarded Early Adolescents. Instrumental Enrichment. Jerusalem: Hadassah-Wizo-Canada Research Institute, 1977.

Feuerstein, R., and Richelle, M. North African Jewish Children. Tel Aviv: Youth Aliyah, 1957.

Feuerstein, R., and Richelle, M. Perception and drawing of the North African Jewish child (in Hebrew). Megamot, 1958, 9:156–162.

Feuerstein, R., and Richelle, M. Children of the Mellah (in Hebrew). Jerusalem: Mossad Szold Press, 1963.

Feuerstein, R., Tannenbaum, A. J., Krasilowsky, D., Hoffman, M., and Rand, Y. The effects of group care on the psychosocial habilitation of immigrant adolescents in Israel, with special reference to high risk children. International Review of Applied Psychology, 1976, 25.3:189–201.

Filler, J. W., Robinson, C. C., Smith, R. A., Vincent-Smith, L. J., Bricker, D. D., and Bricker, W. A. Mental retardation. In N. Hobbs (ed.), Issues in the Classification of Children. Vol. 1. San Francisco: Jossey-Bass, 1975, 194–238.

Findley, W. G., and Bryan, M. M. Ability Grouping, 1970: Status, Impact, and Alternatives. Athens, Ga.: Center for Educational Improvement, 1971.

Foster, M. The effects of different levels of enriched stimulus imput on the abstracting ability of slow learning children. Unpublished masters thesis. George Peabody College, Nashville, Tenn., 1970.

Freidson, E. Disability and social deviance. In M. Sussman (ed.), Sociology and Rehabilitation. New York: American Sociological Association, 1965, 71–99.

Fuller, G. B., and Laird, J. The Minnesota perceptuo-diagnostic test. Journal of Clinical Psychology, Monograph Supplement 16, 1963.

Gagnè, R. M. The acquisition of knowledge. Psychological Review, 1962, 69:465–568.

Gagnè, R. M. (ed.). Learning and Individual Differences: A Symposium of Learning Research and Development Center, University of Pittsburgh. Columbus, Oh.: Merrill Books, 1967.

Gagnè, R. M. Learning hierarchies. Educational Psychologist, 1968, 6:1–9.

Gagnè, R. M. The Conditions of Learning. New York: Holt, Rinehart and Winston, 1970.

Gagnè, R. M. Task analysis—Its relation to content analysis. Educational Psychologist, 1974, 11:11–18.

Gallagher, J. J. The special education contract for mildly handicapped children. Exceptional Children, 1972, 38:527–535.

Galton, F. Classification of men according to their natural gifts. In S. Wiseman (ed.), Intelligence and Ability. Baltimore: Penguin Books, 1967, 21–32.

Gardner, W. I. Behavior Modification in Mental Retardation. Chicago: Aldine Atherton, 1971.

Ginsberg, H. Some problems in the study of schooling and cognition. Quarterly Newsletter of Institute for Contemporary Human Development. Rockefeller University, October, 1977, 1, No. 4.

Gitmez, A. S. Instructions as determinants of performance: The effect of information about the task on problem solving efficiency. Paper distributed at the NATO Conference on Cultural Factors in Mental Test Development, Turkey, July, 1971.

Goldstein, H., Arkell, C., Ashcroft, S. C., Hurley, O. L., and Lilly, M. S. Schools. In N. Hobbs (ed.), Issues in the Classification of Children. Volume 2. San Francisco: Jossey-Bass, 1975, 4–61.

Goodenough, F. L. Measurement of Intelligence by Drawings. New York, Chicago: World Book Co., 1926.

Goodenough, F. L., and Harris, D. B. Studies in the psychology of children's drawings: 1928–1949. Psychological Bulletin, 1950, 47:369–433.

Gordon, E. W. A question of culture. American Child, 1963, 45:11–14.

Gordon, E. W. Characteristics of socially disadvantaged children. Review of Educational Research, 1965, 35:377–388.

Gordon, J. E., and Haywood, H. C. Input deficits in cultural-familial retardation: Effect of stimulus and enrichment. American Journal of Mental Deficiency. 1969, 73:604–610.

Guilford, J. P. The Nature of Human Intelligence. New York: McGraw-Hill, 1967.

Guralnick, M. J. (ed.). Early Intervention and the Integration of Handicapped and Non-handicapped Children. Baltimore: University Park Press, 1978.

Guttman, L., and Schlesinger, I. M. Systematic construction of distractors for ability and achievement test items. Educational and Psychological Measurement, 1967, 27:569–580.

Haeussermann, E. Developmental Potential of Pre-school Children. New York: Grune and Stratton, 1958.

Hamburger, M. Measurement issues in the counselling of the culturally disadvantaged. International Conference on Testing Problems, Princeton, N.J.: Educational Testing Service, October, 1964, 71–81.

Hamburger, M. The milieu is the message: Some observations on powerful environments. In M. Wollins and M. Gottesman (eds.), Group Care: An Israeli Approach. New York: Gordon and Breach, 1971, 264–274.

Havighurst, R. J. The Public Schools of Chicago. Chicago: City Board of Education, 1964.

Hawkes, T., and Koff, R. H. Differences in anxiety of private school and inner city public elementary school children. Psychology in the Schools, 1970, 7:259–264.

Haynes, J. M. Educational Assessment of Immigrant Pupils. Slough: National Foundation for Educational Research in England and Wales, 1971.

Haywood, H. C. (ed.). Socio-cultural Aspects of Mental Retardation. New York: Appleton-Century-Crofts, 1970.

Haywood, H. C., and Heal, L. W. Retention of learned visual associations as a function of IQ and learning levels. American Journal of Mental Deficiency, 1968, 72:828–838.

Haywood, H. C., and Switzky, H. N. Children's verbal abstracting: Effects of enriched input, age, and IQ. American Journal of Mental Deficiency, 1974, 78:556–565.

Haywood, H. C., Heal, L. W., Lucker, W. G., Mankinen, R. L., and Haywood, N. P. Learning and retention of visual associations under passive visual and visual-motor presentations. Unpublished manuscript, George Peabody College, Nashville, Tenn., 1970.

Haywood, H. C., Filler, J. W., Jr., Shifman, M. A., and Chatelanat, G. Behavioral assessment in mental retardation. In P. McReynolds (ed.), Advances in Psychological Assessment. Vol. 3. San Francisco: Jossey-Bass, 1975, 96–136.

Hebb, D. O. The Organization of Behavior. New York: John Wiley and Sons, 1949.

Herrnstein, R. Is equality bad for you? Cited in Time, August 23, 1971, 45.

Herrnstein, R. IQ in the Meritocracy. Boston: Atlantic, Little, Brown, 1973, 3–59.

Hilgard, E. Theories of Learning. New York: Appleton-Century-Crofts, 1948.

Hobbs, N. The Futures of Children. San Francisco: Jossey-Bass, 1975a.

Hobbs, N. (ed.). Issues in the Classification of Children. Vols. 1 and 2. San Francisco: Jossey-Bass, 1975b.

Hoffman, B. The Tyranny of Testing. New York: Crowell Collier, 1962.

Hunt, D. E. Learning style and meeting the needs of the child. Paper presented at the 2nd International Symposium on Learning Problems. Ontario Institute for Studies in Education, 1973.

Hunt, D. E. Person-environment interaction: A challenge found wanting before it was tried. Review of Educational Research, 1975, 45:209–230.

Hunt, J. McV. Intelligence and Experience. New York: Ronald Press, 1961.

Hunt, J. McV. Heredity, environment and class or ethnic difference. In Proceedings of the 1972 Invitational Conference on Testing Problems: Assessment in a Pluralistic Society. Princeton, N.J.: Educational Testing Service, 1973, 3–36.

Inhelder, B., and Piaget, J. The Growth of Logical Thinking from Childhood to Adolescence. New York: Basic Books, 1958.

Ivnik, R. J. Uncertain status of psychological tests in clinical psychology. Professional Psychology, 1977, 8:206–213.

Jastak, J. A rigorous criterion of feeblemindedness. Journal of Abnormal and Social Psychology, 1949, 44:367–378.

Jensen, A. Learning ability in retarded, average, and gifted children. Merrill-Palmer Quarterly, 1963, 9(2):123–140.

Jensen, A. R. Social class, race, and genetics: Implications for education. American Educational Research Journal, 1968, 5:1–42.

Jensen, A. How much can we boost IQ and scholastic achievement? Harvard Educational Review, 1969, 39:1–123.

Jensen, A. A theory of primary and secondary familial mental retardation. In N. R. Ellis (ed.), Research in Mental Retardation. Vol. 4. New York: Academic Press, 1970, 33–105.

Jensen, A. Educability and Group Differences. London: Methuen, 1973.

John, V. The intellectual development of slum children. American Journal of Orthopsychiatry, 1963, 33:813–822.

Johnson, O. G. Special education for the mentally retarded—A paradox. Exceptional Children, 1962, 29:62–69.

Jones, R. L. Labels and stigma in special education. Exceptional Children, 1972, 38:553–564.

Kagan's Question: Can children make a comeback after a poor start? Carnegie Quarterly, Summer, 1975, 6–7.

Kamin, L. J. The Science and Politics of IQ. New York: Penguin Books, 1977.

Karp, J., and Sigel, I. E. Psychoeducational appraisal of disadvantaged children. Review of Educational Research, 1965, 35:401–412.

Katz, I. Experimental studies in Negro-white relationships. In L. Berkowitz (ed.), Advances in Experimental Social Psychology. New York: Academic Press, 1970.

Kirp, D. Student classification, public policy, and the courts: The rights of children. Harvard Educational Review, 1974, I, II, 44:7–52.

Kirp, D. A., Kuriloff, P. J., and Buss, W. G. Legal mandates and organizational change. In N. Hobbs (ed.), Issues in the Classification of Children. Vol. 2. San Francisco: Jossey-Bass, 1975, 319–382.

Kohs, S. C. Intelligence Measurement: A Psychological and Statistical Study Based upon the Block-Design Test. New York: Macmillan, 1923.

Krasilowsky, D., Hoffman, M., Feuerstein, R., and Tannenbaum, A. Youth Aliyah Graduates Entering the Army: A Study of the Differential Effects of Some Youth Aliyah Programs. Jerusalem: Hadassah-Wizo-Canada Research Institute, 1971.

Kugelmas, S., and Lieblich, I. Relation between ethnic origins and GSR reactivity in psychological detection. Journal of Applied Psychology, 1968, 52, 2:159–162.

Labov, W. Social Stratification of English in New York City. Washington, D.C.: Center of Applied Linguistics, 1966.

Labov, W., Cohn, P., Robbins, D., and Lewis, J. A Study of Non-Standard English of Negro and Puerto-Rican Speakers in New York City. New York: Columbia University, 1968.

Leary, M. E. Children who are tested in an alien language: Mentally retarded? The New Republic, 1970, 162:17–18.

Leland, H. Mental retardation and adaptative behavior. Journal of Special Education, 1972, 6:71–80.

Leland, H. Adaptive behavior and mentally retarded behavior. In R. K. Eysman, C. E. Meyers, and G. Tarjan (eds.), Sociobehavioral Studies in Mental Retardation. Washington, D.C.: American Association for Mental Deficiency, 1973, 91–100.

Lennon, R. T. Testing and the Culturally Disadvantaged Child. New York: Harcourt, Brace and World, 1964.

Lesser, G. S., Fifer, G. and Clark, D. H. Mental Abilities of Children of Different Social Class and Cultural Groups. Chicago: University of Chicago Press for the Society for Research in Child Development, 1965.

Levinson, P. J., and Carpenter, R. L. An analysis of analogical reasoning in children. Child Development, 1974, 45:857–861.

Lewandowski. D. G., and Saccuzzo, D. P. The decline of psychological testing. Professional Psychology, 1976, 177–184.

Lindquist, E. F. Design and Analysis of Experiments in Psychology and Education. Boston: Houghton Mifflin, 1953.

Lindsley, O. R. Precision teaching in perspective. Teaching Exceptional Children, 1971, 3:114–119.

Lingoes, J. C. An IBM 7090 program for Guttman-Lingoes smallest space analysis. Behavioral Science, 1965, 10:183–184.

Lingoes, J. C. The multivariate analysis of qualitative data. Multivariate Behavioral Research, 1968, 3:61–94.

Lippman, W. The abuse of tests. New Republic, 1922, 32:297–298.

Lorge, I. Difference or bias in tests of intelligence. Proceedings of 1952 Invitational Conference on Testing Problems. Princeton, N.J.: Educational Testing Service, 1953, 76–83.

Lovell, K., and Butterworth, I. Abilities underlying the understanding of proportionality. Mathematics Teaching, 1966, 37:5–9.

Lunzer, E. Problems in formal reasoning. In P. Mussen (ed.), European Research in Cognitive Development. Chicago: University of Chicago Press for the Society for Research in Child Development, 1965, 19–46.

Luria, A. R. The Role of Speech in the Regulation of Normal and Abnormal Behavior. New York: Liveright Publishing Corporation, 1961.

Luria, A. R. The Working Brain. (Translated by B. Haigh). New York: Basic Books, 1973.

MacMillan, D. L., Jones R. L., and Aloia G. F. The mentally retarded label: A theoretical analysis and review of research. American Journal of Mental Deficiency, 1974, 79:241-261.

McCall, R. B. Intelligence quotient patterns over age: Comparison among siblings and parent-child pairs. Science, 1970, 170:644-648.

McCarthy, J., and Kirk, S. Examiner's Manual. Illinois Test of Psycholinguistic Abilities. Experimental Edition. Urbana: University of Illinois Press, 1961.

McClearn, G. E. Genetics and behavior development. In M. L. Hoffman and L. W. Hoffman (eds.), Review of Child Development Research. New York: Russell Sage Foundation, 1964, 433-480.

McClearn, G. E. Genetic influences on behavior and development. In P. Mussen (ed.), Carmichael's Manual of Child Psychology. Vol. 1. New York: John Wiley and Sons, 1970, 39-76.

McNemar. A. The so-called test bias. American Psychologist, 1975, 30:848-851.

McReynolds, P. (ed.). Advances in Psychological Assessment. Vol. 3. San Francisco: Jossey-Bass, 1975.

Machover, K. Personality Projection in the Drawing of the Human Figure: A Method of Personality Investigation. Springfield, Ill.: Charles C Thomas, 1949.

Masland, R. L., Sarason, S. B., and Gladwin, T. Mental Subnormality. New York: Basic Books, 1958.

Matarazzo, J. D., and Wiens, A. N. Black intelligence test of cultural homogeneity and Wechsler Adult Intelligence Scale scores of black and white applicants. Journal of Applied Psychology, 1977, 62:57-63.

Mercer, J. R. Socio-cultural factors in the education of black and Chicano children. Report on the 10th National Conference on Civil Human Rights in Education, on Violations of Human and Civil Rights: Tests and Use of Tests. Washington, D.C.: National Educational Association, 1972.

Mercer, J. R. Labelling the Mentally Retarded. Berkeley: University of California Press, 1973.

Mercer, J. R. Latent functions of intelligence testing in the public schools. In LaMar P. Miller (ed.), The Testing of Black Students. Englewood Cliffs, N.J.: Prentice-Hall, 1974, 77-94.

Mercer, J. R. Psychological assessment and the rights of children. In N. Hobbs (ed.), Issues in the Classification of Children. Vol. 1. San Francisco: Jossey-Bass, 1975, 130-159.

Mercer, J. R., and Lewis, J. System of Multicultural Pluralistic Assessment. New York: Psychological Corporation, 1977.

Miller, G. A., Galanter, E., and Pribram, H. H. Plans and the Structure of Behavior. New York: Holt, Rinehart and Winston, 1960.

Miller, L. P. (ed.). The Testing of Black Students. Englewood Cliffs, N.J.: Prentice-Hall, 1974.

Moss, J. W. Disabled or disadvantaged: What's the difference? A response. Journal of Special Education, 1973, 7:387-391.

Narrol, H., and Bachor, D. An introduction to Feuerstein's approach to assessing and developing cognitive potential. Interchange. 1975, 6:2–16.

Neifeind, U., and Koch, J. Problemlösen bei Retardierten Schülern. Darmstadt: Institute für Psychologie, 1976.

Ortar, G. R. Improving test validity by coaching. Educational Research, 1960, 2:137–142.

Ortar, G. R., MILTA Intelligence Test. Jerusalem: Hebrew University School of Education, 1966.

Pascual-Leone, J. Cognitive development and cognitive style: A general psychological integration. Doctoral dissertation. University of Geneva, 1969.

Patterson, G. R., Cobb, J. A., and Ray, R. S. Direct intervention in the classroom. A set of procedures for the aggressive child. In F. W. Clark, D. R. Evans, and L. A. Hamerlynck (eds.), Implementing Behavioral Programs for Schools and Clinics. Champaign, Ill.: Research Press, 1972, 151–186.

Piaget, J. The Origins of Intelligence in Children. New York: Norton, 1952.

Piaget, J. The Construction of Reality in the Child. New York: Ballantine, 1954.

Piaget, J. Nécessité et signification des recherches comparatives en psychologie génétique. International Journal of Psychology, 1966, 1:3–13.

Piaget, J., and Inhelder, B. The Psychology of the Child. New York: Basic Books, 1969.

Porteus, S. D. Guide to Porteus Maze Test. Vineland, N.J.: The Training School, 1924.

Porteus, S. D. Maze Tests and Mental Difference. Vineland, N.J.: The Training School, 1933.

Porteus, S. D. The Porteus Maze Test and Intelligence. Palo Alto, Cal.: PCC Books, 1950.

Rand, Y. Styles cognitifs et personnalite dans une situation de rencontre inter-culturelle. Doctoral dissertation. Paris: University of Paris, Sorbonne, 1971.

Raven, J. C. Progressive Matrices, Sets I and II. Dumfries: The Chrichton Royal, 1947.

Raven, J. C. Coloured Progressive Matrices, Sets A, Ab, and B. London: H. K. Lewis, 1956.

Raven, J. C. Standard Progressive Matrices, Sets A, B, C, D, and E. London: H. K. Lewis, 1958.

Raven, J. C. Guide to Using the Coloured Progressive Matrices, Sets A, Ab, and B. London: H. K. Lewis, 1965.

Rey, A. D'un procédé pour évaluer l'éducabilité: Quelques applications en psychopathologie. Archives de Psychologie, 1934, XXIV, 96:326–337.

Rey, A. Six Epreuves au Service de la Psychologie Clinique. Brussels: Etablissements Bettendorf, 1950.

Rey, A. Etude d'un freinage volontaire du mouvement graphique chez l'enfant. Liege: Cahiers de Pedagogie et d'Orientation Professionnelle, 1954.

Rey, A. Test de copie d'une figure complexe. Manual. Paris: Centre de Psychologie Appliquée, 1959.

Rey, A. Six Études de Psychologie, Problèmes de Psychologie Génétique. Geneva: Ed. Gauthier, 1964.

Rey A. Les Troubles de la Mémoire et Leur Examen Psychométrique. Brussels: Charles Dessart, 1966.

Rey, A. Épreuves Mnémoniques d' Apprentissage. Chaudefont: Delachaux and Niestlé, 1968.

Rey, A., and Dupont, J. B. Organization des groupes des points en figures geometriques simples. Monographs de Psychologie Appliquée, 1953, 3.

Rey, A., Feuerstein, R., Jeannet, M., and Richelle, M. Report concerning some pedagogical problems. Unpublished manuscript. 1953.

Rey, A., Feuerstein, R., Jeannet, M., and Richelle, M. Quelques études de l'état psychologique des enfants juifs marocains. Geneva, 1955. (Unpublished manuscript).

Richelle, M. Contribution a l'etude des mecanismes intellectuels chez les Africains du Katanga. E. Bull. Trimestrial CEPS No. 43. (N.D.)

Riessman, F. The Culturally Deprived Child. New York: Harper and Row, 1962.

Rivers, L. W., Henderson, D. M., Jones, R. C., Ladner, J. A., and Williams, R. L. Mosaic of labels for black children, In N. Hobbs (ed.), Issues in the Classification of Children. Vol. 2. San Francisco: Jossey-Bass, 1975, 213–245.

Rohwer, W. D., Jr. Learning, race, and school success. Review of Educational Research, 1971, 41:191–210.

Rohwer, W. D., Jr., and Ammons, M. D. Elaboration training and paired-associate learning efficiency in children. Journal of Educational Psychology, 1971, 376–383.

Roper, S. S. Race and assertive classroom behavior. Integrated Education: A Report on Race and Schools, 1972, 10, 5:24–31.

Rosenthal, R., and Jacobson, L. Teachers' expectancies, determinants of pupils' IQ gains. Psychological Reports, 1966, 19:115–118.

Ross, S. L., Jr., De Young, H., and Cohen, J. C. Confrontation: Special education, placement, and the law. Exceptional Children, 1971, 38:5–12.

Samuda, R. J. Psychological Testing of American Minorities: Issues and Consequences. New York: Dodd, Mead, 1975.

Sarason, I. G., Johnsonn, T. H., and Siegel, J. M. Assessing the impact of life change: Development of the Life Experience Survey. Presented at Western Psychological Association Conference, Seattle, 1977.

Sattler, J. M. Racial experimenter effects in experimentation, testing, interviewing, and psychotherapy. Psychological Bulletin, 1970, 73:137–160.

Sattler, J. M. Assessment of Children's Intelligence. Philadelphia: W. B. Saunders, 1974.

Savage, J. E., Jr., and Bowers, N. D. Testers' Influence on Children's Intellectual Performance. Washington, D.C.: U.S. Office of Education, 1972. (ERIC Microfilm No. 064 329.)

Schacter, E. The problems and difficulties implied in the cognitive assessment of the culturally different and educable mentally retarded adolescent: A contribution to the solution: The Learning Potential Assessment Device (LPAD), its psychoeducational significance. Masters thesis. St. Hughes College, Oxford University, 1971.

Schiefelbusch, R. L., and Lloyd, L. L. (eds.) Language Perspectives—Acquisition, Retardation, and Intervention. Baltimore: University Park Press, 1974.

Schmidt, F. L., and Hunter, J. E. Racial and ethnic bias in psychological tests. American Psychologist, 1974, 29:1–8.

Schucman, H. The development of an educability index for the trainable child. In B. W. Richards (ed.), Proceedings of the 1st Congress of the International Association for the Scientific Study of Mental Deficiency. Reigate (Surrey): M. Jackson, 1968.

Schwebel, M. Who Can Be Educated? New York: Grove Press, 1968.

Schwebel, A., and Bernstein, A. J. The effects of impulsivity on the performance of lower-class children on four WISC subjects. American Journal of Orthopsychiatry, 1970, 40:629–636.

Segal, R. M. Advocacy for the Legal and Human Rights of the Mentally Retarded. Ann Arbor, Mich.: Institute for the Study of Mental Retardation and Related Disabilities, 1972.

Shalom, H., and Schlesinger, I. M. Analogical thinking, a conceptual analysis of Analogy Tests. In R. Feuerstein, et al., Studies in Cognitive Modifiability: Learning Potential Assessment Device. Vol. 2. Jerusalem: Hadassah-Wizo-Canada Research Institute, 1972, 152–178.

Shapiro, A. H., Rosenblood, L., Berlyne, G., and Finberg, G. The relationship of test familiarity to extreme response styles in Beduin and Moroccan boys. Journal of Cross-cultural Psychology, September, 1976, 7(3):357.

Shuey, A. M. The Testing of Negro Intelligence. 2nd Ed. New York: New York Social Science Press, 1966.

Sigel, I. E. How intelligence tests limit understanding of intelligence. Merrill-Palmer Quarterly, 1963, 9:39–56.

Silberzweig, P. Learning Potential Assessment Device Matrix Test as a way to test the abilities of culturally deprived children. Unpublished masters thesis. Bar Ilan University, Ramat Gan, Israel, 1975.

Skeels, H. M. Adult status of children with contrasting early life experiences. Monograph of Society for Research in Child Development, 1966, 31:3.

Skeels, H. M., and Dye, H. B. A study of the effects of differential stimulation on mentally retarded children. Proceedings of the American Association on Mental Deficiency, 1939, 44:114–136.

Skinner, B. F. The Technology of Teaching. New York: Appleton-Century-Crofts, 1968.

Skinner, B. F. Cumulative Record: A Selection of Papers. 3rd. Ed. New York: Appleton-Century-Crofts, 1972.

Skodak, M. Adult status of individuals who experienced early intervention. In B. W. Richards (ed.), Proceedings of the 1st Congress of International Association for the Scientific Study of Mental Deficiency. Reigate (Surrey): M. Jackson, 1968.

Skodak, M., and Skeels, H. M. A final follow-up of one hundred adopted children. Journal of Genetic Psychology, 1949, 75:85–125.

Stott, D. H. Behavioral aspects of learning disabilities. Paper presented at the Annual Convention of the Council for Exceptional Children, Washington, D.C., 1972.

Stott, D. H. A preventive program for the primary grades. Elementary School Journal, 1974:299–308.

Sundberg, N. D. Assessment of Persons. Englewood Cliffs, N.J.: Prentice-Hall, 1977.

Tannenbaum, A. J. Critical review of the IPAT. In Oscar Buros (ed.), Sixth Mental Measurements Yearbook. Highland Park, N.J.: Gryphon Press, 1965, 721–723.

Temp, G. Validity of the SAT for blacks and whites in thirteen integrated institutes. Journal of Educational Measurement, 1971, 8:245–251.

Temp, G. Psychometric barriers to higher education. In L. P. Miller (ed.), The Testing of Black Students. Englewood Cliffs, N.J.: Prentice-Hall, 1974. 31–40.

Terman, L. M., and Merrill, M. A. Directions for Administering Forms L & M: Revision of Stanford-Binet Tests of Intelligence. Boston: Houghton Mifflin, 1937.

Terman, L. M., and Merrill, M. A. Stanford-Binet Intelligence Scale: Manual for the Third Revision, Forms L & M. Boston: Houghton Mifflin, 1960.

Thorndike, R. L. Review of R. Rosenthal and L. Jacobson, Pygmalion in the Classroom. American Educational Research Journal, 1968, 5:708–711.

Thorndike, R. L. Educational Measurement. Washington, D.C.: American Council on Education, 1971.

Throne, J. M. The assessment of intelligence. Towards what end? Mental Retardation, 1972, 10:9–11.

Thurstone, L. L. Primary Mental Abilities. Chicago: University of Chicago Press, 1938.

Thurstone, L. L., and Thurstone, T. G. Factorial studies of intelligence. Psychometric Monographs, 1941, No. 2.

Tyler, F. T., and Chalmers, T. M. Effect on scores of warning junior high school pupils of coming tests. Journal of Educational Research, 1943, 37:290–296.

Tymchuk, A. J. Effects of concept familiarization vs. stimulus enhancement on verbal abstracting in institutionalized retarded delinquent boys. American Journal of Mental Deficiency, 1973, 77:551–555.

Ullman, L., and Krasner, L. A Psychological Approach to Abnormal Behavior. Englewood Cliffs, N.J.: Prentice-Hall, 1969.

Uzgiris, I. C., and Hunt, J. McV. Assessment in Infancy: Ordinal Scales of Psychological Development. Urbana: University of Illinois Press, 1975.

Vale, J., and Vale, C. Individual differences and general laws in psychology. A reconciliation. American Psychologist, 1969, 42:1093–1108.

Vernon, P. E. Intelligence and Cultural Environment. London: Methuen, 1969.

Vygotsky, L. S. Thought and Language. Cambridge, Mass.: MIT Press and John Wiley and Sons, 1962.

Wagner, J. Die Intelligenz u Psychologische Welt von Beduin kinder in der Negev wüste Israels. Frankfurt-am-Main: Peter Lant, 1977.

Warburton, F. W. The ability of the Gurkha recruit. British Journal of Psychology, 1951, 42:114–133.

Wechsler, D. Measurement of Adult Intelligence. Baltimore: Williams and Wilkins, 1944.

Wechsler, D. Wechsler Intelligence Scale for Children. Manual. New York: Psychological Corporation, 1949.

Wechsler, D. Intelligence Scale for Children. Rev. Ed. New York: Psychological Corporation, 1974.

Weintraub, F. J. Recent influences of law regarding the identification and educational placement of children. Focus on Exceptional Children, 1972, 4, No. 2.

Wesman A. G. Intelligent testing. American Psychologist, 1968, 23(4):267–274.

White, R. T. Research into learning hierarchies. Review of Educational Research, 1973, 43:361–375.

Whiteman, M., and Deutsch, M. Social disadvantage as related to intellective and language development. In M. Deutsch, J. Katz, and A. Jensen (eds.), Social Class, Race and Psychological Development. New York: Holt, Rinehart and Winston, 1968, 86–114.

Williams, E. B. Testing the black minority. Strategies and problems. In L. P. Miller (ed.), The Testing of Black Students. Englewood Cliffs, N.J.: Prentice-Hall, 1974.

Williams, R. L. Abuses and misuses in testing black children. The Counselling Psychologist, 1971, 2:62–73.

Willner, A. An experimental analysis of analogical reasoning. Psychological Reports, 1964, 15:479–494.

Wishner, J. Efficiency: Concept and measurement. Personality Research, 1962, 2:161–187.

Witkin, H. A., Dyk, R. B., Faterson, H. F., Goodenough, D. R., and Karp, S. A. Psychological Differentiation: Studies of Development. New York: John Wiley and Sons, 1962.

Yando, R., and Zigler, E. Outerdirectedness in the problem-solving of the institutionalized and non-institutionalized normal and retarded children. Developmental Psychology, 1971, 4(2):277–288.

Zigler, E., and Butterfield, E. C. Motivational aspects of changes in IQ test performance of culturally deprived nursery school children. Child Development, 1968, 39:1–14.

APPENDIX

LPAD CLINICAL BATTERY

Tests included in the clinical battery and described in the text are:

Organization of Dots (See pp. 132–141)
Raven's Progressive Matrices A, Ab, B
LPAD Variations I of Raven's Matrices A, Ab, B (See pp. 148–156)
Raven's Progressive Matrices C, D, E
LPAD Variations II of Raven's Matrices C, D, E (See pp. 156–157)
Plateaux Test I (four buttons) (See pp. 141–147)
Plateaux Test II (eight buttons) (See pp. 147–148)
Representational Stencil Design Test (See pp. 157–165)
Numerical Progressions (See pp. 165–167)
Positional Learning Test 5 × 25 (See pp. 148–149)
Verbal and Figural Analogy Tests (See pp. 281–285, 361–406)

Tests included in the Clinical Battery that are not described in detail in the text and were not included in the study are:

Complex Figure Drawing of André Rey (See Figure 6, p. 83)

Examinee is requested to copy a complex figure. Qualitative evaluation is based upon the way the examinee organizes and structures the figure. The quantitative examination takes into account the presence and location of details and the accuracy of the figure. In the LPAD, the examinee is offered the training after the examiner has established the kind of assistance needed after the examinee's spontaneous production of the figure. Following this, the effects of the training are measured on subsequent productions of the task.

Human Figure Drawing (See Figure 13, p. 130)

In administering the test, the examiner may select from a variety of instructions, such as those presented by Machover, by the Witkin Sophistication Scale, or Rey's FAY test, the one he wishes to use. However, dynamic training is applied whenever developmental cognitive factors determine a low level of representation of the human figure. Training mainly focuses on the articulation of the human body and helping the child discover the body schema, without affecting the static or personal expression. Evaluation of change is mainly qualitative.

Associated Recall Test (Rappelle Associative)

Associated Recall is a test described by Rey (1966) and studies the capacity of the individual to use increasingly reduced stimuli as a support for his memory of 20 figures presented to him in the first phase of the test. Comparison of the results obtained in free recall permits the assessment of the preferential mnemonic modality for perceptual support of free recall.

Memory of Fifteen Words

This test, described by Rey (1968), permits the drawing of a learning curve for 15 words across 10 learning exposures.

SAMPLE EXAMINER-EXAMINEE
INTERACTION FOR LPAD INDIVIDUAL TEST

The following excerpt is a sample of the interaction between the examiner and the examinee in a task that is relatively easy but that can be used to elicit from the examinee important prerequisites for higher level functioning in the more complex tasks with which he will be confronted in the assessment. (This task is based on the Raven Matrices; see Figure A-1.)

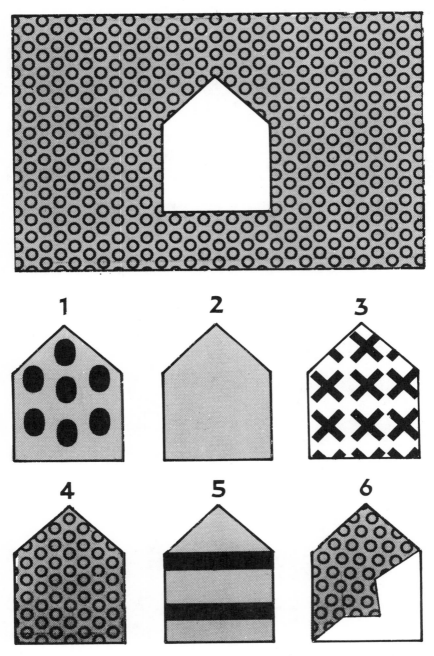

Figure A-1.   LPAD pretest task.

Interaction sequence	Instructor's question	Rationale	Subject's response	Interpretation of subject's response
1	"Look at this page. What must be done here?"	Request for definition of a problem.	"I don't know" (or incorrect or irrelevant response).	No definition of the problem.
2	"Look at this rectangle. What do you see in it? Look at the bottom and you will see 6 pieces."	Produce in the child a state of disequilibrium or a need to fill in the missing part.		
3	"This square is gray. Is it all gray?"	Produce explicit analytic perception of a whole and a missing part. The concept "missing" produces the need for completion.	"No. There is a white part. Some gray is missing."	Possible reason: sweeping perception; impulsivity; use of only one source of information.
4	"Yes. You are right. There is a missing part. What must you do about it?"	Reinforce previous (1, 2, 3) rationales. Orient the child toward the need to solve the problem.	"I have to color it gray."	No relationship has been established between the gray rectangle with the missing part and the choices at the bottom of the page.
5	"No, you cannot color it. We need the booklet. Can you find another way of filling in the missing part?"	Make the child aware of reality (as defined by the examiner) and look for a more appropriate solution.	"No."	
6	"Look at the bottom of the page. What do you see there?"	Make the child gather the information that will be necessary for the solution of the problem.	"I can take one of these and put it in here."	The child has established the relationship between the two parts of the page: the problem and the alternatives for solution.

—continued

Interaction sequence	Instructor's question	Rationale	Subject's response	Interpretation of subject's response
7	"Yes. Right you are. Now could you show me the one that you could put in there to make it look like nothing is missing?"	Induce the child to match two disparate percepts by comparing them on relevant dimensions (e.g., an irrelevant dimension in this task is the shape).	"Number two."	The child has used only one source of information, i.e., only one dimension of discrimination (gray) and has not considered the black circles. Possible reasons: impulsive behavior or lack of systematic exploration that did not permit him to see a more appropriate alternative.
8	"It's almost good; it is the right color. But there is a better one."	Minimize the child's failure since the child has identified one of the correct dimensions (color). Point to the need for a search for a more appropriate answer.		
9	"If you want to find it, look at all the possible choices at the bottom of the page, from 1 to 6. Look at each one, to see which one of them is the right one."	First attempt to produce systematic exploration, accompanied by gestural modeling.		The child needs assistance and orientation to reinstitute his activity.
	The examiner exhibits in front of the child systematic exploratory behavior in looking for the		"Four."	The examinee is taught systematic exploratory behavior by the examiner's modeling

	Examiner	Purpose	Child's Response
10	various alternatives by pointing to each in order from 1 to 6. "Yes. Four is the right one. Six is not. Can you tell me why six is not right? (In asking about the reason for the inadequacy of number six, the examiner states clearly that six is not appropriate. Make the *fact* clear, then ask for the reason.)	Elicit explicit reasoning, including a repetition of a concept of "missing," applied here to a smaller part.	"It's no good because it's not complete. A part of it is missing." Or, "It's no good because it's not enough—it's not big enough."
11	"Very good! That's right! A part of it is missing. It is not complete. You have done very well. Now, could you show which one of these six is the worst (one that cannot fit at all)? (Repeat) I want you to tell me which one is the worst and give me two (hold up two fingers) reasons it is not good."	Teach the use of the appropriate concepts of completeness and missing so they will be useful for later tasks. The three goals are: (1) To produce analytic perception: bring two dimensions of the solution, color and figure to bear on the problem; (2) to produce the need for logical evidence on an elementary level, i.e., all statements have to be supported by a reason; and (3) to enumerate distinct reasons, i.e., first, . . . and second, . . . All of these three elements will be followed throughout the test.	"Three!"

—continued

Interaction sequence	Instructor's question	Rationale	Subject's response	Interpretation of subject's response
12	"You are right. Number three is worst of all. Now give me two reasons."		"It has no gray."	Uses only one source of information.
13	"That is true. It has no gray. But there is another reason."		"It has black."	Black as a color is used inappropriately, without pointing to figure as the relevant dimension. (Fails to consider that black is needed.)
14	"Let's look at the task again. Isn't there any black in it?"	Explicit direction to scan the standard to gather the missing information.	"Yes, it has black circles."	
15	"That's right. There is black in the figures of the circles. Can you tell me the second reason that number three is not good?"	Elicit response based on comparison between the newly perceived and the previous information.	"It doesn't have circles."	Little, if any spontaneous comparative behavior.

#				
16	"That's right. It has a different figure. It has X's. Let's summarize. What are the two reasons that number three is not good?"	Introduce concept of "figure." Call for summative behavior.	"It's white and it doesn't have the black circles."	No effort to initiate categorization.
17	"Very good. Its color and its figures are not right. Now can you tell me why number two is not the right answer?"	Generalize to higher order concepts. Reinforce the use of figure as a criterion.	"It is just gray. It does not have the circles."	
18	"Correct. It has the right color in the background but it doesn't have the figures. You did very well. Now let's turn the page."	Model the use of superordinate concepts in elaborating data.		Examiner will determine if examinee's difficulty is one of concepts or labels in the next tasks.

SAMPLE CATEGORIES OF EXAMINER-EXAMINEE INTERACTIONS FOR THE LPAD*

Examinee response	Examiner response
Types of response	
Correct response	Correct responses are always amplified; given positive feedback and approval
	Request for analytic, rather than impressionistic, intuitive reasons
	Request for logical evidence
	Production of insight into reason for success
	Request for broader meaning of proper response
	Analysis of functions and behavior involved in arriving at correct response
Spontaneous, self-initiated correction of response	As above. Feedback of failure is always given, but meaning of failure is kept localized and moderate
	Questioning of reasons for initial failure as stemming from one or another of deficient functions, such as the use of only one source of information, impulsivity, or lack of spontaneous comparative behavior.
Correction after feedback	Teaching examinee how to independently evaluate response and accordingly to seek ways of correcting errors
	Training for confirmation or rejection of hypotheses by hypothesis testing
	When answer is corrected, approval and positive feedback are given
Correction after intervention	Determination of the nature of intervention that proves to be most efficient and repetition of this intervention as various opportunities arise
	Production of an awareness of the examinee to the particular modality in which the error was best corrected
Partially correct response	Response is not rejected because it is incomplete or not entirely correct. Positive reinforcement is given for the correct dimensions of response
	Fostering examinee's distinction between correct and incorrect parts of answer, with awareness of reasons for response
	Creation of generalization by bringing similar examples of answers

—*continued*

Examinee response	Examiner response
Incorrect response	Probe for reasons for incorrect answers
	Use of incorrect answers as point of departure for correcting prerequisite functions, in accordance with needs revealed in the response
	Emotional, negative meaning of failure should be moderated by the active approach to its correction and should be turned into a source of learning rather than viewed as a passive registration of an irreversible act which, once produced, cannot be corrected
No answer	Probe for reasons for blocking as an emotional reaction to anticipated or actually experienced failure
	Assisting the examinee to overcome his inhibitions
	In cases in which these prove to be resistant, examiner may help examinee by modelling the tasks, and/or assisting the examinee to reinstitute his activity
Modality of response	Intervention will aim at eliciting the same response in modalities other than that used by examinee as a way of enriching his communicational repertoire and making him generalize his responses across modalities initially difficult for him
Motor modality of response	Initiation of motor manipulation in tasks such as Gestalt completion or closure wherever visual perceptual analysis proves to be inefficient
	Exposure to model of manipulation executed by the examiner. In more resistant cases, examinee's hand may be guided in performing the graphic response
Gestural or verbal choice in search of alternative answer	Suggestion and orientation of examinee toward use of code (e.g., "use the number of the correct answer instead of pointing at it with your finger"), and in describing the answer verbally rather than simply coding it or pointing to it
Internalized, anticipatory response	Wherever the structure makes it possible, an anticipatory, representational response will be required prior to or instead of its motor execution or its choice by visual inspection

—continued

Examinee response	Examiner response
	Such anticipatory behavior, once instituted, may become the modality of response throughout the assessment for a variety of tasks and should be interpreted as indicating a shift from concrete to abstract representational modalities of thought
	Must be subjected to the same intervention as detailed above in the examiner's reaction to correct or incorrect responses
Input	The examiner must ensure variations in exposure to stimuli necessary for the examinee's appropriate input of data necessary for solving the task. He must cause the delay of response by repeatedly pointing to source of data and by obstructing exposure to irrelevant data in the visual field
Unsystematic exploration	Teaching the examinee to systematically explore by exposing him to the examiner's own activities as a model of systematic scanning
	Pointing out unsystematic exploratory behavior as a source of failure whenever it occurs.
	With pencil tip, pointing out the order in which exploration must take place
Inhibition of impulsivity	Treatment in a variety of ways, including imposing a latency period between input and output, and delaying the response

* Additional categories of examiner-examinee interactions may be found in the manuals (in preparation) accompanying the Learning Potential Assessment Device.

INSTRUCTIONS FOR ANALOGIES PRE AND POST TESTS

Required personnel	One examiner and one assistant
Materials	1. Two booklets: Versions A and B of the Analogies
	2. Answer sheet in two colors
	3. Poster of enlarged page of analogies
	4. Class seating arrangement chart
Time required	No time limit; however, a testing session usually takes 40–50 minutes

In the pretest procedure, the examiner hangs the poster of the enlarged page of analogies on the blackboard and says:

Hello. We are here to see how teenagers learn to think. We brought this poster so we can all work on the task together. The booklets you will receive contain similar tasks, only they will be smaller. Let's look at the top of the poster. The number of this problem is 98. We always look at the number of the problem first. (Points). Let's see what is in the upper left frame (points). There is a white triangle, completely empty. Nothing is in it. Now, let's look at the upper right frame (points). We have a triangle with diagonal stripes in it. Pay attention. This triangle is empty (points), and this triangle has diagonal stripes (points). Everything that happens on the top row also happens in the next row, beneath

Fig.
A-2

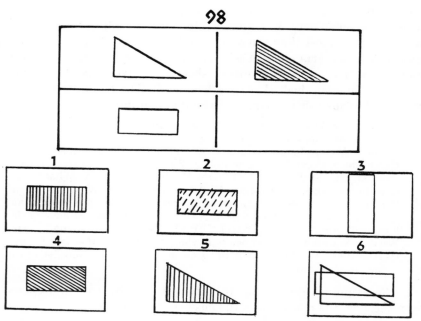

Figure A-2.   Chart presented to children as sample problem.

it. What do we have in the lower left frame? We have a white rectangle, completely empty (points). Nothing is in it. The same thing will happen to it that happened to the triangle. The rectangle will be filled with diagonal stripes. We have six possible answers (points to them), but *only one* is correct. There are answers that are almost right. Try not to allow yourself to be confused by them. Let's look first at number 1. Is it correct or not? CLASS PARTICIPATION. It is incorrect because it has straight lines and we need diagonal lines. What about number 2? It is incorrect because it has diagonal lines but they are broken and not whole. Number 3 is not correct for two reasons. What are they? CLASS PARTICIPATION. The rectangle is standing up (vertical) instead of lying down (horizontal); it is empty (has no diagonal lines). What about number 4? (After deciding that #4 is correct) This is the correct answer. But, let's look further. Maybe there is something better. (Continues until all six answers have been analyzed.) Number 4 is correct. Let's see how we show which one was the correct answer."

Examiner illustrates the problem numbers and answers on the blackboard according to the format of the answer sheet.

Number four was correct so we circle number four. (Circles number 4 on the blackboard). *We do not write in the test booklets.* If you make a mistake and want to correct it, mark an X over it. Do not erase it. (Circles an incorrect answer and marks an X on it).

Assistant distributes the white and yellow answer sheets so that neighboring children do not have the same color. Alternate sheets are given to adjacent rows. Examiner explains how to fill in the personal history data requested on the sheets, and writes the children's names on the seating arrangement chart. Assistant distributes the test booklets so that those with answer sheet A receive booklet A, while those with answer sheet B receive booklet B. The children are then instructed to open their booklets. Examiner continues:

Fig.
A-3

The two booklets are different from each other. However, the first four problems are the same so we'll do them together now. This is the first problem. We see here (points to the number 1 at the top) that it is the first problem because of the number 1. What is in the upper left frame? (points). CLASS PARTICIPATION. We have a small X. What do we have in the upper right frame? CLASS PARTICIPATION. Pay attention to what happened. The small X grew into a large X. The same thing that happened above will happen below. What do we have in the lower left frame? CLASS PARTICIPATION. We have a small circle. What do you think will happen to it when it moves into the right frame? CLASS PARTICIPATION. It will grow into a big circle. Now, let's turn to the possible answers.

The examiner reviews all the answers, one by one, and elicits from the class the reasons why the answers are not appropriate.

Number 5 is the correct answer. Now, let's see how we indicate which is the correct answer. Remember we write *nothing* in the *booklet*. (Shows

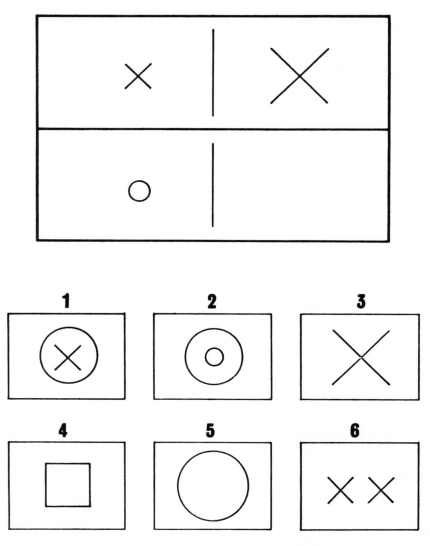

Figure A-3.   Sample problem 1 from Analogies Test.

answer sheet). Look at number 1 on the answer sheet and circle number 5 in the column next to it.

Now, let's turn to page number 2. What is in the upper left frame (points)? We have a circle and a square. Where is the circle and where is the square? CLASS PARTICIPATION. The circle is above and the square is below it. Now what happened to them when they moved to the upper left frame? CLASS PARTICIPATION. They *reversed* positions. Now the square is above and the circle below. (Any spontaneous use of

Fig.
A-4

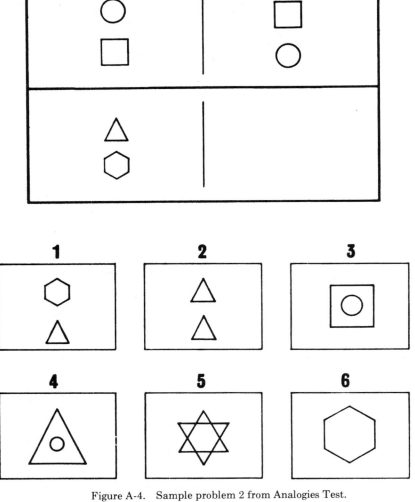

Figure A-4. Sample problem 2 from Analogies Test.

the word "reversal" or "opposite" is reinforced verbally, e.g., "that's wonderful," "excellent") The same thing will happen in the row below. What do we have below? CLASS PARTICIPATION. We have a triangle and a hexagon. Where is the triangle and where is the hexagon? CLASS PARTICIPATION. What will happen to them when they move to the lower right frame?" CLASS PARTICIPATION. They will reverse positions. Now let's turn to the possible answers. (Reviews answers.) Number 1 is the correct answer. Remember, write *nothing* in the *booklet*. (Shows answer sheet). Look at number 2 on the answer sheet and circle the number 1 in the column next to it.

Now we will turn to page number 3. We will do the same thing we have been doing, but this time we will be using words. What do we have in the upper left frame? CLASS PARTICIPATION. A fur coat. What do we have in the upper right frame? CLASS PARTICIPATION. Winter. Now, I want you to give me a short sentence that connects the two words, "fur coat" and "winter." CLASS PARTICIPATION. (Reinforces sentences that express the idea that a fur coat is worn during the winter.) Remember, the same relationship that exists in the row above must be found in the row below. What do we have in the left frame below? CLASS PARTICIPATION. A bathing suit. What is the word that should be in the right frame if we use the sentence we used above? CLASS PARTICIPATION. One wears a bathing-suit during the summer.

Fig. A-5

Examiner reviews all the answers, eliciting replies as to the reason they are not appropriate.

If you choose number 1, "a swimming pool," it is not the correct answer because the question is *when* do you wear a bathing-suit, and not *where* do you wear it. The same reason applies to number 4, "beach." Number 5, "season," could be correct, but it is too general because there are four seasons. Number 2, "clothing," is not correct because it tells us what a bathing suit is and not when it is worn. Number 3 is the correct answer

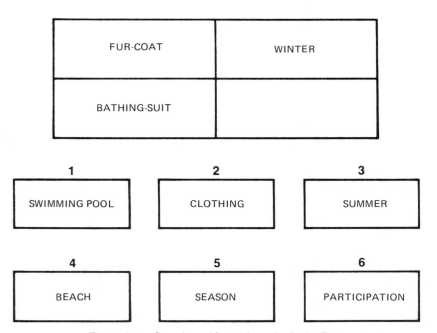

Figure A-5.   Sample problem 3 from Analogies Test.

because it is the specific season, just as winter is a specific season. (Continues with the same format as above).

Now, let's turn to page four. (Examiner follows the same format for sample problem #4 as used in the preceding three sample problems.)

Fig.
A-6

The examiner completes the analysis of the four samples from the analogies test booklets and is sure that the students comprehend what they must do. He continues:

From now on, you'll be working alone. Please work slowly and carefully. You have as much time as you want. Remember that whatever happens on the top row happens on the bottom row. Pay attention to the number on top of the page.

Before you start, I want to remind you of some of the things we have learned. (Examiner makes sure that he has the attention of all of the students). Look carefully at the problem to be sure that you understand what is happening in the top row before you start to look for the answers. Be sure to look at all six answers before you decide which one of them is correct. Remember that in some of the problems we worked on, an answer seemed to be nearly correct, and then we found a better one. When you are certain that you have found the correct answer, make sure that you write it in the proper place. Check the number of the problem; find it on the answer sheet; and then circle the number of the answer which is correct.

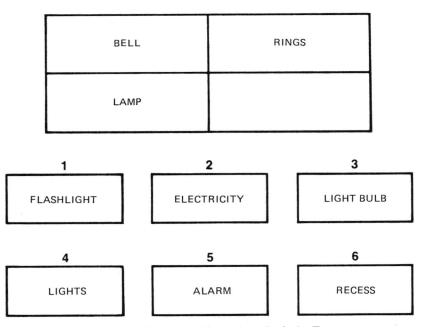

Figure A-6.   Sample problem 4 from Analogies Test.

No help is to be given except in response to a child's questions. In the figural analogies, the standard response is, "Look at what happens in the top row. The same thing happens below." In the verbal analogies, the examiner may explain the meaning of a word that is not understood, but not the analogy.

TRAINING

Training may be given with or without mediated learning. Training precedes mediated learning by a day or two, if both are given.

Required personnel	One examiner
Materials	One of three training booklets, according to the training to be given:
	1. Verbal (16 pages)
	2. Figural (16 pages)
	3. Verbal-figural (16 pages, containing half verbal and half figural tasks)
Time required	$\frac{1}{2}-\frac{3}{4}$ hour/group
Procedure	The examiner says, "Remember when we were here last month? We gave you a test. You did very well on it, but we want you to do even better in 2 weeks when you will repeat the same test. So today we will learn to solve the problems on such a test."

The examiner elaborates on the meaning of the training in order to elicit motivation on the part of the examinees.

The examiner distributes the booklets. Each problem is solved orally, with the maximum participation of the class. Solutions are requested from a number of children and are discussed and analyzed. No writing is done.

Verbal Training

To solve the verbal problems, sentences should be constructed using the terms in the upper frames. These sentences should reflect the relationship between the two terms of the analogy. For example:

Fig. A-7   In the upper left frame, we have the word "hut," and next to it is the word "house." Let's look for a sentence that connects the two words, but shows the difference between them. CLASS PARTICIPATION. The hut is small but the house is big. What is bigger than the hut? The house. (Then, using the word in the lower left frame, a sentence should be elicited, using the same relation). Now what we found above, we will look for below. We have the word "bush," and we ask the same question we asked above. What is bigger than a bush? The correct answer is number 4, a tree.

Fig. A-8   In the upper left frame, we have the word "noise" and next to it the word "quiet." Let's look for a sentence connecting the two words that shows that one is the opposite of the other. Now the relationship we found in the top row we will look for below. We have the word "more" and we ask the same question we asked above. What would be the opposite of "more?" The right answer is number 1, "less."

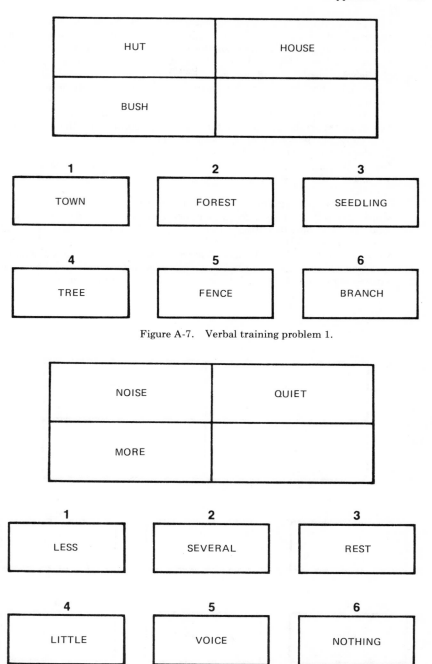

Figure A-7.   Verbal training problem 1.

Figure A-8.   Verbal training problem 4.

Fig.
A-9

In the upper left frame, we have the word "house" and next to it the word "door." Let's look for a sentence connecting the two words but showing the difference between the two. "We enter the house through the door." Now what we found above, we will look for below. We have the word "garden" and we ask the same question we asked above. "Through what do we enter the garden?" The right answer in number 1, "gate."

Fig.
A-10

In the upper left frame, we have the word "bandage" and next to it the word "wound." Let's look for a sentence connecting the two words and showing the relationship between the two. "When do we need a bandage? For a wound." Now what we found above, we will look for below. We have the word "consolation" and we ask the same question we asked above. "When do we need consolation?" The right answer is number 1, "grief."

Fig.
A-11

In the upper left frame, we have the word "sand" and next to it the word "grain." Let's look for a sentence connecting the two words and find the relationship between them. CLASS PARTICIPATION. What is sand made of? It is made of many grains. Now what we found above, we will look for below. We have the word "water" and we ask the same question we asked in the first row. What is water made of? The right answer is number 4, "drop," because water is made up of many drops.

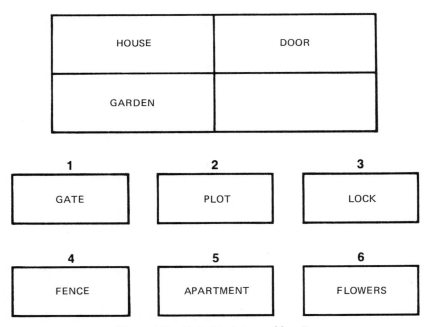

Figure A-9.   Verbal training problem 5.

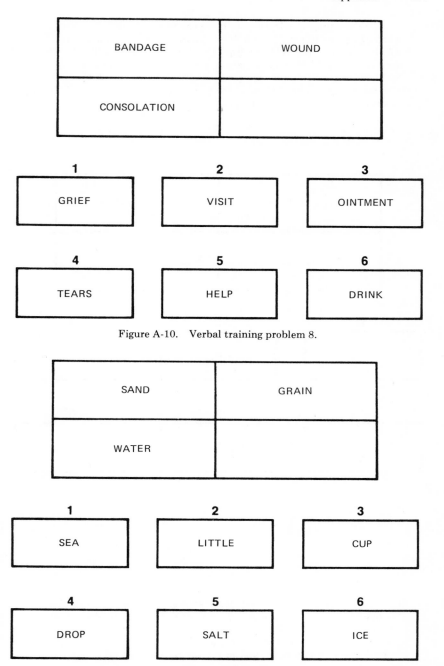

BANDAGE	WOUND
CONSOLATION	

1 GRIEF   **2** VISIT   **3** OINTMENT

4 TEARS   **5** HELP   **6** DRINK

Figure A-10.   Verbal training problem 8.

SAND	GRAIN
WATER	

1 SEA   **2** LITTLE   **3** CUP

4 DROP   **5** SALT   **6** ICE

Figure A-11.   Verbal training problem 10.

Fig.
A-12

In the upper left frame, we have the word "fight" and next to it the word "reconciliation." Let's look for a sentence connecting the two words and find the relationship. CLASS PARTICIPATION. "We put an end to a fight by reconciliation." Now what we found above, we will look for below. We have the word "problem" and we ask the same question we asked above. "How do we put an end to a problem?" The right answer is number 6, by "solution."

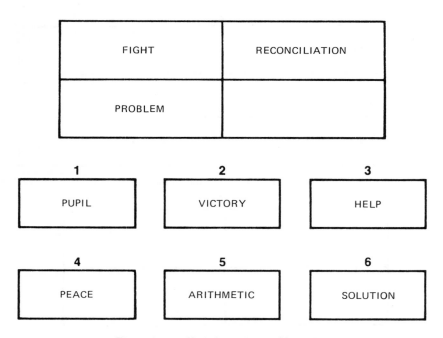

Figure A-12.   Verbal training problem 12.

Fig.
A-13

In the upper left frame, we have the word "dollar" and next to it the word "money." Let's look for a sentence connecting the two words. "A dollar is a unit of money." Now the relationship we found above, we will look for below. We have the word "kilogram" in the lower left frame and we ask the same question we asked above. "The unit of what is a kilogram?" The right answer is number 6, "weight."

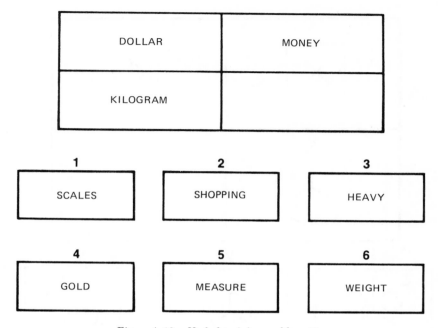

Figure A-13.   Verbal training problem 13.

Figural Training

To solve the figural analogy problems, sentences are constructed in a manner similar to that used in the verbal problems. The transformations between the figures in the upper left and right frames are described verbally. The examiner then explains that the same transformations are imposed on the terms in the set below. Thus, the correct answer is anticipated. Class participation is encouraged throughout the training.

Let's look at the upper left frame. There is a square with an X in it. The square is bigger than the X. What do you see in the upper right frame? CLASS PARTICIPATION. The X became bigger than the square, and the square became smaller. Notice that the X now extends over and beyond the square. Now the same transformation should happen below. In the lower left frame, there is a circle with three lines in it. What will happen when they move to the next frame? CLASS PARTICIPATION. The circle will become smaller, while the three lines become bigger. They will extend over and beyond the circle. Now let's find the right answer. CLASS PARTICIPATION. The right answer is 5. (The other alternatives should be explored and analyzed for the reasons they are not correct). Fig. A-14

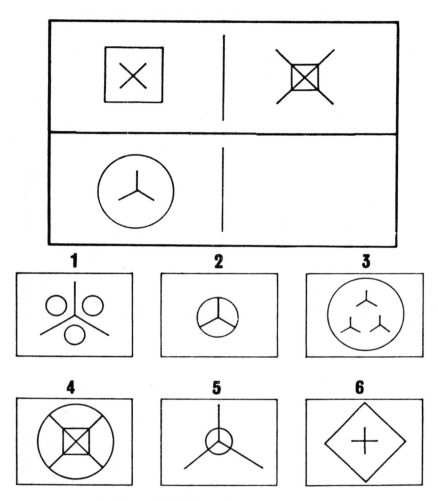

Figure A-14.   Figural training problem 1.

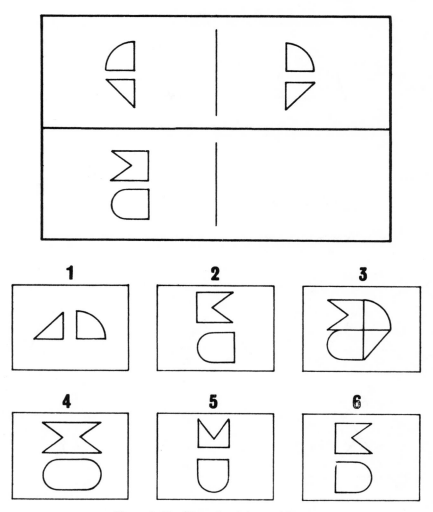

Figure A-15.   Figural training problem 3.

What do we have? CLASS PARTICIPATION. A quarter of a circle and below it a triangle. On the other side they are flipped over, like in a mirror. The same will happen below. There is a flag and half an ellipse. They will be reversed like in a mirror. The right answer is number 6.

Fig.
A-15

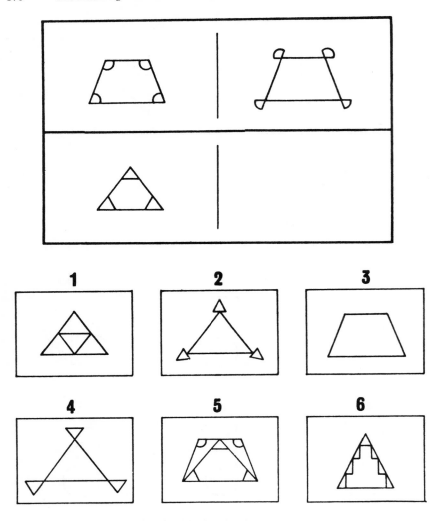

Figure A-16.   Figural training problem 4.

Fig.
A-16
            Here is a trapezoid. It has four sides. In each corner, we see a small
half circle. To its right, we see the same trapezoid with the half circles
outside of it. Notice their orientation. Below, we have a triangle. In each
of its corners, there is a small triangle. What will happen when they will
come out? Number 2 isn't correct because the orientation of the small
triangles isn't correct. They are not reversed. The correct answer is
number 4.

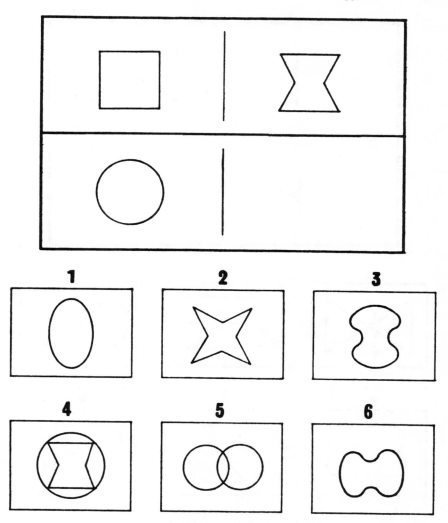

Figure A-17.   Figural training problem 5.

In the upper left frame, we see a square. When it moved to the other frame, it got squeezed on the sides. Below we have a circle. What will happen to it when it moves to the other frame? It will also get squeezed on the sides. Answer 6 isn't correct because the circle got squeezed on its top and bottom. The correct answer is number 3.

Fig. A-17

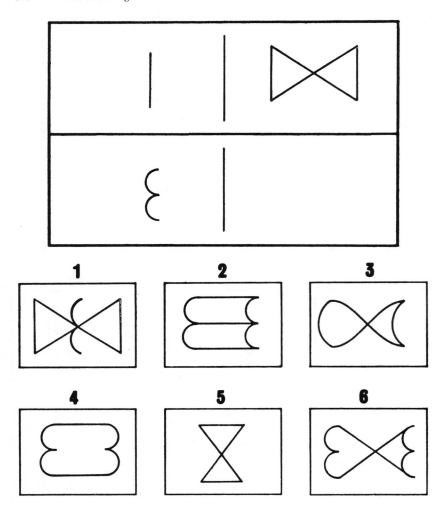

Figure A-18.   Figural training problem 6.

Fig.
A-18   In the upper left frame, we have a line and in the frame next it
another line parallel to the first with an X connecting the two. Below we
have an E (a backwards 3). What will happen when it will move to the
other frame? There will be another E parallel to the first and an X connecting the two. The correct answer is number 6.

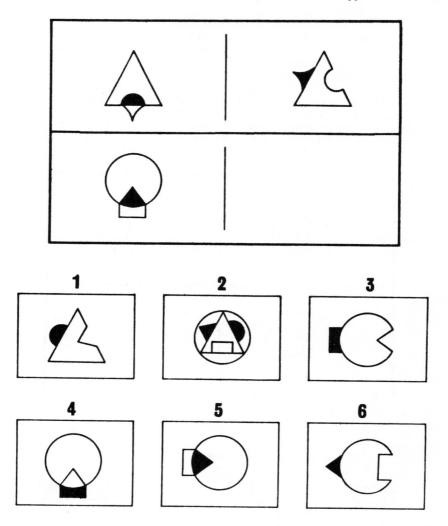

Figure A-19.   Figural training problem 8.

In the upper left frame, we have a triangle with half a black circle inside it and a small triangle outside of it. In the next frame, the small triangle moved to the left side and became black; the half-circle moved to the right side and was removed. Below, we have a circle with a black triangle inside it and a small rectangle outside of it. What will happen when it moves to the next frame? The rectangle will move to the left side and become black while the black triangle will move to the right side and be removed. The correct answer is number 3.

Fig.
A-19

In the upper left frame, we have three forms, one inside the other. The square is on the outside, the diamond is in the middle, and the circle is inside. Let's call the square, number 1; the diamond, number 2; and the circle, number 3. In the upper right frame, the figures have changed places, and sizes. The outside figure, the square, has gotten small and is now the inside figure. When we remove the square from the outside, the diamond is now the outside and the circle is in the middle. Number 1 has become number 3, number 2 moved up to number 1, and number 3 has become number 2. In the lower left frame, we have a trapezoid in place number 1 on the outside; a triangle in place number 2, the middle; and an ellipse in place number 3, the inside. They will

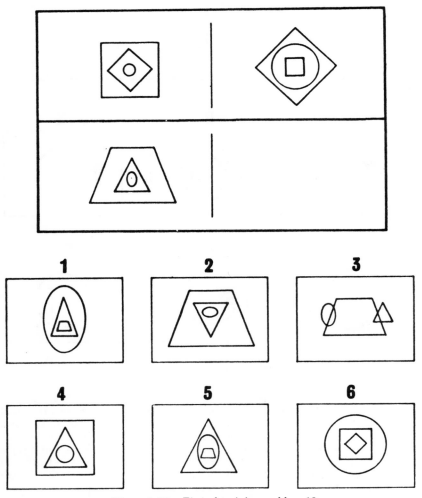

Figure A-20.   Figural training problem 10.

trade places and sizes in the same manner. Number 1, the trapezoid, will be on the inside, place number 3; the triangle, number 2, will move into the outside position, number 1; and the ellipse, number 3, will move into the middle position, number 2. Number 5 is the correct answer.

In the upper left frame, we have a triangle. In the upper right, the triangle has reversed its position and another triangle has been added symmetrically beneath it. (Explain "symmetrically" if necessary.) In the lower right frame, we have a quarter of a circle. When it moves to the next frame, it will also reverse its position and another will be added

Fig. A-21

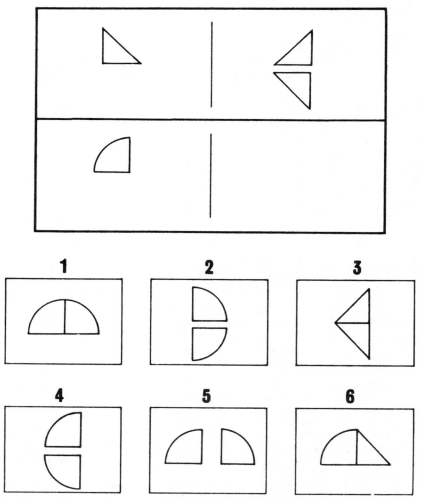

Figure A-21.   Figural training problem 12.

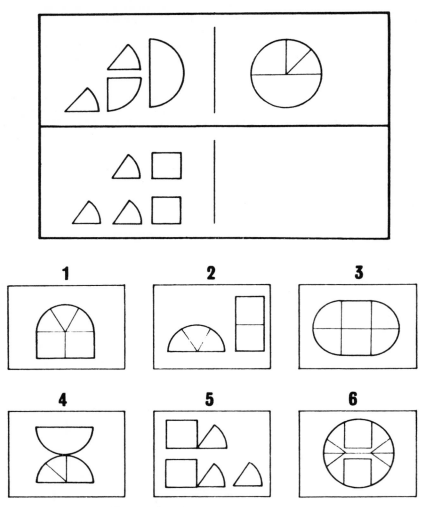

Figure A-22.   Figural training problem 13.

symmetrically beneath it. The correct answer? Number 4. Why is number 2 not good? The quarter-circles face in the wrong direction.

Fig.
A-22   In the upper left frame, there are various parts of a circle: a half, a quarter, and two eighths. In the upper right frame, these parts have all been put together and form a complete circle. What do we have in the lower left frame? Various parts that also must be put together when they move into the next frame. Which is the correct answer? Number 1. Why are the others not correct? CLASS PARTICIPATION.

Fig.
A-23   In the upper left frame, there is a square with a horizontal line dividing it. On either side of the square there is a half-circle. When they move into the

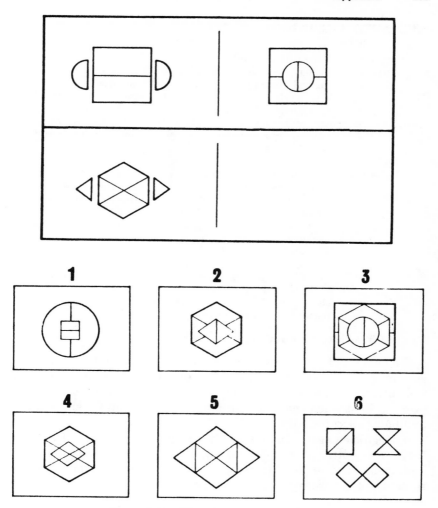

Figure A-23.   Figural training problem 15.

next frame, the two half-circles meet and form a full circle, and are inside the square. Because the circle is not transparent, it hides the part of the horizontal line of the square that is underneath it. Now what happens in the next row? In the lower left frame, we have a hexagon with two diagonal lines. On either side of it is a small triangle. What will happen in the next frame? The triangles will join together in the middle of the hexagon. Part of the intersecting diagonal lines of the hexagon will be hidden. The correct answer? Number 2. Why are the others not good? (CLASS PARTICIPATION).

MEDIATED LEARNING

Personnel	One examiner and one assistant.
Materials	Verbal analogies training booklet (7 pages)
	Figural analogies training booklet (10 pages)
	The verbal treatment group receives the verbal analogies booklet; the figural treatment group receives the figural analogies booklet; the verbal-figural treatment group receives a combination of figural and verbal items.
Time	1½–2 hours/group
Procedure	The initial instructions given to the examinees are as follows: "Remember when we were here last month we gave you a test? You did well on it. But we want you to do even better in 2 weeks when you will repeat it. So today we will work together to learn how to solve the problems on the test."
	The assistant distributes pencils and page one of the analogies to the children. To ensure an equal pace for all of the examinees, successive pages are distributed only after the entire group has completed each page. At the end of the session, the children are permitted to take the completed pages home.

Verbal Mediated Learning

Exercise I The tasks in exercise I are intended to develop systematic classificatory behavior and the ability to gather data from two different sources. The purpose of the mediated learning in this exercise is to teach the children how to identify categorizing criteria and how to ascertain the suitability of a certain term for membership in a specific category. In addition, the examinee learns to distinguish between the attributes of specific objects. By quantifying the criteria appropriate to membership in a specific class, the examinee learns to rank items according to their proximity or distance from a given word.

The exercises consists of 10 problems that range from the concrete to the abstract. Each task consists of a word with two or three criteria that characterize it. Beneath are four words to which the examinee must apply the categorizing criteria.

Fig.
A-24

What is a couch? CLASS PARTICIPATION. First of all, a couch belongs to a class of things we call "furniture." What can we say about this piece of furniture? CLASS PARTICIPATION. We can talk about how it looks—but its upholstery or its age aren't important in defining it as a couch. What is important is its function, what it is used for. What is it used for? CLASS PARTICIPATION. It is used to sit on and to lie on. If you would look in a dictionary you would see that that is its definition and that every couch has those characteristics. Let's look at

1.   COUCH   Furniture. To sit on. To lie on.

       bed   chair   table   key
       [3]   [2]   [1]   [0]

4.   LAMP   Illumination. Artificial. Electric.

       moon   candle   sea   flashlight
       [ ]   [ ]   [ ]   [ ]

5.   EVIL   Character trait. Negative.

       loveable   cruel   pretty
       [ ]   [ ]   [ ]

6.   STABLE   Structure. Dwelling. For animals.

       chicken coop   hotel   book   tower
       [ ]   [ ]   [ ]   [ ]

7,   JUICE   Liquid. For drinking. Cold.

       gasoline   soup   beer   fire
       [ ]   [ ]   [ ]   [ ]

10. RUNNING   Bodily state. Movement. On foot.

       standing   glasses   lying   walking
       [ ]   [ ]   [ ]   [ ]

Figure A-24.   Exercise I. Sample problem, verbal mediated learning.

the four words underneath and see if there is one that also has all three of the characteristics that a couch has. Furniture to sit on and to lie on. CLASS PARTICIPATION. We will write 3 under 'bed' because it has all three of the characteristics. Now let's see if there is something that has two of the characteristics. CLASS PARTICIPATION. "Chair" is a piece of furniture and you can sit on it, but you cannot lie on it. So we write 2 under chair. Why is "table" not good? CLASS PARTICIPA-

TION. It is furniture, but you cannot lie on it and it's not made for sitting on. So how many characteristics does "table" have? One. Write a 1 under table. Now what about "key"? CLASS PARTICIPATION. It is not furniture, and you cannot sit on it or lie on it. So what will we write beneath it? CLASS PARTICIPATION. That's right, a zero. Now let's do the next task.

The examiner follows the same procedure for all of the tasks in the exercise. It is necessary to explain some of the characterizing criteria. In number 5, for example, "character trait" must be explained as an inner quality and contrasted with something that is visible externally, like "beauty." It must also be discriminated from other adjectives that may not be visible externally and describe an individual, like "old" or "rich." The concept of "negative" must also be explained as being basically bad or undesirable, as opposed to "positive" as good and desirable.

Another problem of which the examiner must be aware is that the examinees are not accustomed to associating a "hotel" and "a stable," or "gasoline" and "juice" as members of the same semantic category. In these items, it is important to emphasize the commonality of the category membership. Although the exploration must be systematic, it is important that the examiner be flexible, sometimes starting from the terms that are most similar to the given word and possess all of its attributes, and sometimes starting with an exploration of the term that is most distant from the given word and share none of its characterizing criteria.

Exercise II   This exercise is intended to develop systematic exploration, discrimination, and summative behavior. It consists of nine tasks, ranging from the concrete to the abstract. In each task, there is a given category and various words, some of which definitely belong to it, while others are either marginal or clearly not members. The examinees must find the items that belong to the category, count them, find the sum for each row, and the total for the problem. Discrimination is achieved by encouraging discussion about the marginal items.

Fig.
A-25

In each task of exercise II, we are given the name of a class of objects. Beneath it are rows of objects we must inspect to find those that belong to the given class. Whenever we find one we will underline it. We will count all the objects we find in each row and write the sum on the line next to each row. Finally, we will add the numbers at the end of each row and write the total in the space provided.

The examiner reads all of the items aloud and asks whether or not each belongs to the category specified in the task. When the children seem to be proficient, they are allowed to work on the prob-

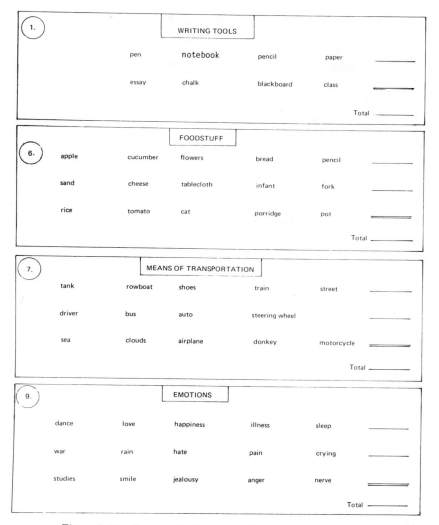

1.

WRITING TOOLS

pen	notebook	pencil	paper	_____
essay	chalk	blackboard	class	_____
			Total	_____

6.

FOODSTUFF

apple	cucumber	flowers	bread	pencil	_____
sand	cheese	tablecloth	infant	fork	_____
rice	tomato	cat	porridge	pot	_____
				Total	_____

7.

MEANS OF TRANSPORTATION

tank	rowboat	shoes	train	street	_____
driver	bus	auto	steering wheel		_____
sea	clouds	airplane	donkey	motorcycle	_____
				Total	_____

9.

EMOTIONS

dance	love	happiness	illness	sleep	_____
war	rain	hate	pain	crying	_____
studies	smile	jealousy	anger	nerve	_____
				Total	_____

Figure A-25.   Exercise II. Sample problem, mediated learning.

lems independently. However, the process is then reviewed orally, referring to the answer sheet. Within each category there will be objects that arouse controversy. For example, in task 1, is paper a writing tool? In task 7, is a donkey a means of transportation? Is happiness an emotion? The examiner must discuss the categories with the children so that they can arrive at the answers themselves; he must explain why certain answers are incorrect.

Exercise III Exercise III induces comparative behavior and divergent thinking. It consists of eight tasks in which the child determines the commonality or the denominator of two given words, and the differences between them on the given parameter.

Fig. A-26 The first task in Exercise III is completed as an example of what is expected. All the remaining tasks should be solved through class discussion, with constant reference to the answer sheet. It should be made clear that there are many answers possible for the differences between things, all of which are correct. For example, in task 5 an airplane and a ship are both means of transportation, but there are many differences between them. An airplane flies, a ship sails; one is for the air, the other for water travel; one uses high octane gasoline, the other diesel fuel; etc. There is no unique answer that is correct. Therefore, the examiner should encourage the children by asking for more and different answers, and reinforcing originality and imagination. His instruction should close with: "All the answers you have given are correct. You may write down the one you like the best."

Exercise IV This exercise consists of four tasks intended to develop logical thinking. The given categories at the head of each task are the product of logical multiplication. The given objects may be classified according to their membership in one, the other, both, or neither of the two categories that combine to form the given one.

1.	HAMMER		Carpenter's tool
		Tools	
	NEEDLE		Tailor's tool
2.	HOUSE		________
		________	
	BARN		________
4.	SUN		________
		________	
	STOVE		________
5.	AIRPLANE		________
		________	
	SHIP		________

Figure A-26. Exercise III. Sample problems, mediated learning.

1.	MEANS OF TRANSPORTATION – ON THE GROUND					
	bus	ladder	bicycle	airplane	1	_____
	boat	train-tracks	fish	helicopter	2	_____
	tractor	submarine	train	cloud	3	_____
					4	_____

4.	ANIMATE – SMALL					
	infant	hill	elephant	penny	1	_____
	fly	wall	mouse	giant	2	_____
	pin	giraffe	bead	water tower	3	_____
					4	_____

Figure A-27.   Exercise IV. Sample problems, verbal mediated learning.

Numbers are assigned to each one of the possibilities and then are appropriately listed beneath the given items.

Fig. A-27

In the first task, our category is "means of transportation—on the ground." Number 1 will be the class of means of transportation on the ground. We will write a 1 under all the items that belong to that class. What will they be? CLASS PARTICIPATION. Bicycle, bus, tractor, train. Why is "train-tracks" not good? CLASS PARTICIPATION. Number 2 will be those things which are means of transportation, but not on the ground. What will that cover? CLASS PARTICIPATION. Write a 2 under all of the items we mentioned. Number 3 will only be on the ground, but not means of transportation. Where will we write a 3? CLASS PARTICIPATION. And number 4 will be neither means of transportation nor on the ground. Now, after we have numbered the items, we will add those that belong to each category and write their sum on the line next to the appropriate category.

The examiner works on each item with the class, always referring to the answer sheet. The pupils do none of the tasks alone. Venn diagrams should be used by the examiner to aid in explanations.

Exercise V   Although this exercise is not being used at present, it is included as a sample. It consists of eight tasks intended to develop structural thinking. Each task consists of three words that must be linked to form a sentence. The criterion is grammatical correctness. A few of the tasks are:

1.   soccer—boys—street
3.   policeman—roof—house
5.   seedling—tree—years
6.   night—sun—cold

Exercises I–V in the verbal mediated learning have equivalents in the figural mediated learning exercises. There are additional exercises in the figural mediated learning that have no parallel tasks in the verbal modality.

Figural Mediated Learning

Exercise I   This exercise is intended to develop the ability to categorize, to gather information from two sources, and to work systematically. It has five tasks, and parallels exercise I of the verbal mediated learning. In each of the tasks, the problem is to rank alternatives according to their proximity to a given model, on three or more parameters. The tasks become progressively more difficult when both the model and the alternatives are less familiar and more complex.

Fig. A-28   In each of these tasks, there is a model figure in the upper left corner of the frame. Next to it are listed the criteria for describing the model. Below, there are three figures in a row. You must find one that is most similar to the model in the given criteria, and mark a "+" in the box beneath it. Then you must find one that is least similar to the given model, and mark a " − " beneath it. In order to do this, you will have to look at each of the alternatives carefully to see how many of the criteria it shares with the model. Let's look at the sample exercise at the top of the page. What is this? (Points to model figure). CLASS PARTICIPA-TION. Let's use the given criteria to describe it: form, size, and color. Its form? A triangle. Its color? White. Its size? CLASS PARTICIPA-TION. Yes, we can only tell that it is small when we compare it with the other figures. Now we must find the one that is most like it. Let's start with the first on the left. Its form? A square. Its size? Large. Its color? White. How many of the criteria of the model does it share? Only one, its color. The next. Its form? A triangle. Its size? Small, the same as the model. Its color? Black. How many criteria does it share? Two, form and size. Now the last figure. Its form? A circle. Its size? It's larger than the model. Its color? Spotted. How many characteristics does it share? None. We must mark a + under the one which has the most criteria in common, and a − under the one with the least. Where do we put the + and the −? CLASS PARTICIPATION. You will notice that the model changes from task to task, as do the criteria. Only those criteria that are listed are those we must consider in describing the model and looking for the figure closest to it.

Mark the most similar with a `+`

Mark the least similar with a `−`

Example:

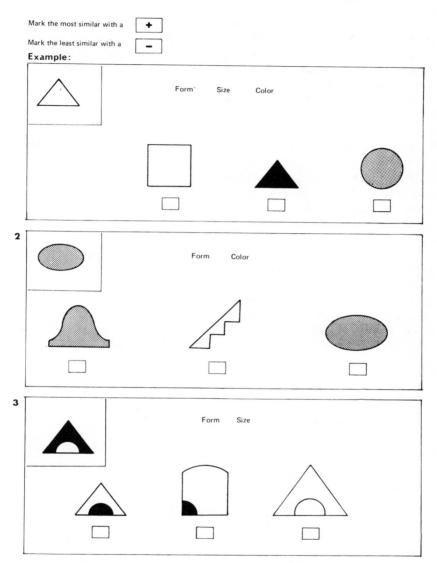

Figure A-28.   Exercise I. Sample problem, figural mediated learning.

Examiner elicits full class participation in the description of the model in terms of the given criteria and in the analysis of the alternatives. He follows the same procedure for all of the tasks, always referring to the answer sheet. It should be noted that in mediated learning, the examiner emphasizes the process necessary for the solution of the tasks. Through his orienting questions, he models the definition of a figure in terms of given parameters and the systematic exploration of alternatives using two or more sources of information. He must be sure that the examinees are aware of the differences that exist between the alternatives and the model and their relevance. Thus, in task 2, he must point out that the fact that the ellipse is larger than the one in the model is not relevant because size is not given as a criterion; and that the relative position of the colors in task 3 must not be considered, since it is irrelevant.

Exercise II   Exercise II is intended to develop discrimination, systematic exploration, and summative behavior. It consists of six tasks and parallels exercise II in the verbal mediated learning. In each of the tasks, there is a model figure and three rows of open and closed forms. The problem is to find those figures that are similar to the model in each of the rows, to write the number found in each row, and then to total the sums. The only criterion for discrimination is form, so that color, size, and orientation are irrelevant.

Fig.
A-29

In these tasks, there is a model in the upper right corner of the frame. We must look at it carefully and label it. Then we will see how many times a figure similar to the model appears in each row. We will work slowly and systematically, and inspect each figure carefully. If there is any doubt as to whether it is the same as the model or not, what do you suggest we do? CLASS PARTICIPATION. Yes, we'll look back at the model. We will underline all those that have the same form as the model. We'll count the number in each row and note it on the line next to that row. When we have finished, we'll add up the sums of each row and note the total next to the word "total." Let's look at the first task. What is the figure in the model? CLASS PARTICIPATION. Is it just a star? CLASS PARTICIPATION. It's a five-pointed star and it's a closed figure. Is the fact that it is white important when we say that we are going to be looking for the same form? CLASS PARTICIPATION. No. We are not interested in color. We are only interested in *form* in this task, the outside lines of the figure. So, the size, the color, and the orientation are not important. Let's start with the first row. (Examiner moves from figure to figure, allowing class to answer. When he receives the answer that a figure is not appropriate, he probes for the reason. He stops at the large star). Is this the same as the model? CLASS PARTICIPATION. Yes, because we are not interested in the size, but only the fact that it is five-pointed star. (Continues until the first figure on

How many designs in each row are similar to the model?   Write the total on the line next to each row and then the sum total.

Figure A-29. Exercise II. Sample problem, figural mediated learning.

the left). Some people draw a star like this. Shall we underline it? CLASS PARTICIPATION. It is not a closed star with five points. How many did we find? Two. Where shall we write the number? (CLASS PARTICIPATION). (Moves to second row). What about the first figure on the right? CLASS PARTICIPATION. It's a closed star, but it only has four arms. (Continues) What about this black star? CLASS PAR-

TICIPATION. The color is irrelevant. We're only interested in the shape. The last figure in this row? CLASS PARTICIPATION. It has six points. (Examiner continues item by item, eliciting class responses.) Which of the figures is the hardest to decide about? CLASS PARTICI-PATION. Those that are quite similar to the model but that differ in the number of arms. The figures that are not at all like the model are easy for us, and those just like the model are easy. What is hard is when they are nearly like the model, but not quite.

The examiner encourages discrimination by the discussion of marginal items. He works with the examinees in the analysis of the various task items until he is sure they have all grasped the principle.

Exercise III This exercise consists of three tasks and is intended to induce comparative behavior. It is not in use at present.

Exercise IV This exercise consists of four tasks that develop logical thinking. In each task, there are two given figures that represent categories. The figures in each of the three rows may be classified according to their membership in one, the other, both or neither of the two categories. Letters are assigned to each one of the four categories, and are listed appropriately beneath each of the figures. The total number of members of each of the sets is listed next to the letter standing for the set. Merely the class of the geometric form is relevant.

Fig.
A-30

Let's look at task 1. What are we given in the model? CLASS PAR-TICIPATION. A hexagon and a triangle. In these tasks we are only interested in the geometric forms we are given in the model. The size, color, and orientation are not important to us. Each of the two forms represents a set. How many sets do you think we can make? We can have the family of hexagons; the family of triangles; the family that is made up of both hexagons and triangles together; and a set of neither hexagons nor triangles. Four altogether. Let's give each set a letter, and draw next to the letter the form the letter represents. So we have A for hexagons and B for triangles. What will we draw in the space for the set that is both hexagon and triangle? CLASS PARTICIPATION. What is the set that is neither? CLASS PARTICIPATION. That's right, D. Now let us inspect the figures carefully, working systematically. Under each figure, we will write the letter of the set it belongs to. (Examiner and class assign the letters to the sets.) Let's look at the first on the right in the top row. What are we looking for? CLASS PARTICIPATION. Where does this belong then? CLASS PARTICIPATION. It has neither a hexagon nor a triangle, so it belongs in D. What will we put under it? Yes, a D. The second figure? CLASS PARTICIPATION. Yes, D. The third? It has both a triangle and a hexagon. What is the letter for that class? C. It's hard to see that it is a hexagon because the triangle is inside it. But how can we be sure that we have a hexagon here? CLASS PARTICIPATION. We can count the sides. How many sides do we need? CLASS PARTICIPATION. Six. The next figure? Only a triangle. What letter do we put beneath it? Yes, a B. The last? Both, so we have

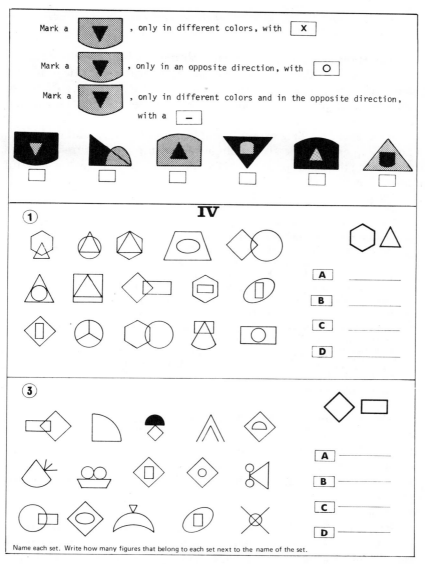

Figure A-30.   Exercise IV. Sample problem, figural mediated learning.

to write a C. Does the position make any difference? No, we are only looking for the family of hexagons and triangles, so the only criterion is that they have to belong to that family. (Examiner continues through the items with the students until all the designs have been labeled). Have we finished the task? CLASS PARTICIPATION. No. Now we have to count the members of each set and write the total next to the letter designating the set.

The examiner should use Venn diagrams to indicate the intersection of two sets that is the product of logical multiplication. By encouraging responses from the members of the group, the examiner makes sure that the principles of the exercise are understood and that the strategy of the process is clear.

Exercise V   This exercise provides practise in visual transport. The task in each of the six problems is to complete a figure or figures by choosing the appropriate part from among alternatives. Successful closure involves an awareness of the size, orientation and form of the missing part.

Fig.
A-31

In each of these tasks, we are given an incomplete figure and must choose the part that completes it from the alternatives at the bottom of the frame. When we think we have found it, we will carry the mental picture of it to the place it belongs in the figure, and see if it is correct. Let's look at task 1. What is the figure? CLASS RESPONSE. What part of it is missing? CLASS RESPONSE. Any corner? No. the upper right corner. Try to imagine what the missing part looks like. Can you describe what you will be looking for? CLASS RESPONSE. That's right. The closed part will be on the right. Which one is it? The second from the left. Why is the third from the left not good? CLASS RESPONSE. Because it is the upper left corner, and that is already there. It faces in the wrong direction. Why are the other two not good? CLASS RESPONSE. Because they are tilted. The lines must be horizontal and vertical.

The examiner continues with the other tasks in the same manner. In both tasks 5 and 6, there are parts similar to one another that must be discriminated between on the basis of their respective sizes, and there are others that are partially but not entirely correct. The examiner must be sure that the examinees are aware of these differences and that their choice is the result of discrimination and reflection.

Exercise VI   The six tasks of this exercise elicit acuity in visual perception, and comparison. In each of the tasks there are two designs, one of which is incomplete in comparison with the other. The purpose is to add the missing parts so that the two designs will be identical.

Fig.
A-32

In each of these tasks there are two designs. You must complete design B so that it looks like design A. How do you suggest we work? CLASS RESPONSE. It will be as if we lay one design over the other, to see what parts they share and what parts appear in design A that don't appear in design B.

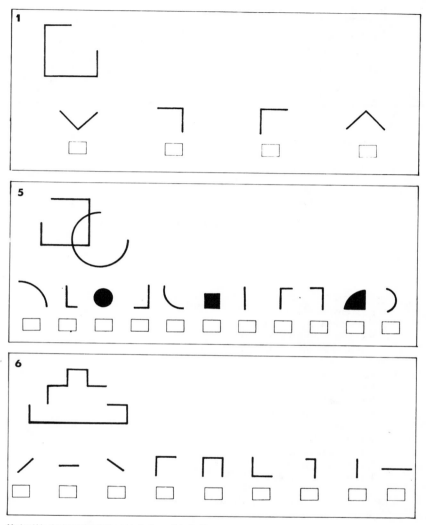

Mark a X in the box beneath the parts that complete the figure.

Figure A-31.   Exercise V, problems 1, 5, and 6, figural mediated learning.

Figural-Verbal Mediated Learning

The figural-verbal mediated learning consists of the following problems from the figural and verbal exercises:

Figural mediated learning
Exercise 1, problems 3–5
Exercise 2, problems 4, 5

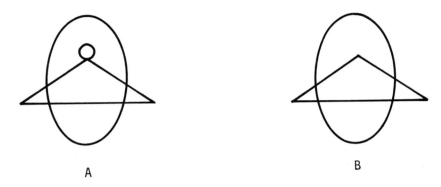

A   B

Complete design B so it looks like design A.

Figure A-32.   Exercise VI, figural mediated learning.

Exercise 3, not in use
Exercise 4, problems 3, 4
Exercise 5, problems 4–6
Exercise 6, problems 4–6

Verbal mediated learning
Exercise 1, problems 6–10
Exercise 2, problems 7–10
Exercise 3,problems 5–8
Exercise 4, problems 3, 4
Exercise 5, none
Exercise 6, none
Exercise 7, none
Exercise 8, problems 5–8

The instructions are identical to those found in the figural and verbal mediated learning sections.

Figural-Verbal Training

The figural-verbal training consists of problems 1–8 from the verbal training booklet and problems 9–16 from the figural training booklet. The instructions are identical to those found in the verbal and figural sections.

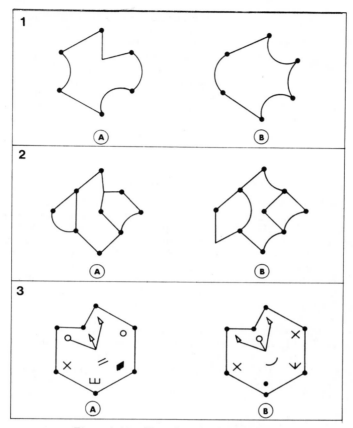

Figure A-33.   Figural mediated learning.

THE SHIFT TEST

Required personnel	One tester and one assistant
Materials	Booklets consisting of 17 pages of material distributed in two versions, one in which figural problems precede verbal problems and one in which verbal precedes figural
Time required	40 minutes
Procedure	The instructions to the children are: "Once again we are going to give you an analogy test to do. This time, though, it will be different from those you have already done. The missing item won't always be where

you are accustomed to finding it but will sometimes be in a different place. Sometimes there may be more than one missing item and you will have to find all of them. At the end of the booklet, you will even find some analogies that are wrong and you will have to correct them. I think you will enjoy doing these analogies. If you have any questions, call either of us over and we will explain what you have to do. Now let's do one figural and one verbal example together."

The tester goes over one example with the class.

Fig. A-33
In the first row we have two circles. The one on the left has diagonal lines. What has happened to the circle on the right in the first row? CLASS PARTICIPATION. We have to put in two figures from the same family in which there are changes that took place in the first row. What will they be? CLASS PARTICIPATION. The two triangles. Which one will be on the left side? Number 4. Why? CLASS PARTICIPATION. Because the diagonal lines have to be the same as in the circle above. The change is in the figure from circle to triangle. And on the right? CLASS PARTICIPATION. Number 3, because it is an empty triangle.

Fig. A-34
In this example we are given "summer" and "winter" in the first row. And we have the word "night" where we are accustomed to filling in the answer. We must look for the relationship between summer and winter. CLASS PARTICIPATION. One is the opposite of the other. The same relationship must hold for the second row, too. What is the opposite of night? CLASS PARTICIPATION. Day, number 3. Very good.

In the other problems, you will sometimes have to fill in one word, and sometimes more. But remember these are all analogies. We must look for the relationship between one set of words and then apply the same relationship to the other set of the same problem.

Now you can start on your own. Good luck! If you have a problem, raise your hand and one of us will come over to help you.

The examiner walks around the room, checking the child's first sheet and helping when necessary. The examiner is *not to give the child the answer*. He may explain unfamiliar words and what must be done.

Additional examples from the Shift Test are given in Figures A-35–A-39. In Figure A-35 the task is to find and correct the error. In Figures A-36–A-39 the task is to complete the analogy by filling in the missing item in the range, domain, or both.

SUMMER	WINTER
	NIGHT

1 SUN	2 SPRING	3 DAY
4 RAIN	5 YEAR	6 COLD

Figure A-34.   Verbal Shift Test training example.

lid	pot
wine	bottle

1	2	3
lock	tin	table
4	**5**	**6**
cork	cup	glass

Figure A-35.   Verbal Shift Test problem 9.

sidewalk	pedestrian

motor	automobile	airplane
ship	road	sea

Figure A-36.   Verbal Shift Test problem 8.

to laugh	to cry
to raise	
	to erase

1	2	3
to write	to clean	to open
4	**5**	**6**
to study	to close	to lower

Figure A-37.   Verbal Shift Test problem 4.

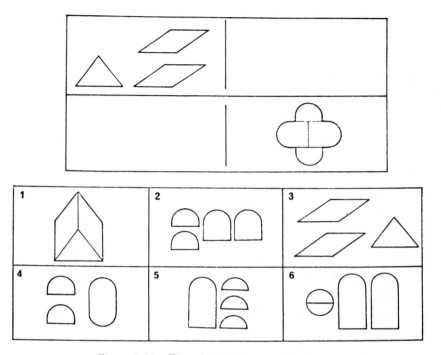

Figure A-38.   Figural Shift Test problem 6.

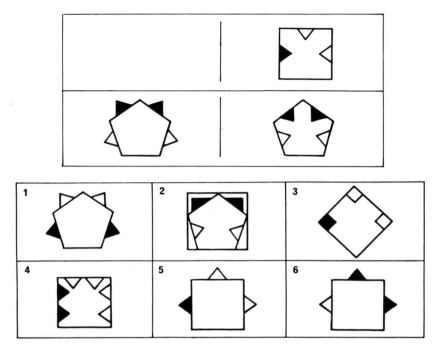

Figure A-39.   Figural Shift Test problem 3.

INDEX

The companion volume...

INSTRUMENTAL ENRICHMENT
Redevelopment of Cognitive Functions of Retarded Performers

By **Professor Reuven Feuerstein**, in collaboration with **Ya'acov Rand, Mildred B. Hoffman**, and **Ronald Miller**. Illustrations by **Eitan Vig**.

Instrumental Enrichment describes the brilliant, successfully implemented program destined to radically change many long-entrenched ideas about education generally and the education of mentally retarded persons in particular. For the many teachers, psychologists, and scientists who have worked with or heard of Professor Feuerstein's Piagetian-based strategy for modifying cognitive ability in retarded and low performing adolescents, the very existence of a book on **Instrumental Enrichment** will be cause for celebration. FIE is a radical departure from conventional educational strategies in that it uses a *learning to learn* approach. Professor Feuerstein's theory is that retarded performance often occurs because the child has never been taught how to focus his attention on significant events and ideas in his environment. FIE thus provides a step-by-step mediated learning experience to directly modify the child's cognitive abilities. It is designed to supplement and enrich the classroom and has already been implemented as a middle-school curriculum in several major American school districts.

Representing the culmination of Professor Feuerstein's theoretical concepts, research, pilot tests, clinical studies, and highly successful application of FIE with tens of thousands of low functioning adolescents over the past two decades, this book now fully describes its actual use in practice, with examples from the instruments themselves, numerous case histories, and a wealth of clinical and experimental data. The text covers the theoretical basis and rationale for cognitive modifiability, FIE strategies, the FIE program, the populations for which it is designed, teacher training and supervision, and bridging over from FIE to other curricula. Together with Professor Feuerstein's other major work, **The Dynamic Assessment of Retarded Performers**, this volume challenges the critical-period-of-development theory and shows that cognitive strategies can be modified at least as late as adolescence. Carefully applied, this approach has potential for revolutionizing existing concepts and practices in education. **Instrumental Enrichment** is essential reading for everyone working in the fields of education, special education, cognition, psychology, and mental retardation.